HC

THE CROMWELLIAN
GAZETTEER

AN ILLUSTRATED GUIDE TO BRITAIN IN THE
CIVIL WAR AND COMMONWEALTH

Samuel Cooper's water-colour is one of the most striking likenesses of
Oliver Cromwell. Painted in 1651–3, Cromwell appears markedly older
and heavier than in Robert Walker's portraits of the 1640s. The
miniature is unfinished and may have served as a 'master' from which
numerous copies and derivatives were taken.

THE CROMWELLIAN
GAZETTEER

AN ILLUSTRATED GUIDE TO BRITAIN IN THE CIVIL WAR AND COMMONWEALTH

PETER GAUNT

The great seal of the Protector by
Thomas Simon. Cromwell is shown
mounted and in armour; behind him
are the arms of the Commonwealth.

WRENS
PARK

A Sutton Publishing Book

First published in 1987 by Alan Sutton Publishing Limited, an imprint of
Sutton Publishing Limited · Phoenix Mill · Thrupp · Stroud · Gloucestershire

This edition published in 2000 by Wrens Park Publishing, an imprint of
W.J. Williams & Son Ltd

A catalogue rcord for this book is avialble from the British Library

ISBN 0 905 778 480

Printed in Great Britain by
Redwood Books,
Trowbridge, Wiltshire.

CONTENTS

Acknowledgements   vi

Foreword   vii

Introduction   ix

The Gazetteer
   England   1
   Wales   175
   Scotland   195
   Ireland   213

A Cromwell Itinerary   224
   Maps   228

Genealogical Tables   236

Select Index of Names   240

Picture Credits   242

ACKNOWLEDGEMENTS

No book, particularly one of this nature, can be the work of a single hand and I have pleasure in acknowledging the many debts which I have incurred: to Trewin Copplestone, Professor Ivan Roots and the Cromwell Association, who initiated the study and offered unfailing help and encouragement throughout its preparation; to the many individuals and organisations who responded to general appeals for information – that restrictions of scope and space have sometimes forced the omission of sites in no way diminishes my gratitude to all who responded; to the staffs of the British Library and Students' Room, the Institute of Historical Research, the Local Studies Centre of Guildford Library, and the Victoria University and Turnbull Libraries, Wellington; and to the many other librarians, archivists and individuals who gave of their time and knowledge in response to personal and written enquiries. My debts to the writings of others are also many and can only be partly reflected in the select list found within my Introduction.

The first draft of the book was prepared during a glorious New Zealand summer, whilst a Fellow of the Victoria University of Wellington. I am extremely grateful to the authorities of the Victoria University for awarding me a Fellowship and enabling me to spend a very happy and rewarding year in New Zealand.

The appearance of a paperback edition has provided the opportunity to correct some minor factual errors, though neither substantial rewriting nor the addition of new entries was possible. For all errors and omissions which remain and which have passed uncorrected in this edition, either because of the author's ignorance or the constraints imposed by reprinting from existing pages, the author begs to be forgiven. Finally, it is important to stress again a point made in the original Introduction – that information on whether a site or building is open to the public and, if so, its times of opening, will inevitably have changed since this book was compiled and readers are strongly advised to make enquiries before visiting.

FOREWORD

The Cromwell Association's decision to commission as part of its Jubilee Commemorations a Gazetteer of Cromwellian Britain is to be commended. Cromwell's name is attached – rightly or wrongly – to so many places that it is worth while bringing them together with appropriate annotation into an accurate and comprehensive work of reference, and to extend it to cover places of interest in the Cromwellian period even where they are not directly related to the man himself. The compilation has been made with skill and scholarship by Dr Peter Gaunt, a young scholar of enterprise and dedication. The result of his efforts is a work that should have a wide appeal – to students of the period, to admirers of 'our Chief of Men' and to tourists – something in fact of a *vade mecum*.

As a biographer and historian, the idea of a Gazetteer of a major historical personage greatly appeals to me. I have always found it essential to relate together people, places and dates as accurately as possible, something which is surprisingly often overlooked.

As for Cromwell, he has for centuries been regarded as the average Englishman on, as it were, a grander scale. His career illustrates the irreconcilable contradiction between ethics and politics – the age-old problem of every statesman – and his struggle to balance morality and expediency, the desirable with the possible, makes him an example and a warning not only to rulers and politicians but to the peoples of a democracy.

C. VERONICA WEDGWOOD

INTRODUCTION

That great God, which is the searcher of my heart, knows with what a sad sense I go upon this service, and with what a perfect hatred I detest this war without an enemy . . . We are both upon the stage and must act those parts that are assigned us in this tragedy; let us do it in a way of honour, and without personal animosities, whatsoever the issue be . . .

Waller's letter to Hopton, written a few days before the two clashed at Lansdown, is rightly famous as an eloquent expression of the reluctance and disdain with which some went to war. But neither commander drew back from the approaching engagement and both won justified renown for their skill and energy on the battlefield. And against the cool phrases and civilized tone of Waller's letter should be placed the unmistakable evidence of an altogether fiercer approach – the thousands of dead at Marston Moor, Naseby and Worcester, the reign of terror and mayhem let loose during the sack of Bolton, Leicester and other unfortunate towns, the massacres at Barthomley, Chapel en le Frith, Hopton Castle, Newark Castle in Scotland and, later, at Drogheda and Wexford in Ireland, and the summary executions of Irishmen, Catholics, turncoats and other unfortunates.

The decade of intermittent but extensive conflict which formally opened on 22 August 1642, when Charles I raised his Standard at Nottingham, affected different people in different ways. Despite the tales of bemused farmers leaning on their gates, amazed at the appearance of an army and supposedly ignorant of the conflict, in reality few if any could have been unaware of, and unaffected by, the Civil War. At the very least, they would have been hit in the pocket by the heavy and repeated exactions which both sides levied to finance the war effort. Some lost lands and property and were ruined by the war; others made a fortune out of it. Military glory and political power accrued to those who backed the winning side and lived long enough to share in the spoils. Some volunteered and fought with enthusiasm; others served under a degree of duress and sought to desert at the earliest opportunity. Some tried not merely to avoid service in person but to keep the conflict as a whole at a safe distance – in several regions the gentry attempted at the outbreak of war to agree and observe pacts of neutrality and non-hostility, thus saving their county from the terrors of war, and in different circumstances during the mid-1640s the Clubmen, too, tried to keep the warring factions from their localities. The possibility of mutilation or death awaited all in arms, from the lowliest trooper to the highest officer – an array of titled aristocrats fell on both sides and at times Cromwell, Fairfax, Rupert, Newcastle and even the King himself were in real danger on the battlefield. For Charles, the war eventually brought defeat and death, for Cromwell wealth, power and political supremacy.

Civil War Britain was overwhelmingly rural and sparsely populated. London, with over 200,000 inhabitants, was far and away the biggest urban centre, and few other towns had populations over 10,000. The uneven distribution of population and wealth was matched by the variable standard of communications. Supplies could be moved by sea – the Thames and Severn were navigable far upstream and York, Nottingham, Cambridge, Stratford and many other inland towns were still serviceable ports at this time – and the century saw significant advances in land drainage and canalisation. But the primary and often only means of transport was the road system. The shortcomings of this system are often exaggerated and it is clear that the area around London and the Home Counties had quite passable roads. Cromwell was able to commute between London and Cambridgeshire without difficulty or inordinate delay and he covered impressive distances during his campaigns in southern England. Further afield, however, only the principal routes radiating from the capital were maintained to a reasonable standard and most roads were at best difficult, at worst completely impassable. Communications and transport were correspondingly slow and although neither side in the war observed a strict 'season' or abandoned campaigning entirely during the winter, operations inevitably lagged as bad weather reduced roads to seas of mud or hid them under a blanket of snow. Unseasonably good weather could bring the armies to the field – in January 1643 Fairfax was able to resume operations in West Yorkshire, catching the local Royalists off guard; unseasonably poor weather hindered Derby's operations before Manchester in August 1642 and a year later ruined the King's attempt to bring down the walls of Gloucester. In part, at least, the course of the war turned on the state of the roads and the skies.

In 1642 Britain possessed no standing or regular army and both sides set about the urgent task of raising, training and equipping troops. General commissions of array and calls to arms were issued; individual members of the gentry and peerage were also commissioned colonels of regiments, which they then raised and equipped themselves. In addition, King and Parliament could call upon the Trained Bands, part-time local defence militias organised at town or county level and possessing limited training and equipment. As the war dragged on, both sides resorted to a degree of duress or conscription to raise troops. Inevitably, the resulting army was a rather mixed bunch. Some troops and officers had gained considerable experience of warfare on the Continent during the 1620s and 1630s, but most had never seen action before. Trained Bands and others often considered their primary role to be the defence of their locality and were reluctant to march too far from their home county. Desertion was always a problem and the standards of uniform, weapons, training and discipline varied enormously. As time progressed, both sides set about reforming their military organisation, streamlining the cumbersome command system and improving army discipline, but the results were always piecemeal. Throughout the war, it was very unusual for either side to have a single army of more than 20,000 men in the field; an army of 12–14,000 was large by Civil War standards.

Poor maps, crude optical instruments, dilatory communications, often rather wayward discipline and frequent divisions between senior officers together made it difficult to manoeuvre a large army and almost impossible to retain tight control on the battlefield. Moreover, neither side seems to have developed a single national strategy or a unified plan of campaign – the Royalists' triple advance on London of 1643 almost certainly owes more to later historians than to anything within the King's mind. Instead of one Civil War there were numerous regional conflicts, often with little cooperation or communication between the various theatres, and sometimes producing very different results – as the King was pursuing Essex's Parliamentary army into the south-west in a campaign which would lead to one of the most crushing Royalist victories of the war, Prince Rupert was virtually losing the North at Marston Moor. In consequence, perhaps, major battles involving the principal or combined armies were rare and the war in England and Wales soon settled into a pattern of regional conflicts, each involving only a fraction of the total Royalist or Parliamentary strength. Territory was controlled or conquered through garrisoning, raiding and limited engagements, in which even total defeat rarely put paid to the cause within the region and was but a setback in the overall conflict.

The Civil War, then, was a regional conflict, and it affected different areas in very different ways. Scotland and Ireland both played a major role in the outbreak of the conflict, Scotland through the religious war which first compelled Charles to call Parliament in 1640 and then ensured that he could not dissolve it, Ireland through the rebellion of autumn 1641 which necessitated the raising of an English army, thereby bringing to a head the growing distrust between King and Parliament. But once the English Civil War was underway, events within the two countries played only a limited and indirect role in the course of that war. Their real importance lay in their potential as a source of troops to fight in England and Wales. The King had grand plans for bringing over soldiers from Ireland, but in reality only a few thousand ever arrived. Scotland proved altogether more fruitful. Despite the optimism aroused in Royalist circles by Montrose's thrilling campaign, the Marquis suffered a fatal reverse before he was able to have any real impact on the war in England. Instead, it was Parliament's alliance with the Scots and the arrival in England of a large Scottish army in early 1644 which really altered the course of the war and tipped the balance decisively in Parliament's favour. The crucial element in the renewed conflict of 1648 and 1651 was the arrival in England of Scottish Royalist invasion forces.

The war in England and Wales, too, followed very different courses in different areas. In Warwickshire, for instance, the Parliamentarians retained control of almost the whole county throughout the period and suffered nothing more than occasional raids; yet the neighbouring regions of north Gloucestershire, former Worcestershire and Oxfordshire were not only under the King's control but also suffered considerable bloodshed as Massey and others struggled to free Gloucestershire from Royalism and as Waller, Fairfax and Cromwell attempted to break the circuit of bases protecting Oxford. The area in and around London was controlled by Parliament throughout the war and most of the south-east, East Anglia and the Home Counties escaped serious fighting. Conversely, Cornwall, much of Wales and the central Marches and Oxfordshire were firmly in the King's hands and saw no significant fighting until the latter stages of the war. Large parts of the Welsh heartlands and of northern England were bleak uplands, neither garrisoned nor fought over during the war. Other areas were not so fortunate and witnessed frequent bloodshed as the armies repeatedly fought for supremacy in the region: Gloucestershire was contested for much of the war; south-west and central southern England was invaded by the King in 1643–44 and slowly reconquered by Parliament; Cheshire, Shropshire and Staffordshire were very thickly garrisoned and suffered incessant raiding and counter-raiding; there were frequent and bloody clashes in the southern half of Lancashire and Yorkshire during the opening two years of the war; and the circuit of bases around Oxford and Oxfordshire was slowly whittled away. In general, Parliament controlled the southern and eastern half of the country during the opening phase of the war, including the arsenals at Portsmouth, the Tower and Kingston upon Hull; most of the fleet declared for Parliament, and control of the crucial ports of Milford Haven, Plymouth, Portsmouth, London and Hull gave Parliament supremacy at sea and all the benefits which accrued. The King controlled the west and north, including Cornwall and almost the whole of Wales.

The first major engagement of the war, at Edgehill in October 1642, was indecisive and despite his advance on the capital, the King was unable to take London. It became clear that neither side would gain a speedy victory and both made preparations for a long and complex conflict; Charles retired to Oxford and established his HQ and Royal capital there. The following year saw considerable Royalist successes. True, Charles failed to take Gloucester or seriously to threaten London, but his forces had been victorious in many areas and had gained extensive territory in the north, the east, north and west Midlands and south-west and central southern England. By the end of 1643 the King controlled up to three-quarters of England and Wales. But the entry of Parliament's Scottish allies significantly altered the balance of power to the detriment of the King. In July 1644 the Royalist cause in the north was all but destroyed at Marston Moor and thereafter the King retained a mere handful of isolated bases beyond the line linking the Humber and Mersey estuaries. Royalism was still a potent threat in the south, but the arrival of troops freed from service in the north, the appearance of the Scottish army and the reorganization of the Parliamentary army under a more vigorous and dynamic command structure together turned the tide there, too. The King was eventually brought to battle at Naseby in June 1645; the fight was close but eventually brought a crushing Parliamentary victory. Thereafter the war became a grand mopping-up operation, as the New Model Army retook the south and south-west and isolated the remaining Royalist bases. In 1646 Charles surrendered to the Scottish army before Newark. On his orders Newark itself, Oxford and most of the other surviving outposts surrendered to Parliament.

The Civil War brought to the fore the MP for Cambridge, Oliver Cromwell. Cromwell came from a middling gentry family in the Fenlands. When the Short Parliament assembled he had no previous military experience and only very limited experience in Parliament, gained during the late 1620s. Nonetheless, he soon became prominent as one of the most vigorous critics of Royal government within the House. At the outbreak of war Cromwell acted quickly to secure the town and university of Cambridge for Parliament and to organize the defence of East Anglia. He spent much of the following year on campaign in Lincolnshire, where he gained a reputation as an energetic cavalry commander. Commissioned a lieutenant-general in 1644, he rose to national prominence during the Marston Moor campaign. In 1645–46, as Lieutenant-General or second-in-command of the New Model Army, he worked closely with Fairfax to clear Royalism from southern and south-western England; he played a crucial role at Naseby. His appearances in Parliament were inevitably infrequent during the war, but when there he spoke with great authority and was widely respected. By 1646 Cromwell was potentially one of the most powerful men in the country.

Thereafter Cromwell occupied a unique position, for he was both a very senior army officer and a leading politician and MP, and thus had a foot in both the military and the civilian camps. This placed him in a very awkward position in 1646 as rifts grew between the Parliamentary army — which wanted religious and political reforms and strict constitutional limitations on the King – and Parliament itself – which seemed to favour a very lenient agreement with Charles and which showed little sign of instituting reforms. Cromwell eventually sided with the army as it seized the initiative by abducting the royal prisoner and negotiating with him direct; the troops camped in and around London to ensure Parliament's acquiescence. Increasing divisions within the Parliamentary army and the futile and – on Charles's part – insincere negotiations were both cut short by Charles's flight to the Isle of Wight in 1647 and his treaty with the Scots. In line with this a Scottish Royalist army under Hamilton entered England in summer 1648 but was crushed by Cromwell at Preston. Royalist risings in Kent, Surrey, Essex, South Wales, Yorkshire and elsewhere were poorly coordinated and no match for the experienced Parliamentary army. In this manner was the Second Civil War fought and lost. In its wake Parliament was purged by the army, the King tried and executed and monarchy and the House of Lords abolished.

Cromwell's military career was by no means over. In 1649–50 he went on campaign in Ireland, crushing the Catholic/Royalist rebellion which had smouldered on since 1641. In spring 1650 he was summoned back to the mainland to meet the renewed threat from Scotland, where Charles' son, the Prince of Wales, had been crowned King and was gathering an army. Fairfax had been unwilling to move against his former allies and Cromwell became Lord General of the army in his place. From July 1650 to August 1651 he campaigned in the Lowlands, attempting unsuccessfully to bring the main Scottish army to battle. Eventually, by accident or design, the Scottish army was able to march south into England; on 3 September it was caught and destroyed at Worcester. Despite occasional conspiracies and rebellions thereafter, Royalism was effectively ended as a serious threat; Cromwell's military career, too, was at an end.

Politically, however, the greatest achievement still lay ahead. With the departure of the remnant or Rump of the Long Parliament and the failure after a mere six months of the experiment with a supreme Nominated Assembly, the powers that be – the senior army officers – turned to a written constitution restoring certain elements of the pre-war system. There was to be an assured succession of triennial Parliaments possessing extensive legislative power; a permanent and independent executive Council of State; and a Lord Protector, serving to lead and unite the two arms of government, but possessing very strictly limited powers in his own right. Oliver Cromwell became Lord Protector for life. With his unique military and political background, Cromwell succeeded in containing the enormous stresses caused by the presence of a large, expensive and powerful standing army within a basically civilian and cost-cutting regime and was able to make the system work reasonably well. After his death in September 1658 no one was able to repeat the performance – certainly young Richard Cromwell lacked the necessary background – and the Protectoral edifice quickly collapsed. The repeated changes in government of the following year are difficult to follow and almost impossible to explain, but in spring 1660 the whole experiment in republicanism or government without a king was brought to a close with the Restoration of Charles II. Waller, now a gouty old Royalist in his sixties, was there to see the final curtain fall on the tragedy in which he had unwillingly played a leading role.

The Cromwellian Gazetteer is designed as a guide to sites in Britain and Ireland associated with the Parliamentary cause during the Civil War and Interregnum, 1642–1660. It covers sites of important Civil War battles, skirmishes and sieges and locations connected with the leading Parliamentary soldiers, politicians, clerics and artists of the period. Wherever possible, however, the emphasis is on Cromwell himself, and sites connected with Oliver and his family have been given particular prominence.

This volume is intended neither as a biography of Oliver Cromwell nor as a history of the Civil War. It is, instead, a topographical guide or gazetteer to the physical remains of Civil War and Cromwellian Britain, focussing particularly upon sites and buildings which still bear evidence of their mid-seventeenth-century connections. Moreover, the gazetteer reflects the Parliamentary side in the conflict, to the ruthless exclusion of the Royalist. Thus the homes or tombs of Fairfax, Essex and Warwick figure, but not those of Rupert, Hopton or Newcastle; Charles I's movements as a prisoner of Parliament and the Parliamentary army are covered, but not his itinerary between battles 1642–46; and his son's exploits on the battlefield of Worcester are included, but not his dramatic wanderings and arboreal adventures thereafter.

An itinerary of Oliver Cromwell appears as an appendix to the gazetteer. It includes only the more reliable records of Cromwell's travels, those mentioned in his own letters or described in apparently well-informed contemporary accounts. Many of the locations listed in this itinerary do not appear in the main body of the work: where there is no reliable evidence to indicate the building in which Cromwell lodged, it seemed pointless to create a separate entry in the gazetteer merely to record his presence in that town or village on a particular date. Where precise locations are known, sites and buildings connected with Cromwell are covered in detail, as are some of the more persistent traditions concerning his whereabouts, many of them unsupported by contemporary evidence – and thus usually omitted from the itinerary – some of them quite implausible.

Several other leading figures fall within the scope of the gazetteer, and entries record where they resided in life and lie in death. They include not only Cromwell's close relatives and descendants of the male line down to its extinction in 1821 – a detailed genealogy is to be found appended – but also other prominent members of the Parliamentary cause, senior army officers of the Civil War, leading opponents of the King in the Long Parliament, Cromwell's Major-Generals and Protectoral Councillors and the artists who painted the Lord General and his colleagues in verse as well as oils.

Careful selection proved vital in compiling the Civil War entries, for it would have been quite impossible to include every skirmish fought and every building fortified and defended. In some areas of the country there was almost perpetual fighting, with small local forces disputing territory or settling old scores. Major centres such as Gloucester, Oxford and Chester stood amid very thickly garrisoned territory, surrounded by concentric circuits of defensive outposts and enemy bases, and at the height of operations almost every village or defensible building in the area housed troops. A large army on the move would be engaged in near-continuous skirmishing, as raiding parties worried its van or rear. Temporary quarters were particularly vulnerable and frequently attacked. Clearly, it would be neither possible nor particularly illuminating to include every conflict and outpost. In general, all the major actions have been covered, even where battlefields have been completely built over – as at Seacroft Moor, West Yorks or Aberdeen, Grampian – or where nothing remains of the besieged stronghold – Lathom House, Lancs, for example, and the seventeenth-century defences of Plymouth, Devon. Lesser engagements have been included where something of the ground or building caught up in the war can still be traced.

The coverage for England and Wales is quite straightforward, with examination of the three wars of 1642–51 and of the handful of minor rebellions of the 1650s. The situation in Scotland and Ireland was less clear, for much of the bloodshed of the period in these two countries was only indirectly or distantly related to the main struggle between the King and the English Parliament. The coverage of Scotland is confined to Montrose's campaigns, Cromwell's visit of October 1648 and his campaign of July 1650 to August 1651, and a small number of other sites, usually castles, involved in the fighting of the late 1640s and early 1650s; the troubles of the mid to late 1650s and Monck's efforts to quell them have been omitted. Similarly, Irish coverage rarely extends beyond Cromwell's campaign of August 1649 to May 1650.

The sites are listed under their post-1974 counties. These, in turn, run alphabetically for each of the four countries covered. Further division seemed necessary in Greater London, and the entries have been rather loosely divided into Greater London Central and Greater London Suburbs. Approximate locations of sites in England, Scotland and Wales are indicated by four-figure references from the standard national grid; Ireland has its own, slightly different grid. Street names have often been added to help locate a site or building in London and other large towns. Where appropriate – usually when describing a specific site or building outside urban centres – a six figure reference is given. Large scale maps – preferably the Ordnance Survey 1:50 000 series – will often be indispensable for locating or understanding a particular site.

Wherever possible the entry indicates whether the site or building is open to the public and, if it is, outlines the current (1985) periods of opening. This information will, no doubt, rapidly become outdated and inaccurate and anyone planning a visit is strongly advised to check details of opening in advance. Inclusion in this gazetteer is no indication that a site or building is open to the public. Many of the entries describe sites and buildings which are strictly private, with no public right of entry. Please respect this privacy and view only from public roads or footpaths, however distant from the site itself.

Many published works have proved invaluable in the preparation of this volume. For Cromwell's itinerary – W.C. Abbott, *The Writings and Speeches of Oliver Cromwell* (Cambridge, Mass., 1937–47); the newspapers and pamphlets of the period in the Thomason Collection in the British Library, many extracts from which are reprinted in J. Caulfield, *Cromwelliana* (London, 1810); W.S. Douglas, *Cromwell's Scotch Campaigns* (London, 1898); D. Murphy, *Cromwell in Ireland* (London, 1883); J.R. Phillips, *Memoirs of the Civil War in Wales and the Marches* (London, 1874). For the military events of the war – the many books of Brigadier Peter Young are indispensable, particularly P. Young and A.H. Burne, *The Great Civil War* (London, 1959) and P. Young and R. Holmes, *The English Civil War* (London, 1974); the works consulted for the war in specific counties or regions, both collections of contemporary writings and secondary narrative accounts, are legion and far too numerous to list individually. For the buildings – N. Pevsner and others, *Buildings of England* series (London, 1951+); H.M. Colvin, *History of the King's Works* (London, 1963+); and the many counties covered in the two collections, *Victoria History of the Counties of England* (London, 1900+) and *Royal Commission on Historical Monuments* (London, 1910+).

P.R. Newman, *Atlas of the English Civil War* (London, 1985) is a useful guide to military events, including a concise statement of Newman's reinterpretation of the Battle of Marston Moor. *Royal Commission on Historical Monuments, Newark on Trent; The Civil War Siegeworks* (London, 1964) is a superb account, giving a wealth of detail impossible to reproduce here, and remains essential reading for dedicated explorers.

Despite the research and preparation, a volume of this kind is bound to contain errors and to omit much which, on reflection, is worthy of inclusion. With the possibility of a revised edition in mind, we would be very grateful for having errors and omissions pointed out in as much detail as possible. These should be addressed to the publishers at Phoenix Mill, Far Thrupp, Stroud GL5 2BU.

ENGLAND

AVON

Secured for Parliament at the outbreak of war, Avon passed under Royalist control during the summer and autumn of 1643 and remained in the King's hands for two years. The siege and capture of Bristol in September 1645 effectively ended the Royalist cause in Avon. Cromwell was present throughout this operation, the only recorded occasion on which he was involved in military action within the area covered by the modern county.

Bath (ST7564) Initially held by Parliament, Bath served as a base for Waller in late June 1643 and it was in its defence that he marched out to meet Hopton at Lansdown on 5 July. Following his dismal showing there, Waller evacuated the town and Bath fell under Royalist control. Thus it remained for two years until, on 30 July 1645, Col. Okey launched an early morning raid on Bath, surprising and expelling the small garrison.

In the south transept of Bath Abbey is a monument to Waller's first wife (d1633) with reclining figures of Waller and his late wife. The Parliamentary General was not buried here, but lies in an unmarked grave in London.

Bristol (ST5872) In the seventeenth century Bristol was the second city of England, a rich trading centre and the main west coast port. In consequence, control of the town became one of the chief objectives of both armies. The large and sprawling town was defended by two lines of fortifications. A long circuit of dry ditches, stone walls or earth banks with five interval forts and numerous gates surrounded the suburbs north of the Avon and Redcliffe in the south-east. The inner city was protected by the rivers Frome and Avon on all sides except the north-east, where a huge medieval castle blocked the headland between the meandering rivers. The fortifications appeared very strong, but their great length — the outer circuit was over three miles long — meant that huge numbers of troops were needed to hold them. It was the fate of two governors to have insufficient men to defend Bristol and to be severely criticised for its fall.

Bristol was held by Parliament at the outbreak of war, but on 23 July 1643 Rupert arrived before the town with up to 20,000 men; to defend the town, Nathaniel Fiennes had just

1,800 troops. Rupert bombarded the defences for two days and then stormed the town in the early hours of the 26th. Although attacks on the north wall and Redcliffe were repulsed, Col. Wentworth eventually broke through around Brandon Hill and Fiennes surrendered as the Royalists were preparing to storm the inner city. For this action he was subsequently sentenced to death but reprieved.

Two years later, in summer 1645, the main Parliamentary army under Fairfax retook Bristol, besieging and bombarding the place for a fortnight and then storming the outer defences on 10 September. Prince Rupert surrendered once the outer circuit had been breached, earning the King's extreme displeasure. Cromwell was present throughout the siege, lodging first at Keynsham to the south-east and later at Fairfax's HQ in a farmhouse at Stapleton. On 10 September he supervised the action around Priors Hill fort, north-west of the town centre. Cromwell stayed in Bristol for several days after its fall; he returned in 1649 on his way to Ireland, lodging at Joseph Jackson's house for a fortnight from 14 July while he awaited the arrival of money for the campaign. He passed through the town again in May 1650 on his return from Ireland.

Despite its large and eventful role in the Civil War, there is little to be seen in Bristol today. The seventeenth-century defences have been overrun and obliterated in the later expansion of the city and even the mighty castle has gone, slighted in the 1650s and now surviving only in the name of a green and several streets on the north bank of the Avon (around ST593732). There is a modern plaque by Christmas Steps to Col. Henry Lunsford, a Royalist officer shot dead here on 26 July 1643 as he led an assault on the Frome Gate.

William Penn, one of Cromwell's Admirals

Right: Bath Abbey, Avon. Epiphanius Evesham's fine monument to Sir William Waller's first wife, Jane (d1633), was desecrated by Royalist troops during the Civil War and the features of Waller and his wife badly damaged.

Below: Donnington Castle, Berks. The huge gatehouse stands before the shattered remains of the medieval stronghold. To the left is part of the earthwork fort thrown up by Sir John Boys's Royalist garrison.

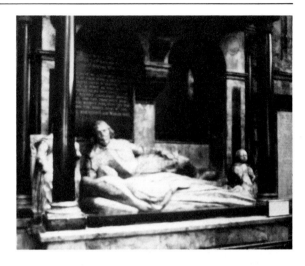

and a colleague of Blake, lies buried near a mural monument in St Mary's Redcliffe.

Lansdown (ST7268)

Lansdown was the only significant battle of the Civil War in Avon, and although inconclusive, it contributed to the erosion of the Parliamentary hold on the area during summer 1643. Hopton's army was in Bradford on Avon by 2 July and then spent three days trying to march around the east side of Bath and sever Waller's communications with Wiltshire. By the 5th Hopton had pushed his way up the Avon valley, driving in Parliamentary outposts from Claverton, Batheaston and Monkton Farleigh (Wilts), and was preparing to attack Lansdown Hill.

Lansdown is a large hill with steep sides and a long flat top which runs north-west from Bath. Waller had occupied the hill on 4 July and by the morning of the 5th had drawn up his men behind hastily dug earthworks near the northern crest, facing north (around ST721703). Hopton advanced from Marshfield via Tog and Freezing Hills and a confused mêlée developed in the muddy valley between Lansdown and Freezing Hills. Hopton at first planned to withdraw, but when the Cornish Infantry threw back the Parliamentary Horse and began assaulting Lansdown Hill he ordered a general attack. Parties of musketeers set out on either flank to support Grenville's Cornishmen as they struggled up the hill straight towards Waller's line. The Royalist Horse were badly mauled, but at the third attempt the Cornish Foot took the ridge and Waller fell back to a stone wall 400 yards south of his original position. Darkness fell and the Parliamentarians slipped away during the night leaving the Royalists in control of the hill. It was an expensive semi-victory: the Royalists had all but exhausted their ammunition, their Horse were in tatters, Sir Bevil Grenville and many other officers were dead and on the following day Hopton was badly injured and many more killed when a cartload of powder exploded on Tog Hill.

Lansdown Hill is still open ground above Bath, crossed by a minor road. The northern slopes, where the fighting was fiercest, are more heavily wooded now than they were during the seventeenth century. By the road at the crest of the hill is a monument to Sir Bevil Grenville, an obelisk erected by his son John, 1st Earl of Bath.

Thornbury Castle (ST633907)

The castle, really a grand domestic residence with slight military pretensions, was begun by the 3rd Duke of Buckingham in 1511. Garrisoned by both sides during the war to cover the road from Bristol to Gloucester, it survived intact and was remodelled in the eighteenth and nineteenth centuries. The ornate mansion, with round and polygonal towers, heraldic decorations and impressive chimney stacks, stands in private grounds north of the church.

Yate Court (ST713860)

Yate Court, the thirteenth-century fortified mansion of the Berkeley family, changed hands several times during the Civil War, serving alternately as an outpost of the Bristol garrison and as a base to disrupt communications with that town. By the end of the war the house had been reduced to ruins by repeated attacks. The surviving parts were incorporated in the modern farm buildings on the site. Yate Court Farm is private, but the exterior and the remains of the square moat and embankment which surrounded the medieval mansion can be viewed from the public footpath which runs by the farm.

BEDFORDSHIRE

Secure for Parliament throughout the Civil War, the county saw little military action beyond brief and infrequent Royalist raids. Cromwell probably passed through the eastern fringe of the county from time to time during the 1640s when following the westerly of the two routes between Huntingdon and London. He was certainly in Bedford on several occasions.

Ampthill (TL0338)

On 4 October 1643 400 Royalist Horse under Sir Lewis Dyve raided Ampthill, surprising and capturing the county's Parliamentary committee meeting there. During the 1650s the regicide and Major General, John Okey, acquired property in and around the town, including Ampthill Park House. The house which he owned has gone, and the present Park House dates from the very end of the seventeenth century.

Bedford (TL0549) Sir Lewis Dyve's Royalist raiding party briefly occupied the town in October 1643, skirmishing with a small Parliamentary unit around the bridge. Before moving on, the Royalists made a futile effort to refortify the very dilapidated Norman castle, which survives as a low motte to the west of Newnham Road. A Royalist force passed through the town again in August 1645, once more clashing with Parliamentary soldiers around the bridge.

Cromwell was certainly here on 11 June 1645 and in July 1647 and he probably passed through the town quite frequently on his way to and from Cambridgeshire and Lincolnshire. In March 1644 he directed that any letters and messages for him be addressed to the Swan in Bedford, where he would collect them. The present Swan Inn in the High Street dates from the late eighteenth century, but probably stands on the site of the earlier Swan known to Cromwell.

Brogborough (SP9638) The Round House, also known as Brogborough Park Farm, stands amid the brickfields near the village of Brogborough. The building is of three storeys – a flight of steps leads to the first floor entrance – under a steep-pitched roof. Several windows are false. The house is large and square, and is known as 'The Round House' not because of its external shape but because interconnecting rooms make it possible to walk around the inside of the building in a single circuit. Probably built by John Stone in the first half of the seventeenth century, there are rather dubious stories that the house was fortified for Parliament in the Civil War, that Cromwell stayed here on several occasions and that he fought off a Royalist attack here. John Okey bought the property in 1650 and lived here for most of the following decade. The Round House is still a private residence, though now much dilapidated and semi-derelict.

Bromham (TL017513) In the seventeenth century Bromham Hall was the home of the Dyve family, the most prominent supporters of the Royalist cause in Bedfordshire. Sir Lewis fortified the hall in summer 1642, but it was quickly taken by Parliamentary forces at the outbreak of the war. The late Tudor brick hall survives as a private residence.

Clifton (TL165393) Cromwell's cousin Thomas, third son of Sir Philip Cromwell, lived at Clifton during the 1650s. While his brothers Oliver and Philip had both fought and died for Parliament in the previous decade, Thomas had served the King, become Major of a Horse Regiment and survived unscathed. He died in 1658 and lies buried in an unmarked grave in All Saints Church.

Dunstable (TL0121) A Royalist party raided the town in June 1644, plundering and looting, disrupting a church service and taking pot-shots at the minister in the pulpit – they missed. The landlord of the Red Lion, High Street North, was not so lucky, for he was shot dead when he refused to supply the Royalists with horses.

Pertenhall (TL095652) Hoo Manor or Farm, a modest Tudor building surrounded by a moat, was the home of the Rolt family during the seventeenth century. Cromwell's cousin Mary, youngest daughter of Sir Oliver Cromwell, married Edward Rolt in the 1620s and the couple spent the rest of their lives at Hoo Manor. Both lie buried in St Peter's Church (TL084654) and a monument to Edward (d1652) survives on the south wall of the nave.

Upper Dean (TL046677) Cromwell's cousin Anna, daughter of Henry Cromwell, lived at Dean with her husband John Neale, who represented the county in the first Protectorate Parliament. Anna (d1651) and John (d1680) both lie buried in All Saints Church, near a mural monument to them in the south chapel.

Woburn (SP965326) On 19 June 1647 Charles I, prisoner of the Parliamentary army, was lodged for the night at Woburn House. The Russells' early seventeenth-century house on the site of the demolished medieval abbey was itself largely demolished in the following century and the present grand mansion is almost entirely Georgian.

BERKSHIRE

The new, much reduced county has lost most of its Civil War sites to Oxfordshire, and surprisingly few important sites remain within Berkshire. The western half of the county fell under the control of Royalist Oxfordshire, whilst the Parliamentarians were usually dominant in the east and south. Not until the closing year of the war did Parliament gain the upper hand throughout the county. Cromwell frequently travelled through Berkshire in 1644–45 but, with the exception of the Second Battle of Newbury, he was involved in no serious fighting within the county.

The Blue Boar Inn (SU455742) According to an unconfirmed tradition, Oliver Cromwell lodged at the Blue Boar Inn before the Second Battle of Newbury. The inn still stands by the road, two miles west of Chieveley.

Donnington Castle (SU461692) Donnington was of great strategic importance, for it commanded the Great Bath Road from London to the West and the road from Oxford to Portsmouth and the south coast. It was secured by the Royalists in 1642 and held for the King by Col. John Boys throughout the Civil War, enduring repeated attacks and sieges. On 31 July 1644 Parliamentary forces under Middleton tried to storm the castle but they were fiercely repulsed and, lacking artillery, posed no further threat to the garrison. Two months later Col. Horton returned with a larger force and heavy cannon which eventually shattered three of the castle's towers. But on 18 October the Parliamentarians, by then commanded by Manchester, fell back before the main Royalist army. Although Waller briefly renewed the siege after the Second Battle of Newbury, a second Royalist force relieved the castle on 9 November. Safe for another year, the castle was under siege again from November 1645 and on 1 April 1646 Boys finally surrendered the place to Col. John Dalbier. The castle was sacked and reduced to ruins.

The fourteenth-century castle was square, the outer walls linked by round corner towers, with additional square towers set in the north and south walls. Little more than the outline of this building survives above ground and only the eastern gatehouse remains intact. A huge three storey building flanked by twin drum towers rising a further two storeys, the gatehouse contains a collection of Civil War relics. In 1643 Boys strengthened the castle by adding an artillery fort beyond the walls, an irregularly shaped double banked earthwork with arrowhead bastions on the north, east and south sides. The fort is somewhat eroded but still clearly visible. The castle is open daily.

Eton (SU9677) Francis Rous – Puritan divine, veteran Parliamentarian, Speaker of the Nominated Assembly and Protectoral Councillor – died in January 1659 and was buried beneath a monument in the Church of the Blessed Mary, the Chapel of Eton College. He had been Provost of Eton during the 1650s.

Horton (TQ013758) In the chancel of St Michael's is an inscribed floor slab to Sarah (d1637), mother of John Milton. The house in which the young Milton and his retired parents lived during the 1630s has long since disappeared.

Newbury (SU4767) Newbury shared with Lostwithiel the dubious distinction of having two major Civil War battles fought in the immediate vicinity. In consequence, Newbury Museum contains a fine collection of Civil War artefacts.

First Battle (around SU4565). In September 1643 the Parliamentary army under Essex relieved Gloucester and then marched east, heading back to London. Essex made curiously slow progress, and on the evening of the 19th the Royalists swept into Newbury ahead of him, blocking the road to London. The King's men spent the night south of the town, occupying the plateau of Wash Common. Essex responded by occupying the rising ground to the west and north-west of the common. Fighting began when Wentworth and Lisle tried unsuccessfully to clear this area, falling back under heavy fire; Lord Falkland, Charles's Secretary of State, was amongst those killed. A confused battle developed around the Parliamentary positions on the western edge of the common and continued until nightfall when the Royalists marched away, their ammunition exhausted.

The eastern side of the battlefield, the area occupied by the Royalists, now lies under a south-western suburb of Newbury. A monument to Lord Falkland stands by the main road at SU460650, near the Gun Inn, traditionally the King's HQ during the battle. The western edge of the common, where fighting was fiercest, is still open ground and has changed little since the seventeenth century. The so-called burial mounds on Wash Common are probably ancient earthworks of some kind and not Civil War graves.

Second Battle (around SU4668). The Second Battle of Newbury, of 27 October 1644, followed a much clearer pattern. The King offered battle to relieve the besieged Royalist bases of Banbury and Donnington Castles and Basing House. His steady advance eastwards persuaded the hesitant Manchester to gather his forces and give battle. By 26 October the two armies were facing each other on open ground to the north of Newbury. Charles occupied the land between the villages of Speen and Shaw, taking in Donnington Castle and Shaw House. The Parliamentary army to the east decided to divide and launch a co-ordinated attack from the front and rear. To this end Waller set off in a wide arc to the north of the Royalist position. By the afternoon of the 27th he was in place to the west of Speen and attacked immediately, quickly taking the village and breaking the west end of the Royalist line. But Cromwell and others were slow to follow up the attack and the Royalists were able to reorganise and counter-charge. A fierce but inconclusive fight developed around Speen. To the east, meanwhile, Manchester had failed to launch a major attack to coincide with Waller's and not until dusk did he attack Shaw and Shaw House, to no great effect. Charles's army was outnumbered and marched away to Oxford under cover of darkness. The losses were about equal – around 500 men apiece – but the Royalists had succeeded in relieving a number of key bases.

The area of the battle is now crossed by a number of roads, but it has not yet been engulfed by the expansion of Newbury. The villages of Speen and Shaw retain their separate identities, and Shaw House also survives, a magnificent Elizabethan mansion surrounded by an ancient earthwork.

Reading (SU7272)   Straddling the main road to the west and the rivers Thames and Kennet, Reading was a key base between the opposing capitals of London and Oxford. The town was secured for the King by Sir Arthur Aston and a garrison of 2,000 in November 1642, and they spent the winter building or strengthening the wall and bank around Reading, using stone from Reading Abbey. On 15 April 1643 Essex laid siege to the town with 4,500 men, overrunning the outer trenches and bombarding the inner works. On the 25th a relieving force from Oxford was halted and repulsed at Caversham Bridge, the crossing of the Thames immediately to the north of seventeenth-century Reading. Two days later Col. Fielding, acting governor in place of the injured and supposedly dumb Aston, surrendered to Essex, an action for which he was later tried and sentenced to death but reprieved. The town changed hands twice more, but with little further fighting. In September 1643 Essex abandoned the place after the First Battle of Newbury, and Aston entered unopposed. During the spring of 1644 the Royalists in turn pulled out, slighting the defences as they went, and by May the Parliamentarians were back in Reading, hastily repairing the fortifications.

The Parliamentary army was based at Reading for three weeks in July 1647, and the King was lodged at Caversham Court. It was a period of intense negotiation, and Fairfax and Cromwell were frequently with the King.

The great nineteenth- and twentieth-century expansion of Reading has obliterated the medieval and Civil War defences of the town. Caversham has been absorbed into the main urban sprawl, and its thirteenth-century timber bridge over the Thames replaced by a modern concrete construction (SU712747). Caversham Court, where the King was held, has been demolished and Southcote House, the Elizabethan building used by Fairfax and Cromwell as their HQ, has fared little better – only the moat and gatehouse survive (SU692717). Earthworks in Forbury Gardens may be the remains of a Civil War redoubt, Forbury, built by Aston in 1642–3.

Windsor (SU960770)   The Royal castle of Windsor comprises a mass of buildings of widely differing dates – the central strongpoint, the Round Tower in the middle of the three wards, was begun by Henry II in the twelfth century and strengthened by George IV over 600 years later. Windsor Castle was held by Parliament without serious challenge throughout the Civil War, a base for operations and often the HQ of the army's high command. Cromwell was frequently at Windsor during the mid and late 1640s, consulting with Lord General Fairfax and attending meetings of the General Council of the Army. The castle is open to the public when the royal family is not in residence.

BUCKINGHAMSHIRE

The county saw few major engagements during the Civil War and, with the exception of a handful of Royalist strongholds – particularly in the west under the influence of Oxfordshire – the area was Parliamentarian throughout the period. The county is rich in Parliamentary connections because many senior politicians and soldiers lived and died here. There are a number of Cromwellian associations, though many are based on tradition rather than clear evidence.

Aylesbury (SP8113) Aylesbury was almost within the range of Royalist raids from Oxford and stood in something of a frontier zone. There was frequent minor skirmishing in the surrounding district, but Aylesbury itself seems to have escaped most of the bloodshed and was held by Parliament throughout the war. A Royalist detachment advancing on London from the northwest after Edgehill was halted and repulsed outside the town by Col. Balfour, and Prince Rupert was beaten off when he moved against the town in January and June 1644. In July 1646 Aylesbury was degarrisoned and the earthwork defences demolished. No trace of them survives.

Cromwell probably stayed in Aylesbury on many occasions during his campaigns in the area. He was certainly here on 29 May 1645 and again on 9 September 1651 when he halted in Aylesbury on his way back to London after the battle of Worcester to receive a delegation of MPs bearing congratulations and money. According to tradition he stayed at the King's Head off Market Square, a grand, late medieval coaching inn with a stable yard and gateway, now owned by the National Trust. On display is a chair supposedly used by Cromwell during his stay.

A modern bronze statue of John Hampden, the local Parliamentary hero, stands nearby in the Market Square. The Parliamentarian and regicide Thomas Scott also came from Aylesbury.

Boarstall (SP624142) Boarstall House or Castle was a late medieval fortified manor-house surrounded by a moat. In the very west of the county, barely ten miles from Oxford, it served as a Royalist outpost for most of the war. The King's men garrisoned Boarstall unopposed at the beginning of 1643 to protect Brill and the north-eastern approaches to Oxford. In April 1644 it was evacuated on the approach of Parliamentary forces and briefly held by them, but on 10 June Col. Gage led 1,000 men from Oxford against the place. The outbuildings and the nearby church, also held by Parliamentary soldiers, were taken and on the 24th the main garrison surrendered. It was held by Royalists for two more years, its deep moat thwarting

attempts by Skippon and Fairfax to storm it in June 1645. Not until 10 June 1646, following a long blockade, did the Royalist garrison surrender, the last stronghold in the county to hold out for the King. Only the gatehouse survives, a mighty fourteenth-century pile with turrets, battlements and seventeenth-century windows, now owned by the National Trust. Beyond, the remains of the moat encircle the site of the demolished medieval mansion.

Brill (SP6513) In the west of the county and on the frontier between Royalist Oxfordshire and Parliamentary Buckinghamshire, the area around Brill witnessed frequent skirmishing during the war. The village itself was held by the Royalists at the beginning of the war and their hastily erected earthwork bank and ditch enabled them to beat off an attack by Goodwin and Hampden's troops from Aylesbury in January 1643. By the end of the year, however, the pressure on the weakly defended village was too great, and the Royalists pulled out. It was later occupied by Parliamentary troops who used the village as an operational and supply base. In open ground to the north of the church are the slight remains of earthworks, possibly part of the Civil War defences thrown up by the Royalists in 1642–3.

Buckingham (SP6933) Buckingham castle was very ruinous by the seventeenth century and the town was neither formally garrisoned nor of real importance in the war. There is no clear evidence that Cromwell ever lodged at Buckingham, but tradition has it that he stayed here at some point, either in Castle House or in an adjoining property, perhaps the Swan and Castle, formerly the White Swan or simply the Swan, in Castle Street.

Cromwell's cousin Elizabeth (d1666) and her husband Sir Richard Ingoldsby (d1656) were buried in St Peter and St Paul, but most of the medieval church and any monuments to them were destroyed in the fire which devastated the town in 1725.

Chalfont St Giles (SU9893) According to tradition, Cromwell stopped in Chalfont in October or November 1642 on his way back to London

Right: Chalfont St Giles, Bucks. The brick and timber-framed cottage, where John Milton lived in 1665–6 to escape the London plague, is the only one of his many houses to survive.

Below left: Boarstall Gatehouse, Bucks. The medieval gateway was renovated in the seventeenth century, when the large arch, bay windows and balustrading were added. Very little remains of the great house or castle which it once defended.

Below right: Hillesden Church, Bucks. Civil War bullet holes riddle the fifteenth-century north door of All Saints', almost obliterating the earlier, astronomical decorations.

after the battle of Edgehill, lodging at The Stone, the home of the Ratcliffe family. The old hall was demolished long ago but a modern private residence which stands on the site, 400 yards north of the church, is still called The Stone. Cromwell's men supposedly quartered in the grounds of the Pheasant Inn.

In Vache Lane stands The Vache, an Elizabethan manor owned and occupied in the mid-seventeenth century by the regicide George Fleetwood. It passed to the Duke of York after the Restoration.

In 1665 Milton sought refuge from the London plague and took a cottage in Chalfont, finishing *Paradise Lost* and beginning *Paradise Regained* during his stay. The brick and timber cottage in Deanway is now a Milton museum, open Tuesday to Saturday from February to October.

Chalfont St Peter (TQ0090)

Sir Isaac Pennington, City financier and sometime Lord Mayor of London, acquired The Grange in the 1650s and used it as his country seat for the remainder of the decade. Sir Isaac, a strong supporter of the Parliamentary cause, was prominent in ensuring that the City gave moral and financial backing to Parliament during the Civil War; he also served as Colonel of the City forces. He was imprisoned in the Tower at the Restoration and died there in December 1660. His son, Isaac junior, the Puritan and Quaker, also spent much time at The Grange. Pennington's old house was demolished in the nineteenth century and a modern school, also known as The Grange, stands on the site.

Chenies (TQ014984)

Chenies Manor, the seat of the Earls of Bedford, was a meeting place for Hampden and other opponents of the Royalist government during the 1630s. In 1642–3 the house served as a garrison for Hampden's regiment, who quartered in the huge armoury, still known as 'The Barracks'. Chenies Manor is open to the public on certain summer weekends.

Dinton (SP765118)

Dinton Hall, a late medieval red brick mansion, remodelled in the sixteenth century when the distinctive Tudor chimneys and gables were added, stands close to the village church. In the seventeenth century it was the seat of the Mayne family, including Simon Mayne, regicide and friend of Cromwell, who died in the Tower in 1661. Cromwell supposedly stayed at Dinton Hall after the battle of Edgehill or Naseby – accounts vary. His movements after Naseby are well-documented and he was certainly not in the area, but he may well

have passed through Buckinghamshire in October or November 1642 after Edgehill. In 1669 Richard Beke, widower of Cromwell's late niece Levina, and a distant relation of the Maynes, came to live at Dinton Hall and stayed here until his death.

Dinton Hall is private but the exterior can be viewed from the road and from the vicinity of the Church of St Peter and St Paul. The latter contains memorials to many members of the Mayne family, including the regicide's father and son. Richard Beke (d1707) and his second wife lie beneath an inscribed black marble slab in the south aisle.

Ellesborough (SP8406)

Chequers Court was owned in the eighteenth century by the Russell family, descendants of Cromwell's youngest daughter Frances by her second husband John Russell. The house contains a fine collection of Cromwellian portraits, though for obvious reasons the Prime Ministerial home is not open to the public. The Church of St Peter and St Paul nearby (SP863068) contains the tombs of many eighteenth-century Russells, including Cromwell's great-great-grandson Sir John.

Fawley (SU765842)

Fawley Court, 1¼ miles south-east of the village, was built in the 1680s and is now a private school. It stands on the site of an earlier Fawley Court, the home of Bulstrode Whitelock during the 1630s, which was sacked and destroyed by Rupert in the opening months of the war. Whitelock lived elsewhere after the Restoration, but in 1675 his body was brought back to Fawley and buried in the south transept of the church. Although the church contains several monuments to the Whitelock family, there is none to Bulstrode himself.

Great Hampden (SP848024)

The Hampden family were not only Cromwell's relatives by marriage but also the most prominent Parliamentarians in the county. Cromwell's aunt Elizabeth married William Hampden of Hampden Hall, Great Hampden in the early 1590s. Before his early death, William produced two sons, the elder of whom, John, became one of the leading opponents of Charles I's government. A cousin and friend of Cromwell, Hampden was one of Pym's closest political allies during the early stages of the Long Parliament and was one of the five Members whom Charles attempted to arrest in January 1642. At the outbreak of war he took up arms for Parliament and embarked on a brief but distinguished military career which ended the following year with his fatal wounding on Chalgrove Field.

Hampden Hall, the family's late medieval home, remodelled in the eighteenth century, is not usually open to the public, but footpaths run by it to the adjoining Church of St Mary Magdalene. Many members of the family are buried here, including William (d1597) and Elizabeth (d1665) and their two sons John (d1643) and Richard (d1659). Another Cromwell, Anna, a granddaughter of Sir Oliver, was buried at Great Hampden in 1669. Amongst the many memorials to the family are an inscribed tablet to John's wife and an elaborate eighteenth-century monument to John himself, with cherubs, a sarcophagus and an oval relief featuring the Hampden family tree growing out of a representation of John's wounding at Chalgrove.

In Honorend Land, just outside the village (SP863020), is a nineteenth-century memorial to John Hampden, with an inscription commemorating his refusal to pay Ship Money in the 1630s.

Greenlands House (SU775856)   A private nineteenth-century mansion now stands outside the village of Hambleden on the site of the medieval manor-house which was badly damaged in the Civil War and completely demolished thereafter. In May 1644 Sir John Doyley fortified Greenlands House for the King but within a month it was under siege. Although a relieving force from Oxford lifted the siege in early July, the Parliamentary forces soon returned. During the heavy bombardment which followed the Royalist magazine was hit and exploded, persuading the King's men to abandon the then ruined house and surrender to Col. Browne on 12 July.

Haddenham (SP7408)   The late fourteenth-century Wealden type house next to the church and facing the village green was the home of the Beke family in the seventeenth century. In February 1656 Levina Whitestone, daughter of Cromwell's sister Catherine and the Protector's favourite niece, married Richard Beke at a ceremony at Whitehall Palace attended by the Protector and his wife. The couple lived at Beke's house in Haddenham, then known as Beke House or Place, but their time together was brief, for within two years Levina was dead. In the 1660s Richard Beke sold up and moved to Dinton. The house is private, but the exterior can be viewed from the road.

Hartwell (SP795125)   The Church of St Mary the Virgin was built in the mid-eighteenth century on a Gothic octagonal plan, apparently modelled on the Chapter House of York Minster. Several worthies were buried or reburied in vaults beneath the church, including Richard Ingoldsby (d1685), regicide turned servant of Charles II, Cromwell's first cousin once removed. Inscriptions commemorating Ingoldsby and others are to be seen above the north and south doors.

Hillesden House (SP685287)   Nothing survives above ground of Hillesden House, the late medieval mansion which stood next to the church and was destroyed during the Civil War. In February 1644 Parliamentary forces fell back before a Royalist assault, and the King's men occupied and fortified Hillesden House, strengthening their position by digging a half-mile trench around the house and church. On 4 March Cromwell and Sir Samuel Luke led 2,000 men against Hillesden, overrunning the trenches and expelling a small Royalist outpost from the church. Capt. Smith surrendered the house as Cromwell was preparing to storm it. The search for treasure was stepped up when some plate and coin were found hidden within the house, and the ransacked building was then burnt to the ground. A new house built on the site in 1648 was itself demolished in the nineteenth century. Slight traces of the Civil War earthworks survive to the west of the church, and the north porch doors of All Saints bear bullet marks supposedly made during the storming of the church. The capture of Hillesden is the only clearly documented occasion on which Cromwell was engaged in military action within Buckinghamshire.

Lee (SP898044)   Modern stained glass in the east windows of the restored Saxon church include representations of Cromwell, Hampden and Hobart.

Lenthenborough (SP698314)   The present Manor Farm incorporates the remains of the former manor-house, partially demolished in the eighteenth century, which in the previous century had been the home of the Ingoldsby family. Cromwell's cousin Elizabeth and her husband Sir Richard Ingoldsby (d1656) lived here, and their children – including Richard, the regicide turned Royalist – were all born here. The farm is private, but a public footpath runs past the building.

Lilies (SP8118)   On the outskirts of the village of Weedon stands Lilies House, a Victorian successor to the Tudor mansion on the site which was destroyed by fire in 1860. Amongst the relics on display within the house are deeds and letters of Cromwell and John Hampden. According to a rather vague tradition, Cromwell quartered in the grounds of the old house during his Oxfordshire campaign.

Middle Claydon (SP719254) Claydon House,

a sixteenth-century manor-house remodelled in the eighteenth, still remains the seat of the Verney family. In the seventeenth century Sir Edmund Verney, Knight Marshal of England, loyally supported the King, but his military career was brief: he was killed at Edgehill, clinging desperately to the Banner Royal. Various relics of the Civil War are on display, including a letter written by Cromwell. Claydon House is open to the public on certain summer weekends.

Nether Winchendon (SP7312)   Nether Win-

chendon House, a quadrangular stone medieval mansion, extended and remodelled in the sixteenth and seventeenth centuries, contains a small selection of seventeenth-century furnishings and portraits. On display is a warrant summoning Joachim Mathews as a member of the Nominated Assembly; the document is dated 6 June 1653 and is signed by Cromwell. Nether Winchendon House is open on certain days during the summer.

Newport Pagnell (SP8743)   Although small

and quite weakly defended in 1642, Newport Pagnell's position on the main road between Oxford and East Anglia and the East Midlands made it of great importance to both sides in the war. In 1643 Sir Lewis Dyve secured the place for the King and began to throw up earthworks around the town. Because of a terrible mistake, probably the mis-reading of an order, Dyve evacuated the town in October 1643 and the grateful Parliamentarians promptly moved in. Sir Samuel Luke and his garrison strengthened the bank and ditch around the town and added a stone wall round Back Lane. Although Luke complained frequently and with some justice that his garrison was under-manned and under-supplied, he held the town for Parliament for the rest of the war, repelling several Royalist raids during 1644. None of the Civil War defences of the town survive.

Padbury (SP7230)   On 2 July 1643 500 Par-

liamentary soldiers under Middleton clashed with Lucas's Royalists around Padbury. The Parliamentarians were outnumbered and suffered heavy casualties as they fell back on Aylesbury. The village served as Cromwell's base in early March 1644 during operations against Hillesden.

Quarrendon (SP806156)   In open ground to

the south-east of Church Farm are the remains of Civil War earthworks, comprising three lines of entrenchments with embrasures for guns and four gun platforms. There is no record of any fighting here.

Steeple Claydon (SP704267)   According to tra-

dition, Cromwell and his troops spent the night of 3–4 March 1644 in Steeple Claydon before launching their dawn raid on Hillesden House. Cromwell supposedly slept in Camp Barn, west of the church at the southern end of the village, where Camp House now stands. The remains of two lines of entrenchments, possibly dating from the Civil War, run south and west of Camp House.

Stoke Mandeville (SP827103)   Moat Farm, an

'L'-shaped late Tudor brick and timber building partly surrounded by a moat, survives as a private farmhouse about ½ mile west of the modern church. It was owned by the Hampdens in the seventeenth century and garrisoned for Parliament throughout the war, but saw no significant fighting.

Wendover (SP8708)   One of several uncon-

firmed traditions concerning Cromwell's journey through the county after Edgehill has it that he spent a night in Wendover, sleeping in an upstairs room of the Red Lion Inn, an early seventeenth-century brick and timber coaching inn on the south side of the High Street. The town itself was garrisoned for Parliament during the Civil War.

Woodrow High House (SU933966)   This

modern private residence, 1½ miles south-west of Amersham, stands on the site of an earlier mansion, traditionally linked with the Cromwells. It was supposedly occupied at one time by the Protector's wife and daughters, though the association is extremely dubious.

CAMBRIDGESHIRE

The new county of Cambridgeshire, incorporating all of former Huntingdonshire, was firmly Parliamentarian throughout the war and suffered nothing more than isolated Royalist raids. More important, perhaps, it was Cromwell country, the area in which he and his family were born and brought up and in which he began his military career during the opening years of the Civil War.

Alconbury (TL1875)   In the early seventeenth century Cromwell's uncle, Sir Oliver, acquired the wardenship of Weybridge Forest and other lands in and around the village. Weybridge Lodge was occupied at various times by several members of the family, including Sir Oliver's brother Sir Philip, before the wardenship was sold off in the late 1620s. The timber framed lodge, Tudor but with seventeenth- and eighteenth-century additions, still stands surrounded by a moat in the private grounds of Weybridge Farm, about two miles south of Alconbury. At least one of Sir Philip's children, Joan (d1606 aged 1 year), lies buried in an unmarked grave in the Church of St Peter and St Paul.

Burghley House (TF050060)   Burghley House, one of the finest Elizabethan houses in England, was built for William Cecil, 1st Lord Burghley, in the late sixteenth century, incorporating the smaller hall which he and his father had erected earlier in the century. The house, which is open to the public, comprises four ranges around a central courtyard with four square corner towers topped by domes and two more domed towers flanking the gatehouse.

Burghley House was secured for the King without opposition in July 1643 and a small garrison installed to threaten the Parliamentary heartlands to the east. Cromwell returned from Lincolnshire to counter the threat and by 19 July he was before the house. A brief bombardment caused little damage and produced no response, but when Cromwell drew up his men to storm the place, the Royalists opened negotiations and surrendered Burghley later that day. Cromwell and his men probably spent the night in and around the house before hurrying back to Lincolnshire. A portrait of Cromwell, attributed to Walker, hangs in the Pagoda Room and a pair of boots, supposedly Cromwell's, are on display in the Great Hall.

Cambridge (TL4458)   Although Cromwell never lived in Cambridge for any length of time, he had many close links with the town. He was an undergraduate here in 1616–17 and he returned 23 years later to be admitted a burgess, preliminary to representing the town in the two Parliaments of 1640. Cambridge was one of the HQs of the Eastern Association during the war and Cromwell was often here, securing the university plate for Parliament in August 1642 and returning frequently over the following three years to supervise military operations. Three hundred years later his severed head was laid to rest in Cambridge.

During his year at Sidney Sussex, Cromwell is traditionally said to have occupied rooms on the north side of the first floor of Hall Court, overlooking Sidney Street. The College retains many Cromwellian links, including three portraits of the Protector, a document bearing his signature, a bible of 1658 supposedly owned by him and an oak chair inscribed 16 OC 58. On 25 March 1960 a semi-mummified human head, believed to be Cromwell's, was buried within the walls of the College; a plaque on the wall of the ante-chapel records the ceremony. One of the courts leading to the College has been named 'Cromwell Court'.

Queen's College, off Silver Street, contains a number of mid-seventeenth-century paintings, including portraits of Cromwell, Hugh Peter and George Monck. A bust of Cromwell is on display in King's College, off King's Parade.

By the seventeenth century most of the medieval castle had been demolished and only the south-west gatehouse and the Great Hall remained, used as a gaol and courthouse respectively. However, the site, on high ground at the north end of the town, was refortified in 1643: the Great Hall was partially rebuilt and converted to barracks, a bastioned earthwork fort was thrown up around the motte and 1,000 men were garrisoned here. They left in 1647 after an uneventful war and the defences were slighted. Of the circuit of ramparts and ditches constructed around the town in 1642–3, no trace survives. The castle barracks were demolished in the nineteenth century, but the remains of the Civil War fort survive, with the north and east bastions still visible around the edge of the Norman motte.

In 1640 Cromwell stayed at the White Bull Inn in Bridge Street while he was admitted a burgess and elected the town's MP; the inn no longer exists. From 1642 the Parliamentary committee were based at the Bear, and it is likely that Cromwell would have stayed here during his many war-time visits to the town. The inn referred to is probably the Black Bear, long since demolished, which stood off an alleyway north-west of the junction of Market and Sidney Streets.

Childerley Hall (TL355616)

Charles I was lodged at Childerley Hall on 5–7 June 1647 by the Parliamentary army, then stationed around Newmarket and Cambridge. On the 7th Cromwell, Fairfax and Ireton rode to Childerley to hold brief discussions with the King but by the evening all had left, the officers back to the army and Charles on to Newmarket. Childerley Hall is a fairly plain two-storey Tudor hall, remodelled in the nineteenth century, standing in private parkland between Great and Little Childerley. 'King Charles's Chamber' is the principal room on the upper floor, above the hall.

Chippenham (TL6669)

Chippenham Park was the seat of the Russell family, who were doubly linked with the Cromwells. In May 1653 Cromwell's son Henry married Elizabeth Russell; five years later her brother John became the second husband of Cromwell's youngest daughter, Frances. When not in Ireland, Henry and Elizabeth lived at Chippenham until 1660, when they moved to Spinney Abbey nearby. John and Frances lived here until John's death in 1669, when the estate passed to the eldest of their surviving children, Sir William.

Frances continued to live here for a further thirty years, but she ended her life in London, living with her sister Mary at Chiswick. The early Stuart mansion at Chippenham was demolished in the following century, and the present great house is nineteenth-century.

In the Church of St Margaret (T663698) lie many members of the family, including John Russell (d1669), at least two of his children and his niece, Elizabeth Cromwell (d1659), daughter of Henry Cromwell.

Earith (TL393750)

On low, flat ground between the Old and New Bedford Rivers, just north of the main A1123, stand the remains of a Civil War fort. The earthwork stronghold is square, with double ramparts and diamond shaped bastions enclosing an area of nearly five acres. There is no record of fighting here.

Elsworth (TL3163)

In 1656 Samuel Disbrowe, brother of Major General John and himself a prominent Parliamentarian and member of the Scottish Council, bought lands at Elsworth and had a new house built here. His two storey 'U'-shaped manor house in whitewashed brick still stands to the north of the church. Samuel (d1690) is buried in Holy Trinity beneath an inscribed slab in the chancel.

Eltisley (TL2759)

John Disbrowe, soldier, Protectoral Councillor and Major General of the south-west, was born and brought up in Eltisley. He lived as a child in the 'Old House', the 'L'-shaped two storey, half-timbered house built for his father James around 1611, which still stands at the west end of the village green near the church. It was in St Pandionia and St John that Disbrowe married Cromwell's sister Jane on 23 June 1636. Although Disbrowe acquired further property in the village during the 1650s, including the manor-house, he never returned to live at Eltisley and instead spent the rest of his life in London.

Ely (TL5380)

During the sixteenth century several generations of the Stewart family, farmers of the cathedral tithes, acquired lands and property in and around Ely. When Sir Thomas Stewart died childless in January 1636 he left his estates to a nephew, his sister Elizabeth's only surviving son. Thus it was that Oliver Cromwell inherited lands at Ely. The Cromwells lived here for ten years up to 1646–7, when they moved permanently to London; although Parliamentary and military duties kept Oliver away from Ely for much of the time after 1640, he visited his wife and children as often as possible during the Civil War.

The Cromwells lived in a half-timbered house off St Mary's Street, 300 yards west of the cathedral, known at that time as The Sextry, today called variously Cromwell House, Rectory House or St Mary's Vicarage. The house survives almost unaltered since Cromwell's day, a two storey black and white building, mainly late medieval but with an early seventeenth-century extension at the west end. Traditionally the Cromwells' bedroom was the upper room in this western portion, overlooking the yard. The house is now open to the public and houses a small Cromwell museum, including displays, restored rooms and an audio-visual presentation.

In Cromwell's time the property also comprised an adjoining barn, Sextry Barn, but this was demolished in the nineteenth century and only a fragment of walling survives – including a thirteenth-century double lancet window – now incorporated in the vicarage garage.

Cromwell's maternal grandfather William Stewart (d1594) and his uncle Sir Thomas Stewart (d1636) lie buried in the Cathedral, and it was here in January 1646 that John Claypole

Sidney Sussex College, Cambridge. Cromwell's semi-mummified head (*above*), the cranium sliced open in the original embalming, was returned to his old college in 1960 and buried or immured near the chapel (*below*). A seventeenth-century chair (*left*) owned by the college is traditionally linked with Cromwell.

Near to this place was buried on 25 March 1960 the head of **OLIVER CROMWELL** Lord Protector of the Commonwealth of England, Scotland & Ireland, Fellow Commoner of this College 1616-7 married Cromwell's daughter Elizabeth. Cromwell's youngest child, Frances, was baptised in St Mary's in December 1638.

Great Staughton (TL124647)

In 1627 Cromwell's cousin Anna, daughter of Sir Oliver, married John Baldwin of Ramsey, and although the couple lived in Ramsey for many years, they moved to Great Staughton towards the end of their lives and both died here. Anna (d1663) and John (d1657) lie under inscribed floor slabs in the chancel of St Andrew's.

Horsey Hill (TL223960)

On the slopes of Horsey Hill, one mile east-south-east of Stanground, stand the remains of a Civil War fort. The pentagonal earthwork fort with angle bastions comprises a single or double rampart and outer ditch, with traces of an outer parapet on the east side, and covers an area of 5½ acres; the enrance was in the southern curtain. The fort is situated on rising ground east of the old River Nene near the bridge carrying the main road to Peterborough. Modern buildings have encroached upon the site, but the earthworks themselves are well preserved. The fort never saw serious action.

Huntingdon (TL2472)

Huntingdon abounds with Cromwellian connections. Cromwell was born, brought up and educated in Huntingdon, he lived over half his life here, and many of his family were baptised or buried in the town's churches. Huntingdon became one of the centres of the Eastern Association and Cromwell was frequently here during the first half of the war. The town was the scene of almost the only serious fighting within Cambridgeshire during the first Civil War. Here, too, can be seen the finest collection of Cromwellian relics in Britain.

In 1568 Sir Henry Cromwell, formerly Williams, bought a plot of land at the north end of Huntingdon and gave it to his second son, Robert. Robert largely demolished the ruined Augustinian friary which stood on the site, though parts of the western cloister range and of the church were incorporated in the new house he built here. Robert lived at Huntingdon for nearly fifty years, marrying and raising a family here. On his death in 1617 the property passed to his son Oliver who, in turn, lived here with his wife and young family. In 1631 he sold up and moved to St Ives. The house was largely rebuilt in the early eighteenth century, though the room in which Cromwell was supposed to have been born and the chamber below were preserved. They survived until 1810 when the site was completely cleared and the present Cromwell House built. Above the front door, facing the High Street, are Cromwell's coat of arms and an inscribed plaque recording the Cromwellian connection.

From 1610 to 1616 Cromwell attended the grammar school in the High Street, just off Market Square. The building was originally part of the twelfth-century infirmary hall of the Hospital of St John the Baptist, which extended to the north and east, laid out on the standard plan of four ranges grouped around a courtyard or cloister. In 1565 most of the building was converted into a grammar school. Only the two western bays of the infirmary hall survive, heightened in the nineteenth century and with a blocked ornamental west doorway. In 1961 the building was opened as the Cromwell Museum, and despite limited space, the museum displays an unrivalled collection of Cromwelliana, including portraits and prints of Cromwell, his family and many other senior Parliamentarians, a number of Cromwell's personal possessions, such as his walking-stick, ring, sword, seal and hat, and a selection of letters and documents. The museum is open daily except Mondays, admission free.

Cromwell and most of his children were baptised in St John's Church and his day-old son, James, was buried here in January 1632. St John's stood on the west side of the High Street, opposite Ambury Road. Badly damaged in the Royalist attack of August 1645, it was demolished in the 1650s and today nothing survives except fragments of the churchyard wall.

St Mary's Church, near the south end of the High Street, was extensively renovated in the early seventeenth century and the south aisle arcade was rebuilt. Inscribed stones, originally fixed to the new pillars, commemorated the local worthies who had contributed to the work, and a stone bearing the names of I. Turpin and R. Cromwell, Oliver's father, is now fixed to the east wall of the nave, north of the chancel arch.

St Benet's Church, which stood on the west side of the High Street opposite the present Chequers Court, was badly damaged by Royalists in 1645. The nave and chancel were destroyed and though the tower and spire survived for another 150 years, they too were demolished in 1800.

All Saints Church, immediately north of the Market Square, was also damaged in the Royalist attack, when cannon fire shattered the tower; it was later repaired in red brick. Inside is a medieval font found near St John's churchyard; it may have belonged to St John's, in which case it could be the font in which Cromwell was baptised in 1599. Cromwell's grandfather Sir

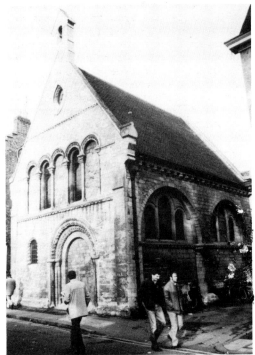

Left: Huntingdon, Cambs. The old grammar school in which Cromwell was educated in 1610–16 now houses a museum devoted to his life. Samuel Pepys was a pupil here in the early 1640s. *Top:* Ely, Cambs. For ten years from 1636 Cromwell lived in this substantial stone and timber-framed house, inherited from a wealthy uncle, which stands almost in the shadow of the cathedral. *Above:* Huntingdon, Cambs. Despite later extensions and modernizations, the Falcon Inn remains at heart the late Tudor building which probably served as Cromwell's base while on campaign in Huntingdon during the opening year of the war.

Henry (d1604) and Sir Henry's two wives, his father Robert (1617), uncle Ralph (d1581) and several of uncle Sir Oliver's children and grandchildren were buried in All Saints. Any monuments to them were probably damaged or destroyed by Royalists during the Civil War and certainly none survive today. Because of present-day vandalism, All Saints is often kept locked.

During the war Huntingdon became a base for the Eastern Association and Cromwell and Manchester were frequently here 1642–4. According to tradition, Cromwell usually lodged during the war at the Falcon Inn in Market Square, a late sixteenth-century brick and timber building with many later additions.

A ditch and bank were dug around the town to protect it – no traces survive – and gates were placed acrosss the north and south entrances to the High Street. Half a mile north-east of the town centre stand the weathered remains of a Civil War fort, a rectangular earthwork with corner bastions surrounded by a ditch. Thrown up to command the main road to the north-east, the present Hartford Road, it now stands by Clayton's Way amid a modern housing estate.

On 24 August 1645 the King led an army of 2,400 Horse south from Stamford; 500 Parliamentarians marched out of Huntingdon to meet them. The two forces clashed at Stilton, where the outnumbered Parliamentarians were quickly broken, Col. Gibb and 60 colleagues falling prisoner and the remainder hurrying back to Huntingdon. The King attacked the north entrance to Huntingdon, pushing back Col. Bennet's force as it tried to hold the bridge over the Town Brook at the north end of the High Street — bridge and brook have both disappeared. The Parliamentarians made a series of stands in the churches down the High Street, but the Royalist bombardment forced them to abandon each in turn until the whole town was under Royalist control. Charles spent the night either in the George or in the Old Chequers Inn, the remains of which lie beneath a modern shopping precinct. The Royalists left on the following day, closely followed by Parliamentary troops.

Half a mile west of the town stands Hinchingbrooke House, built by the Cromwell family in the sixteenth century on the site of a twelfth-century nunnery acquired by them at the Dissolution; parts of the medieval church and ranges were incorporated within the new house. Hinchingbrooke was the principal summer residence of Sir Oliver Cromwell until mounting debts forced him to sell it in 1627. After the Restoration it was bought by Edward Montagu, 1st Earl of Sandwich, Parliamentary soldier, admiral and politician turned ardent Royalist, who extended the western ranges. Now a school, Hinchingbrooke is at heart an Elizabethan mansion of four ranges around a central courtyard, though it has since been extended and remodelled on many occasions. It is open to the public on summer Sundays.

Kimbolton (TL0967)

Kimbolton Castle, a medieval fortress largely rebuilt in the sixteenth and early seventeenth centuries in the form of a quadrangular mansion, was the seat of the Earls of Manchester. It was the main country residence of the 2nd Earl, Parliamentary politician and General and the commander under whom Cromwell served in East Anglia and the East Midlands in 1643–4. The castle was remodelled and rebuilt by Vanbrugh in the eighteenth century, and is now a school, open to the public on summer Sundays.

The 2nd Earl was buried in 1671 in the Montagu vault beneath the north chapel of St Andrew's Church (TL099679). There are monuments to many members of the family within St Andrew's, particularly in the north and south chapels.

Linton (TL5646)

In 1648 Sparrow's Troop of Horse dispersed a party of Royalist rebels under Reynolds and Appleyard gathering at Linton in preparation for a march to Colchester.

Northborough (TF1508)

Northborough Manor House stands off the main street at the west end of the village, a small, stone-built fortified hall of two storeys under a gabled roof. It was built by Geoffrey De La Mare in the early fourteenth century and renovated and extended in the seventeenth. A gatehouse stands by the road and to the west is a large, early seventeenth-century barn into which a row of circular gun ports were cut during the Civil War. The house was owned in the seventeenth century by the Claypole family and John Claypole, Parliamentary soldier and politician and a friend of Cromwell, was born and brought up here. In 1646 he married Cromwell's daughter Elizabeth, but the couple seem to have spent most of their married life in London rather than Cambridgeshire. By the time John returned to Northborough at the Restoration his wife was dead, but he brought with him their three surviving children, together with the Protector's widow, Elizabeth, who lived here until her death in 1665. By 1676 John was heavily in debt and he sold Northborough and moved to London.

The south transept of St Andrew's Church, often known as the Claypole Chapel, contains the graves of many of the Claypole family. John and Elizabeth both lie in London, but at least two of their children, Martha (d1664) and Cromwell (d1678?) rest here. The Protector's widow was also buried in the south transept and although no contemporary monument survives, a large broken (and repaired) floor slab is traditionally said to mark her grave. The Cromwell Association have set up an inscribed tablet in her memory on the east wall.

Peterborough (TL1999) Peterborough was one of Cromwell's bases during the early stages of the war and he was frequently here 1642–44. His usual lodgings appear to have been 'The Vineyard' which stood to the east of the cathedral. No such building survives.

To the west of the town centre in the suburb of Longthorpe stands Thorpe Hall (TL170986). The manor of Longthorpe was acquired after the Civil War by Oliver St John, Lord Chief Justice and husband of Cromwell's first cousin, Elizabeth. He demolished the old manor house and had a new mansion built on the site 1653–56. Thorpe Hall was one of the few great houses built during the Interregnum, and almost the only one to survive complete. The main block is rectangular, two rooms deep and 2½ storeys high, with a porticoed entrance reached by a flight of concentric, semi-circular steps. Ancillery ranges adjoin the main house. In the seventeenth century the place was surrounded by a magnificent walled garden. The hall has stood empty for several years and become rather dilapidated. Although it has recently been partially restored, its future remains a matter of uncertainty and controversy. Thorpe Hall is currently closed to the public.

Ramsey (TL2885) This Fenland village was dominated in the Middle Ages by Ramsey Abbey, one of the greatest and richest of the English monasteries. At the Dissolution much of its land and property around the village was acquired by the Cromwells and remained in their hands until the late seventeenth century. The Lord Protector and his descendants had no link with Ramsey for Cromwell's father had moved to Huntingdon in the sixteenth century, but several of his uncles and their children lived here in the seventeenth century.

The abbey buildings were used as a stone quarry after the Dissolution and by the end of the sixteenth century very little remained standing. Around 1600 Sir Henry Cromwell built Ramsey Abbey House on the site (TL292852), incorporating at its east end the thirteenth-century Lady Chapel, almost the only part of the medieval abbey which was still standing. Sir Henry's house was small and simple, a single long block facing north with a central porch and projecting square towers at each end. In 1604 Abbey House passed to Sir Oliver, and it became his principal seat after the sale of Hinchingbrooke in 1627. In May 1643 Oliver Cromwell and his troop paid his uncle a visit, removing plate and arms from Abbey House: Sir Oliver was a Royalist and had raised men and money for the King. The house stayed in the family for a further two generations, but when Sir Oliver's grandson died childless in 1673 Ramsey Abbey was sold off. The building was greatly extended in the eighteenth and nineteenth centuries and Sir Henry's early Stuart house is almost lost amid the later work. In recent years Abbey House has been used as a school, and there is no public access. The ornate medieval gatehouse nearby, once the abbey gatehouse, survives intact and is open to the public.

Bodsey House, 1½ miles north of the village (TL296873), was originally the site of the abbey hermitage and later an abbey grange. The northern half is a thirteenth-century two storey secular building, the lower storey in stone, the upper in wood, beneath a timber wagon roof. The southern part was originally a fourteenth-century chapel of three bays. The house passed to the Cromwells at the Dissolution and the chapel was divided into three floors, with fireplaces and chimneys added. In the seventeenth century the house was owned by Sir Oliver and used at various times by several of his children. By the 1660s it had become the main residence of his grandson Henry, on whose death the house was sold off. Bodsey House survives in good order as a private residence.

The Biggin, between Ramsey and Upwood, was originally a small leper house, converted in the mid-fourteenth century into an abbey grange. It was largely rebuilt in the sixteenth century when it was acquired by the Cromwells. Over the following century several members of the family lived here, including Oliver's uncle, Sir Philip. When the house was demolished in the eighteenth century a late Tudor door bearing the initials 'H.C.' was salvaged and taken to Abbey House. A ruinous range of outbuildings known as The Maltings survives north-west of the site of the former house. Biggin Lane runs close by.

In family vaults under the Church of St Thomas lie many members of the Cromwell family, including Oliver's uncles Sir Oliver and Sir Philip and several of their children and grandchildren. No monuments to them survive.

St Ives (TL3171) Oliver Cromwell and his family lived in St Ives from 1631 to 1636, renting a house and land from Henry Lawrence (who twenty years later served his former tenant as President of the Protectoral Council). There is, however, no clear evidence to indicate exactly which property Cromwell rented. Slepe Manor, a rather grand mansion demolished in the nineteenth century, was owned by the Lawrences at this time, and it is often asserted on no firm evidence that this was Cromwell's home; the building came to be known as Cromwell House or Place. Similarly, a sixteenth-century, brick walled, five bayed outbuilding on Green End Farm, north of the church, was traditionally linked with Oliver and became known as Cromwell's Barn, although once again no evidence firmly links him with the building, which was demolished in the 1960s. In the early 1630s the Cromwells were far from wealthy, and it is likely that Oliver would have rented a fairly small farm around St Ives, something far more modest than Slepe Manor.

In the Market Place stands an impressive statue of Oliver Cromwell, unveiled in 1901. It was originally designed for Huntingdon, but the town authorities refused the statue, and thus Cromwell stands in the middle of St Ives. Nearby, the Norris Museum in The Broadway contains several relics from the Civil War in the area.

In the Market Place, opposite the statue of Cromwell, stands the Golden Lion, a Tudor building which was once an important coaching inn. The coach yard has now been enclosed and the balconies serve as corridors linking the bedrooms of the hotel. According to tradition, Oliver Cromwell's ghost stalks the rooms and corridors, particularly room 13; a green lady also seen in the Golden Lion is reputed to be his mistress!

St Neots (TL1860) After a disastrous rising in Surrey in early July 1648, the 3–400-strong remnant of Buckingham's and Holland's Royalist force reached St Neots on the evening of 9 July and spent an uneasy night quartered in and around the town, aware that a Parliamentary force was on their tail. On the following morning Col. Adrian Scrope and 100 Horse swept into St Neots, brushing aside a small Royalist unit at Eaton Ford and attacking the main rebel force hastily drawn up on Market Hill. The brief clash left 40 Royalists dead, 100 captured and the rest fleeing in all directions. The Duke of Buckingham escaped, but Holland was found at an inn and taken.

Somersham (TL3677) Valentine Waulton, regicide and brother-in-law of Cromwell, acquired property in Somersham in 1654 and lived here until the Restoration, when he fled abroad. It is not clear whether his wife, Margaret Cromwell (b1601), was still alive when he moved to Somersham – she died sometime during the 1650s, but it is not known exactly where or when.

Stuntney (TL555785) After the Dissolution the Stewart family acquired property around Stuntney, including Stuntney Manor, also known as the Old Hall. William Stewart lived in the manor-house in the late sixteenth century, and his two children, Thomas and Elizabeth (Oliver Cromwell's uncle and mother respectively), were born and brought up here. In due course the house was inherited by Thomas, on whose death in 1636 it passed to his nephew. Cromwell never lived in the place. The Old Hall was an early seventeenth-century brick house with a long gabled front range and a second wing to the rear.

Thriplow (TL4346) In mid-June 1647 the Parliamentary army quartered on open land adjoining the Icknield Way around Thriplow village. Although lodging by night at Royston (Herts), Cromwell and the other senior officers paid frequent visits to the army quarters on Thriplow Heath.

Upwood (TL2582) Upwood Manor House, 150 yards west-north-west of the church, was bought by the Cromwell family in the sixteenth century. Oliver's uncle Henry lived here with his family until his death in 1630. The property was sold to Stephen Peasant or Pheasant in 1649, and he demolished the Cromwells' old home and built the present manor-house on the site after the Restoration.

Henry Cromwell, his wife Eluzai (d1620), their son Richard (d1626) and their grandchildren Henry (d1625) and Anna (b1623) were all buried in St Peter's Church, together with another of Oliver's uncles, Richard (d1628). No monuments to them survive.

Whittlesey (TL2797) Cromwell's sister Catherine (b1597) lived here with her first husband Roger Whitestone, a professional soldier who served in the Thirty Years War. He was dead by the early 1650s and Catherine remarried and moved away. Roger and at least one of his children, Henry (d1659), lie in unmarked graves in the parish church.

Above: Northborough, Cambs. The modest medieval and Jacobean manor-house was owned by John Claypole and his wife Elizabeth, the Protector's favourite daughter. The Protector's widow (*left*) spent her last years here and was buried in the village church in 1665. *Below:* Peterborough, Cambs. Thorpe Hall, one of the largest and grandest country houses of the Civil War and Interregnum, survives almost unaltered. Probably designed by Peter Mills, it was built for Oliver St John in 1653–6. *Right:* St Ives, Cambs. Pomeroy's bronze statue of Cromwell, originally intended for Huntingdon but refused by the town, was erected in the Market Place in 1901.

Wicken (TL5770) Cromwell's son Henry moved to Wicken after the Restoration, living in retirement at Spinney Abbey, one mile north-west of the village (TL554718). The building and surrounding land had once been part of a thirteenth-century Augustinian abbey. Henry lived here quietly for fourteen years with his wife, their surviving children, and his spinster aunt Elizabeth. The present Spinney Abbey, now a farmhouse, dates from the 1770s; many of the stones certainly came from the earlier house, and the eighteenth-century builders may have incorporated complete standing sections of the old Abbey House within the new.

Henry Cromwell (d1674) and his wife Elizabeth (d1687) lie beneath black marble slabs near the altar of St Laurence's Church. Nearby are the graves of their eldest son Oliver (d1685) and Henry's aunt Elizabeth (d1672). At least one of their grandchildren, Henry (d1692), also lies within the church. The modern oak chancel screen was erected in memory of the Lord Deputy and his wife, a small inscribed brass plate recording the dedication.

Wisbech (TF4609) John Thurloe acquired property around Wisbech in the 1650s and became Lord of the Manor. He demolished the fifteenth-century fortified palace which stood on the site of the Norman castle, and had a new mansion built in its stead. Resembling Thorpe Hall and probably designed by Peter Mills, Thurloe's mansion stood near the Museum Square. It was demolished in 1816 and the present Castle House was built on the site. Of Thurloe's mansion, only the garden walls and the massive gate piers survive *in situ*, though the balcony of the old house was removed before its demolition and was later added to the new building. Wisbech Museum contains various relics of Thurloe's house.

Wistow (TL2881) The Tudor manor-house was bought by the Cromwells in the sixteenth century and although Oliver's uncle, Sir Oliver, sold the place in 1649, the family retained a connection with Wistow until the end of the century.

Oliver's sister Anna lived at Wistow with her husband John Sewster, and several of their children remained in the village throughout their lives. In unmarked graves in or around St John's Church lie John (d1680/1) and Anna (d1646) and five of their six children (d between 1642 and 1705).

Woodcroft Castle (TF140045) On the outskirts of Etton stand the remains of Woodcroft Castle, a small fortified manor-house begun in the late thirteenth century – the double towered gatehouse dates from this period; the internal domestic ranges were built or rebuilt 300 years later. According to several accounts the castle was attacked by Parliamentary soldiers in the Civil War, the Royalist owner was killed and his chaplain was hurled from the battlements to his death. Woodcroft is haunted by this unfortunate priest.

CHANNEL ISLANDS

The two main islands followed very different courses during the Civil War. The people of Guernsey were strongly Parliamentarian and they controlled the island throughout the war, keeping the Royalist governor in Castle Cornet under perpetual siege. On Jersey Parliamentary sympathies were stifled by Sir George Carteret's Royalist invasion of 1643 which reduced the island for the King. Prince Charles visited Jersey on several occasions and was proclaimed King here in 1649. The island was invaded and conquered by Parliamentary troops in 1651.

Guernsey Castle Cornet, open daily, stands on a rocky outcrop off St Peter Port, linked to the mainland by a pier. It was built in the thirteenth century and became the principal stronghold of the island and the residence of the governor. The Royalist governor at the outbreak of the Civil War, Sir Peter Osborne, held out in the castle under a state of siege from 1643 until its surrender at the end of 1651. Thereafter Castle Cornet became a prison for political undesirables, holding Lilburne and others during the Protectorate and then several regicides and former Parliamentarians after the Restoration. Although John Lambert was held on Guernsey throughout the 1660s, only his first two years here were spent in close confinement within the castle. In the late seventeenth century much of the castle was demolished when the magazine exploded, and the present buildings within the curtain wall are mostly post-Civil War. The castle museum contains many relics from the Civil War, and the armoury has weapons and armour of the period.

Jersey In 1651 the Parliamentary invasion force was landed by Admiral Blake at Grand Etaquerel at the north end of Ouen's Bay and quickly overran two of the three strongpoints on the island, St Aubin's Fort and Mont Orgueil. Elizabeth Castle offered greater resistance, and did not fall until the end of the year.

St Aubin's Fort stands on a rocky offshore island, cut off from the mainland at high tide. Constructed in the sixteenth century as a defence against French raids, it was largely rebuilt in the eighteenth century and saw action as recently as the Second World War. The small Royalist garrison here put up no serious resistance in 1651.

Mont Orgueil stands on a granite headland on the east coast of the island. Built in the thirteenth century, the development of gunpowder and cannon two hundred years later rendered it vulnerable to attack and Somerset Tower and the Grand Rampier were added in an attempt to hold the high ground above the fortress. The castle, which promptly surrendered in 1651 and survived the Civil War unscathed, was reno-

vated in the eighteenth century and refortified during the Second World War. Open during the summer, Mont Orgueil is a complex of buildings laid out on a concentric plan, with three separate wards blocking the approach to the north-eastern keep. Most of the work is medieval, albeit much renovated and remodelled. The Queen's Gate leading from the Lower Ward was built by Carteret in 1648.

In 1651 Sir George Carteret made his stand in Elizabeth Castle, another island fortress linked to the mainland by a causeway. The island, which stands off St Helier, was a monastic site in the Middle Ages, but was converted for military use in the sixteenth century when French raids threatened the developing port. The layout of the triple-warded castle, built 1594–1668, was dictated by the shape of the long, narrow island. In the mid-seventeenth century many of the old priory buildings survived in the lower ward and here Carteret established his HQ. The 50 day Parliamentary siege during autumn 1651 caused havoc within the castle, for on 9 November a mortar scored a direct hit on the Royalists' ammunition dump in the priory's crypt and the massive explosion destroyed most of the buildings in the lower ward. The Royalists held out for a further month before surrendering on generous terms. The castle is open daily in the summer, tides permitting.

CHESHIRE

During the opening months of the war the county was divided into two almost equal sections, the Royalists controlling the north and west, the Parliamentarians the south and east. From 1644 the Parliamentary forces gradually gained the upper hand, though not until 1645–46 did they secure the county town and the western fringes of the county along the Welsh border. Indeed Chester was a major Royalist base throughout the war, gradually surrounded and isolated by a circuit of Parliamentary outposts until by 1645–46 the north-west quarter of the county was dotted by a large number of bases and minor garrisons involved in the operation against Chester. Cromwell entered the county only once, in August 1648, when he pursued the remnant of the Scottish Royalist invasion force through Winwick to Warrington.

Adlington Hall (SJ905805) Adlington Hall, the late Tudor home of the Legh family, was garrisoned for the King in 1643. It was attacked by Fairfax in February 1644 and a heavy bombardment, which caused much damage to the building, induced the garrison to surrender on the sixteenth. The house was repaired by Thomas Legh after the war and it survives today in the form of a quadrangular mansion. The south and west ranges are eighteenth-century brick but

the north and east are mainly sixteenth-century black and white half-timbering, enclosing an early Tudor Great Hall with an open hammer-beam roof. The hall is open on summer Sundays and on other days in August.

Barthomley (SJ767524) Barthomley was the scene of a massacre at Christmas 1643 when the Royalists stormed the village. The pro-Parliamentary inhabitants sought refuge in the tower of St Bartoline's Church, but the Royalists burst into the building and lit a bonfire under the tower to smoke them out. The villagers were killed as they emerged.

Beeston (SJ537592) Beeston Castle, the thirteenth-century stronghold of the Earls of Chester, stands on a hilltop dominating the extensive plain below. Garrisoned initially by Parliamentary forces under Capt. Steele, the castle was captured by a small Royalist raiding party under Col. Sandford on 13 December 1643. Steele was subsequently condemned and shot at Nantwich for surrendering the place. Thereafter the castle suffered frequent though brief Parliamentary sieges and held out until November 1645, when it was surrendered and slighted. The ruins, open daily, comprise the remains of the gatehouses, curtain walls and mural towers of the inner and outer wards.

Chester (SJ4066) Chester stood as a Royalist stronghold and key base for operations over a wide area throughout the Civil War, its garrison secure behind a circuit of Roman and medieval walls which were repaired and strengthened in 1642–3. From summer 1643 the city was often attacked or under siege, but lines of communication across the Dee into Royalist North Wales were not broken and the Parliamentary effort was in vain. Not until 1645 did Brereton attempt a more thorough blockade, establishing a number of bases around the city. Pressure gradually increased as more and more outposts fell to Parliament and in September Brereton overwhelmed most of the extra-mural suburbs. For a time the King and others were still able to slip into Chester but after the defeat of the relieving forces at Rowton Moor, the city's fate was sealed. Even then the King was able to get away and Lord John Byron was able to hold out for another winter of siege and bombardment, broken by occasional and futile attempts to storm the walls. He surrendered on 3 February 1646. Thirteen years later, in summer 1659, Chester became the centre of Sir George Booth's Royalist rising, but surrendered to Lambert without serious resistance on 20 August after the destruction of the Royalist force at Winnington.

The city walls are almost complete and although most of the mural towers and gates have gone, the north-east tower, from which the King watched the defeat of Langdale's Horse after Rowton, survives intact. Then known as the Phoenix Tower, now usually called King Charles's Tower, it serves as a museum of local history concentrating on Chester during the

Civil War. It contains a model of Rowton Moor and the siege, together with arms and armour of the era.

Cholmondeley Hall (SJ536514) The fortified Tudor mansion at Cholmondeley changed hands several times in the course of the war. The Parliamentarians held and garrisoned the place in 1642 but they pulled out towards the end of the following year and the Royalists took possession. The King's men endured repeated Parliamentary raids from Nantwich and occasionally abandoned the hall, only to return once the raiding party had left the area. Surprisingly, the Elizabethan brick and timber hall survived the war almost unscathed, but in the following century it was partly demolished and a new mansion built on the site. This, in turn, was demolished at the end of the eighteenth century to make way for the present hall and only three bays survive from the original Tudor house. Cholmondeley Hall is private but the grounds are open on summer Sundays.

Christleton (SJ4465) Christleton Old Hall served as a Royalist outpost for most of the war, guarding the eastern approaches to Chester. In 1645–46 it became a base for the Parliamentary army besieging the city. The village and its immediate vicinity witnessed frequent skirmishing throughout the war. The present manor-house, adjoining the churchyard, is post-seventeenth-century.

Crewe Hall (SJ732540) Built by Sir Randolph Crewe in the 1620s, Crewe Hall has had a stormy history. It was garrisoned for Parliament in spring 1643, taken by Royalists in December, but retaken by Fairfax in the following year after a bombardment which caused considerable damage to the building. Early nineteenth-century restorations and a fire in the 1850s completed the destruction of the old building, and although the east end of the present hall retains a Jacobean appearance, it is almost entirely late nineteenth-century work.

Doddington Hall (SJ708465) The fourteenth-century tower house at Doddington was ruinous by the seventeenth century and the building fortified and held during the Civil War was probably the Jacobean hall nearby. Garrisoned for Parliament in 1643, it fell to Royalist forces in January 1644 only to be retaken by Fairfax five months later following a brief siege and bombardment. The Jacobean hall was completely demolished in the eighteenth century and a Georgian mansion built on the site. The only

Above: Guernsey, Channel Islands. Beyond the church and rooftops of St Peter Port stands the island fortress of Castle Cornet. Sir Peter Osborne's isolated force survived here until the end of 1651 and was one of the last Royalist garrisons to fall. The castle, far removed from the mainland and beyond reach of habeas corpus, was used by both the Protector and Charles II to hold political undesirables.

Right: Chester, Cheshire. It was from the Phoenix or King Charles's Tower, at the north-east angle of the city walls, that Charles watched the destruction of one of the last Royalist armies in September 1645. The medieval tower has been repaired and refaced on several occasions and has lost most of its original defensive features.

parts of the earlier hall to survive are balustrading and statues from the porch; they now adorn the ruined medieval tower house in the grounds of the hall.

Dodleston (SJ3661) The village served as an outpost of Chester until autumn 1645, when the Royalist garrison was forced back into Chester. Thereafter Dodleston became an important centre of operations during the siege of Chester and was Brereton's HQ for much of the winter. The Royalist garrison and Parliamentary command were based in Dodleston Old Hall, a Tudor mansion of the Egerton family which stood next to the church within the bailey of an early medieval castle. The old hall has been demolished – the present Dodleston Hall is a modern building on a different site to the north of the village – but the medieval earthworks in which it stood remain.

Eaton Hall (SJ414608) A grand late Stuart house, recently demolished, stood on the site of an earlier hall which guarded the southern approaches to Chester. Eaton also commanded a ferry across the Dee a little to the north. The Royalist garrison of Sir Richard Grosvenor was ejected by Parliamentarians in 1645 and the old hall then became a Parliamentary base during the siege of Chester.

Farndon (SJ413545) In the seventeenth century only two bridges spanned the lower reaches of the Dee and one of them, the Chester crossing, was firmly under Royalist control until 1646. Thus the fourteenth-century bridge immediately west of Farndon became a vital and much disputed passage between England and North Wales. The Parliamentarians hoped not only to keep the North Wales Royalists out of England but also to cross the Dee themselves and attack Chester from the west. For their part, the Royalists were determined to hold the crossing and keep open their lines of communication. Although the strongest fortifications lay on and west of the bridge, the village of Farndon to the east also served as a base to cover the passage. Farndon Church changed hands several times as first one side then the other established a garrison here. The Royalists were usually in control 1642–44, the Parliamentarians from late 1644. Repeated attacks caused extensive damage to the church, and much of the present interior dates from the rebuilding of the 1650s and 1660s. The windows of the Barnston Chapel date from this period and depict in coloured glass the officers and men of Col. Sir Francis Gamul's Foot regiment, part of the Royalist garrison at Chester during the Civil War. Gamul is shown standing by his tent, together with pikemen, musketeers, a standard-bearer, pipers and drummers and a number of weapons and trophies from the war.

Halton (SJ5381) The fragmentary remains of the medieval castle stand behind the present Castle Hotel. The castle was garrisoned by Royalists in 1643 and fell to Parliamentary forces during the following summer after a heavy bombardment. Badly damaged during the war, the fortress was subsequently slighted and now only small sections of the curtain wall and of one of the mural towers survive above ground.

Huxley (SJ497623) Lower Huxley Hall, one mile north-west of the village, was garrisoned for Parliament from late 1644 and served as one of many bases in the area for the siege of Chester. The Jacobean brick hall has been partly demolished, but part remains, remodelled and still a private residence, surrounded by the old moat.

Middlewich (SJ7066) The scene of frequent skirmishing throughout the Civil War, the unwalled and weakly defended town changed hands several times. The biggest engagement took place on 13 March 1643 when Brereton led a combined Cavalry and Infantry force against Aston's Royalist garrison. The inexperienced Royalist Cavalry fled at the approach of the Parliamentarians, leaving Col. Ellis and a small Infantry unit to hold the town. Ellis's men were pushed back into an ever-decreasing area around St Michael's Church and sought refuge within the church itself. Surrounded, outnumbered and enduring a heavy bombardment, the Royalists soon surrendered. Marks on the outside of St Michael's tower are attributed to Parliamentary cannon-fire during this action.

Nantwich (SJ6552) Nantwich stood on the main road south-east of Chester in something of a Civil War frontier zone; the Royalists, secure to the north-west, and the Parliamentary forces, dominant to the south and east, frequently clashed in and around the town. Nantwich was secured for the King by Lord Grandison in September 1642 but his tenure was brief, for in the following January Brereton took the town at the second attempt. It remained a Parliamentary base for the rest of the war, defended by a circuit of banks and ditches, but the garrison was often under threat and had to endure repeated Royalist sieges and assaults. The most serious fight took place in January 1644 when Byron and the Royalist besieging force were routed by Fairfax's unit sent to relieve the town. On the 24th Fairfax approached Nantwich from the northwest, sweeping aside 200 Royalists attempting to block his passage around Delamere. That night melting snow turned the Weaver into a torrent, destroying the town bridge and cutting the Royalist force in two. Byron and his men on the east bank rode north to cross the river at Minshull and so rejoin their colleagues to the west of the Weaver, but they were still absent when Fairfax arrived before Nantwich around mid-day on the 25th. The west bank Royalists under Col. Gibson had lifted the siege and drawn up around Acton Church (SJ632530) to the north-west of the town to meet the Parliamentary force, but they were outnumbered and effectively surrounded, with Fairfax's men before them and the town garrison under Col. Booth approaching from behind. There was a fierce fight around the church, the Royalists making a last stand within St Mary's before surrendering; 1,500 prisoners were taken. Byron and most of the Royalist Horse never appeared, possibly turned back by units which Fairfax had posted to block the northern approaches to the town.

Northwich (SJ6573)

On 19 August 1659 Parliamentary forces under Lambert intercepted and destroyed Booth's Royalist rebels at Winnington, now a north-western suburb of Northwich.

Thirty Royalists were killed and the remainder scattered in the one-sided fight around Winnington Bridge (SJ642749) which spanned the then unfordable river Weaver. Today a modern bridge crosses the rather depleted river, for much of the water is now taken by the adjoining canal.

Rowton Heath or Moor (SJ445645)

The battle at Rowton Heath was in reality only one in a series of engagements – almost a running fight – which took place on 24 September 1645 in the area south-east of Chester. The city had been under siege for much of the year and by September the Royalist garrison was under great pressure. On the 23rd Charles slipped into Chester from the west, having sent Langdale's 3,000 Horse into England at Holt with orders to march east and then swing north to attack the rear of the Parliamentary force before Chester. Langdale's march towards Chester on the 24th was disrupted by a pursuing Parliamentary force

under Poyntz which had come north from the Worcester area. A series of clashes between the two armies as they picked their way towards Chester culminated in a major engagement on Rowton Moor, three miles south-east of the city. Langdale was caught between Poyntz's force to his rear and 800 men under Michael Jones who had left the siege to bar his approach to the city. Surrounded and outnumbered, the Royalist force soon broke and galloped in disorder towards Chester. A confused and bitter fight developed beneath the city walls as Langdale's Horse and some of the city garrison who had come to his aid were destroyed by the combined forces of Poyntz and the besieging army. The area of this final engagement is now built over, but the scene of the earlier battle around the village of Rowton is still open heathland.

Tarvin (SJ4867)

Tarvin was the scene of numerous skirmishes during the Civil War, in one of which, during August 1644, Brereton and Middleton surprised a party of Royalist Horse stationed in the town, forcing them back into St Andrew's Church and capturing them all. The town was formally garrisoned by Parliament towards the end of 1644 and served as one of the bases during the siege of Chester.

Warrington (SJ6088)

Warrington was held for the King at the outbreak of war and two attempts by Brereton to take the town early in 1643 were repulsed, the first in a skirmish on Stockton Heath, then open land, now a southern suburb (SJ6186), the second in a fight at Great Sankey (SJ5788) around the Black Horse, an impressive black and white timbered building which survives largely unaltered. At the third attempt, however, in June 1643, Brereton successfully expelled the Royalist garrison and the Parliamentarians held the town without serious challenge for the rest of the first Civil War.

On 19 August 1648 the Scottish Royalist army, broken at Preston and Winwick, struggled into Warrington. Making no attempt to stand and fight, Hamilton headed south with the Horse leaving Baillie and up to 4,000 Foot to hold the place or surrender on whatever terms they could obtain. Thus the grand invasion ended with a mass surrender and only minor skirmishes, including a fight at the bridge and action around St Elphin's Church, which a group of Royalists occupied and attempted to hold – the Parliamentary bombardment which persuaded them to surrender has left its mark on the outer chancel wall. The museum in Bold

Street contains a recently discovered cannon, together with boots, armour and other relics of the Civil War found in and around the town.

Cromwell and the army halted at Warrington for several days awaiting not only the arrival of fresh horses and men but also the completion of repairs to Warrington bridge, damaged by the fleeing Royalists. Cromwell stayed here 19–22 August before turning round and heading north. He lodged at a house or inn in Church Street, long since demolished, on the site of which the General Wolf inn now stands. A plaque on the adjoining, possibly seventeenth-century house, records Cromwell's stay.

A modern bronze statue of Cromwell with bible and sword in hand and mace and hat resting at his feet, stands near the restored Academy Building in the town centre. The Academy dates from the eighteenth century and claims that Cromwell lodged here are therefore incorrect. Similarly the tradition that he stayed at Bradleigh Old Hall, five miles north-west of the town (SJ572939) seems unfounded. He may have paid a passing visit and it is possible that Parliamentary soldiers were quartered in the late medieval hall, of which only the ruined gate-house remains – the rest was demolished in the eighteenth century and replaced by the present Georgian mansion. The tradition linking Cromwell with a cottage near Prescot, ten miles west-north-west, is also rather dubious.

Winwick (SJ6092)   On 19 August 1648 the Scottish Royalist invasion force marched through Winwick, closely pursued by Cromwell and the Parliamentary army. Part of the Scottish Infantry made a stand in the sunken lane and adjoining enclosures just north of the town. They put up a fierce fight, but Cromwell eventually cleared the road and continued the pursuit south. Some of the Royalists tried to hold St Oswald's Church but were quickly overcome and captured as the main Parliamentary army swept through the town.

CLEVELAND

This small county escaped serious fighting during the Civil War. Although several of its ports and inland towns were expanding rapidly in the seventeenth century, they were overshadowed by established centres such as Newcastle and Durham to the north and York and Hull to the south, and none was of great significance in the war. Moreover the county lay to the east of the main road between Yorkshire and the North. There is no evidence that Cromwell ever set foot in the area now covered by Cleveland.

Guisborough (NZ6116)   In January 1643 Sir Hugh Cholmley and a Parliamentary force from Scarborough surprised and scattered Col. Slingsby's Royalist detachment at Guisborough. The victory seems only to have increased Cholmley's doubts and within weeks he had gone over to the King.

Hartlepool (NZ5032)   Hartlepool was held for the King in 1643–44, but when the Scottish army appeared before the town in summer 1644 the Royalists offered no resistance and surrendered the place on 24 July. The town walls were semi-ruinous by the time of the Civil War and were subsequently slighted. Only fragments now survive, particularly around the harbour.

Stockton (NZ4418)   Held for the King during the first half of the war, Stockton was promptly surrendered to the Scots in July 1644. The town's medieval castle, probably derelict by the seventeenth century, played no significant part in the war. Nevertheless, it was later slighted on Parliament's orders.

Yarm Bridge (NZ418132)   On 1 February 1643 Cholmley's Parliamentary force was repulsed by Royalists guarding the bridge across the Tees into North Yorkshire.

CORNWALL

Cornwall was overwhelmingly Royalist in the 1640s: most of the county was secure for the King from the outbreak of war until 1646 and was one of the last regions of England to remain firmly Royalist. The eastern fringes of the county were contested by Devonshire Parliamentarians during the winter and spring of 1642–3 but thereafter Royalist control was complete and was not seriously disrupted by Essex's doomed march into Cornwall in the following year. Cromwell was here in February and March 1646 during a largely bloodless campaign which saw Cornwall rapidly fall to Parliament.

Beacon Hill (SX1259) The Battle of Beacon Hill, also known as the Second Battle of Lostwithiel, was in reality a series of disorganised skirmishes which took place over a fairly wide area on 21 August 1644. Earlier in the month Essex had established a number of outposts protecting the approaches to his army's base in Lostwithiel. At dawn on the 21st the King's men launched well-planned and co-ordinated attacks on these outposts, quickly driving the Parliamentarians from Druid's Hill, 1½ miles northeast of the town (SX1261) and from Beacon Hill itself. The Parliamentary forces regrouped on an unnamed hill immediately north-east of Lostwithiel on the north side of the Liskeard road (around SX1160) and only after further fierce fighting in the afternoon and evening did the Royalists end a very successful day by taking this hill too.

The hills to the east and north-east of Lostwithiel are still open and largely undeveloped, skirted or crossed by a number of main and minor roads. The slopes of Druid's Hill are now wooded much more thickly than they were in the seventeenth century.

Boconnoc (SX146605) The late medieval mansion served as Hopton's base on 18 January 1643 immediately before the Battle of Braddock Down. Eighteen months later, in August 1644, Boconnoc was the King's HQ throughout the operation to seal up and capture Essex's army on the west bank of the Fowey. The old house was largely demolished in the eighteenth century when the Pitt family built the present Georgian mansion, which stands in private parkland.

Bodmin (SX0767) Although Bodmin was secure in Royalist hands for most of the war, on two occasions it fell briefly under Parliamentary control. In mid-May 1643, with Hopton's army away in north-east Cornwall trying to intercept Stamford, Sir George Chudleigh led 1,200 Parliamentary Horse west and took the town after bitter street-fighting; he hurriedly departed on hearing of Hopton's victory at Stratton. In the

following summer the Parliamentarians returned, Essex and the main army taking the town almost unopposed on 28 July 1644. Bodmin was the most westerly point reached during the doomed Cornish venture and by early August the Parliamentarians had fallen back on Lostwithiel. Grenville retook Bodmin on the 11th, quickly expelling the small Cavalry unit which Essex had left in the town. Bodmin remained in the King's hands until Fairfax and the main Parliamentary army entered Cornwall in February 1646. Hopton evacuated the place on 1 March and fell back on Truro, and on the following day Fairfax entered unopposed. Cromwell stayed at Bodmin on 3–6 March and again on the 21st on his way back to Devon.

Braddock Down (SX160618) On 19 January 1643 the first serious fighting of the Civil War in Cornwall took place on open ground one mile north-east of Boconnoc House. A Parliamentary force under Ruthin had entered south-east Cornwall at the beginning of January and advanced as far as Lostwithiel before turning northeast to join Stamford's Parliamentary army around Launceston. Hopton's army, recently re-equipped from the contents of three Parliamentary warships driven by storm into Falmouth, set out to engage Ruthin before he could link up with Stamford. On 19 January Hopton's 8,000 Royalists advanced east to face Ruthin's men, who were drawn up at the eastern end of Braddock Down, then an open area of gently sloping high ground, dotted with trees and bushes and encircled by hedged enclosures. Hopton drew up on the western edge of the Down, his guns and possibly part of his army hidden from Ruthin by the contour of the land. The ensuing battle, known variously as the Battle of Braddock Down or the First Battle of Lostwithiel, opened with two hours of indecisive skirmishing. The Parliamentary forces may then have begun a general advance, only to be halted by a volley from Hopton's previously concealed guns. Certainly at this point the Royalist front line charged, quickly breaking Ruthin's force and driving it back to Liskeard and beyond, taking up to 1,500 prisoners in the process.

The battlefield is now covered by thick woods, broken only by long avenues or ridings. The obelisk in a clearing ½ mile south-west of the battlefield has no connection with the Civil War.

Castle Dore (SX104548) By 31 August 1644 Essex's army was in a terrible position. Most of the Horse had escaped to Plymouth, but the Foot was trapped around Lostwithiel, hemmed in by Royalists to the west, north and east. On the last day of August Essex began a pointless retreat south towards Fowey closely pursued by the Royalists, and a running fight developed along the muddy road. In the early evening the Parliamentarians halted around Castle Dore and drew up in a line across the hilltop immediately north of the ancient earthwork. After fierce fighting they were driven back into the fort, but nightfall prevented further action and Essex's men were able to slip away. The area around the fort is still open common and farmland and Castle Dore itself, a circular double-ramparted earthwork fortress, is well-preserved and open to the public.

Cotehele House (SX423685) Cotehele is one of the best preserved late medieval manor houses in England, a fairly small stone house amid extensive grounds. Although the house played no significant part in the Civil War, the large collection of arms and armour on display in the Great Hall includes many items from the period. The richly furnished house is open daily during the summer.

Falmouth (SW8032) A Royalist port throughout the Civil War, Falmouth relied for defence upon twin castles guarding the entrance to Carrick Roads, and it was these castles rather than the town itself which offered resistance to the Parliamentary force in 1646. Pendennis on the western bank of the straits and St Mawes on the eastern were built by Henry VIII in the early 1540s to command the neck of Carrick Roads and thus control access to the port of Falmouth and to the mass of navigable waterways stretching as far as Truro. They were held for the King throughout the Civil War.

St Mawes (SW841327) comprises a central circular keep with three adjoining semicircular bastions providing additional gun positions. Designed to cover the straits below, the fort had only weak defences on the landward side. When Fairfax's troops appeared before the castle on 12 March 1646 the Royalist governor, Lt.

Bonython, immediately entered into negotiations and surrendered on terms later that day. St Mawes Castle, open daily, is a near perfect example of the Henrician coastal forts of the early sixteenth century.

Pendennis Castle (SX825319), with a three storey central keep, a semicircular bastion and a massive outer curtain wall, was much the stronger of the two forts. A Royalist base throughout the war, visited by the Queen in 1644 and by the Prince of Wales in February 1646, it offered serious resistance to the Parliamentarians in spring and summer 1646. Sir John Arundell refused to surrender when summoned by Fairfax on 18 March and his garrison held out for five months under siege by land and sea. Arundel was eventually starved into submission on 17 August, and his garrison marched out on the following day. Thus Pendennis was probably the last English base to have held out for the King in the first Civil War. The well-preserved castle, open daily, houses a small museum tracing the history of Pendennis during the Civil War and other eventful periods.

Dennis Fort, a small earthwork position adjoining Pendennis, surrendered to Fairfax without serious resistance in March 1646.

Fowey (SX1251) On 2 September 1644 the remains of the Earl of Essex's army surrendered to the King at Fowey. The 6,000 men were allowed to march away, and eventually reached Portsmouth, but large quantities of arms and ammunition fell to the Royalists.

Hexworthy (SX3681) Hexworthy was the country seat of Robert Bennet, a prominent Parliamentary soldier and politician and a colleague of Cromwell during the 1640s. According to unconfirmed but plausible stories, Cromwell lodged at Hexworthy in late February 1646 while based around Launceston. Bennet's house has long since disappeared and the present Hexworthy is a later property.

Ince Castle (SX402565) Ince Castle, the Tudor fortified mansion of the Killigrew family, stands on the banks of the Lynher. During the Civil War it was held by Royalist forces and served as a base guarding the southern road into Cornwall and as an outpost for operations against Plymouth. There is no record of fighting here, and the garrison probably withdrew before Fairfax's invasion force in 1646. The brick mansion, with pyramidal corner towers and an embattled gateway, survives intact as a private residence.

Lanhydrock House (SX085636) The Jaco-

Top: Falmouth, Cornwall. Pendennis Castle, guarding the entrance to Carrick Roads, was a Royalist stronghold throughout the war and the last English mainland base to fall to Parliament. *Above:* Restormel Castle, Cornwall. The Black Prince's castle, one of the best preserved shell keeps in Britain, was hastily refortified by Essex's army in summer 1644; it fell to the King with equal speed. *Left:* Lostwithiel Church, Cornwall. According to a contemporary report, it was around this finely decorated fourteenth-century font in St Bartholomew's that Essex's soldiers held a ceremony in August 1644: 'They brought a horse to the font . . . and there . . . did, as they called it, christen the horse and called him by the name of Charles in contempt of his Sacred Majesty.'

bean quadrangular house of the Robartes family became a shortlived Parliamentary base in August 1644. Lord Robartes, one of Essex's chief advisers on the Cornish venture, made his house available at the beginning of August as an outpost guarding the new Parliamentary base at Lostwithiel. Within a fortnight Grenville had retaken Lanhydrock without a fight, the small Parliamentary garrison falling back before the Royalist advance. The house survived the war intact, but partial demolition in the late eighteenth century and a fire in 1881 destroyed much of the old house. The north wing and part of the west are Jacobean, and the gatehouse dates from 1658, but the rest of the present building is Victorian. The richly furnished house and surrounding gardens are open to the public during the summer.

Launceston (SX3384)

In the very east of the county, Launceston was almost the only Cornish town to be secured by Parliament at the outbreak of war. By the beginning of October, Hopton had assembled an army of 3,000 men around Bodmin and when they approached Launceston on the 4th Sir Richard Buller and his 700 strong garrison abandoned the place and fled east. However, while Devon remained Parliamentarian, the town was always vulnerable to attack. Thus in January 1643 Stamford reoccupied Launceston but quickly fell back at the approach of Hopton's army. On 23 April James Chudleigh led 2,500 Devonshire Parliamentarians against the town, attacking Hopton's position on Windmill or Beacon Hill. Hopton had drawn up behind the ancient earthworks which crowned the hill and the hedges which then covered the lower slopes. Parliamentary losses during the day-long attack were moderate but steady, and by evening Hopton felt strong enough to launch a major counter-attack on Chudleigh's tired and depleted force. The Parliamentarians were thrown back, though nightfall saved them from complete destruction and the young Major General conducted an orderly retreat. With the Royalist conquest of Devon later in 1643 Launceston's position was secure, and it remained in Royalist hands until 1646. In February most of the garrison retreated westwards at the approach of the main Parliamentary army and on the 25th Fairfax and Cromwell entered the town, quickly expelling the small Royalist Infantry unit which had been left here. Cromwell stayed in or near Launceston until the 27th.

Windmill or Beacon Hill, the steep hill to the south of the town centre, is still crowned by open parkland, but its lower slopes have now been built over. Launceston Castle, a dramatically-sited Norman fortress, was derelict and probably indefensible by the seventeenth century – it is noticeable that Hopton chose to hold the hill, not the castle – and played no significant part in the Civil War.

Lostwithiel (SX1059)

The town became the HQ of Essex's army at the beginning of August 1644, the small Royalist garrison abandoning the place at the approach of the Parliamentary force. A band of Royalists took refuge in the tower of St Bartholomew's Church and in an effort to flush them out the Parliamentarians set off a barrel of gunpowder beneath the tower. The explosion lifted part of the roof, which was subsequently rebuilt at a different level and pitch; the line of the earlier roof can be traced on the east wall of the tower. According to Royalist allegations, the Parliamentarians then held mock services within the partly ruined church, christening a horse 'King Charles' in a ceremony around the font. Although the arc of Parliamentary outposts to the north fell on the 21st, the King's men made no real attempt to retake Lostwithiel until the end of August, and part, at least, of Essex's army remained in the town until driven out by the advancing Royalists on the 31st.

Mawgan in Meneage (SW710251)

In May 1648 a number of pro-Royalist demonstrations took place in west Cornwall and although Parliamentary soldiers quickly restored order in Helston and Penzance, they failed to prevent a Royalist gathering around Mullion and Goonhilly. On 23 May the rebels, under Capt. Pike, advanced to Mawgan, where they were caught by a Parliamentary force under Col. Bennet. The Royalists were no match for the professional soldiers and after a clash around St Mauganus's Church, they fell back in disorder to the Gear, an ancient earthwork above Mawgan Creek (SW720249). At the approach of Colonel Bennet's men they scattered, many seeking refuge on the rocks and shore below.

In the chancel of St Mauganus's Church are the sword and armour of Sir Richard Vyvyan, a prominent local Royalist.

Mount Edgecumbe (SX4552)

The Tudor mansion, seat of the Royalist Edgecumbe family, was garrisoned for the King for most of the war and served as one of the principal bases for operations against Plymouth. It was frequently raided by the Plymouth Parliamentarians and was finally surrendered to Fairfax by Col. Piers Edgecumbe on 3 March 1646. The old house was largely destroyed during the Second World War and the present mansion is a modern restoration, though incorporating surviving sections of the Tudor and Stuart building. The house is open during the summer, the fine gardens and park which surround it all year.

Restormel Castle (SX104614) By the seventeenth century Restormel was semi-derelict, but the fortifications still afforded some protection and in August 1644 it was garrisoned as an outpost guarding the approach to the new Parliamentary base at Lostwithiel. On the 21st, however, Sir Richard Grenville took the castle for the King, Col. John Weare's garrison offering no resistance and abandoning the place at the approach of the Royalists. The castle played no further part in the war. Although the interior apartments are very ruinous, the curtain wall of the circular shell keep survives almost to its original height. The castle is open daily.

St Gennys (SX1597) The Church of St Genesius contains an inscribed slate memorial to Capt. Braddon, member of the Long Parliament and an officer in the Parliamentary army.

St Michael's Mount (SW5130) The military potentials of this rocky island have long been appreciated, and although a Benedictine priory stood here from the twelfth century, the Mount was frequently taken over by troops. In the fifteenth century the monks were permanently ejected and a castle built on the summit of the island; it incorporated large parts of the old priory buildings. The place was held for the King throughout the Civil War, the defences strengthened, and batteries added on the north side to cover the main approach path from the causeway. By March 1646 the Mount was isolated and blockaded by Parliamentary forces and on 16 April Sir Arthur Bassett was persuaded to abandon the hopeless struggle and surrender to Col. Hammond. The present castle buildings clustered on the 195 foot pinnacle owe much to post-Civil War renovation and remodelling, but large parts of the medieval priory and of the late medieval and early modern military works survive. The castle is open for guided tours on certain weekdays throughout the year.

St Tudy (SX0676) On 1 March 1646 Cromwell and his men occupied St Tudy to counter any attempt by Hopton to strike north-east from Bodmin and outflank the main Parliamentary army approaching from Launceston. In fact, Hopton made no such move, and St Tudy's distinguished visitor had a peaceful day. On the 2nd he moved on to rejoin Fairfax, who had just entered Bodmin unopposed, but Cromwell was still vigilant and travelled via Wadebridge, where he left a troop of Dragoons to guard the bridge (SW9972).

Saltash (SX4259) Clinging to the hillside above the river, Saltash's importance in the Civil War lay in its position on the Tamar at the lowest point at which it could be crossed safely and easily by fairly small boats. The town was taken by Parliament at the end of 1642 only to be retaken by Hopton in January 1643. It remained in Royalist hands for most of the war although it was captured and briefly occupied in September 1644 by Parliamentary Horse who had cut their way through from Fowey, and fell again in October to a raiding party from Plymouth. Saltash was finally surrendered to Fairfax in February 1646.

Stratton (SS227071) In May 1643 the Earl of Stamford gathered his Parliamentary army, over 5,500 strong, at Torrington and marched west to invade northern Cornwall. He entered the county on the 15th and by nightfall had reached Stratton. Meanwhile, Hopton was marching north-east from Bodmin to oppose him, and arrived before Stratton in the early hours of the 16th; he had just 3,000 men. Moreover Stamford had taken up a strong position behind ancient earthworks on the top of a long, narrow hill running north of the village, its eastern slopes steep and thickly wooded, its western gentler and fairly open. Despite his numerical disadvantage, Hopton decided to attack and at dawn on the 16th he launched a three-pronged assault up the south, west and north slopes of the hill. An inconclusive struggle ensued and continued into the afternoon, until Major General Chudleigh ill-advisedly left the hilltop and led a counter-attack down the slope. Initially successful, Chudleigh soon found himself cut off and surrounded. Even worse, the Parliamentary force on the hilltop had been significantly depleted, particularly at the southern end, and here the Royalists at last gained a foothold and pushed north into the Parliamentary flank. By 4 p.m. the hill was taken; 300 Parliamentarians were dead, 1,700 captured and the remainder fleeing back to Devon.

A minor road now runs north from Stratton, across the hilltop and on to Stibb, and along it modern housing has begun to encroach upon the battlefield. The north end of the hill and the eastern and western slopes are still open ground, however, and the prehistoric earthworks survive. The place is now known as Stamford Hill, a curious honour for a defeated commander. Marks on the north-west corner of the tower of St Andrew's Church in Stratton are attributed to wayward shots from the Royalist cannon, intended for the southern end of the Parliamentary line. The dead of both sides were buried in unmarked communal graves in St Andrew's churchyard and relics found on the battlefield are now on show within the church. According to tradition, the Royalists established their HQ in the Tree Inn, Stratton.

Trematon Castle (SX410580)   The medieval castle, held for the King throughout the Civil War, served as a base guarding the southern road into Cornwall and as an outpost for operations against Plymouth. There is no evidence of any fighting here and it was probably eighteenth-century neglect and nineteenth-century partial demolition rather than Parliamentary cannon which have reduced the castle to its present sorry state. The ruins of the keep, gatehouse and bailey wall stand in the grounds of a private Regency mansion.

Tresillian (SW869465)   On 10 March 1646, at the bridge over the river Tresillian, Hopton agreed in outline to a cessation of hostilities. After three days of negotiation at Tresillian and Truro the final terms of surrender were agreed and the remnant of Hopton's army dissolved. A plaque on the outer wall of the Sunday school by the village church facing the bridge records the events of March 1646 and commemorates 'all brave Cornishmen who died in the Great Civil War'.

Truro (SW8244)   Truro served as a Royalist recruiting base at the outbreak of war and remained a stronghold for the King throughout the Civil War. In March 1646 Fairfax and the Parliamentary army entered the town unopposed and the final details of Hopton's surrender were arranged here. Cromwell was in Truro on 10–21 March.

CUMBRIA

The county was notionally Royalist at the outbreak of war and was conquered by the Scots in 1644–45, but in reality there was very little military action here during the first Civil War. Most of the fighting in the county occurred in 1648, when the Scottish Royalist invasion force marched through Cumbria taking and garrisoning key towns and castles on their way south. Even then fighting was rare; the major clashes took place in Lancashire and Cheshire to the south, and the Royalist bases within Cumbria then fell to Parliament without further bloodshed. Cromwell participated in no military actions within Cumbria and his one recorded visit to the county, to Carlisle in October 1648, took place after order had been restored to the area.

Appleby (NY686199)   On his arrival in Cumbria in April 1648, Lambert established his HQ in Appleby Castle, a good centre from which to watch the Royalists at Carlisle and Penrith and to block possible lines of advance south into Lancashire or south-east into Yorkshire. In fact, his surveillance proved rather poor for his troops were surprised by the Scots on 17 July and only with difficulty did the Parliamentary Foot hold Hamilton off while the Horse regrouped. Lambert withdrew to Bowes and Barnard Castle leaving a small garrison in Appleby Castle, which in due course fell to the Scots. Town and castle were retaken without serious resistance at the end of the summer. The Norman castle, largely rebuilt by the Cliffords in the fifteenth century, was repaired by Lady Anne Clifford, Dowager Countess of Pembroke, after the Civil War. The remains of the castle stand on high ground to the south of the town centre and are not open to the public.

Brougham Castle (NY537290)   The Cliffords' medieval castle was occupied by Sir Marmaduke Langdale's Royalists in April 1648 but abandoned by them in the following month when Lambert's forces approached. The fortress was modernised and extended by Lady Anne Clifford in the 1650s but fell derelict in the eighteenth century. The extensive ruins, which include the remains of the keep, the inner and outer gatehouses and the domestic buildings within the inner ward, are open daily.

Carlisle (NY3955) Carlisle occupies a key position near the Scottish border and on the main western route between Scotland and England. The Romans established a fort here, and it remained a strong point throughout the Middle Ages, heavily fortified and suffering repeated Scottish raids. A Royalist base from the outbreak of the Civil War, Carlisle became important only after the fall of York in July 1644. Thereafter Carlisle served as the Royalists' northern HQ, its garrison was enlarged and Sir Thomas Glemham became governor. Under siege from October 1644 and encircled by Parliamentary forces stationed at Newtown, Stanwix, Wetheral, Dalston Hall and elsewhere, Glemham held out until 25 June 1645 when he surrendered on terms to Leslie. In the following October Digby and Langdale made a rather half-hearted attempt to recover the town, but were repulsed by the Scots in a skirmish on Carlisle sands.

In 1648 Carlisle became one of the centres of the second Civil War. Sir Philip Musgrave secured the town for the King in April, and in July it became the base from which the Scottish Royalist invasion force launched their grand operation. The small garrison left in Carlisle surrendered on 1 October and a fortnight later Cromwell paid a brief visit to the town on his way back from Scotland.

A substantial section of the medieval town wall survives on the west side of the town centre, running along West Walls Road; elsewhere, the wall has been destroyed and none of the three town gates survive. The outer ward of the medieval castle disappeared in the nineteenth century but the rectangular twelfth-century keep survives, extensively repaired in the eighteenth and nineteenth centuries and now housing a military museum, open daily; nearby stand the remains of the gatehouse, walls and towers of the inner ward. Carlisle Cathedral owes its present modest dimensions to the Civil War, for in 1645 the Scots demolished the chapter house, cloisters and part of the nave to provide stone for repairing the town's defences.

Cockermouth (NY125310) Above the river stand the remains of the double-warded castle begun by William de Fortibus in the thirteenth century but extended later in the Middle Ages and heavily restored in the eighteenth and nineteenth centuries. The castle was garrisoned for Parliament in 1648 and unsuccessfully besieged by the Scottish Royalists as they marched past in July.

Levens Hall (SD495851) Originally a twelfth-century peel tower, Levens was converted into a grand Elizabethan mansion towards the end of the sixteenth century. The fine Tudor and Stuart interiors survive in good order and the Hall contains a fine collection of sixteenth- and seventeenth-century furniture, paintings and other fittings, including a small selection of Civil War arms and armour. Levens Hall is open most days during the summer; the exotic eighteenth-century gardens are open all year.

Lindale (SD4180) On 1 October 1643 Col. Rigby's Parliamentarians intercepted a force of local Royalists marching south to relieve Thurland Castle (Lancs) and scattered them in a skirmish outside Lindale.

Millom (SD172814) The late medieval fortified home of the Huddlestones served as a minor Royalist outpost during the first Civil War and again in 1648, when it was besieged and captured by Parliamentarians. The substantial remains of the quadrangular castle, with an eastern gatehouse, western great hall and a fifteenth-century peel tower, stand on private farmland.

Penrith (NY5130) The town and castle stand in a key position on the main road into England and changed hands several times in 1648. Taken by Langdale for the King in April, the Royalists fell back before Lambert in early July and the Parliamentarians established a base here to block the road south. But on 15 July Langdale returned with Hamilton and the main Scottish army, and Lambert, heavily outnumbered and under instruction not to engage the enemy until Cromwell had arrived, abandoned the town and retreated to Appleby. Penrith was retaken by Parliament without a fight in September, its defences were slighted and the stone sold. The remains of the castle stand in public parkland.

Rose Castle (NY371462) Partly restored as a Bishop's Palace in the nineteenth century, Rose Castle was begun in the thirteenth century and extended by Bishop Strickland 200 years later. A minor Royalist outpost in the Civil War, it fell to Parliament in 1645; three years later it was retaken and briefly held by the Scottish Royalists. By the end of the seventeenth century the building was in ruins. Although the south and east ranges were completely demolished, the north and west ranges of the present 'castle' incorporate much of the medieval fortress.

Scaleby (NY449624) The medieval double-moated castle served as a Royalist garrison in 1644–45, falling to Parliament in spring 1645 only to change hands twice more before the end of the year. In 1648 it was secured by Musgrave for the King in April, fell to Lambert after a brief siege in May, was abandoned by him in July and finally retaken by Parliament after the destruction of the Scottish Royalist army at Preston and Warrington. The substantial remains, part medieval, part nineteenth-century reconstruction, stand on private land.

DERBYSHIRE

Most of the county was secured for Parliament by Sir John Gell in autumn 1642 and remained largely Parliamentarian throughout the Civil War. Despite the proximity of Royalist territory to the north, west and south-west in 1643–44, Derbyshire suffered nothing more than occasional raids launched from Royalist bases outside or around the fringes of the county. Cromwell marched through Derbyshire in August 1651, the only occasion on which he is known to have set foot within the county.

Ashbourne (SK1846) Ashbourne was the scene of two minor skirmishes during the Civil War. On 12 February 1644 a Royalist unit from Tissington Hall was ambushed outside the town by Major Saunders's forces. Surprised and outnumbered, the Royalists were quickly overwhelmed and 170 captured. During summer 1645 the main Royalist army marched through, brushing aside a small local force which vainly tried to block their path.

Barton Blount (SK2134) Barton Blount, a decayed medieval village, now comprises nothing more than a few scattered farms and an isolated hall. Barton Hall was garrisoned for Parliament during the Civil War to guard against incursions from Staffordshire Royalists. It was badly damaged by fire, presumably the result of one such raid, and the present hall is largely eighteenth- and nineteenth-century, though incorporating fragments of the earlier building which saw action in the Civil War.

Bolsover (SK470708) Bolsover stands in the north-east of the county, an area susceptible to Royalist influence during the first half of the war. Bolsover Castle was secured for the King by spring 1643 and the garrison held out until summer 1644, when the King's cause in the area collapsed after the disaster at Marston Moor. The castle fell to Major General Crawford's Parliamentarians on 12 August. The medieval castle had been demolished in the early seventeenth century, and the building which saw action in the Civil War was a mock castle, a square house with battlements and turreted angle towers, built by Sir Charles Cavendish during the reign of James I. The main house probably stands on the site of the Norman keep, and the massive seventeenth-century walls to the south follow the line of the inner bailey wall. The terrace range running along the west edge of the site was probably erected just before the Civil War. Bolsover Castle is open daily.

Boyleston (SK182359) In July 1644 a detachment of 200 Royalists under Col. Eyre quartered for the night at Boyleston Church. Failing to set a proper watch, they received a rude awakening, surprised at dawn by local Parliamentary troops who had surrounded St John's. The Royalists had no choice but to surrender and emerged one at a time through the small south door in the chancel, whereupon each was searched and stripped of weapons and valuables.

Bretby (SK300225) Although the Earl of Chesterfield's Jacobean mansion was garrisoned for the King at the outbreak of war, it was almost immediately besieged by Gell's forces, reinforced in December by Major Molloner's troop of dragoons. Faced by such numbers, the Royalist garrison promptly abandoned the place and, after a brief exchange of fire, fled across the surrounding parkland in the direction of Lichfield. The house was then plundered by the Parliamentarians. Bretby Hall was largely demolished in the eighteenth century, though the present nineteenth-century castellated mansion on the site incorporates fragments of its Jacobean predecessor.

Carsington Chapel (SK2553) The fourteenth-century church was 're-edified' in 1648 by the Gell family of neighbouring Hopton Hall. There are several memorials to the Gells, including

Top: Brougham Castle, Cumb. The imposing fortress by the river Eamont, seized and briefly occupied by Scottish Royalists in spring 1648, was repaired by the indomitable Lady Ann Clifford after the war; she died here in 1676. *Bottom:* Bolsover Castle, Derbs. Sir Charles Cavendish's grand early Stuart mansion changed hands repeatedly during the opening years of the war. It was in this fine Gallery range, now a gutted shell, that Charles I and Henrietta Maria had been lavishly received in happier days before the war, enjoying a Jonson masque – 'Love's Welcome to Bolsover' – and other entertainment costing over £15,000.

windows bearing their crest and family tree. The sundial of 1648 was almost certainly provided by the Gells.

Chapel en le Frith (SK0680)

The fourteenth-century Church of St Thomas à Becket became both prison and grave for many Scottish Royalists in 1648. After the defeat and disintegration of the invasion force, large numbers of Scottish prisoners were herded into St Thomas's and held there for sixteen days in early September. Overcrowded and kept in very unsavoury conditions, at least 40 died during their captivity and many more were so weakened that they collapsed and expired on the subsequent march through Derbyshire.

Chatsworth (SK260702)

In the sixteenth century Sir William Cavendish built a quadrangular fortified mansion here, a four storey house with square angle towers and a western gatehouse. Garrisoned for the King under Col. Eyre early in 1644, the house fell to Parliament at the end of the summer and was partially slighted – the gates were removed and certain defensive walls breached. The 1st Duke of Devonshire completed the destruction at the end of the seventeenth century, clearing the site in preparation for his new mansion, the present Chatsworth House.

Derby (SK3536)

The town was occupied unopposed by Sir John Gell in October 1642 and became his HQ throughout the war. Derby had neither a castle nor stone walls and Gell set about constructing earthwork defences around the town. They were not put to the test, for the Royalist raids into south Derbyshire never penetrated as far as Derby. Gell's HQ, garrison and magazine were sited in the Tudor town hall, long since demolished.

Eastwood Hall (SK3463)

One mile east-north-east of Ashover stand the remains of Eastwood Hall, the Tudor manor house owned by Immanuel Bourne during the Civil War and slighted by Royalists in 1646. The house could not be brought down by canon and the King's men eventually set off a barrel of gunpowder in the base of the tower. The ivy-covered ruins include sections of this tower and of adjoining apartments.

Egginton Heath (SK2628)

In February 1644 Gell marched south-west from Derby to meet Royalist forces advancing on the town from Burton upon Trent. They clashed on Egginton Heath, just within the county boundary.

Although the two parties produced very different accounts of the skirmish and its aftermath – Gell claiming to have routed his opponents and forced them back over the river Dove, the Royalists talking of a drawn battle and an orderly retreat – it is clear that the Parliamentarians emerged victorious, if only because they had halted the Royalist advance on Derby.

Hardwick Hall (SK463637)

The massive and richly decorated Elizabethan mansion played no significant part in the Civil War. Nonetheless, amongst the many items on display is a small but fine selection of Civil War arms and armour. The house is open most days during the summer.

Hopton Hall (SK256533)

The Elizabethan Hall was the home of the Gell family in the seventeenth century, including Sir John Gell, bart., one of the leading lights of the Parliamentary cause in the North Midlands. Gell secured most of Derbyshire for Parliament during the opening months of the war and, whatever his moral weaknesses – accusations of adultery abounded – he proved a very active and successful military commander, not only keeping most of his native county clear of Royalists but also prominent in the struggle against Royalism in Staffordshire and west Nottinghamshire. He fell from favour with Parliament during the early 1650s and welcomed the restoration of Charles II. He continued to live at Hopton Hall and in London, where he died in 1671. Hopton Hall remains at heart an Elizabethan mansion, but the exterior was extensively remodelled in the eighteenth century and has been repeatedly renovated since. The hall is not open to the public.

Staveley (SK4374)

Staveley House, a Jacobean hall standing next to the parish church, was owned during the early 1640s by John Frecheville. A staunch Royalist, he garrisoned the place for the King in spring 1644. Royalist occupation was brief, for in August the house was invested and captured by Major General Crawford's Parliamentarians. Staveley House survived the Civil War intact, was remodelled in the eighteenth century, and now serves as council offices.

Sutton Scarsdale (SK442688)

The present Sutton House stands on a site occupied from the fifteenth century onwards by a succession of grand houses. The seventeenth-century hall was garrisoned for the King by Lord Deincourt early in 1643, but at the end of April it fell to a Parliamentary force under Thomas Gell, Sir John's brother, and played no further part in the Civil War. By the eighteenth century the house was ruinous and a new mansion was built on the site, incorporating part of the old hall. Georgian Sutton House or Hall was one of the grandest mansions in the county, richly decorated inside and out, but sadly this building, too, is now a ruined shell. Although the weathered earthworks still discernible in the grounds have occasionally been described as Civil War defence works, there is no clear evidence to link them with the war.

Swarkestone (SK3628) For much of the Civil War southern Derbyshire was very vulnerable to Royalist raids launched from bases in northwest Leicestershire and north-east Staffordshire. In response, Gell established a series of defences at all the main crossing points over the Trent, including Wilne Ferry at Great Wilne and King's Mills, where 200 Royalists were captured in a skirmish in February 1644. But fighting was generally fiercest at the crossing at Swarkestone, just five miles south of Derby, where a bridge and a ¾ mile elevated causeway carried the road across the Trent and the low, marshy ground around it. In autumn 1642 the Parliamentarians garrisoned Swarkestone Hall, at the northern end of the causeway, to guard the passage, but in the opening days of 1643 bridge and hall both fell to Col. Hastings and a Royalist force from Ashby de la Zouch. Aware of the grave threat to his HQ in Derby, Gell immediately despatched Sir George Gresley to retake the crossing. The two forces clashed on 5 January and after a fierce fight the Royalists were driven off and the bridge secured. Despite frequent Royalist attacks, Swarkestone remained Parliamentarian thereafter. The garrison in the hall dismantled the earthworks which the Royalists had hastily thrown up to the north and constructed their own bank and batteries on the southern side to cover the bridge and the river.

Swarkestone Hall, a Tudor and Jacobean mansion built by Sir John Harper, was partially demolished after the Civil War and is now very ruinous. The remains, including a barn, a gateway, and two domed towers joined by a three-bayed crenellated wall (possibly part of the banqueting house) stand by the river (SK375285) on land crossed by a public footpath. The medieval bridge and causeway survive, though the arches which span the river were heavily restored or rebuilt in the eighteenth century.

Tissington Hall (SK174524) The early Jacobean hall was garrisoned for the King by Col. Fitzherbert in January 1644, the Royalists thus gaining a foothold in the very west of the county on the fringes of the Staffordshire peaks. In the following month, however, most of the garrison was ambushed and routed at Ashbourne, and the survivors hastily retreated. The hall saw no further action in the Civil War and emerged unscathed. Although the west front was remodelled in the eighteenth century, much of the hall, including the east front with its central porch, retains the appearance of a rather plain, two storey Jacobean house. The exterior can be viewed from the road and public footpath which run close by.

Wingfield House (SK374548) Begun in the mid-fifteenth century by Lord Cromwell and completed several decades later by the Earl of Shrewsbury, Wingfield House or Manor changed hands several times in the course of the Civil War. Garrisoned for Parliament for most of the war, it was vulnerable to Royalist raids from north Nottinghamshire. Thus in December 1643 it fell to Newcastle's men after the three day siege; within weeks the new Royalist garrison was itself under siege and surrendered on 20 March 1644. Wingfield was retaken by the Royalists in the late spring, but in mid-August it fell to Parliamentary forces returning from South Yorkshire. It remained Parliamentarian for the rest of the war. Remodelled and partially demolished in the late seventeenth and early eighteenth centuries, the house is now an extensive and spectacular ruin, open daily. It is double quadrangular in plan, the two courts divided by a cross range with a central gateway and a western great tower. The remains of the state rooms and great hall lie in the north range of the northern or inner court.

Wirksworth (SK2854) In October 1642 Sir John Gell attacked and scattered a small band of local Royalists under Sir Francis Wortley who had gathered around Wirksworth. Sir John returned nearly thirty years later, his body brought from London in a slow and stately procession, the bearers distributing alms wherever the cortège spent a night on its six week journey. Gell was laid to rest in St Mary's Wirksworth, a large thirteenth-century church restored by Scott in the nineteenth, which contains tombs of many of the family, including an inscribed memorial to Sir John himself.

DEVON

Although the county was secured for Parliament at the outbreak of the Civil War, the Royalists successfully invaded Devon during the summer of 1643 and by the end of the year all the major towns and strongholds, with the exception of Plymouth, had fallen to the King. From autumn 1644 the county was slowly retaken by Parliament, but not until the arrival of the main army under Fairfax in winter 1645–46 was the Royalist hold over large areas of Devon finally broken. Cromwell campaigned with the Parliamentary army and was based in Devon from October 1645 to April 1646.

Ashburton (SX7569) According to a plaque on the former Mermaid Inn in North Street, Fairfax lodged here on 10 January 1646 after driving a small Royalist force from the town.

Barnstaple (SS5533) The northern ports of Appledore, Bideford and Barnstaple were secured for Parliament in 1642 and taken by Royalists in 1643, but of the three only Barnstaple saw serious fighting during the Civil War. Barnstaple was by far the largest town in north Devon in the seventeenth century, a prosperous and growing port and a convenient base for sea-borne routes to South Wales and southern Ireland. The medieval castle and the town wall, which ran from the Yeo to the Taw, were both rather dilapidated by the mid-seventeenth century but still quite defensible. Garrisoned for Parliament in 1642, the town surrendered to Prince Maurice on 2 September 1643 after a brief siege. It remained Royalist for the rest of the war, with a brief interruption in summer 1644 when the pro-Parliamentary townspeople rose up and expelled the small Royalist garrison, repelling an attack by Digby on 1 July before abandoning the hopeless venture and surrendering to the besieging Royalists on 18 September. Despite the sympathies of many of the townspeople, Barnstaple was the last important centre in Devon to hold out for the King, finally surrendering to Fairfax's men on 19 April 1646, ten days after Exeter had fallen. Of its medieval and Civil War defences almost no trace survives: the town wall has been completely destroyed, and de Totnes's Norman castle is now nothing more than a scattering of masonry fragments on and around a small mound in public gardens behind the cattle market. Bullet holes in the woodwork of Penrose Almshouses in Litchdon Street were supposedly made during the Civil War in action around the southern entrance to the town.

Bickleigh Castle (SS936068) The Norman castle, long-time seat of the Courtenay family, was garrisoned for the King by the Carews in 1643 and held by the Royalists for 2½ years before being bombarded into submission by Fairfax in autumn 1645. By the end of the Civil War much of the old fortress was ruinous and was demolished. The massive Norman gatehouse in red sandstone stands before a medieval chapel and a number of seventeenth-century domestic buildings. The armoury contains a collection of weapons and armour from the Civil War. Bickleigh Castle is open on certain summer weekdays.

Bovey Tracey (SX8178) On 9 January 1646 Cromwell led his men south from Crediton and routed Lord Wentworth's Horse just south of Bovey Tracey. Wentworth had quartered for the winter on Bovey Heath, then known as 'Heathfield', 1¼ miles south-south-east of the town centre, and had built or strengthened embankments across the heath to protect camp and town from attacks from the south-east. But on the 9th Cromwell advanced from the north along the Moretonhampstead road, entering Bovey Tracey without opposition in the afternoon and capturing many of the Royalists relaxing in town, including a party of officers in the Tudor manor-house, which still stands in East Street. The Parliamentarians swept on and at dusk they attacked the surprised and unprepared Royalists camping on the heath. Over 100 prisoners were taken and the remainder fled in all directions. Some took refuge in Ilsington Church (SX785762), but rode off when Cromwell's men approached. An impression in the shape of a horseshoe on a slate tombstone at Ilsington was supposedly made by a fleeing Royalist, one of many traditions and supernatural tales in the area which stem from the battle.

Today Bovey Heath is something of a mess, hemmed in between two main roads and a railway, with industrial premises encroaching at the north and south ends and the open land in between often churned up by motorcycles. The area around which fighting was fiercest, at the town end of the heath, is still open ground; the battle symbol at SX822768 on the O.S. map is probably accurate. In the 1970s a simple wooden cross bearing the date 1645 (presumably the Old Style date of the battle) was erected on the remains of one of the embankments on the heath, probably built or renovated by Wentworth. To the south-west of the town, by the public footpath to Challabrook Farm, stands a damaged stone cross, an ancient relic said to have been reused in 1646 to mark the grave of a Royalist officer killed in battle. In common with many towns which Cromwell visited, a number of features and buildings in Bovey Tracey with no known Cromwellian link now bear his name. Thus the stone archway over the main street is often known as 'Cromwell's Arch' and the Oliver Cromwell public house stands at the junction with the Moretonhampstead road.

Buckland Abbey (SX487668)   The thirteenth-century Cistercian Abbey was converted for secular use at the Dissolution and was remodelled by Sir Francis Drake in the latter half of the sixteenth century. It became a Royalist base during the siege of Plymouth in 1643 and remained in Royalist hands until spring 1646, when it was stormed and captured by Fairfax's troops. The buildings, which survived the Civil War intact, are open to the public.

Chagford (SX7087)   On 8 February 1643 a Royalist party of Horse and Dragoons under Berkeley and Ashburnham attacked Northcote's Parliamentarians quartered in Chagford. An inconclusive street fight developed in the early morning, memorable only for the death of the Royalist poet Sidney Godolphin, who was shot in the leg and bled to death in the porch of the Three Crowns. His body was carried to Okehampton for burial.

Colcombe Castle (SY248947)   The medieval castle of the Earls of Devon was garrisoned for the King 1643–44 but evacuated in autumn 1644 at the approach of Parliamentary forces. The fortress was probably semi-derelict by the time of the Civil War and today only fragmentary ruins survive around, and incorporated within, post-seventeenth-century farm buildings.

Crediton (SS8300)   During winter 1645–46 Fairfax's Parliamentary army quartered in a number of towns and villages in a wide arc around Exeter, including Ottery St Mary to the east, Tiverton to the north and Crediton to the north-west. Cromwell probably visited all the bases during the winter and he certainly lodged in Crediton in October 1645 and January and

February 1646; he passed through the town again in March on his way back from Cornwall to Exeter. Fairfax and Cromwell attended services in the Church of the Holy Cross in the High Street, Crediton. A small museum and governors' room above the church vestry contains a number of relics recalling the Parliamentarians' stay in Crediton, including armour, a buff coat, a saddle and military boots.

Dartmouth (SX8751)   The flourishing port of Dartmouth was secured for Parliament without opposition at the outbreak of war. Twelve months later Prince Maurice laid siege to the place, taking the castle on 4 October and the town on the following day. Dartmouth was garrisoned for the King in 1643–46, its defences strengthened in 1645 by the addition of an earthwork fort above the town. On the other side of the estuary, Kingswear was also occupied and fortified. Fairfax launched a carefully planned and co-ordinated land and sea attack in January 1646, storming the town and castle on the 18th and securing the remaining Royalist outposts around Dartmouth and Kingswear on the 19th.

The early Tudor blockhouse at Baynards Cove, at the southern end of Dartmouth (SX878510), apparently played little part in the Civil War and fighting centred around Dartmouth Castle, ¾ mile south-east of the town at the mouth of the Dart (SX887503). Built in the late fifteenth century, the three storey artillery fort comprises two linked towers, a round tower containing the principal living quarters and gun emplacements and a square entrance tower. It remained in military use until the early twentieth century, but is now a scheduled historic monument, open to the public daily. The Church of St Petrox nearby was used as an additional magazine and store by the Royalist garrison. On the hillside above are the remains of Gallants Bower, the earthwork fort thrown up by the King's men in 1645 (SX886502).

On the opposite bank of the Dart stands Kingswear Castle (SX892503). Built in the late fifteenth century, it was derelict and ruinous by the seventeenth and was not occupied during the Civil War. Instead the Royalists built an earthwork fort, Mount Ridley, on the hillside above Kingswear, but unfortunately the subsequent expansion of the town has obliterated all trace of it. The Redoubt Hotel probably stands on the site.

Exeter (SX9292)   Modern Exeter is very much the second city of Devon, but in the seventeenth century the still-thriving port rivalled if not exceeded Plymouth in size and wealth. The city was defended by a circuit of Roman and medieval walls, within the northern angle of which stood a Norman castle. Exeter was held by a Parliamentary garrison during the opening months of the war, but by late November 1642 Royalist forces had appeared before the walls. Although Hopton's initial assault was repulsed, there followed ten months of intermittent sieges and repeated attacks, ending on 7 September 1643 when the beleaguered garrison, by then isolated in a largely Royalist county, surrendered to Prince Maurice. Exeter became the Royalists' HQ in the south-west, garrisoned by them and frequently visited by members of the royal family. By October 1645, however, the city was threatened by Fairfax's Parliamentarians who – like the Royalists two years before – quickly established a ring of bases around the city, including Exmouth, Topsham, various points along the Clyst, Stoke Canon, Poltimore, Powderham and Dunsford. Fairfax made no serious attempt to storm Exeter, preferring to blockade it until either starvation or the collapse of the Royalist cause throughout the area persuaded the garrison to surrender. Sure enough, by early April 1646 Sir John Berkeley had opened negotiations, and talks in Poltimore House led to the surrender of the city on lenient terms on 9 April. Nine years later the Royalist cause was again brought low in Exeter, when in late spring 1655 the rebel John Penruddock was tried here and executed on a scaffold in front of the castle.

Most of Norman Rougemont Castle has been demolished and the site is now occupied by eighteenth- and nineteenth-century court buildings. The much restored Norman gateway survives at the top of Castle Street and twelfth-century Rougemont Tower stands at the northern angle of the city walls. Long stretches of the walls survive to a good height, particularly on the southern side between the cathedral and Southernhay West and down to Quay Hill, and to the north along Bartholomew and Paul Streets and on through Rougemont Park. The medieval guildhall in Fore Street contains many fine seventeenth-century paintings, including a portrait of George Monck.

Great Fulford (SX790918)   The medieval home of the Fulford family stands in private grounds three miles north-west of Dunsford. The house was garrisoned for the King from 1643 and fell to Fairfax in autumn 1645 after a ten day siege. The house was then used to quarter Parliamentary troops over the winter. The circular earthwork 500 yards south of the mansion,

guarding the southern approach road, may date from the Civil War.

Hemyock (ST134133)   On 6 March 1644 Royalists from east Devon attacked Col. Butler's Parliamentary force stationed in Hemyock. Butler and 200 of his men took refuge in the old castle but gave themselves up on the following day. The castle, which stood just west of the church, was subsequently slighted and only the gatehouse remains intact, a late medieval structure with twin flanking towers. Surviving fragments of the keep and great hall were incorporated in the later farm buildings, and slight traces of the castle moat are still visible, particularly on the west side. The farm and surrounding land are private and should be viewed from the road or the churchyard.

Modbury (SX6651)   In the early morning of 7 December 1642 Col. Ruthin and 500 Parliamentary Horse from Plymouth swooped down upon the 3,000 Royalist volunteers gathering at Modbury to enlist in the King's army. Hopton and other officers managed to escape and their would-be soldiers were scattered by Ruthin's men. Ten weeks later the Parliamentarians were back, for on 21 February 1643 a Parliamentary force moving to relieve Plymouth came across Slanning's and Trevanion's Royalists stationed here. The two forces clashed on a hilltop immediately east of the village (around SX667515) and the Royalists were eventually pushed west through Modbury and fell back on Plympton, losing 100 dead and at least as many captured. The tombs and effigies in St George's Church were allegedly mutilated by Parliamentary troops.

Plymouth (SX4755)   Although it was repeatedly assaulted, besieged and blockaded by Royalist forces, the town of Plymouth held out for Parliament throughout the Civil War, the only important base in Devon to do so. Under intermittent siege from November 1642 to January 1646, the garrison also endured several Royalist attempts to storm the town. The most determined attempt by the Royalists to capture Plymouth began with the arrival of Prince Maurice on 30 September 1643. He closely invested the town, establishing bases in an arc from Plymstock, Plympton, Egg Buckland, Tamerton, Saltash and Mount Edgecumbe to Mount Stamford. Against him, the Parliamentary garrison under Col. James Wardlaw manned a defensive line of forts and walls or embankments stretching from the Tamar to the Plym. In deteriorating weather Maurice abandoned the main siege on

Above: Powderham Castle, Devon. The seat of the Courtenay Earls of Devon for nearly 600 years, Powderham is partly fourteenth century, but Civil War damage and later rebuilding and modernization has destroyed or concealed most of the medieval stronghold which fell to Fairfax in 1646. Despite the imposing military frontage, Powderham is largely a grand eighteenth- and nineteenth-century house.

Right: Dartmouth Castle, Devon. The waterside fort guarding the river Dart and the approach to the town was the focus of action when Dartmouth fell to Maurice in October 1643 and to Fairfax in January 1646. The castle, built by townspeople in the early 1480s as a defence against possible French attacks, was one of the earliest coastal fortresses designed specifically for artillery.

22 December but the blockade continued and the threat to the town was not lifted until the Parliamentary invasion in winter 1645–46. On 25 March 1646, old New Year's Day, Fairfax and Cromwell led a triumphant procession through the loyal town.

In less happy times for the Parliamentary cause after the Restoration, Drake's or Nicholas's Island in the Sound became a prison for several enemies of the regime, including the political philosopher James Harrington and Robert Lilburne, soldier, regicide and deputy Major General of Yorkshire in 1655, who ran the area in the absence in London of Major General Lambert. Lambert himself was imprisoned here from 1670 until his death in March 1684, when he was laid to rest beside his wife (d1676) in St Andrew's Church.

Almost nothing now survives of Civil War Plymouth. The great urban expansion of the nineteenth and twentieth centuries had obliterated all trace of the earthwork defences thrown up by the Parliamentarians in 1642 and the bombs of the Second World War reduced medieval St Andrew's Church to a ruined shell, since rebuilt.

Powderham (SX9684)

Powderham Castle (SX968836) was garrisoned for the King at the end of 1642 and remained in Royalist hands as an outpost of Exeter for three years. In winter 1645–46 Fairfax's troops attacked the castle as part of the operation to surround and isolate Exeter. Their first assault in mid-December 1645 was repulsed and although the retreating Parliamentarians briefly occupied and fortified St Clement's Church (SX973844), they fell back in the face of a Royalist counter-attack. On 25 January 1646 they returned, however, and successfully stormed the castle. The medieval stronghold of the Courtenays, Powderham Castle was extensively redesigned and rebuilt in the eighteenth and nineteenth centuries, and only two medieval towers and the Elizabethan domestic wings remain of the fortress which saw action in the Civil War. Open during the summer, the castle contains a fine collection of furniture and fittings, including a portrait of the Parliamentary General William Waller.

Salcombe Castle (SX733382)

Known variously as Salcombe Castle, Fort Charles and the Old Bulwark, this Henry VIII coastal fort was garrisoned for the King by Sir Edmund Fortescue in 1645. The small but well-equipped garrison was under siege by the following January and finally surrendered on 9 May 1646, the last base in Devon to fall to Parliament. The ruined castle stands near the water's edge at North Sands, south of Salcombe.

Shute House or Barton (SY253974)

The late medieval manor-house was garrisoned for the King from early 1643 until May 1644, when it was surrendered to a Parliamentary raiding party. The house apparently played no further part in the war. The fourteenth- and fifteenth-century castellated mansion and its Jacobean gatehouse remain a private residence, not usually open to the public.

Sourton Down (SX5491)

On the night of 25–26 April 1643 Hopton led his 3,500 strong Cornish army into Devon, advancing with incautious speed on James Chudleigh's quarters at Okehampton. The Parliamentarians were aware of Hopton's plans, and Chudleigh was waiting with his Horse on Sourton Down, an area of fairly flat, high ground on the fringe of Dartmoor, 1½ miles north-north-east of Sourton village. The Royalist van stumbled straight into the ambush, scattering in panic when Chudleigh's men fired a volley at close range and then charged. At least 60 Cornishmen died before the approach of Hopton and the Royalist rear restored order and persuaded Chudleigh to fall back. While Chudleigh awaited the arrival of his Infantry from Okehampton, Hopton took up a defensive position behind prehistoric earthworks on the Down. However, the expected second attack never in fact took place, and after a brief exchange of shots the two armies marched away in opposite directions amid a heavy downpour.

South Molton (SS7125)

On the evening of 14 March 1655 John Penruddock's Royalist rebellion ended in this quiet north Devon market town. The rebel army, less than 400 strong, was caught by Unton Crook's troop of Horse from Exeter, and after a three hour street fight the Royalists broke and fled. Some escaped, but large numbers of rebels – including the leaders Grove, Jones and Penruddock himself – were captured.

Tiverton (SS9512)

The town and castle were taken for the King early in 1643 and remained in Royalist hands for 2½ years. On 17 October 1645 Fairfax's army approached from the east and quickly overran the town, the Royalist garrison taking refuge in the castle. Fairfax bombarded the fortress for three days until a lucky or skillful shot broke the chains of the drawbridge and brought it crashing down. The 250 Royalists within promptly surrendered.

Tiverton became one of the bases for the Parliamentary army over the winter, and Cromwell and Fairfax were probably frequent visitors.

Most of the fortress which saw action in the Civil War has gone, destroyed in the war itself or demolished thereafter. A fourteenth-century gatehouse, the medieval south-west and south-east angle towers and parts of the Tudor rebuilding survive, largely incorporated within a Georgian mansion. The castle, which stands by St Peter's Church (SS954129), is open on certain Sundays and weekdays during the summer.

Topsham (SX9688) The thriving port on the Exe Estuary served as an outpost of Exeter and its capture was a crucial preliminary to any attack on the city itself. In winter 1642–3 Hopton's forces stormed and captured Topsham, expelling the small Parliamentary garrison, thereby cutting the water route to Exeter and preventing supplies reaching the city by sea. In July 1643 Warwick tried and failed to retake Topsham and thus reopen the estuary in a combined land and sea operation. In autumn 1645 the Parliamentary army, in turn, made the capture of Topsham one of its first priorities in the operation to isolate and starve out the Royalists in Exeter.

Torrington (SS4919) At the end of January 1646 Hopton took to the field in an attempt to draw the Parliamentary forces away from Exeter. On 10 February his army of 2,000 Foot and 3,000 Horse occupied Torrington, now Great Torrington, and set about fortifying the place with a circuit of earthworks and barricades of treetrunks across the approach roads. Leaving a unit before Exeter to continue the siege, Fairfax and Cromwell led the Parliamentary army north-west through Crediton and Chumleigh and approached the town on 16 February, driving in several Royalist outposts, including a party at Stevenstone House (SS528194) – the present house is Victorian. Fearing that any delay would enable Hopton to slip away under cover of darkness, Fairfax ordered an immediate attack on Torrington. Thus the last battle of the Civil War in Devon took place in the failing light of a winter's afternoon as the Parliamentarians fought their way across the barricades and then through the streets of Torrington. At this point a stray spark ignited the Royalist gunpowder stored in the parish church, and the resulting explosion not only killed many Royalist soldiers and Parliamentarian prisoners in and around the church but also effectively ended the battle. Falling debris narrowly missed Fairfax, and in the resulting confusion Hopton and the remnant of his army slipped away and fled back to Cornwall. On the following day Hugh Peter preached amid the ruins in the market square, warning the Devonians of the evils of King Charles and his Irish Catholic allies. The Parliamentarians soon moved on, some back to the operations before Exeter, but most – including Fairfax and Cromwell – west into Cornwall in pursuit of Hopton.

Only the south-east chapel of the old parish church survived the explosion of 1646. The rest of St Michael's was rebuilt in 1651 and despite Victorian extensions and renovations, much of the present building dates from the Interregnum.

DORSET

The county was divided in allegiance during the early months of the war, some towns – particularly the south coast ports – declaring for Parliament, other regions for the King. The Royalists gradually gained the upper hand during 1643 and by the end of the year only Lyme and Poole held out. Most of the county was retaken by Parliament during the following year, but not until 1645–46 did the Royalists relinquish control over several strongholds. Cromwell was frequently in Dorset between March and October 1645, but he fought no major engagements here. Indeed, there were no significant battles or skirmishes in the field within Dorset, the war quickly developing into a dour struggle for control of a number of key towns and fortresses.

Abbotsbury (SY5785) In 1643 Sir John Strangeways fortified the Abbey House for the King and installed a Royalist garrison; at the same time he occupied the adjoining church as an outpost and store. The garrison survived for eighteen months until November 1644, when Sir Anthony Ashley Cooper led a party of Musketeers and Horse against Abbotsbury. The Church of St Nicholas was stormed by the Musketeers and the dozen or so Royalists within quickly expelled. The capture of the main house proved far more difficult and only after six hours of fierce fighting did the Parliamentarians reach the walls of the house. They wrenched open the windows and threw in blazing furze, forcing the Royalists to abandon the soon blazing and smoke-filled house. As Parliamentary troops rushed in to plunder a spark set off the Royalist magazine, killing over 50 Royalists and Parliamentarians and demolishing much of Abbey House. Cooper withdrew with the 130 surviving Royalist prisoners.

Nothing now remains of the Strangeways' Elizabethan mansion built on the site of a Benedictine Abbey. The present Abbey House is much later and the adjoining ruins are apparently no earlier than the eighteenth century. St Nicholas's Church has survived several renovations largely unaltered; bullet holes in the Jacobean pulpit were supposedly made by Cooper's forces as they stormed the church.

Chideock (SY4292)

Chideock Castle, also known as Whitechurch Castle, stood on high ground immediately north of the village. A late medieval fortified manor-house defended by a moat, it was owned during the mid-seventeenth century by Henry, Lord Arundel, who garrisoned it for the King in 1643. In March 1644 it was stormed and taken by a detachment of Parliamentarians from Lyme led by Capt. Thomas Pyne, who subsequently garrisoned it for Parliament. Retaken by Royalists in the autumn, it changed hands for the third and final time in July 1645 when the 100-strong Royalist garrison fell to the Lyme Parliamentarians. By the eighteenth century only the gatehouse remained, and today nothing survives above ground. The site of the castle, however, is still clearly visible, indicated by a number of earthworks – particularly the dry ditches of the former moat – in a field 300 yards north-east of the church.

Christchurch (SZ150926)

Held for the King by Sir John Mills during the opening eighteen months of the war, Christchurch was attacked and taken by Waller's Horse on 3 April 1644. Nine months later, on 15th January 1645, Goring stormed the town, forcing Major Lower and his 200-strong garrison to take refuge in the castle. Reports that a Parliamentary relieving force was approaching prompted Goring to fall back. Much of the medieval motte and bailey castle has since been destroyed, but the ruins of the fourteenth-century keep survive, and to the east stands the Castle or Constable's Hall, a well-preserved medieval hall which once stood

within the castle bailey. Keep and hall are open daily.

Corfe Castle (SY959823)

One of the most spectacular ruins in England, Corfe Castle stands on a steep hillock overlooking the village. The Normans built the keep on the site of an earlier Saxon fortress, and over the following centuries the castle was strengthened with the addition of curtain walls, wall towers, and gatehouses on the slopes below. The castle was garrisoned for the King in 1642 and, despite frequent attacks, it held out until 1646, ably defended by Lady Bankes and other members of the family. It finally fell through treachery: on 26 February Lt.-Col. Pittman rode out from the castle to collect reinforcements, defected to Parliament, and led 50 Parliamentary soldiers back into the castle under a Royalist banner. The castle was slighted after the war and rendered indefensible. The extensive ruins are open daily.

By the road ¼ mile south-west of the castle stand the Rings, the remains of a siegework thrown up by King Stephen in the twelfth century. Five hundred years later the stronghold was reused by the Parliamentarians as a battery. Inevitably, the site became known as 'Cromwell's Battery', although Cromwell himself played no recorded part in the siege.

Dorchester (SY6990)

In common with many Dorset towns, Dorchester changed hands several times in 1643–44 as the two sides disputed control of the county. Despite the addition of earthworks around the town to strengthen the much-decayed Roman defences, Dorchester remained very vulnerable to attack, the occupying garrison usually retreating without a fight at the approach of a larger force. Not until November 1644 was the town finally secured for Parliament by Col. Sydenham. Cromwell was frequently in the area during 1645 and there is an unconfirmed tradition that in March of that year he clashed with local Royalists at Fordington, now a western suburb of Dorchester.

Most of the Civil War defences have been destroyed. The exception is Maumbury Rings, a Neolithic henge and Roman amphitheatre south of the town centre by Weymouth Avenue. In 1642 the Parliamentarians threw up gun emplacements within the circular earthwork to cover the main road to Weymouth. The internal terracing and the gun platform in the south-west corner are still visible.

Denzil, Lord Holles, was buried in St Peter's Church in 1680. MP for Dorchester in the Long Parliament, he was one of the most prominent

Corfe Castle, Dorset. The spectacular medieval castle (*above*), with a Norman keep and a complex of later walls, towers and gatehouses crowded on the steep slopes below, was held for the King throughout the war. Lady Bankes's garrison eventually fell by subterfuge in 1646 and Capt. Thomas Hughes of Lulworth was ordered to slight the castle by mining and explosives. The south-west gatehouse (*right*), a thirteenth-century ashlar pile guarding the entrance from the outer bailey, was destroyed by undermining the southern of its twin towers. In consequence, the gatehouse broke in two above the central arch and the southern tower (on the left) slipped roughly 8 feet down the slope, while remaining largely upright and intact.

political opponents of the King during the early 1640s and was one of the five Members whom Charles tried to arrest in January 1642. He lies with his son and grandson in the family vault beneath the church, near a large standing monument to the Holles family.

East Lulworth (SY855822) Lulworth Castle, in reality a Jacobean lodge or fortified house, is a three storey embattled block with round corner towers. Garrisoned for the King at the outbreak of war, by 1644 it had fallen to Parliament and was being used as a base to cover the Royalists in Corfe. Although the Corfe garrison launched several raids on Lulworth, it was a twentieth-century fire rather than Civil War cannon which reduced the castle to its present state. Roofless and gutted, but otherwise complete, the spectacular shell can be viewed from the public footpaths which run close by.

Hambledon Hill (ST8512) Hambledon is a large, irregular-shaped hill standing between the rivers Stour and Iwerne and topped by the remains of an extensive, multi-ramparted hillfort. In early August 1645 a large body of Clubmen, somewhere between 2,000 and 4,000 strong, gathered on the hilltop. Cromwell and Disbrowe came under fire as they approached up the western slopes in the hope of parleying with the Clubmen; they returned later on 4 August at the head of a full-scale assault. Cromwell led one party up the western slopes to distract the Clubmen whilst Disbrowe launched the main attack from the Child Okeford side. Overwhelmed by the professional soldiers, the Clubmen scattered. Five hundred were rounded up and held overnight in St Mary's Church in Iwerne Courtney or Shroton (ST860125). Cromwell and his men quartered in and around the village before returning to Sherborne on the 5th.

Lyme Regis (SY3492) A small but prosperous port and cloth town, Lyme was strongly Parliamentarian during the 1640s. Despite its rather weak position, overlooked by high hills and with no stone walls for defence, Lyme held out for Parliament throughout the Civil War, a vital land and sea base in an area which was overwhelmingly Royalist in 1643–44. On 20 April 1644 Prince Maurice appeared before Lyme with 6,000 men, quickly driving in the Parliamentary outposts and establishing an arc of bases around the north of the town. Below them Cols Were and Ceeley defended the town behind a hastily constructed ring of earth banks and turf and earth blockhouses – all traces of these

defences have long disappeared and their precise layout and location are not known. The siege continued for nearly two months, the King's men keeping up a heavy bombardment and launching several unsuccessful attacks, the Parliamentarians occasionally sallying out to hinder Royalist operations. A prolonged siege was futile – Lyme was kept supplied by sea and could not be starved out – and having failed to take the town by storm, Maurice fell back on 15 June at the approach of the main Parliamentary army under Essex. Various relics of the siege and of the town's heroic defence are now on display in the Philpot Museum in Bridge Street.

Poole (SZ0190) A Parliamentary stronghold throughout the Civil War, Poole held out even during the Royalist high-tide of 1643–44. In July 1643 Sir Walter Erle fell back into Poole from his position before Corfe and he organised the subsequent defence of the town against frequent attacks from Lord Crawford and others. The Parliamentary fleet in the bay not only kept the town supplied by sea but also broke up Royalist operations with heavy artillery fire. Old St Michael's Church at Hamworthy (SY9991), one mile north-west of Poole, was wrecked in the course of this naval bombardment.

Portland (SY685744) Secured for Parliament at the outbreak of war, the 'Isle' of Portland and its strongpoint, Portland Castle, changed hands several times during 1643. According to tradition the castle was captured on one occasion by subterfuge: two groups of Horse approached the castle and the first, flying Parliamentary colours and apparently fleeing from Royalists, were immediately admitted by the garrison, whereupon they attacked and overpowered the unsuspecting Parliamentarians. By the end of 1643 the castle was garrisoned by a large Royalist force and it remained under the King's control for over two years, resisting blockades by land and sea and repelling occasional attacks. The garrison finally surrendered on 6 April 1646, by which time the Royalist cause in the south-west had collapsed. The castle, built by Henry VIII in rich Portland ashlar, survived the Civil War in surprisingly good order, and remained in military use until the nineteenth century. Open to the public daily, the castle comprises a tower, externally round but internally octagonal, standing at the centre of an artillery emplacement shaped like a segment of a circle, the outer curved wall of which faces north towards the sea.

Sherborne (ST648167) The old castle, built by

the Bishop of Salisbury in the twelfth century, was one of the few medieval fortresses in Dorset still defensible during the Civil War. The Marquis of Hertford occupied the castle for the King in August 1642 and repaired its defences, which had been partly destroyed in the late sixteenth century when Raleigh began converting the place along more domestic lines. In early September the Earl of Bedford arrived at the head of a 7,000-strong Parliamentary army and set up camp to the north of the castle. However, repeated raids by Hopton and others persuaded the Earl to depart on the 6th without having launched a serious attack on the castle. Hertford himself marched off later in the month. The castle changed hands several times in 1643–44, but by 1645 it was under the control of Sir Lewis Dyve and his large Royalist garrison. The main Parliamentary army laid siege to the castle at the end of July and the King's men endured a fortnight of heavy bombardment and mining. Cromwell was present during the early stages of the siege and again on 15–17 August when Dyve and his 400-strong garrison surrendered. The badly damaged castle was slighted later in the year and much of the stone was taken away to build an extension to St Mary Magdalene's in Castleton.

The castle stands on a slight knoll to the east of the town and comprises a curtain wall with gatehouses and angle towers enclosing a large, roughly rectangular ward in which stand the keep and adjoining domestic and religious buildings. Open daily, the castle is now very ruinous. Several earthworks beyond the curtain wall are ascribed to the Civil War, particularly the triangular bastion to the west, immediately beyond the moat and south-west gatehouse, thought to be a gun emplacement thrown up by the besieging army in summer 1645.

Sturminster Newton (ST7813)

On 29 June 1645 a large body of Dorset Clubmen, aided and abetted by local Royalists, clashed with Massey's Parliamentarians outside Sturminster. Surprised and outnumbered, Massey's men fell back in disorder.

Wareham (SY9287)

Wareham changed hands several times during the Civil War, the earth ramparts which had protected the town in the tenth century proving no real obstacle in the seventeenth. Though derelict, the Norman castle was still defensible during the early 1640s and was slighted by Parliament after the Civil War. Today nothing survives except a slight mound off Castle Close.

Weymouth (SY6778)

Despite the attempts of both sides during the Civil War to strengthen Weymouth and Melcombe Regis with earth banks and ditches, the towns could offer little resistance to a determined assault and accordingly changed hands at least six times during the course of the war. Col. Sydenham and the Parliamentary garrison attempted to bolster Weymouth's defences in autumn 1644 by erecting two earth and turf forts, North Fort and Chapel Fort, around the town. They did not stop Dyve's forces taking Weymouth for the King on 9 February 1645, and Sydenham fell back on Melcombe. However, the Parliamentarians returned at the end of the month and finally secured Weymouth. The great expansion during the eighteenth century and later has not only effectively united Weymouth and Melcombe Regis as a single urban centre but also obliterated all trace of the Civil War defences, including Sydenham's two forts.

Wimborne St Giles (SU0312)

St Giles House, the seat of the Ashley family (later the Ashley Coopers and later still the Earls of Shaftesbury), was the birthplace and home of Anthony Ashley Cooper, the 1st Earl. Although the earldom and much of his career belong to the period after the Restoration, Ashley Cooper rose to prominence in the mid-seventeenth century. He joined the King's army at the outbreak of war but soon adopted the Parliamentary cause and saw action in Dorset and Wiltshire. He was one of Cromwell's principal supporters in 1653–54, serving in the first Protectorate Parliament and in the Protectorate Council. For reasons which remain unclear, he broke with Cromwell early in 1655 and became an outspoken critic of the Protectorate.

The present St Giles House was begun by Ashley Cooper in the 1650s on the site of the family's late medieval mansion. Originally a modest brick house with a five or seven bay front and a hipped roof, it has been extensively remodelled and extended since the late seventeenth century.

After a frequently stormy career the 1st Earl was buried in St Giles's Church in 1683 (SU032120). The elaborate monument in the church, featuring a statue of Ashley Cooper standing before an obelisk, was erected nearly fifty years later.

Wynford Eagle (SY5895)

The Tudor and Jacobean Manor Farm was the seat of the Sydenham family and here was born William Sydenham, Parliamentary soldier, governor of

Weymouth, Melcombe and the Isle of Wight, a leading supporter of Cromwell in the 1650s and a member of the Protectorate Parliaments and Councils. Sydenham demolished the old house in the 1630s and built the present, rather plain Manor Farm.

DURHAM

Secured for the King at the outbreak of war, County Durham suffered only minor Parliamentary incursions until the appearance of the Scottish army in March 1644. The departure of the Scottish Parliamentarians southwards into Yorkshire and the approach of Montrose's band of Royalists led to a brief Royalist recovery in summer 1644, but the destruction of Newcastle's army at Marston Moor in July was rapidly followed by the collapse of the King's cause throughout the area. Cromwell passed through County Durham in 1648 and again in 1650–51 on his way to and from Scotland.

Barnard Castle (NZ0516)   The town and the medieval castle guarding the crossing of the Tees lay well to the west of the principal north–south routes, in territory firmly held by the Royalists in 1642–44 and then abandoned by them without a fight. Thus Barnard Castle escaped serious bloodshed in the Civil Wars. In October 1648 Cromwell visited the area while making his way south from Scotland in rather leisurely fashion, and he stayed at Barnard Castle on the 24th and 25th. The castle was semi-derelict by the seventeenth century and it is possible that Cromwell lodged at a humbler building within the town.

Bishop Auckland (NZ214301)   Little remains of Auckland Castle, the medieval fortified palace of the Bishops of Durham. Charles I was lodged here as a prisoner of the Scots in February 1647. Later in the year the estate was sold to Sir Arthur Hesilrige, who demolished large sections of the palace, including the medieval chapel and great hall. The site was restored to the Church in 1660 and the surviving buildings refurbished; the medieval banqueting hall was converted into a chapel. The palace, which was extended and remodelled in the eighteenth century, stands amid an extensive and carefully landscaped park. Parts of the palace, including the state rooms and the chapel, are open to the public on certain weekdays in summer.

Brancepeth (NZ223377)   Cromwell usually travelled to and from Scotland via Durham, but in August 1651 he bypassed that city and stayed instead at Brancepeth on the 15th. He may have lodged in the castle, the medieval seat of the Neville family, heavily restored in the nineteenth century and still a private residence.

Chester le Street (NZ2751)   The town was the scene of a brief skirmish on 20 March 1644 when a Scottish raiding party surprised and captured a detachment of Royalist Horse from Newcastle's army.

Durham (NZ2742)   Secured for the King in 1643, Durham became the temporary HQ of Newcastle and the Royalist army in March and early April 1644. The Earl had fought a series of delaying actions, hindering the southern advance of the Scottish army, but by mid-April the Scots had overcome the forces sent to contain them and, having abandoned the attempt to take the town of Newcastle, were marching south once more. Their approach and the news that Selby had fallen and that York was therefore threatened persuaded Newcastle to hurry south rather than attempt to hold Durham. The Royalists marched out on 13 April and the Scots passed through unopposed soon after.

Cromwell was in Durham in September and October 1648 – he attended a Thanksgiving service in the cathedral on 8 September – and in July 1650 on his way to and from Scotland. Despite a local tradition that on at least one occasion he lodged at a farmhouse in Shincliffe, south-east of Durham (NZ2940), it is probable that he usually stayed at Durham Castle, the medieval stronghold of the Prince-Bishops of Durham.

The castle, with its central courtyard surrounded by domestic ranges to the north and west, the gatehouse and curtain wall to the south and the much restored keep on a motte to the east, is open on certain weekdays throughout the year.

Above: Durham, Co. Durham. The city skyline is dominated by the castle and cathedral, the twin seats of the Prince-Bishops of Durham. Cromwell probably lodged in the much-restored castle on several occasions in 1648–50 and attended services in the Norman cathedral.

Right: Saffron Walden, Essex. In May 1647 the Sun Inn was the venue for a series of discussions attended by Cromwell, Ireton, Fleetwood and other officers. The late medieval building was decorated in the seventeenth century with a form of elaborate plaster work known as pargeting. The gable on the left bears the date 1676; that on the right, probably earlier, shows the Cambridgeshire folk-hero, Tom Hickathrift, and the Wisbech giant whom he slayed.

Lumley Castle (NZ288511) A very impressive and almost perfectly preserved late medieval castle, Lumley was built in the late fourteenth century for the family of that name. It was garrisoned for the King by Sir Richard Lumley from 1642 but was evacuated without a fight in April 1644 when the Earl of Newcastle abandoned his bases in the area and retreated to York. The quadrangular castle, with large corner towers and a central square courtyard, remains a private residence.

Piercebridge (NZ212155) Dere Street, one of the principal routes linking Yorkshire and the north, crosses the Tees here. At the end of 1642 the younger Hotham tried to hold the crossing against Newcastle's Royalist army heading south towards York. Heavily outnumbered, Hotham sent up a barrage of cannon and musket fire which succeeded in holding the Royalist advance for a time. However, Newcastle's 8,000 men eventually forced their way across the sixteenth-century five-arch bridge and brushed aside the Parliamentarians. The bridge survives, albeit widened and renovated in the eighteenth century.

Raby Castle (NZ129218) A late medieval stronghold of the Neville family, Raby Castle was bought by Sir Henry Vane senior in 1626. Garrisoned for Parliament in the Civil War, the castle was captured by Royalists in 1645 but swiftly retaken by a small local force led by Sir George Vane. Scottish Royalists unsuccessfully besieged the place three years later. Throughout the period Raby was the principal country seat and occasional residence of Sir Henry Vane senior and junior. Their seventeenth-century work has largely disappeared and the present castle is a mixture of medieval fortress – including Lady Joan's, the Kitchen and the Chapel towers – and eighteenth- and nineteenth-century remodelling. Raby Castle now houses a fine collection of furnishings from many periods and is open to the public during the summer.

EAST SUSSEX

The county saw no significant action during the Civil Wars and was held by Parliament without serious challenge throughout the period. The Royalist raids of 1643 along the south coast were halted in West Sussex and the disturbances in Kent five years later did not spread to its western neighbour. Cromwell seems never to have set foot within East Sussex.

Glynde (TQ456093) Col. Herbert Morley was born and brought up at Glynde Place. MP for Lewes during the 1640s, Morley was one of the leading lights in the defence of Sussex, raising troops, levying money, sequestrating estates and generally administering the area for Parliament. His zeal and enthusiasm won him praises from Parliament but many enemies in Sussex. By the 1650s, however, he had broken with Cromwell and army and became an outspoken critic of the Protectorate. He purchased a pardon at the Restoration and spent the last years of his life in retirement at Glynde. The fine Tudor house, built by William Morley around 1560, was extensively remodelled by the Bishop of Durham in the mid-eighteenth century. The eastern range is now largely Georgian, but the western retains its original Tudor appearance. The finely furnished house is open on certain weekdays during the summer. Col. Morley lies beneath an inscribed monument near the altar of St Mary's Church, the medieval church next to Glynde Place which was rebuilt in exuberant style by Bishop Trevor in the eighteenth century.

ESSEX

Essex was secure for Parliament throughout the first Civil War and saw serious fighting only in the second, when, in summer 1648, Colchester became one of the centres of Royalist rebellion. There are several Cromwellian traditions connected with Essex – for example, the dubious tale that Cromwell almost drowned in the spring or well at Maldon which now bears his name – but clear and well-documented links are few.

Abbess Roding (TL5711) John Thurloe, Cromwell's Secretary of State and Secretary to the Protectorate Council, was born and brought up at the old rectory here; his father was rector of St Edmund's.

Boreham (TL735103) New Hall or Newall, 1½ miles north-north-west of the village, is the surviving part of the early Tudor royal mansion of Beaulieu which stood on the site. The quadrangular house, remodelled in the 1570s, has been largely demolished, and little remains of the Tudor building beyond the impressive southern façade. Cromwell acquired the property in 1651 but seems never to have visited the place. A later story that he and his family held a reunion at Newall on 25 April 1652, Cromwell's 53rd birthday, rests on no contemporary evidence and is highly implausible: Cromwell attended Council meetings in London on 23 and 27 April and others who supposedly attended the gathering, including his brother-in-law John Disbrowe, were definitely far away from Essex on the 25th. Now a convent, both Newall and the surrounding land are private, but the exterior of the building can be viewed from the public footpath which runs close by.

Chipping Ongar (TL55030) Jane Palavicini, daughter of Sir Oliver Cromwell and first cousin of the Protector, lies buried in the Church of St Martin of Tours. In 1606 she married Sir Toby Palavicini, then of Babraham, Cambridgeshire, but Sir Toby later sold off his extensive Cambridgeshire estates and the couple moved to Essex. Jane (d1637/8) lies beneath an inscribed black marble floor slab in the chancel of St Martin's.

Colchester (TM0025) In early June 1648 the remnant of the Earl of Norwich's Royalist force left Kent and marched north to join the Essex Royalists led by Sir George Lisle and Sir Charles Lucas. The combined army swept through the southern half of the county, sacking the magazine at Braintree and briefly occupying Chelmsford before moving on to Colchester on 12 June. Fairfax was in hot pursuit and approached Colchester on the following day, attacking immediately. Lucas had drawn up his men across the London road, covered by cannon in St Mary's churchyard and on the castle. Despite the initial success of his right wing under Barkstead, Fairfax was compelled to fall back under heavy musket fire and a Royalist counter-attack. The Parliamentary forces settled down for a long, formal siege, cutting the roads and rivers into Colchester and surrounding the town with ten earthwork forts, linked to the south of the Colne by a bank and ditch. The extra-mural suburbs were overrun and Royalist outposts driven back within the walls. By late July the heavy Parliamentary bombardment was no longer answered by Royalist cannon, for within the town both ammunition and food were running very low. Starvation and disease compelled the Royalists to surrender the town unconditionally at the end of August. Fairfax entered Colchester on the 28th and promptly executed Lucas and Lisle in the castle yard.

Although the Parliamentary siege works have completely disappeared, much of the circuit of Roman and medieval walls which sheltered the Royalists survive in good order, particularly in the south east around Priory Street and on the west side by Balkerne Hill and Lane where a Roman gateway, the West or Balkerne Gate, also survives. Just beyond the wall by Priory Street stand the remains of the Norman church of St Botolph's Priory, wrecked during the Parliamentary bombardment. Nearby in Abbey Gardens, the fifteenth-century gatehouse of the otherwise demolished Abbey of St John bears marks caused by Civil War cannon and the timber frame of an early Tudor house in East Street – now called Siege House – is riddled with Civil War bullets. The massive castle keep now houses Colchester Museum in which many relics from the siege are on display; the museum is open every weekday. An obelisk in Castle Park marks the spot where Lucas and Lisle were shot. In 1661 they were honoured with a solemn service in St Giles's Church and a black marble monument was later erected over the Lucas vault in the north chapel where both had been unceremoniously buried. In 1648, immediately after the surrender of the town, they and the other rebels had been held in the yard of the Red Lion, a well preserved Tudor inn which still stands in the High Street.

Felsted (TL676204) This small town has several Cromwellian connections. Oliver's sons were all educated here in the Old School House, a timber frame and plaster Tudor hall with a projecting upper storey which survives in good order near Holy Cross Church. His eldest son, Robert, died at Felsted and lies buried near the south porch of the church. The Rich family, Earls of Warwick, had their country seat nearby and many of them lie in vaults beneath Holy Cross, including Robert, the 2nd Earl (d1658), Parliamentary Admiral during the first Civil War and his grandson, another Robert, who married Cromwell's youngest daughter in November 1657 but died just three months later. Cromwell's father-in-law, Sir James Bourchier, also acquired extensive property around Felsted and he, too, may be buried here.

Hatfield Broad Oak (TL5416) Cromwell's aunt Joan and her husband Sir Francis Barrington lived at Barrington Hall, one mile north of the village, where they brought up their large family of nine children. The Tudor and Jacobean hall has completely disappeared and the present Barrington Hall (TL550177) is eighteenth-century. Joan and Sir Francis were buried in the Church of St Mary the Virgin (TL547166) but no monument now marks their graves.

High Laver (TL5208) Otes, the family home

of the Mashams during the seventeenth century, stood one mile north-north-west of the church. Sir William Masham was a prominent opponent of Charles I's government and according to tradition Cromwell visited Otes to confer with him on several occasions in the late 1630s. The house no longer exists.

Little Stambridge (TQ888907) Little Stambridge Hall was the principal country seat of the Bourchier family during the sixteenth and early seventeenth century. Sir James Bourchier became a very wealthy City merchant and he acquired property elsewhere in Essex and East Anglia but he retained Stambridge Hall and it was probably here that his daughter Elizabeth – later the wife of Oliver Cromwell – was born and brought up. The present hall is largely Georgian but sections of the earlier Tudor building are incorporated at the rear and parts of the old moat also survive. The hall is private, but it can be viewed from the adjoining public footpath.

Saffron Walden (TL5438) The increasingly restless Parliamentary army was stationed around the town from March to May 1647. Cromwell was here on 2–20 May, holding talks with other senior officers about military grievances and possible remedies in the Sun Inn, at the corner of Market Hill and Church Street. The late medieval building comprised a central hall flanked by gabled wings; the storey above the hall was added in the late sixteenth century and the rich pargeting in the seventeenth. The building is owned by the National Trust and is open to the public.

GLOUCESTERSHIRE

Although Gloucestershire was largely Parliamentarian in 1642–43, from the outbreak of the war the Royalists held a number of bases around the fringes of the county and by 1643–44 they had taken all but a triangle of land around and to the east of Gloucester. The defence of the city became one of the major contests of the war and the surrounding area – on both sides of the Severn – was very thickly garrisoned with a circuit of Parliamentary outposts protecting the approaches to Gloucester and further circles of Royalist bases beyond. Cromwell passed through eastern Gloucestershire in June 1645 on his way to Dorset and in summer 1648 he stopped in Gloucester en route to and from South Wales, but there is no evidence that he took part in any fighting within the county.

Beachley (ST5490) During the Civil War the bare flat promontory between the mouth of the Wye and the Severn Estuary made an ideal

military base, protected on three sides by water and by a bank and ditch across the neck of the headland to the north. In September 1644 500

Horse, sent to Beachley by Rupert to cover the lower reaches of the Wye and the Aust passage, were surprised by Massey's Parliamentarians and over 100 Royalists were killed or captured before the survivors managed to cut their way out. Nothing daunted, in the following month Col. Winter briefly re-established a Royalist base here, only to fall to a combined land and sea attack by Massey on 14 October. A party of Royalists under Winter escaped northwards along the east bank of the Wye and, according to a rather fanciful tale, the Royalist commander escaped the pursuing Parliamentarians by leaping from the cliff into the river at a spot now known as Winter's or Wintour's Leap (ST541963). The headland around Beachley is still occupied by a military camp, now overshadowed by the Severn Bridge.

Berkeley (ST685989)   The grim medieval castle was secured for Parliament in 1642 but the garrison withdrew in February 1643 at the approach of Rupert and for the following 30 months it served as a Royalist base. In September 1645 the Parliamentarians returned, established a battery in the churchyard of St Mary's and bombarded the castle for three days, wrecking the outer defences. The castle was stormed and captured on the 25th. Repairs were carried out after the war, particularly to the north and west sides facing the church, which had sustained most damage during the bombardment. The castle, which is in good order, comprises a curtain wall with four mural towers enclosing a roughly circular ward in which stand the Norman keep and a number of medieval and post-medieval domestic buildings. Berkeley Castle is open daily except Mondays during the summer.

Beverstone (ST860940)   The remains of the thirteenth-century quadrangular castle, including parts of the west range, the south-west drum tower and the eastern gatehouse, stand on private land near St Mary's Church. A modern house on the site of the southern range may incorporate further sections of the old fortress. The castle was garrisoned for the King in 1642 and held without serious challenge until 1644, when it was twice attacked and taken by Massey's men. It fell to the Parliamentarians on 23 May but was promptly retaken by the Royalists and not until the autumn, following a second siege and bombardment, was it finally secured for Parliament.

Boddington (SO8925)   The Tudor manor-house, extensively rebuilt or redesigned in 1820 in mock-Tudor style, was garrisoned for the King in 1643–44.

Brookthorpe (SO8312)   The area of the village saw frequent clashes during the war, the most serious in August 1643 when a party of Gloucester Parliamentarians stumbled into a Royalist troop here and were hard put to cut their way back north. The Royalist force covering Gloucester was probably based in Brookthorpe Court, the timber frame and stone mansion, late Tudor but heavily restored in the nineteenth century, which stands east of the church.

Chavenage (ST872951)   Chavenage House, an 'E'-shaped Elizabethan manor house, open to the public on certain days during the summer, was supposedly visited by Cromwell and Ireton during 1648. They came, the story runs, to persuade the owner, Col. Stephens, to take part in the trial and execution of the King and were lodged during their stay in two bedrooms in the south-east wing, now known as the Cromwell and the Ireton Rooms. However, a number of factors weigh against this colourful tale. Cromwell passed through Gloucestershire in May and July 1648 but on both occasions he was moving quickly to meet Royalist rebellions elsewhere and it seems unlikely that he would have spent time at Chavenage. The story assumes that by summer 1648 Cromwell not only had firm plans for the removal of the King but was also willing to reveal them to others who were unconvinced or hostile. Perhaps the most telling point against the tradition is the claim that Cromwell and Ireton visited Chavenage together, for throughout summer 1648, the only time of the year when Cromwell could possibly have been here, Ireton was serving in Kent and Essex, putting down Royalist rebellions there.

Cheltenham (SO9522)   A small village in the seventeenth century, little more than the single High Street, Cheltenham was one of the bases for Royalist troops during the siege of Gloucester and was taken by Essex on 6 September 1643 *en route* to the city.

Chipping Campden (SP1539)   Campden manor-house, a modest Tudor hall extensively rebuilt by Sir Baptist Hicks in the early seventeenth century, was garrisoned for the King under Lord Molineaux in 1644–45. The Royalists evacuated the place in May 1645, burning the house as they left to prevent it being used by Parliamentary forces. The stable block, the Jacobean lodges and the gateway survive intact by the southern entrance to St James's churchyard; in the field beyond stand the fragmentary remains of the manor-house itself.

Cirencester (SP0202)

Cirencester was important in the Civil War because it lay on one of the principal routes linking the Midlands and the south-west. With Royalist Oxfordshire firmly controlling the less direct routes to the east and Parliamentary Gloucester blocking the western road, control of Cirencester and of the road which passed through it became a major objective of both sides. In consequence, the town saw frequent skirmishing and, defended by nothing more than decayed and outgrown Roman walls and banks, changed hands several times during the course of the war.

The fiercest fighting took place on 2 February 1643, when Rupert and Hertford launched an early morning raid on the large Parliamentary garrison, which had been cut off by snow for much of January and was dangerously short of supplies. The Royalist forces attacked from the north and south-west while their guns pounded the east side of the town and although the garrison resisted fiercely, by noon Rupert had captured the town, together with 1,000 prisoners with 1,000 prisoners and five guns.

The prisoners were held in the Church of St John the Baptist; on the wall of the south aisle is a memorial tablet to Hodgkinson Paine, a local clothier who perished during Rupert's attack. The town's museum contains several items from the Civil War.

Coleford (SO5710)

By February 1643 Lord Herbert had gathered a 2,000-strong Royalist army in South Wales and was marching east through the Forest of Dean towards the Parliamentary stronghold of Gloucester. On 20 February he clashed at Coleford with a Parliamentary detachment under Col. Berrows, which had been sent to engage and halt the Royalists. Although more experienced than their opponents, the Parliamentarians were heavily outnumbered and were thrown back in disorder, losing over 50 men.

Eastington (SO7805)

The outlying Parliamentary garrison, protecting the approaches to Gloucester, probably occupied Eastington Manor, the Elizabethan manor-house of the Stephens family. The large three storey house, which stood close to the west end of the church, fell derelict and ruinous in the eighteenth century and was demolished in 1775. Marks on the tower of St Michael's Church were reputedly caused by cannon-fire.

Gloucester (SO8318)

The city of Gloucester controlled not only the lowest bridgeable crossing of the Severn but also the main road linking south-west England with Wales, the Marches and the West Midlands. Garrisoned for Parliament without opposition in autumn 1642, it remained a crucial Parliamentary stronghold throughout the Civil War, even in 1643–44, when Bristol and most of the region had fallen to the King. In the opening months of 1643 Col. Edward Massey, the young Parliamentary governor, hastily repaired the city's derelict defences, the Roman walls which stood to the north, east and south and the large medieval castle to the west. His work was soon put to the test, for the main Royalist army appeared before the city on 10 August 1643 and laid siege to the place. Charles I established his HQ at Matson House, to the south of the city (SO847155), and Rupert lodged at Prinknash Park (SO879134). The Royalists quickly overran the extra-mural suburbs and closely invested the city, but bad weather hindered their operations and heavy rain flooded the tunnels which they had dug under the city walls, ruining the mines just as they were ready to be sprung. Meanwhile Essex and an army of 15,000 were hurrying west from London to the relief of the city and their approach on 5 September persuaded the demoralised Royalists to abandon operations and depart. Although much of the county remained under Royalist control until 1644–45, the high-tide of Royalism in the region had passed and the county town was never again under serious threat. In 1648 Cromwell passed through the city on his way to and from South Wales, but his stay was brief and it is not known exactly where he lodged.

After the Restoration, Gloucester suffered for its Parliamentary past and its walls, gates and castle were slighted on Royal orders. Almost no trace of them remains – the base of the Eastgate tower and adjoining ditches have been revealed by excavation. During the Civil War Massey had his HQ in a sixteenth-century timber-framed inn in Westgate Street; now No. 26, it can be viewed from Westgate Street and from the adjoining Maverdine Passage. Further down Westgate Street stands an early Tudor, three storey, timber-framed building, known as Bishop Hooper's Lodging, now a local museum containing many relics from Civil War Gloucester. The churches of St Mary de Lode and Holy Trinity served as prisons for captured Royalists and St Mary de Crypt as a magazine.

Haresfield Beacon or Hill (SO8209)

The hill affords superb views over Gloucester and

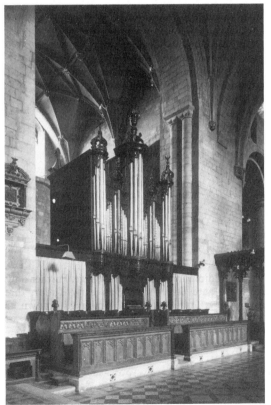

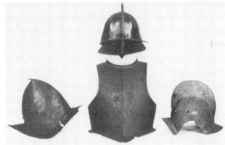

Top: Highnam Court, Glos. The compact 2½ storey red brick house was built sometime around or a little before the Restoration. It stands on the site of an earlier Highnam Court, occupied by Herbert's Royalists in February 1643 but wrecked in the following month when Waller and Massey fell upon and routed the King's men.

Above: Gloucester, Glos. Civil War helmets and breastplates and other items from the period are on display within the city's folk museum in Bishop Hooper's Lodging.

Left: Tewkesbury, Glos. The case of the Milton Organ, probably the oldest organ still in regular use in Britain, was built in Oxford around 1580. Cromwell had the organ moved to Hampton Court where, according to tradition, the blind Milton would play it to soothe the Protectoral brow.

was probably used as an observation point by the Royalist army besieging the city and by Essex's relieving force in 1643. A modern inscribed stone near the summit commemorates the siege. Although it is sometimes referred to as the 'Cromwell stone' Cromwell was not with Essex's army in 1643 and there is nothing to link him to Haresfield Beacon.

Hartpury (SO8025) The Royalist garrison here during the siege of Gloucester was probably based in Hartpury Court. The Tudor building has largely gone and the present farmhouse of that name which stands on the site is a much later mock-Tudor edifice.

High Meadow (SO559105) The Royalist garrison was one of several minor outposts in the area covering the western fringes of the county and the road into South Wales. The home of the Catholic Hall family, the large 'H'-shaped Tudor house set in grand gardens was further strengthened by a series of earthworks. Col. Hall abandoned the place in 1645. The house has been demolished but its site is still evident from the decayed earthworks and foundations around the present, modern High Meadow, north-east of Newland.

Highnam (SO7919) In March 1643 Lord Herbert's newly raised Royalist army occupied Sir Robert Cooke's manor-house at Highnam, quartering in the grounds and throwing up earthworks on the east side to counter possible attacks from Gloucester – traces of these earthworks are still visible in and around the churchyard (SO796195). Aware of Herbert's movements, Massey and Waller planned a joint attack. Some of Massey's men approached Highnam on 23 March and a fierce skirmish developed, but the main attack was launched on the following day. Massey led one assault from the east while Waller, who had ferried his men across the Severn on the far side of Highnam, swooped down from the west. Surprised and surrounded by a larger and more experienced force, the Welsh Royalists broke. At least half the 2,000-strong force surrendered on the spot, but others managed to cut their way clear. One party fled north, along the west bank of the Leadon, but was caught and cut down around Barber's Bridge, east of Tibberton (SO772221). Many bodies, probably those of Herbert's Welsh Royalists, were found buried by the bridge in the nineteenth century and a small monument, made partly of stone from the walls of Gloucester, was erected on the spot, just south of the bridge.

Huntley (SO716198) The remains of a moat north of the church and on the western outskirts of the village may mark the site of the Tudor manor-house. It was held by Parliament as an outpost of Gloucester, but was surprised and captured by Winter's Newnham Royalists in January 1644. Collusion was suspected.

Lancaut (ST5396) Like Beachley to the south, Lancaut is a natural stronghold, a promontory of land protected on three sides by the waters of the Wye. The military potential of the site and of others within adjoining meanders has long been recognised and the area is rich in ancient forts and earthworks, including Offa's Dyke. A line of ditch and bank across the neck of land to the east of Lancaut (around ST542967) is probably ancient, but may have been recut or redug in the Civil War. In the course of the conflict, both sides established a base in the village, garrisoning the manor-house and the church to cover the river-crossing into South Wales. In February 1645 a force of Horse and Foot sent from Gloucester overwhelmed the small Royalist garrison here and finally secured the place for Parliament.

Littledean (SO6713) Following his victory at Highnam in March 1643, Waller advanced through the Forest of Dean into south-east Wales. Two thousand Royalists under Maurice hurried south from the Worcester area to intercept him and block his line of retreat back to Gloucester. Aware of the Royalists' approach, Waller sent most of his Infantry, guns and baggage across the Severn by boat from Chepstow and then he and the Horse moved cautiously along the west bank of the Severn towards Gloucester. On 11 April they entered Littledean and drew up on the hillside immediately south of the town to await the approach of Maurice's men, who were a mile or two north. When the Royalists did not appear, Waller continued his march towards Gloucester, leaving a small garrison at Littledean. At the departure of most of the Parliamentary army, Maurice swooped down on the town and a confused but fierce street fight developed as Waller and the main body of Horse quickly returned. Although the Royalists eventually took the town, they sustained heavy losses and were unable to prevent the Parliamentarians slipping away.

Maurice garrisoned the town, establishing a base at Dean Hall, near the southern end of Littledean. The garrison survived until 7 May 1644, when Massey's men returned, quickly overran the town and negotiated the surrender of the hall. Discussions were broken off when a Royalist sniper shot and killed one of Massey's men. The Parliamentarians responded by storming the place and killing many members of the garrison, including its two commanding officers. The hall survives as a private residence, a largely Tudor building with a Jacobean north wing and a third storey added in the nineteenth century.

Lydney (SO6303)   The Elizabethan home of Sir William Winter, known variously as Lydney, White or White Cross House, stood immediately opposite the lychgate of the parish church. Fortified and garrisoned for the King by Sir John Winter in 1643, it endured a number of Parliamentary raids over the following two years. In May 1645, with the virtual collapse of the Royalist cause in much of the county, Winter evacuated the place, removed the lead and valuables and then burnt the house to the ground rather than see it fall into Massey's hands.

Lypiatt Park (SO886058)   The medieval mansion was garrisoned for Parliament in 1643–44 as an outpost of Gloucester, protecting the southern approaches to the city. On 1 January 1645 Sir Jacob Astley led a Royalist raiding party to Lypiatt, surprising and expelling the small Parliamentary garrison. With most of the county firmly in Parliament's hands, Astley made no attempt to hold the place and instead he sacked and burnt the house and withdrew. Restored after the war and remodelled and extended in the nineteenth century, the house stands in private parkland east of Stroud.

Miserden Park (SO9409)   Miserden Park, an Elizabethan mansion built out of a derelict and partly demolished Norman castle, was garrisoned for Parliament throughout the Civil War as an outpost of Gloucester. The house apparently never saw serious action and survived the war unscathed. The three storey, richly gabled mansion overlooking a steeply wooded valley remains a private residence.

Naunton (SP1123)   Cromwell House, an early Stuart building, originally 'L'-shaped, belonged to the Parliamentary Aylsworth family in the mid-seventeenth century. There is no clear foundation to the story that Cromwell stayed here.

Newnham (SO691115)   Newnham was garrisoned from time to time during the Civil War by Royalist forces to cover Gloucester and to break the lines of communication between the city and South Wales. In early April 1643 the Royalist

garrison fell back at the approach of Waller but returned towards the end of the year, establishing a base in and around the parish church and digging a bank and ditch around the site to protect the landward approaches. These proved insufficient to halt Massey's men, who attacked Newnham on 8 May 1644, pushed Sir John Winter's Royalists back into the church and then took the building by storm. Twenty Royalists perished and over 100 were captured. The Church of St Peter stands at the south end of the town, affording superb views over the Severn. The embankment which runs nearby, from Castle House and the castle mound to the vicarage, may be part of the Royalists' Civil War defences.

Painswick (SO8609)   During the Royalist operations against Gloucester in late summer 1643 Charles established a base in Court House, a Jacobean mansion which stands immediately south of the church. St Mary's itself served as a prison for captured Parliamentarians. One of them, Richard Foot, carved an apt quotation adapted from Spencer's *Fairie Queen* within the church – 'Be bold, be bold, but not too bold'. The village suffered several raids and bombardments, in the course of which both the Court and the church were hit and damaged. The Court House, which was restored after the war and is in good order, is open on certain weekdays during the summer.

Prestbury (SO9724)   The Gloucester Parliamentarians established a base here to protect the approaches to the city. The troops fortified and garrisoned the priory, west of the church, a fourteenth-century timber frame and stone block, originally little more than a single storey hall open to the roof belonging to Lanthony Priory. It was converted to secular use at the Dissolution, when two-storey bays were added at each end. The building was extended and clad in stone in the eighteenth and nineteenth centuries.

Stow on the Wold (SP1925)   A small town possessing neither stone walls nor a castle in the seventeenth century, Stow was nevertheless of great importance in the Civil War as it lay at a crucial junction where no less than eight roads met. There were frequent skirmishes in and around the town and on 21 March 1646 the last important engagement of the first Civil War took place just outside Stow, on a hillside near the village of Donnington (SP1928). Lord Astley had led 3,000 Royalists south from Worcester, trying to avoid Parliamentary units and reach the King at Oxford, but by 20 March he was hemmed in near Stow by converging forces. Astley drew up on open land, at a spot now covered by Horsington Plantation. Attacked at dawn on the 21st by the combined forces of Brereton, Birch and Morgan, Astley's heavily outnumbered army put up a fierce and spirited fight but was eventually broken and put to flight back through Stow and beyond. After the battle many of the 1,000 prisoners were held in St Edward's Church. St Edward's Hall, nearby, contains an extensive collection of contemporary and later portraits of many prominent Royalists and Parliamentarians, including Cromwell, Ireton, Pym and Hampden.

Sudeley (SP032277) Secured for the King by Lord Chandos at the outbreak of war, Sudeley Castle became the Royalist HQ for operations in the north of the county. Although it fell to Massey after a brief siege on 29 January 1643, within a fortnight Rupert had retaken the fortress and it remained under Royalist control until summer 1644. On 10 June 1644 the garrison surrendered to Waller and the castle was subsequently slighted by Parliament. Parts of the ruined late medieval quadrangular fortress remain unaltered, but large sections were incorporated within nineteenth- and twentieth-century rebuilding, and the present castle is a curious mixture of medieval and modern. Marks on the outer face of the northern gateway and on two adjoining towers are attributed to Civil War cannon-fire, and the desecration of Katherine Parr's tomb in the chapel is usually blamed on Waller's men. Sudeley Castle is open on certain weekdays and weekends in summer.

Taynton (SO7322) Taynton stood in a frontier zone hotly disputed by the Gloucester Parliamentarians and the Royalists to the north-west. It was repeatedly raided and frequently changed hands. The strongpoint was probably Taynton House, a Tudor mansion belonging to William Crundall, which still stands, though it was greatly remodelled and modernised in the nineteenth century. The medieval Church of St Lawrence probably served as an outpost or store and was wrecked in the course of the conflict; it was rebuilt in 1647–48 and, although heavily restored in the nineteenth century, much of the

present church remains mid-seventeenth-century in origin, a simple hall orientated north–south. Within is a monument to Thomas Pury (d1693), the Parliamentary politician and MP for Gloucester in the 1640s, who lived at The Grove, a late Tudor timber frame and brick house to the east of the village (SO743216).

Tewkesbury (SO8932) The area around Tewkesbury was the scene of frequent skirmishing during the war and the town, defended by nothing more than hastily erected earthworks, changed hands at least ten times. None of the Civil War defences survive.

The Milton organ in Tewkesbury Abbey was built in the early seventeenth century and was housed at Magdalen College, Oxford, until 1654. It was then acquired by Cromwell and placed in the Great Hall at Hampton Court. There Milton and others would reputedly play it to the Protector and his family.

Westbury on Severn (SO717140) Westbury served as an outpost of Gloucester during the Civil War, Parliamentary forces garrisoning the church and adjoining manor-house to cover the road to and from South Wales and the Forest of Dean. In January 1644 the town fell to a force of Royalists from Newnham led by Col. Winter, but four months later, on 7 May, Massey arrived from Gloucester to retake the place. He expelled the Royalists from the church by tossing in grenades and then captured the main force within the house. Westbury remained in Parliamentary hands until the end of the war. The Church of St Peter, St Paul and St Mary survives intact, complete with its detached northern tower, but the Elizabethan manor-house, Westbury Court, has been completely demolished and modern houses now stand on the site next to the churchyard.

Wotton under Edge (ST7593) In November 1643 Capt. Backhouse and a Parliamentary force swooped down from the hills to attack a convoy of Royalist reinforcements from Ireland moving through Wotton *en route* from Bristol to Oxford. Although they had the initial advantage of surprise, the Parliamentarians were outnumbered by the 1,100-strong convoy and were eventually beaten off with heavy losses.

GREATER LONDON

The county rarely witnessed open fighting during the period. In November 1642 Charles I approached from the west but was turned back at Turnham Green, and a minor Royalist rebellion to the south in summer 1648 was quickly crushed. London's importance stems from its role as the political and administrative centre of the Parliamentary cause throughout the 18 years of Civil War and Interregnum. Most senior Parliamentarians lived in London full or part time and many lie buried here. Cromwell himself was frequently in the capital during the 1640s, and after September 1651 he very rarely left the boundaries of Greater London.

The entries have been divided into Greater London Suburbs and Greater London Central, the latter roughly corresponding to the built up area of the mid-seventeenth century and its immediate environs.

I GREATER LONDON SUBURBS

Acton (TQ2080) Philip Skippon – soldier, leader of the London Trained Bands, one of Cromwell's Major-Generals in 1655 and a Protectoral Councillor – lived for much of the period in Acton, at Acton House, long since demolished. His first wife, Maria Comes (d1655), was buried beneath a monument in the chancel of St Mary's Church. Two years later Philippa, wife of Francis Rous, another Acton resident, was buried nearby. St Mary's was rebuilt in the mid-nineteenth century and most of the pre-Victorian monuments were destroyed.

Brentford (TQ1777) At dawn on 12 November 1642 Prince Rupert stormed the town, expelling and largely destroying the regiments of Brooke and Holles who were holding Brentford for Parliament. The Parliamentarians put up stiff resistance but were slowly pushed back towards the Thames where many were killed. Some tried to swim the river to safety, but most drowned in the attempt. Rupert captured 500 Parliamentary soldiers and their guns and he established a base in Syon House, from where his cannon covered the Thames and hindered the passage of Parliamentary ammunition barges. However, Syon House and Brentford were both evacuated within the week as the Royalists pulled back to Reading and Oxford. The present Syon House (TQ173766) in parkland north of the Thames is a Georgian successor to the mansion which Rupert occupied, a late medieval nunnery converted to secular use at the Dissolution. The placing of the battle symbol on Ordnance Survey maps at TQ175768 is somewhat arbitrary, for there was a running fight through Brentford and around Syon House and the Thames.

Chiswick (TQ2177) The present Church of St Nicholas in Chiswick Mall is largely Victorian, for in the nineteenth century all but the late medieval tower of the old parish church was demolished to make way for the new. Two of Cromwell's daughters, Mary (d1713) and Frances (d1721) lie in unmarked graves somewhere within the church. Mary, Lady Falconberg, had taken a house in Chiswick – Sutton House or Court, to the west of the church – in the 1670s and had lived there permanently after the death of her husband in 1700; she was soon joined by her long-widowed sister Frances. Sutton House no longer exists. According to a rather fanciful tradition, the body of Cromwell himself lies buried within St Nicholas's.

Croydon (TQ319654) The Archbishop's Palace in Old Palace Road was once the summer residence of the Archbishops of Canterbury and is now a church school. It comprises a complex of mostly fourteenth- and fifteenth-century buildings, including the Great Hall, Great Parlour, Library, Long Gallery and Chapel, arranged around two courtyards. Seized by Parliament in the 1640s, the palace was acquired by Sir William Brereton after the war. Brereton, the former leader of the Parliamentary war effort in Cheshire and the surrounding district, seems to have spent most of the 1650s at Croydon and he died here in April 1661. Shortly afterwards the property returned to the church.

Greenwich (TQ3977) The late medieval and Tudor palace of Greenwich was almost completely demolished soon after the Restoration and new buildings erected later in the century. Inigo Jones's Queen's House, completed in 1635, survived the rebuilding and, with the adjoining wings of the former Royal Hospital School, now comprises the National Maritime Museum. Admiral Blake lay in state in the Queen's House in 1657 before burial in Westminster Abbey, and here several relics from the Interregnum navy are to be seen, including portraits of Blake and Penn, some of Blake's personal and professional possessions and a model of the *Naseby*, launched in 1655 and re-named the *Royal Charles* five years later.

Hampton Court (TQ157685)

The mellow red brick palace, begun in the early sixteenth century by Wolsey, was taken by Henry VIII in 1529 and remained a royal residence until the time of George II. The palace is a complex of ranges and quadrangles, the main Base Court leading onto several lesser courts. The Tudor Great Hall and other parts of the original palace survive, but much was demolished and rebuilt by William III in the late seventeenth century. In December 1653 Hampton Court was given over to the new Protector under the Instrument of Government, and it became Cromwell's weekend retreat, used regularly during the summer months and often in winter too. Several officials and dignitaries were allocated lodgings within the palace, as were Cromwell's daughters Elizabeth and Mary and their husbands; indeed Mary married Thomas, Lord Falconberg at Hampton Court. Charles I's bedroom and suite on the upper floor remained unfurnished and unoccupied during the 1650s; Cromwell had his principal bedroom on the ground floor in Charles I's former Day Rooms.

Heston (TQ1277)

Elizabeth Cromwell and her husband John Claypole owned the long de-molished White House at Heston, probably using it as a town house in the period before the Protectorate; under Cromwell they had rooms at Hampton Court and Whitehall. The tradition of Cromwell visiting his daughter and son-in-law at Heston is plausible but unconfirmed by contemporary sources.

Highgate (TQ2887)

Lauderdale House on Highgate Hill was owned by Henry Ireton dur-ing the last three years of his life, and then passed to his brother John, a London alderman and City politician. The late Tudor mansion was largely demolished and rebuilt after the Restora-tion, and it became for a time the home of the Cabal politician whose name it bears. Restored after a serious fire in 1963, it is now a local museum and restaurant.

On the other side of Highgate Hill stand Cromwell House and Ireton House, the former certainly early seventeenth-century, the latter possibly eighteenth. Despite the names, they have no known links with Cromwell and his son-in-law.

Ickenham (TQ0786)

Swakeleys, an 'H'-plan mansion built for Sir Edmund Wright in 1630, passed to his son-in-law, Sir James Harrington, in 1642. Harrington, a prominent MP and Parliamentarian and cousin of the author of *Oceana*, lived here until the Restoration. He made several additions to the house, including a painted screen in the Great Hall which originally bore the busts of many leading politicians and soldiers of the mid-seventeenth century; those of Charles I and Sir Thomas Fairfax remain *in situ*. Swakeleys still stands and was recently con-verted into offices.

The bust of the Earl of Essex, Fairfax's prede-cessor as Parliamentary Lord General, was at some time removed from the screen and is now in the mausoleum attached to St Giles's Church, Ickenham.

Kensington (TQ2579)

The Kensington area has many Cromwellian associations, some of them rather dubious. John Lambert frequently stayed at his father-in-law's house in Kensington during the 1640s and at least two of his children lie buried in St Mary Abbots, the medieval parish church rebuilt by Scott in Victorian Gothic.

According to tradition Cromwell or Thurloe owned an estate around the then village of Kensington, and present street names – Crom-well Road, Mews, Place and Crescent and Thur-loe Street, Square, Close and Place – supposedly recall this former ownership. Tradition, too, has it that Cromwell once owned and lived in Hale House, renamed Cromwell House, a seventeenth-century mansion demolished in the nineteenth, which stood on the south side of Cromwell Road by Queensberry Place; again, there is no clear evidence to support the tradi-tion.

Holland House, off Holland Walk, was used by Fairfax in the late 1640s as both army HQ and residence, and around that time several other senior officers, including Lambert, had temporary lodgings here. According to less reli-able accounts, Cromwell and Ireton often held conferences in the gardens of Holland House, where Cromwell could shout at his rather deaf son-in-law without risk of being overheard. A grand Jacobean mansion built in 1606 and owned from 1623 by the Earl of Holland, whose ineffectual Royalism brought him to the block in 1649, Holland House survived in remarkably good condition until 1940, when much was completely destroyed and the remainder gutted. The standing portions have been restored and the outline of the rest is marked out in the

Top: Hampton Court, Greater London. The royal chambers at the heart of Wolsey's palace, occupied by Cromwell and his court during the Protectorate, were swept away when Wren laid out the colonnaded Fountain Court for William III. *Above:* The great seal of the Commonwealth of 1651, designed by Simon, shows the House of Commons in session in St Stephen's Chapel, Westminster. *Left:* Cromwell's death mask, cast in September 1658, can be seen in the British Museum and elsewhere.

grounds of Holland Park, now open to the public.

The Victoria and Albert Museum in Cromwell Road contains many relics from the period, including a buff coat and other costumes of the 1640s and 50s and a number of mid-seventeenth-century miniatures, including a self-portrait of Samuel Cooper.

Kingston upon Thames (TQ1769)

Kingston's importance in the seventeenth century lay in its bridge, the lowest crossing of the Thames before London Bridge. The town was occupied and garrisoned by Parliamentary forces at the outbreak of war but was evacuated on 12–13 November 1642 at the approach of the King's army. Kingston was held by the Royalists for five days in mid-November before they, in turn, evacuated the place.

The Parliamentary army was frequently based in and around Kingston after the first Civil War and in 1647 Fairfax briefly established his HQ at the fourteenth-century Crane Inn, now demolished.

The town saw military action again in July 1648, for the Earl of Holland's brief Royalist rebellion began and ended around Kingston. Six hundred Royalists gathered at Kingston on 5 July, but retreated into Surrey at the approach of one of Ireton's Horse regiments. They went as far as Reigate but then turned about and headed back towards Kingston, pursued by Livesey's Cavalry. On 7 July Holland made a stand on Kingston or Surbiton Common, one mile southeast of Surbiton station. In a brief exchange the rebels were routed – 20 were killed, including Francis Villiers, the Duke of Buckingham's brother, and the remainder fell back through Kingston and away north. When Parliamentary patrols entered Kingston at dawn on the 8th they found the place deserted.

Putney (TQ2375)

In October and early November 1647 the General Council of the Army held a series of often bitter and ultimately inconclusive debates somewhere in Putney, probably in the parish church of St Mary the Virgin. They were attended by most of the senior officers, including Cromwell, Fairfax and Ireton, and by several more radical junior officers. The discussions ranged over the political settlement of the country, including both the constitutional details of government and the broad principles upon which they were to rest. A Cromwell Association plaque within St Mary's, which was largely rebuilt in the nineteenth century, commemorates the events which took place in or near the building in autumn 1647.

Stoke Newington (TQ3386)

A large red brick mansion on the north side of Stoke Newington Church Street became the home of Charles Fleetwood after his marriage to Mary Hartopp in 1664. The couple lived here for nearly 30 years, surrounded by the many children of their previous marriages. The house, which became known as Fleetwood House, has long gone, and only the name Fleetwood Street, running north to Abney Park Cemetery, recalls the Cromwellian link. Several children of Fleetwood's marriages lie buried in Old St Mary's Church, Stoke Newington. Despite occasional claims to the contrary, Fleetwood's second wife, Cromwell's eldest daughter Bridget, was not buried here but in St Anne's, Blackfriars, which was destroyed in the Great Fire and not rebuilt.

Turnham Green (TQ205785)

By 13 November 1642 the Parliamentary party, seriously threatened by Charles I's march on London from the west, had been stirred into organising the defence of the capital. Twenty-four thousand men, including a large contingent of the London Trained Bands under Skippon, drew up on the common at Turnham Green to oppose the King's men. Charles's army was outnumbered, and after facing the Parliamentarians all day, the Royalists drew off to Hounslow at night. Most of the area has now been developed, and a road and tube station both bear the name Turnham Green. The common was probably a little to the south-west of these, and a small triangle of open land, still called Turnham Green, survives west of the junction of Chiswick High Road and Heathfield Terrace.

Uxbridge (TQ0584)

Parliamentarian throughout the Civil War, Uxbridge saw no serious fighting. It was, however, a convenient base to the west of London, and the Parliamentary army frequently quartered in and around the town. It was also the venue of a peace conference between Royalists and Parliamentarians in January 1645. The Royalist delegation, led by the Duke of Richmond, lodged on the south side of the High Street in the Crown Inn, since demolished, whilst the Earl of Northumberland and the Parliamentary group lodged on the north side in the George. Talks were held at a number of venues, including a Tudor and Jacobean mansion in the High Street, then called Place House. Partly demolished and partly remodelled in the eighteenth century, the building became an inn, The Crown and Treaty House, and still stands at the north end of the High Street.

Wimbledon (TQ2472)   On the hillside to the north of the town centre stood Wimbledon House, an Elizabethan mansion built for Sir Thomas Cecil in 1588. A large and rambling stone and brick building with turrets, several wings and a lead roof, it was surrounded by extensive gardens. It was bought by John Lambert in 1652, and he lived here for the rest of the 1650s, during his period as a senior politician and then in retirement after his fall. According to tradition Cromwell visited him at Wimbledon on several occasions. The house was returned to the Crown in 1660 but was completely demolished in 1717. Over the following century a succession of houses were built on or near the site, the latest, Wimbledon Park House (built 1799), surviving until 1949. Cecil's house probably stood on or near the present Home Park Road. Much of its extensive gardens have been built over or developed as tennis courts, but parts survive as open land, now Wimbledon Park and golf course.

Woolwich (QT4378)   The Museum of Artillery in the Rotunda, Woolwich Common, contains an unrivalled collection of guns and artillery pieces from the fifteenth century to the Second World War. Many items from the Civil War are on display.

II   GREATER LONDON CENTRAL

Apsley House, Picadilly   The late eighteenth-century red brick house is famous as the residence of the Duke of Wellington from 1816 to his death, and is open to the public as a Wellington museum. Cromwell's ghost is said to have appeared in the house during the Reform Bill crisis of 1832, pointing sternly at the riotous crowd outside and then vanishing.

Artillery Grounds, Chiswell Street   A rectangle of open land survives in the area bounded by Chiswell Street, Bunhill Row, Bunhill Fields and City Road. In the seventeenth century it formed the exercise grounds of the Honourable Artillery Company of the City of London, and here Skippon frequently exercised the trained bands and others called upon to defend London. Still used for military purposes, the grounds are not usually open to the public; the present barracks and other buildings are all post-seventeenth-century.

British Museum, Great Russell Street   The museum holds a number of relics from the Civil War and Interregnum, including Cromwell's death mask, seals of the Commonwealth and Protectorate and a selection of Civil War siege pieces. Also on display are examples of Protectorate coins bearing the imperial bust of Cromwell, few of which went into general circulation and survive only as very rare proofs.

Buckingham Street, WC2   Number 12 Buckingham Street, a six bay brick house of the 1670s, was from 1687 the town house of Cromwell's daughter, Mary, Lady Falconberg. It survives as a private residence.

Bunhill Fields, Bunhill Row   One of the main burial grounds of late seventeenth- and eighteenth-century London, Bunhill Fields cover a rectangle of land between Bunhill Row and City Road. South west of the City Road Gate stands the restored table tomb of Charles Fleetwood and his third wife, Mary Hartopp. The tombs of the Puritan divines Dr Thomas Goodwin and Dr John Owen stand nearby, respectively north-east and north-west of Fleetwood's tomb. In the central southern part of the Fields are two Cromwell vaults, containing the remains of the Protector's eighteenth-century descendants – one, Richard and William and their wives, the other, Thomas and Henry – grandchildren of Oliver's son Henry, sometime Lord Deputy of Ireland.

Christ Church, Newgate Street   The medieval Franciscan church, converted to parish use at the Dissolution, was occasionally the venue for official state services in the seventeenth century. On 7 June 1649 senior army officers and MPs, including Cromwell, Fairfax and Ireton, attended a service of Thanksgiving for the apparent end of the wars. Christ Church was badly damaged in the Great Fire and rebuilt by Wren. Sadly this church, too, was largely destroyed in the Second World War and now only the tower survives.

Clerkenwell Close, Clerkenwell   Despite the strong tradition linking Cromwell to Clerkenwell Close, there is no clear evidence that he ever owned or lived in a house here. The large house, popularly linked with Cromwell or Thurloe and renamed Cromwell House, was probably Sir Thomas Chaloner's Tudor mansion. It was demolished in the nineteenth century, but the new house on the site preserved the tradition in its name, Cromwell Place.

Coleman Street, City

Here stood the Star Inn, long since demolished, a favourite meeting place of Cromwell and other Parliamentarian leaders.

Derby House, Canon Row, Westminster

The late Tudor mansion of William, Earl of Derby, was used throughout the Civil War and Interregnum for a variety of state purposes. John Pym died here in 1643 and his body lay in state at Derby House before burial in Westminster Abbey nearby. The building was used by several parliamentary committees, including the Committtee of Both Kingdoms, later of Both Houses, the government's principal executive body, often known as the Derby House Committee. Derby House stood on the east side of Channel or Canon Row, on the west bank of the Thames a little south of Whitehall Palace. The building was demolished in the eighteenth century and Canon Row itself disappeared during nineteenth-century redevelopment. The site of Derby House lies under the present Victoria Embankment and New Scotland Yard.

Downing Street

The area now covered by Downing Street includes the site of Hampden House, the town house of the Buckinghamshire family of that name, including William Hampden and his wife Elizabeth Cromwell, Oliver's aunt. The area was acquired and developed by George Downing, one of several Parliamentarians-cum-Royalists who did well out of the Protectorate and then turned to Charles II.

Drury Lane

Cromwell had a house in Drury Lane in 1646 but its precise location is unknown and no seventeenth-century building linked with him survives.

Falconberg House, Soho Square

On the east side of Soho Square stood the town house of Mary, Lady Falconberg. She lived there from time to time from the early 1670s until 1687. The house has been completely demolished but street names in the area still recall the association – Sutton Row (named after Sutton Court, the Falconbergs' Chiswick house) and Falconbridge Mews and Court.

Grocers' Hall, Grocers' Hall Court

In common with the other halls of the city companies – Goldsmiths', Weavers', Haberdashers' etc. – Grocers' Hall was requisitioned by Parliament at the outbreak of war and used throughout the 1640s and 50s for meetings of various parliamentary and non-parliamentary committees. After the service of Thanksgiving on 7 June 1649 Cromwell, Fairfax, Ireton and other senior soldiers and politicians attended a great banquet in Grocers' Hall. The Elizabethan building has long gone and the present hall on the site was opened in 1970.

Holborn

A principal east–west route through London, in the seventeenth century Holborn was a convenient and fashionable area in which to live and at various times Fairfax, Milton, Pym, Warwick and other parliamentary leaders had houses in or off Holborn.

Just west of the junction with Red Lion Street stood the Blue Boar Inn, demolished in the nineteenth century. According to dubious accounts it was here that Cromwell and Fairfax intercepted the King's 'Saddle Letter' revealing the insincerity of his dealings with the English Parliament and army and his hopes for a treaty with the Scots.

A little further west stood the Red Lion, once the largest and most popular inn in Holborn. A strong tradition has the exhumed bodies of Cromwell, Bradshaw and Ireton resting at the Red Lion overnight on their way to Tyburn, and later accounts claim that Cromwell's body was rescued in the night and quickly buried in an unmarked grave to the north in what was then open land, now Red Lion Square. Sightings of ghostly cloaked figures stalking the Square at night have been linked with this.

Further east, on the north side of Holborn opposite Chancery Lane, stood Warwick House, the town house of the earls of that name, including the 2nd Earl, the Parliamentary Admiral during the first Civil War. His grandson Robert Rich and Frances Cromwell, Oliver's daughter, lived here after their marriage in November 1657 until Rich's death just three months later. The house was demolished in the late seventeenth century and only the name Warwick Court survives.

Jamaica House, Bermondsey

By the junction of Cherry Gardens and Jamaica Road stood a house – long since demolished – said to have been owned by Oliver Cromwell. No surviving evidence supports the Cromwellian tradition.

King Street, Westminster

In the seventeenth century King Street was a main thoroughfare to the west of the Thames, running north from Westminster Abbey, through the western fringes of Whitehall Palace and up to Charing

Cross. The area has changed considerably over the past 200 years and King Street has disappeared – the present St Margaret Street, Parliament Street and Whitehall roughly follow its course. Cromwell had a house in King Street during the latter half of the 1640s and was in residence in 1648. Tradition has it that his house stood on the west side of the street, by the entrance to the Blue Boar's Head Yard, a site now occupied by the north-west corner of Parliament Square and adjoining offices. However the original rent book of the area suggests that Cromwell had a house on the east side of King Street, probably near the northern end.

Lincoln's Inn, Chancery Lane　Although no entry is to be found in the admission rolls, near contemporary accounts report that Cromwell was a student here in 1617, occupying chambers over the gatehouse. His son Richard certainly studied here, as did several other leading Parliamentarians. From 1646 to 1659 John Thurloe occupied a chamber on the south side of the gatehouse, No. 24, which still exists; on the outer wall, facing Chancery Lane, a blue plaque records his residency. From 1660 until his death eight years later Thurloe lodged at Dial Court, since demolished, where his papers were discovered at the end of the seventeenth century. Thurloe lies buried in Lincoln's Inn Chapel, beneath a tombslab bearing a Latin inscription.

London Museum, London Wall　The museum contains relics from all periods of London's history, including the mid-seventeenth century. Civil War armour and several swords from the Hounslow factory are on display, together with some of Charles I's clothing.

Long Acre, Covent Garden　Cromwell owned or rented a house here from 1637 to 1643, somewhere on the south side of the street. The precise location is uncertain, and none of the present houses claim Cromwellian associations.

National Army Museum, Royal Hospital Road　The principal museum of the English army from the sixteenth to the twentieth century, the National Army Museum holds a small collection of Civil War relics, including armour, weapons and a number of documents relating to the Parliamentary army.

National Portrait Gallery, Charing Cross Road　The Gallery holds portraits and miniatures of many of the leading Parliamentary soldiers and politicians, together with their Royalist opponents. Portraits of Cromwell, Fairfax, Ireton and Lambert are usually on display, together with miniatures of Cromwell and Thurloe and a bust of the Lord Protector.

St George the Martyr, Queen's Square　Built as a chapel of ease to St Andrew's, Holborn, St George's gained parish status in the 1720s, and was extensively remodelled a hundred years later. Queen's Square had already been developed when the chapel was built and its graveyard, later the parish burying ground, was sited in then open land 200 yards to the north, a long, narrow, rectangular strip of land immediately north of Foundling Hospital, originally known as Nelson's Burying Ground. Richard Cromwell's daughter Ann or Anna, wife of Thomas Gibson, was buried here in 1727. The burial grounds survive as open land south of Regent Square and north of Coram's Fields.

St George the Martyr, Southwark　The present St George's is a Georgian building on the site of an earlier church in which George Monck was married in 1652. John Rushworth (d1690), Secretary to the Army during the Civil War, was buried near the pulpit of the old church. According to near-contemporary reports Cromwell's body rested here briefly in autumn 1658, where it was met by friends and clergy who accompanied it across the river to Somerset House.

St Giles, Cripplegate, Fore Street　This medieval church, gutted in the Second World War and since restored, has several Cromwellian connections. On 22 August 1620 Oliver Cromwell was married here to Elizabeth, daughter of Sir James Bourchier. Two years later his cousin, Richard Cromwell, married Elizabeth Hake in St Giles's. John Milton (d1674) lies buried here, and there is a memorial to him in the south aisle. Modern stained glass in the west windows include the armorial bearings of Milton and Cromwell. A facsimile of the record of Cromwell's marriage is on display, as is a marble bust of the Lord Protector.

St Giles in the Fields, St Giles High Street　The present building dates from the early eighteenth century, but incorporates fittings and monuments from the medieval church which stood on the site. Andrew Marvell (d1678) lies buried here, on the south side of the church under the pews, and Sir Thomas Widdrington (d1664), Parliamentary lawyer and politician and Speaker of the 2nd Protectorate Parliament, rests somewhere under the chancel.

St Lawrence Jewry, Gresham Street
Wren's late seventeenth-century church, which replaced the medieval church destroyed in the Great Fire, was itself gutted in the Second World War and has since been restored. Dr John Wilkins, sometime Bishop of Chester and the second husband of Cromwell's youngest sister Robina, was buried here in December 1672. Cromwell's niece Elizabeth, daughter of Robina by her first marriage, was married here in 1664 to John Tillotson, later Archbishop of Canterbury. Tillotson was buried in the chancel of St Lawrence's in November 1694 and a memorial to him survives on the north chancel wall.

St Margaret, Parliament Square   The early sixteenth-century building in the shadow of Westminster Abbey has long been the MPs' church, used for parliamentary services and other semi-religious ceremonies. Services were held here regularly during the Civil War and Interregnum as MPs gathered for days of Thanksgiving and Humiliation. Members of the Long Parliament subscribed to the Solemn League and Covenant in St Margaret's, and in 1654, 1656 and 1659 the Lord Protector and his Councillors attended special services to mark the opening of the three Protectorate Parliaments. John Milton married Katherine Woodcock here in 1656. The marriage was a short one for two years later she was buried in St Margaret's. Henry Elsyng (d1654), long-serving Clerk of the House of Commons, and James Harrington (d1677), the political philosopher, also lie in or around the church, though no monuments to them survive. On the north and west sides of the church are modern memorial windows to Blake and Milton.

At the Restoration most of the leading Parliamentarians who had been buried in Westminster Abbey over the previous 18 years were exhumed and reburied in a communal grave in St Margaret's churchyard, now the North Green. A Cromwell Association tablet on the outside west wall of the church commemorates the 21 known to have been so reburied, including Blake, Deane, Popham, Meldrum, Dorislaus and Pym, Cromwell's mother Elizabeth, who died in November 1654, and his sister Jane, wife of John Disbrowe, buried in October 1656.

St Pancras Old Church, St Pancras Road   Within the church is a small monument to the artist Samuel Cooper (d1672) who lies buried here. Cooper painted many of the leading figures in mid-seventeenth-century England and his miniature of Cromwell, though unfinished, is

one of the most striking likenesses of the Lord General.

The Strand   Many grand houses lined the Strand in the seventeenth century, including Essex House, where the Earl and Parliamentary Lord General lived and died, and York House, Fairfax's London residence during the 1650s. Both have been demolished and only the street names remain to mark the sites, Essex Street and Deveraux Court around Essex House and York Street, Buckingham Street and Villiers Street around York House, which had been rebuilt by the Duke of Buckingham in the 1620s.

DEVEREUX

On the south side of the Strand stands Somerset House, a late eighteenth-century mansion on the site of the original palace built in the mid-sixteenth century by Protector Somerset and given over to Protector Cromwell a hundred years later. In fact, Cromwell never took up residence and the buildings, which had stood empty for much of the Civil War, were used for other state purposes, housing ambassadors and conferences. Somerset House also served as a staging post for bodies on their way to Westminster Abbey, and Admiral Blake and Cromwell's daughter Elizabeth both rested here briefly during the Protectorate. Cromwell himself lay in state in Somerset House during the autumn of 1658, and twelve years later the body of his former ally turned Royalist, George Monck, rested here. The buildings known to the two Protectors were demolished in the eighteenth century.

Tower of London   The main fortress of the capital and the kingdom, the Tower is a complex of buildings of many periods, with the Norman White Tower encircled by several lines of later concentric defences. The place was held by Parliament throughout the Civil War and Interregnum and served as armoury, magazine, garrison, prison and place of execution – Strafford and Laud died here. A collection of arms and armour from the Civil War is on display in the present Armoury within the White Tower. The remains of the executed regicide and former Major-General, John Okey, lie within the Chapel of St Peter Ad Vincula, granted a Christian burial by Charles II.

Tyburn   On 30 January 1661 the corpses of Cromwell, Ireton and Bradshaw were posthumously executed at Tyburn and their headless bodies buried nearby. Five other regicides, Hacker and Axtell (ex. October 1660) and Okey, Barkstead and Corbett (ex. April 1662) also suffered here. Tyburn ceased to be a place of execution in the late eighteenth century and has since been engulfed by the westward spread of London. The road complex of Marble Arch probably overlies the site of the permanent scaffold and, despite a number of dubious counter-claims, Cromwell's body almost certainly rests somewhere under the surrounding streets or houses. No. 1 Connaught Place is sometimes suggested as the place of burial, though this seems to depend on the uncertain evidence of sightings of Cromwell's ghost in the house and garden.

Wallace Collection, Manchester Square

The Wallace Collection at Hertford House, Manchester Square, includes a fine selection of British and European armour. Many examples from the English Civil War are on display.

Wallingford House

The late Tudor mansion which stood immediately north-west of Whitehall Palace became the meeting place during the late 1650s for a group of pro-Commonwealth army officers, often known as the Wallingford House Party. It was demolished in the eighteenth century and the Old Admiralty Building stands on the site.

Westminster Abbey, Parliament Square

During the Civil War and Interregnum the Abbey continued to be the favoured burial place for political and military leaders, and many of the prominent Parliamentarians who died 1642–60 were interred here. Most were removed at the Restoration.

The usual place for such burials was Henry VII's Chapel, particularly the east end, now the RAF Chapel. Cromwell was buried here in an elaborate state funeral in November 1658, and nearby were the tombs of Bradshaw and his wife, Ireton, Cromwell's mother Elizabeth and sister Jane, Blake, Deane, Bond, Mackworth, Constable, and a daughter of Charles Fleetwood. All were removed after 1660 either for 'execution' at Tyburn or reburial in St Margaret's graveyard. A large floor tablet in their memory set down by Dean Stanley in the nineteenth century is now covered by the modern carpet of the RAF Chapel, and all that is usually visible is a small slab by the entrance marking 'The Burial Place of Oliver Cromwell 1658–1661'.

Two Cromwellians buried in Henry VII's Chapel survived exhumation. The excavators were probably unable to locate the tomb of Major-General Charles Worsley, buried here in June 1656; a large skeleton, thought to be his, was found in the eighteenth century during a search for James I's body. By accident or design Cromwell's favourite daughter Elizabeth (d August 1658) was also left in peace and a later floor tile just west of Henry VII's tomb marks the spot with the simple inscription 'Elizabeth Crompoole, daughter of Oliver Cromwell, 1658'.

Popham (d1651), Pym (d1643) and Strode (d1645) had been buried around St John the Baptist's Chapel and were duly exhumed at the Restoration. A floor slab in the north aisle outside the chapel records their burial and removal. Popham's elaborate monument within the chapel survived, but its inscription was removed. Rather fortunately, perhaps, the Earl of Essex (d1646) was left undisturbed at the Restoration; a later floor slab over his grave in St John the Baptist's Chapel describes him as 'late Lord General of the Forces Raised and Imployed by the Parliament of England'.

Edward Montagu and George Monck survived the Restoration to become prominent royal servants in the 1660s, rewarded with the Earldoms of Sandwich and Albemarle respectively, and in due course given state funerals in the Abbey. A floor tablet west of the Queen's tomb in the Queen Elizabeth Chapel records many Stuart worthies buried nearby, including Albemarle (d1670) and Sandwich (d1672). There is a larger memorial to Albemarle in a side chapel to the south of Henry VII's Chapel and his funeral effigy survives in the Abbey museum.

There is a modern memorial tablet to Admiral Blake on the south wall of the south choir aisle.

Westminster Palace

Although Henry VIII had moved his court to Whitehall, the former Royal Palace of Westminster remained in the seventeenth century the centre of law and administration. The jumble of buildings included Westminster Hall, the Lords' House, St Stephen's Chapel – in which the Commons sat and Cromwell took his seat as an MP on many occasions – and the Painted Chamber, in which Cromwell received his Protectorate Parliaments on formal occasions. The place was gutted by fire in 1834 and largely destroyed, the new Palace of Westminster (Houses of Parliament) and precincts covering much of the site. The only important part of the medieval palace to survive is Westminster Hall, begun by William II but extended in the folllowing centuries. In the seventeenth century the hall was divided into several courts of law – Common Pleas, King's Bench and Chancery – which continued to meet during the Civil War and Interregnum. Important state trials were also held here, including that of Charles I in January 1649, attended by Cromwell and the other regicides. Nearly four years later Cromwell returned to the hall to be formally installed as Lord Protector. Because of its position within the precincts of the Palace, Westminster Hall is usually closed to the public.

In Old Palace Yard, facing Parliament Square, stands a statue of Cromwell by Sir Hamo Thornycroft, unveiled in 1899.

Whitehall Palace The principal royal residence in London from the reigns of Henry VIII to James II, Whitehall Palace was a rambling collection of buildings which stretched from the Thames to St James's. The buildings were only partly used during the 1640s, split into apartments and allocated to MPs and others. Cromwell's association began in February 1650 when Parliament voted him the Cockpit, formerly the lodgings of the late Earl of Pembroke. Cromwell lived at Whitehall until his death in 1658, and the Palace became his main residence and seat of government during the Protectorate. The new court was established here, most senior politicians and administrators were allocated rooms, and the Protectorate Council met regularly in the Privy Council Chamber on the north side of the Palace.

None of these chambers can be seen today, for almost the whole building was destroyed by fire in 1698. The main part of the Palace occupied a square of land from the river to the present Whitehall (the street), an area now covered by government offices. The Cockpit, a term used to describe the western ranges of the Palace between the Holbein and King Street Gates, lay to the west of the present Whitehall.

The Banqueting House is the only important part to survive. Built by Inigo Jones 1619–22, it stood near the south entrance to the Palace. It was on a scaffold in front of this building that Charles I died on 30 January 1649. The Banqueting House is open to the public on most weekdays.

GREATER MANCHESTER

The area now covered by Greater Manchester saw some of the bloodiest episodes of the Civil War as Royalists and Parliamentarians fought for control of the prosperous north-western towns and as two armies battled their way south along the main western route between Scotland and England. Although the region was generally sympathetic to Parliament, large parts of the county fell initially under the influence of Royalist north Cheshire and not until the latter half of 1644 did Parliamentary forces secure the whole of Greater Manchester. The region saw further fighting as two Scottish Royalist armies marched through in 1648 and 1651. In August 1648 Cromwell pursued the already shattered Royalist force through the area, his only recorded visit to the area now covered by Greater Manchester.

Bolton (SD7209) The 'Geneva of the North' was strongly Parliamentarian in sympathy and became one of Parliament's main bases in the area. Without stone walls, however, Bolton was always vulnerable to attack and although troops and townspeople held off the Earl of Derby in February and March 1643, earthworks and barricades proved no obstacle to Prince Rupert. He stormed the town on 28 May 1644, overwhelming the Parliamentary garrison in a fierce two hour fight and then letting loose a tide of destruction and killing. Garrison and townspeople alike were put to the sword and at least 1,600 died during the sack of Bolton. The Earl of Derby, who was present during the massacre, returned here seven years later to be executed in Churchgate. He spent his last hours held in the thirteenth-century Ye Old Man and Scythe Inn.

An inscribed tombslab in St Peter's Church in memory of John Okey (d1684) records the bloody events through which Okey lived, including the Civil War and the storming of Bolton.

Leigh (SD6500) In one of the many minor skirmishes in the area west of Manchester, a Royalist detachment surprised near Bolton on 27 November 1642 was pursued by Parliamentary Horse in a running fight from Chowbent (now Atherton), through Leigh and on to Lowton Moor or Common, two miles to the south-west (SJ6498). Here the Royalists tried to turn and stand but were quickly routed by the Mancunian Parliamentarians.

Manchester (SJ8398) A Mancunian weaver,

Above: Whitehall Palace, Greater London. The rambling Tudor and early Stuart palace was Cromwell's principal residence and seat of government during the Protectorate. Although Cromwell's own suite was on the far side of the complex, the royal state rooms on and near the Thames continued to serve as government offices and accommodation. On the right, boats are landing at Whitehall Palace Stairs; the small flight on the left are the Privy Stairs. Inigo Jones's Banqueting House, which towers behind the riverside range in this seventeenth-century print, is almost the only part of the old palace to have survived (*right*). In January 1649 Charles I stepped through one of the first floor windows onto a temporary scaffold draped in black. The precise location of that window is disputed – it may even have been in a separate forebuilding at the north end, of which nothing remains. *Below right:* Charles I's death warrant was signed and sealed by 59 regicides; Cromwell's signature appears in the left hand column.

Richard Perceval, was one of the first civilian victims of the confrontation between King and Parliament. He was killed here in July 1642 when Lord Strange (soon to inherit the Earldom of Derby) and his Royalist retinue clashed with the pro-Parliamentarian townspeople. When Derby returned two months later at the head of a 3,000-strong army he found the town defended by mud walls and chains stretched across the streets, the work of Johan Rosworm, a German soldier and engineer. The Royalists tried and failed to storm the town and settled down for a long siege, but when heavy rain flooded their trenches and ruined their powder, a wet and dispirited Derby abandoned the attempt. Manchester remained a Parliamentary base throughout the war, defended so strongly that neither Rupert in May 1644 nor the Scottish Royalists in 1648 and 1651 seriously attempted to take the town.

The Civil War earthworks and most of the small town which they defended have long since disappeared beneath the sprawling industrial city. The only surviving building with clear Civil War associations is Chetham's Hospital in Long Millgate, which was fortified by Rosworm and served as the principal Parliamentary magazine for the region. In origin a late medieval cathedral college, the building has been used at times as a private residence and as a hospital; it is now a music school.

Middleton (SD8606) Sir Ralph Assheton, one of the leading north-western Parliamentarians, was born, brought up and buried here. A member of the Long Parliament, he took up arms at the end of 1642 and proceeded to galvanise a rather lack-lustre Lancashire war effort, initiating a campaign which saw Derby routed at Whalley in April 1643 and most of the Royalist bases in the area fall soon after. Assheton died in 1651 and was buried with his wife in St Leonard's Church. They lie beneath a monumental brass on which Sir Ralph is portrayed in half-armour of the period and his wife in a flowing dress. The Assheton tomb is something of a rarity, for very few monumental brasses were made during the Civil War and Interregnum – a period more often associated with their destruction – and less than twenty are known to survive.

Stockport (SJ8990) A Parliamentary base for much of the Civil War, Stockport was captured by Rupert on 25 May 1644 after Cols Mainwaring and Duckenfield had tried unsuccessfully to hold the approach road. The Royalists plun-

dered the town but quickly moved off towards Bolton.

Turton Tower (SD732152) A fifteenth-century peel tower extended and converted to domestic use in the sixteenth century, Turton Tower stands high on the edge of Turton Moor. Now a museum, open daily, it contains several items rescued from nearby Bradshaw Hall prior to demolition, including a large oak bedstead in which Cromwell supposedly slept on one occasion.

Westhoughton (SD6506) In December 1642 a small Parliamentary unit under Cols Bradshaw and Venables was surprised and captured at Westhoughton by a 1,000-strong detachment from Derby's army.

Wigan (SD5805) Held initially for the King by Major-General Blaine, Wigan was surprised and captured by Assheton in April 1643. Thereafter neither side formally garrisoned the town, which saw no further fighting until 1648.

On 18 August 1648 the rear of the Scottish army under Middleton was caught by Cromwell's advanced guard on Wigan Moor, north of the town, and pushed back into Wigan, creating near panic in the main army. Cromwell marched through the town in pursuit on the following day. He was here again on the 23rd on his return journey northwards.

Although the main Scottish Royalist army marched through unopposed in early August 1651, the Earl of Derby and a force of newly-raised recruits from Lancashire were caught outside Wigan on 25 August as they were marching south to rejoin their colleagues. Robert Lilburne engaged the inexperienced Royalists as they entered Wigan Lane, a broad sandy track bordered by hedges which ran off the moor and south into Wigan. After a very fierce fight at close quarters the Royalists were routed – 300 were killed and 400 captured and the Earl himself was badly wounded. A late seventeenth-century monument to the battle and to Sir Thomas Tyldesley, a Royalist officer killed in the engagement, stands beside the former track, now the main road through the northern suburb of Wigan collectively known as Wigan Lane. According to tradition, the wounded Derby hid from Parliamentary troops after the battle in the Old Dog Inn, which stood in the Market Place, Wigan.

Wybersley Hall (SJ9685) During the sixteenth century the Bradshaw family acquired extensive property in what was then northern Cheshire, including Wybersley Hall. John Bradshaw was born here in 1602 and educated at nearby Stockport. He pursued a successful legal career both in Cheshire and London, culminating in his appointment as President of the court which tried and convicted Charles I in 1649. Bradshaw's republican leanings caused him to break with Cromwell and the Protectorate during the 1650s, much of which he spent in semi-retirement in the north-west. Despite failing health, he returned to national politics in 1659, upon the fall of the Protectorate; he was dead within a year. Of his birthplace, little now remains – fragments of the Tudor hall may survive, incorporated within the grand nineteenth-century castellated mansion which now stands on the site.

Wythenshawe Hall (SJ815898)   A Royalist garrison on the southern fringes of a strongly Parliamentarian area, the hall survived intermittent sieges throughout 1643. On 25 February 1644 Sir Thomas Fairfax arrived with a large force and heavy artillery and proceeded to bombard and then storm Wythenshawe, overwhelming Robert Tatton's small garrison. The hall was repaired after the Civil War and is still in good order. The early Tudor timber framed building with a central hall flanked by projecting gabled wings stands in parkland to the east of Sale. It is now a museum open during the summer and contains a fine collection of furniture, paintings and armour, much of it dating from the seventeenth century. In the nearby parkland is an impressive statue of Oliver Cromwell, standing with sword in hand upon an inscribed block of natural stone.

HAMPSHIRE

Although Hampshire was largely Parliamentarian during the opening year of the war, from the outbreak the King's men held a number of isolated bases within the county and in 1643–44 they overran most of north, west and central Hampshire. The Battle of Cheriton in March 1644 ended Royalist dreams of taking the whole county and of pushing further east to threaten London, and the areas which remained in the King's hands were gradually reconquered by Parliament in 1644–45. Cromwell passed through Hampshire on many occasions during the 1640s on his way between London and the west; he campaigned here in 1645 and saw action at Winchester and Basing.

Alton (SU7239)   Alton was the scene of two fierce engagements during 1643, the first of which has left no visible trace. On 22 February 1,500 Royalist Horse attacked a much smaller Parliamentary reconnaissance party temporarily stationed here. The Parliamentarians repelled the attack by discharging a field gun into the advancing Cavalry at very close range and to devastating effect.

At the end of the year Waller attacked and overwhelmed Major-General Crawford's newly established garrison here. Advancing from Farnham on the night of 12–13 December, the Parliamentarians followed a roundabout route and avoided main roads, thus escaping detection by Royalist scouts. The garrison was surprised before dawn and although the Horse managed to get away, Col. Bolle and the Royalist Foot were surrounded. They put up a brave fight, forced back from their initial position in St Laurence's churchyard into the church itself, where they continued to resist, climbing scaffolding within the church and firing down from the windows onto the advancing Parliamentarians. Even when Waller's men forced their way into the church, the Royalists continued to fire from their position behind the corpses of several horses laid across the aisles. Eighty Royalists were killed during the operation and several times that number were captured when they at last recognised the hopelessness of their position and threw down their arms. The church still bears unmistakable signs of the battle, with marks in the south doors where Parliamentary pikes were driven through to prize them open and a peppering of bullet holes and splashes in the walls and pillars. An inscribed plaque on the wall commemorates the Royalist commander, supposedly struck down as he stood in the Jacobean pulpit. The dead were buried in a pit just outside the north wall of the nave.

Cromwell stayed overnight in Alton on 11 May 1649 *en route* to Burford.

Andover (SU3645)   In October 1644 Waller's 3,000 Horse based here were surprised by Goring's Royalists advancing from the west and the outnumbered and ill-prepared Parliamentarians fell back before the King's men.

Cromwell was probably here on several occasions – Andover stood on one of the main routes between London and the south-west – and he certainly lodged at Andover overnight on 9 March 1645 and 12 May 1649.

Basing House (SU663527)   The Marquis of Winchester's massive fortified palace was a Royalist stronghold throughout the Civil War, a serious threat to communications between London and Salisbury and the south-west. A Norman motte and bailey castle stood on the site and a number of later medieval buildings were added within the bailey; they were known collectively as the 'old house'. In the sixteenth century the 1st Marquis of Winchester built a fortified house – the 'new house' – immediately to the east, a five storey mansion with a great tower in the north-east corner and lesser towers at the other angles. At the same time a four storey brick gatehouse with flanking towers was built at the west entrance to the inner ward. The whole site was surrounded by a dry moat and a curtain wall with interval towers. A large farmhouse to the north, the Grange, was defended by its own high wall.

The 5th Marquis garrisoned Basing House for the King in 1642 and endured frequent attacks over the following years. Richard Norton assaulted the awesome defences in July 1643; Waller spent nine days bombarding the place in the following November; Norton returned in July 1644 and besieged Basing for nearly six months until disease, deteriorating weather and raids from Royalist relieving forces sent from Oxford together persuaded him to depart; and in August 1645 a local force bombarded the house. But the honour of capturing 'old loyalty' fell to Cromwell, who arrived before Basing on 8 October 1645 with heavy siege guns and a plentiful supply of ammunition. A six day bombardment badly damaged the defences and on 14 October Cromwell stormed the place, capturing both the old and the new houses. One hundred Royalists were killed in the assault and twice that number were captured, including the Marquis and Inigo Jones. The houses were sacked and burnt and the stone and brick were subsequently carted off for use in other buildings.

Although the medieval earthworks remain, very little of the old or new houses survives above ground. There are odd fragments of walling, an octagonal summer-house, a dovecote and a small outer gatehouse by the road, but everything else was destroyed in or soon after 1645. The site has been excavated on several occasions and has recently been cleared; a selection of finds and other relics is on display in the small museum at Basing. Although Tudor Grange Farm has also perished – the present building of that name dates from the late seventeenth century – the original brick barn survives nearby. Cromwell's ghost supposedly stalks the site of the former mansion, particularly the area around Grange Farm and the old barn. St Mary's Church often served as an outpost of the garrison and usually fell during the early stages of the Parliamentary attacks. In consequence it was damaged several times during the war, particularly during the final bombardment of October 1645, and much of the present church is mid-seventeenth-century post-war repair work. An earthwork to the north of the village called 'Oliver's Battery' has no known connection with Cromwell or the Civil War. A loopholed barn in Crown Lane may also have been occupied during operations here.

Basingstoke (SU6352)   Cromwell was probably based in the old town during the operation against Basing House in the first half of October 1645. According to tradition, he lodged at the Fleur de Lys Inn in London Street. The former Bell Inn, opposite, housed the Marquis of Winchester and other prominent prisoners after the fall of Basing. Both buildings survive, though converted to shop and office use.

Bishops Waltham (SU550173)   The former palace of the Bishops of Winchester was garrisoned for the King at the beginning of 1644. In early April Col. Bennet's 200 man garrison was besieged by a small Parliamentary force under Col. Whitehead; the arrival of Major-General Brown with reinforcements and heavy artillery sealed the garrison's fate. The palace was bombarded and wrecked and Bennet surrendered on the 9th. The ruined palace was then sacked and burnt. The remains of the largely fifteenth-century quadrangular palace are open daily.

Calshot Castle (SU489025)   This small and simple Henrician coastal fort – a single round stone tower – served as a minor Parliamentary garrison throughout the war, guarding the coast and the approaches to Portsmouth.

Cheriton (SU5928)   The major battle fought outside Cheriton on 29 March 1644 resulted in a decisive Parliamentary victory which halted the Royalist conquest of the region and marked a turning point in the Civil War in Hampshire.

In mid-March Waller had advanced up the Meon Valley to threaten the Royalists in Winchester. Hopton and Forth marched to meet him but Waller at first refused to give battle and the

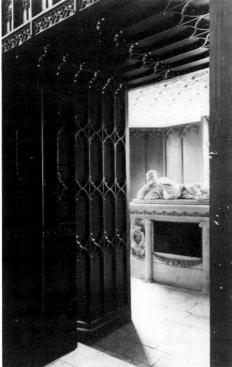

Top: Basing, Hants. The huge early Stuart tithe barn adjoining Basing House is the only part of the Royalists' fortified grange to survive intact. *Left:* The Vyne, Hants. Caloner Chute, resplendent in Speaker's robes, surveys his tomb chamber. Thomas Carter's effigy, executed over a century after Chute's death, is one of the finest monuments of the late eighteenth century. *Above:* Winchester, Hants. The archway of medieval Westgate proved far too narrow for modern traffic and the High Street has been re-routed to the left.

fourth week of March passed with nothing more than indecisive skirmishing in the area around East and West Meon. Waller then drew off towards Alresford but Hopton occupied the town ahead of him and the armies spent 1½ days sparring in the area south of the town. The major engagement finally took place on the 29th on largely open ground to the east of Cheriton. Waller drew up on a slight ridge running east of the village, facing the Royalists who were deployed a mile or so to the north on the other side of a slight depression. Both armies straddled the track which runs from New Alresford to the modern A272 near Bramdean. To the east of this track between the two armies stood Cheriton Wood, and the battle began here when Waller's right wing advanced to occupy the wood. The Royalist left responded by moving forward and a mixture of hand to hand fighting and heavy musket- and cannon-fire forced the Parliamentarians back. This initial Royalist success was squandered when part of the Royalist right wing under Col. Bard charged forward into the depression, where it was engaged and destroyed by Hesilrige's 'lobsters'. The Parliamentary right under Balfour then advanced into Cheriton Wood once more, slowly driving the Royalists back. With both wings under pressure, Hopton regrouped and launched a general assault from the centre, probably charging down the main track, and a fierce mêlée developed in the area west of Cheriton Wood around the point marked by the battle symbol on Ordnance Survey maps (SU598295). The Royalist centre fared badly and, with both wings collapsing, was in real danger of being outflanked and surrounded. Hopton therefore ordered his men to fall back and retreated northwards, through Alresford and eventually back to Oxford.

Cheriton Wood still stands, though its size and dimension have altered somewhat since the seventeenth century; the rest of the battlefield is still open ground and has probably changed little since 1644. A minor road now runs north-north-east from Cheriton through the centre of the battlefield and across the Alresford track or lane. In the nineteenth century, bodies, arms and armour were frequently discovered, both on the battle site and around West Meon.

Crondall (SU7948)

The fine Norman Church of All Saints was a minor Parliamentary outpost for most of the war, guarding the western approaches to Farnham. The building may have been damaged at some point, for it was extensively restored during the 1650s; the grand red brick western tower was added in 1659.

Hursley (SU4225)

In 1638 Richard Maijor, a wealthy Southampton merchant, acquired Merdon Manor in Hursley, complete with the Tudor great house and outbuildings which stood to the west of the village. On 1 May 1649 his daughter Dorothy married Richard Cromwell in Hursley Church; the service was attended by Oliver Cromwell, who lodged at the manor-house overnight. The young couple lived at Hursley until 1658, when Richard took up residence at Whitehall as Lord Protector. They returned to Hampshire in 1660 and although Richard soon fled to the Continent, Dorothy stayed at Hursley until her death in 1676. Richard returned to England towards the end of the seventeenth century but he lived in London and Hertfordshire and paid only occasional visits to Hursley. The house was held by his eldest son, Oliver, until his death in 1705, when it became the subject of a long and bitter family dispute. In 1718, six years after Richard's own death, Merdon Manor was sold to William Heathcote, who completely demolished the Tudor house.

Richard Cromwell and his wife were buried in the chancel of All Saints Church but any contemporary monuments to them were destroyed when the church was largely demolished and rebuilt in the nineteenth century. Of the church known to the Cromwells, the fifteenth-century tower alone remains, at the base of which is a large eighteenth-century monument to many members of the Maijor and Cromwell families buried nearby, including Richard Maijor, Richard Cromwell and Dorothy and six of their children.

Hurst Castle (SZ318897)

Hurst Castle was built in the mid-sixteenth century, one of the many Henrician artillery forts defending the south coast. A twelve-sided central keep surrounded by three semicircular towers, Hurst was derelict by the eighteenth century, but was repaired and refortified during the Napoleonic Wars and again in the Second World War. It is now a scheduled monument, open to the public daily. In November 1648 Charles I was briefly held in Hurst Castle before being taken to London to face trial.

Moyles Court (SU1608)

One mile east of Ellingham stands Moyles Court, the former house of John Lisle, Parliamentarian, judge and regicide; Lisle fled the country at the Restoration and was assassinated on the Continent in 1664. The early seventeenth-century two storey brick house was restored in the nineteenth century and remains a private residence. Fairfax, Cromwell and the military high command may have met or lodged in Moyles Court when around Ringwood in March 1645.

Netley Castle (SU451088)

The Henrician coastal fort, garrisoned for Parliament throughout the Civil War, was later converted into a dramatic domestic house. The simple sixteenth-century fort, a single storey rectangular block with archways on the seaward side and a strong embattled parapet, is all but lost amid the grand mock-Tudor Victorian mansion which engulfed it.

North Stoneham (SU441173)

Cromwell's aunt Dorothy and her husband Sir Thomas Fleming lived at North Stoneham throughout their married lives. Both lie buried in the Church of St Nicholas.

Odiham (SU7451)

Despite frequent Royalist raids, the town and nearby castle were held by Parliament for most of the Civil War. The fiercest clash took place on the night of 31 May–1 June 1644, when Royalist forces from Basing House mounted a supposedly surprise raid on Odiham. In fact, Norton's troops were forewarned and on the alert and the Royalists were repelled with heavy losses following a stiff fight around the town and the castle, which stood nearly a mile to the north-west in the village of North Warnborough (SU7227520). Little survives today except the picturesque ruin of a large thirteenth-century octagonal keep.

The George in the High Street is a Tudor timber framed inn remodelled and refronted in the eighteenth century. The dining-room contains Tudor panelling and a carved Elizabethan chimney-piece said to come from Basing House.

Old Alresford (SU588337)

Richard Norton, Parliamentary soldier and politician and a close friend and correspondent of Oliver Cromwell, lived at Old Alresford House during the mid-seventeenth century. The old mansion stood in the north-west corner of a large park, which gently sloped down to a lake; the house was extensively rebuilt by Lord Rodney in the eighteenth century. Cromwell supposedly visited Norton on several occasions and lodged here in early October 1645 *en route* to Basing.

Portsmouth and Southsea (SU6400)

Seventeenth-century Portsmouth was one of the most important and heavily defended south coast ports, and the Royalist cause received a major boost on 2 August 1642 when the town's governor, George Goring, declared for the King. Waller was despatched to retake the port and

entered the island on 12 August, brushing aside the small Royalist force holding the crossing at Portsbridge. Portsmouth, however, was another matter, for Goring's 400-man garrison was secure behind a circuit of medieval earth ramparts and stone walls. The rest of August passed with nothing more than minor skirmishing and an ineffective bombardment from Parliamentary batteries set up to the north of the town and at Gosport. The stalemate was broken in the early hours of 3 September when Waller surprised and captured Southsea Castle, meeting only token resistance from Capt. Challoner and his 12-man garrison. The fall of Southsea prompted Goring to open negotiations and four days later he surrendered Portsmouth. Despite a brief siege in autumn 1643 and occasional Royalist raids thereafter, the port remained in Parliamentary hands for the rest of the Civil War.

Southsea Castle (SZ642982) was one of the Henrician coastal forts of the sixteenth century, a single large round keep containing fourteen guns. The castle, which is open to the public, survives in good order, though much of the present building is nineteenth-century repair work following an explosion which demolished much of the original Tudor castle.

The earth and stone defences which surrounded seventeenth-century Portsmouth have largely disappeared and there survives only a short stretch of walls and mural towers by the seafront in Old Portsmouth (around SZ630994). No trace of the defences survives on the landward side. The medieval Church of St Thomas was used by the Royalists in August 1642 as a base and lookout point and in consequence suffered several direct hits from Parliamentary cannon which wrecked the tower and nave. Restored after the Civil War, St Thomas's is now the cathedral.

Romsey (SU3521)

The town changed hands several times during the Civil War, usually with little or no fighting, and neither side established a formal garrison here. Marks on the outer wall of the north transept of the abbey are usually attributed to Civil War bullets, possibly fired when Waller attacked Royalist troops here in July 1643.

Southampton (SU4112)

Southampton was held and garrisoned by Parliament throughout the Civil War and the Parliamentary troops hastily repaired the medieval walls which defended the town. Crawford unsuccessfully laid siege to the town in September 1643 and later Royalist raids occasionally reached the extra-mural suburbs. Despite the modern expansion and large-scale rebuilding of Southampton, much of the circuit of thirteenth-century walls survives, particularly along Western Esplanade, behind Queen's Way and by Platform Road and Orchard Place; three of the original town gates and several mural towers also survive.

Southwick (SU6208)

Richard Norton, the Parliamentary soldier and politician, inherited Southwick Park, formerly the estate of a twelfth-century Augustinian priory. The great house, which incorporated parts of the old priory itself, was destroyed by fire around 1750 and the present Southwick House dates from the nineteenth century.

The Vyne (SU637568)

The Vyne is an early Tudor red brick mansion, extended by the Chute family during the seventeenth and eighteenth centuries. Chaloner Chute, lawyer, Parliamentarian, MP and Speaker of Richard Cromwell's Protectorate Parliament, acquired the house at the beginning of the 1650s and resided here until his death in 1659. He was responsible for adding the grand north portico, often described as the earliest domestic portico in England.

As a memorial to Speaker Chute, a tomb chamber was added in the late eighteenth century to the medieval chapel which adjoins the house. Inside is a magnificent monument by Thomas Carter portraying Chute lying on his side, his head propped up on an elbow, dressed in his official Speaker's robes and with his large hat beside him. (In fact, Chute died at his London house at Little Sutton and probably lies not here but in St Nicholas's, Chiswick.) The Vyne is open at weekends and on certain weekdays during the summer.

Warblington (SU728055)

Margaret Pole, Countess of Salisbury, built a large moated manor-house here in the early sixteenth century. The house was garrisoned for Parliament by Col. Norton in January 1644 but fell to Hopton later in the year following a siege and bombardment. The Royalists made no attempt to hold the place, possibly because it had been badly damaged during the bombardment, and Warblington played no further part in the war. Today nothing remains of the Tudor mansion except a tall octagonal turret in stone and red brick – formerly the angle tower of the gatehouse – and parts of the adjoining walls. The present Warblington House is a post-Civil War building which stands to the east of the site of the Tudor manor-house.

Winchester (SU4829)

Town and castle changed hands several times in the course of the Civil War as first one side and then the other gained control of central Hampshire. In December 1642 Waller seized the town and quickly overwhelmed the small Royalist garrison which had taken refuge in the castle. The Parliamentarians soon moved on and the Royalists returned. Although Waller attacked the town again in spring 1643 he was driven off by a relieving force and Winchester remained in the King's hands. By summer 1645 the town was one of the few important bases in central southern England still held by the King and as such it became one of Cromwell's main targets during his Hampshire campaign. He arrived before Winchester on 28 September, overran the town on the following day and laid siege to the large and well supplied Royalist garrison which had taken refuge in the castle. Five days of heavy bombardment from all sides severely damaged the outer defences of the castle and induced the Royalists to open negotiations. The 700-man garrison surrendered to Cromwell on 6 October. The damaged castle was slighted by Parliament after the war and today little remains of the once mighty fortress begun by William I and greatly extended by his successors. The Great Hall alone survived demolition, and is now one of the finest medieval halls in England. The Roman and medieval town walls have also largely disappeared, though odd fragments remain, including a section around College Street, and two of the medieval town gates survive, Kingsgate and Westgate, the latter housing a small museum of local history.

On a hillside to the south-west of the town (SU460278) is an earthwork known variously as Cromwell's or Oliver's Battery or Cromwell's Camp, supposedly a gun emplacement thrown up by Cromwell at the end of September 1645. However, the site is a very long way from the town and castle and the association seems doubtful.

HEREFORD AND WORCESTER

Hereford and Worcester saw frequent fighting during the opening months of the Civil War until the region was secured for the King at the beginning of 1643. It remained overwhelmingly Royalist thereafter and was one of the last counties in England to remain solidly loyal to the King. The area became the centre of renewed Royalist activity in August 1651 as Charles Stuart and his Scottish Royalist army entered the county and established their HQ here. The campaign which culminated in their destruction at the Battle of Worcester was led by Cromwell, his one clearly recorded visit to the area covered by the modern county.

Aconbury Camp (SO506330) Some sources suggest that this large Iron Age hill-fort, west-south-west of the village, was reoccupied and refortified during the Civil War.

Bewdley (SO7875) The town was important during the Civil War as it commanded one of the few bridges across the Severn. Lord Wharton secured the place for Parliament in September 1642 but by the end of the year it had fallen to the King and it remained in Royalist hands for well over a year. In April 1644 Col. Fox and a 60-strong detachment for Edgbaston took the town; they arrived before Bewdley in the early evening, cooly bluffed their way past the guards on the bridge and at the east end of the town and then overpowered the surprised and gullible garrison. They proceeded to capture the governor, Sir Thomas Littleton, and the other senior officers, who had retired for the night to Tickenhill Manor, just outside the town. Fox made no attempt to hold the town and returned at once to Birmingham with his prisoners. He probably destroyed the town's defences as he left, for neither side garrisoned Bewdley thereafter. No trace of the medieval town walls and gates remains and the late medieval bridge across the Severn was long ago replaced by one of Telford's spans. Tickenhill Manor survives on the hillside beyond Park Lane, its Georgian exterior concealing the late medieval and Tudor building which was once a royal manor and a meeting place for the Council of the Marches.

Brampton Bryan (SO370726) A Parliamentary outpost in a largely Royalist area, the small castle held out heroically for many months. It was occupied for Parliament in 1642 and defended by Brilliana, Lady Harley, against Vavasour's besieging Royalists for much of the following year – the King's men lacked heavy artillery and were unable to batter down the outer walls. After a brief winter respite the siege and bombardment were renewed by Col. Woodhouse with greater energy and larger guns in March 1644. On 17 April the Parliamentary garrison surrendered the by then badly damaged and undermined castle. Brampton Bryan was immediately razed and little more than the ruined gatehouse (private property) survives. In the 1650s stone from the demolished castle was used to rebuild the adjoining Church of St Barnabas, which had been occupied as a Parliamentary outpost in 1642–43 and wrecked by the Royalist bombardment of 1643–44.

According to tradition a violent storm on 3 September 1658, which toppled many of the trees in the grounds of the ruined castle, was caused by the Devil dragging Cromwell through the park on his way down to Hell. The Devil supposedly returns every 3 September to rampage through the grounds with Cromwell's soul.

Broadway (SP0937) According to tradition, Cromwell stayed at the Lygon Arms, formerly the Whyte Harte, at some point during his Worcester campaign. The well preserved Tudor building in brown stone contains a room, decorated with seventeenth-century plasterwork and a fine Stuart fireplace, in which Cromwell supposedly lodged.

Canon Frome (SO6543) Canon Frome Court, a late Georgian building, stands on the site of the demolished fifteenth-century manor-house which was garrisoned for the King during the Civil War. On 22 June 1645 the stronghold was stormed and taken by Leven's Scots, who put governor Barnard and most of his garrison to the sword.

Croft Castle (SO449654) The Welsh border castle was garrisoned by both sides during the Civil War as a minor outpost guarding the northern approaches to Hereford. The fine late medieval fortified manor-house, with round corner towers in pink stone, was restored and remodelled in the eighteenth and nineteenth centuries. The richly decorated house is open to the public on certain weekdays during the summer.

Eldersfield (SO8031)   A decisive skirmish, known variously as the Battle of Eldersfield or Redmarley, was fought in open land somewhere between these two villages on 27 July 1644. Col. Mynne's 1,000-strong Royalist force spent the night of 26–27 July in Redmarley (Glos), awaiting the arrival of reinforcements from Worcester before continuing south to attack Gloucester. Meanwhile, Massey had marched north to meet the threat and his men spent the night in Eldersfield. As the dawn mist cleared, the two forces clashed somewhere on the borders of Gloucestershire and Hereford and Worcester, Massey attacking the Royalists before their reinforcements had arrived. The King's men were slowly pushed from their initial position amid an area of enclosures and out onto open land, where their Horse was charged and put to flight by the Parliamentary Cavalry and their Foot then routed by Massey's experienced troops. Mynne and 130 of his men were killed and at least 200 more captured.

Evesham (SP0344)   Control of Evesham became a major objective of both armies during the Civil War, for the town occupied a crucial position in the Avon valley and commanded the two parallel roads which linked the Royalist cities of Worcester and Oxford. The Royalists were anxious to keep this line of communications open, the Parliamentarians to break it, and Evesham thus became the centre of frequent skirmishing. The King's men held Evesham for much of the war and erected earthworks to protect the unwalled town. The Avon afforded protection on three sides and the Royalists concentrated on strengthening the fourth, landward side, linking the meandering river with a ditch and embankment surmounted by a timber pallisade. On 26 May 1645 Massey launched a dawn raid on Evesham, filling the ditch with faggots, scaling the embankment, tearing down the pallisade and breaching the defences in several places. Legg's Royalists resisted fiercely and at first prevented Massey's men entering the town but by mid-morning the Parliamentarians had breached the defences in so many places that the over-stretched garrison could no longer keep them out. The defences were slighted after the Civil War and no trace of them now survives.

Cromwell stayed in Evesham on 27 August and 5–7 September 1651 on his way to and from Worcester.

Ewyas Harold (SO3828)   On 13 November 1642 a Parliamentary detachment under Col. Kyrle surprised and scattered a party of Welsh Royalists here and pursued them back towards Raglan.

Goodrich Castle (SO5719)   The medieval castle was held for Parliament by the Earl of Stamford during 1643 but by December Royalist pressure in the area had compelled the Parliamentarians to withdraw into Gloucester and the outpost was lost. From 1644 until summer 1646 the castle was garrisoned for the King by Sir Henry Lingen. Colonel Birch laid siege to Goodrich in July 1646 and bombarded it with heavy artillery, including a great mortar known as Roaring Meg. By the end of the month the castle's water supply had been cut and when cannon-fire and mines brought down the Ladies Tower, the Royalists within surrendered. The castle was subsequently slighted. The spectacular and extensive remains of the red sandstone fortress stand on a rocky outcrop above the village. The ruins are open daily.

Hartlebury (SO836712)   Hartlebury Castle, built by the Bishops of Worcester in the thirteenth century and extended and renovated in the fifteenth, was one of the few medieval fortresses within the county which survived in fairly good order at the outbreak of the Civil War. It was secured for the King without opposition in 1643 and garrisoned by Col. Sandys until the end of the war. On 9 May 1646 Col. Morgan's Parliamentarians arrived before the fortress; brief negotiations convinced Sandys that the King's cause was hopeless and that no relieving force existed to come to his aid, and the castle was surrendered on terms on the 14th. Hartlebury then served for several years as a minor Parliamentary garrison but the troops were withdrawn at the end of the decade and the castle was slighted. By the late seventeenth century little remained of the medieval fortress and the present 'castle', a long, low building in red sandstone with a central hall flanked by projecting, two storey wings, is almost entirely late seventeenth and eighteenth century. The chapel and the Great Hall are probably medieval, but both were heavily remodelled in the eighteenth century. The north wing now houses a museum, open each weekday during the summer; the rest of the castle is open to the public on Sundays and certain weekdays throughout the summer.

Hereford (SO5139)   Although the strength of Royalism in the area ensured that the former county town was held by the King for most of the war, Hereford suffered several Parliamentary raids from Gloucester and changed hands

Top: Goodrich Castle, Hereford & Worcs. The mighty sandstone fortress stands on a bluff above the Wye. The border fortress fell in 1646 to John Birch, the local Parliamentary leader, who survived and prospered under Charles II. His imperious marble effigy stands in Weobley church (*left*). *Above:* Brampton Bryan Castle, Hereford & Worcs. The twin towered medieval gatehouse alone survived razing after the castle was captured by Parliament in 1644. The mansion to the left is Georgian.

more than once. The Earl of Stamford took Hereford for Parliament in September 1642 but evacuated it in early December; a Royalist garrison under Col. Lawdey promptly moved in. On 25 April 1643 Waller led 2,500 men north from Gloucester, siezed the town and briefly garrisoned it for Parliament; having failed to take Worcester or to break the Royalist hold over the area, Waller fell back at the end of May and the King's men returned once more. In July and August 1645 Leven's Scots unsuccessfully besieged the town and were driven off in early September by the approach of the King. Relief was brief, for in November a larger Parliamentary force appeared before the walls and on 18 December Col. John Birch stormed the place, surprising the garrison and quickly overcoming the very half-hearted resistance – collusion was suspected. Birch held the town for the rest of the war.

The Civil War garrisons sheltered behind a hastily repaired circuit of medieval town walls, several sections of which survive, particularly on the west side, running north from Greyfriars Bridge along Greyfriars Bridge Street and Victoria Street. The medieval castle, probably semi-derelict by the time of the Civil War, was completely demolished at the end of the seventeenth century and nothing now survives but an open space known as Castle Green. Traffic is now carried over the Wye by modern Greyfriars Bridge but Old Wye Bridge still spans the river a little to the east; for defensive purposes the Royalists demolished the third bay from the north in 1644 and replaced it with a draw-bridge, and despite many subsequent renovations the arch rebuilt immediately after the war is still noticeably different from the others. Roaring Meg, John Birch's huge mortar used to devastating effect at Goodrich and elsewhere, is on display in Hereford Museum. Three-quarters of a mile east of Victoria Bridge stands the 'Scots' Hole' or 'Scots' Rowditch', an oval entrenchment cut into the hillside and defended by a now weathered rampart. It was supposedly constructed by Leven's men in 1645 during their unsuccessful siege.

Kilpeck Castle (SO4430)

The medieval motte and bailey fortress, west of the ornate church, was probably derelict by the seventeenth century and there is no record of action here during the Civil War. Nonetheless it was ordered slighted by Parliament in 1645. The fragmentary remains of a twelfth-century polygonal shell keep stand on a motte above a kidney shaped bailey and three outer enclosures.

Ledbury under Malvern (SO7137)

Ledbury was occupied by Massey's Parliamentarians on several occasions during the last two years of the war and frequently served as a temporary base for operations in the south of the county. On one such occasion, in April 1645, it was Massey who suffered defeat, surprised and routed here by Prince Rupert. The Prince marched down from Worcester overnight, arrived before Ledbury at dawn on 22 April and sent a detachment round to the south of the town to block Massey's natural line of retreat. The main Royalist force then attacked from the north, overcoming stiff resistance from Massey's Infantry manning the barricades, pushing on through the streets, and finally pursuing the defeated Parliamentarians out of town. Massey struggled back to Gloucester but lost 120 dead and at least 400 captured. Bullet holes in the panelling of the Talbot Inn, New Street, are said to have been made during this clash.

Madresfield (SO808474)

Madresfield Court, the Elizabethan moated mansion of the Lygons family, was garrisoned for the King throughout the war. The Royalists endured one siege in October 1645 but Col. Aston promptly surrendered the place to Col. Whalley in the following June, allegedly in return for a £200 bribe. The Tudor hall has since been demolished, though fragments of Elizabethan and Jacobean work, including panelling and chimney-pieces, were saved and have been incorporated within the present nineteenth-century house.

Moor (SO9848)

According to tradition Cromwell lodged on 28 August 1651 in the old half-timbered manor-house at Moor, sometimes called Hill and Moor, near Fladbury.

Much Dewchurch (SO4831)

St David's Church contains many monuments to the local Pye family, including James (d1646) and Robert (d1681). Sir Robert Pye (d1701) was a leading Parliamentary soldier and politician – he saw action in much of southern England, led the unsuccessful defence of Leicester against Rupert in 1645 and was a member of most Parliaments of the period. Pye's seat, The Mynde, 1¼ miles south-west of the village (SO470296), was seized and fortified by the King's men in autumn 1642. There seems to have been no serious action here and the house was probably abandoned without a fight towards the end of the war. The present house is a 2½ storey Georgian mansion, though incorporating the remains of the Tudor hall which saw service in the Civil War.

Pembridge Castle (SO488193) Built in the thirteenth century, Pembridge Castle was a small border fortress with curtain walls, angle towers and a double towered gatehouse; a hall, chapel and other buildings were added within the courtyard during the sixteenth and early seventeenth century. Pembridge was occupied by Parliamentary troops in summer 1644, but the garrison was battered into submission in the following November. The castle was badly damaged during the two week bombardment and played no further part in the Civil War. Although the buildings within the ward were renovated in the 1650s, the whole place fell derelict in the eighteenth century. The extensive ruins were consolidated and partly restored in the twentieth century. Pembridge Castle is open on certain weekdays during the summer.

Pershore (SO952462) In June 1644 the King fled from Oxford to Worcester and ordered the bridge over the Avon at Pershore to be destroyed behind him to hinder Waller and Essex and the pursuing Parliamentarians. The Royalists successfully brought down the central arch, but the masonry gave way sooner than expected and 30 soldiers and several civilians were drowned. The old bridge still spans the river immediately north of the modern road bridge, and its central arch, repaired after the Civil War, remains noticeably different from the others.

Powick Bridge (SO835524) Although it was the first serious engagement of the Civil War, the skirmish fought around Powick Bridge on 23 September 1642 involved fairly small numbers and was of little significance in the development of the conflict. Moreover, our knowledge of the engagement rests on several confused and contradictory contemporary accounts.

During the third week of September the Royalists decided to evacuate Worcester and to cover this manouevre Prince Rupert stationed 1,000 men to the south of the city. Meanwhile Cols Brown and Fiennes led an advanced party of Parliamentary Horse towards Worcester, ahead of Essex's main army. By the afternoon of 23 September Brown and Fiennes were in Powick Ham, an area of open land between the village and the bridge across the Teme. The Parliamentarians decided to advance, the main body waiting near the bridge while Col. Sandys led a detachment over the Teme and north up the lane towards Worcester. Surprised by the Parliamentary advance, Rupert quickly drew his force together and counter-charged. A confused and bloody mêlée ensued as the isolated Parliamentary unit was pushed back south to the

bridge. After more fighting around the bridge itself, the main Parliamentary force turned tail and rode away to rejoin Essex's army. The Royalists had won the first battle of the Civil War, taking 70 prisoners and killing or wounding at least twice that number, but the evacuation of Worcester went ahead as planned.

The fifteenth-century bridge at Powick still spans the Teme to the west of the Victorian construction which now carries the road. Although the south-western suburbs of Worcester are approaching Powick, the area around the bridge where fighting was fiercest is still open land. Marks on the outside of the tower of the Church of St Peter and St Lawrence in Powick may have been made by Civil War bullets fired as Rupert pursued the fleeing Parliamentarians through the village. (For further action around Powick in 1651 see 'Worcester' below).

Ripple (SO8637) A minor battle was fought here on 13 April 1643 as Waller's Parliamentarians advancing north from Tewkesbury clashed with a Royalist force under Prince Maurice marching south from Upton to intercept them. Waller was following the old Worcester road which ran to the west of the present A38 and took him through the village of Ripple. At this point he could see Maurice's 2,000 men drawn up on flat ground away to the north, blocking his path. In response the Parliamentarians deployed across a slight hill – Old Nan's Hill – 3–400 yards north of Ripple around Uckinghall. Waller had fewer than 1,500 men and little artillery and after an initial exchange he decided to fall back. He posted his Dragoons ahead to guard his front as he moved most of his army to his right into the lane the leading back to Ripple (around SO875382). Maurice saw this movement and decided to attack; one party was sent straight down the lane while Maurice led the main Royalist force south along the river bank before swinging left up the gentle western slopes of the hill and so into Waller's left flank. The Royalist units tore into the redeploying Parliamentary force causing confusion and panic. Although Hesilrige's lobsters made a temporary stand, they too were broken and forced back and Maurice then pursued the Parliamentarians into Ripple and beyond. Although most of Waller's men headed for the comparative safety of Tewkesbury, some fled west towards the ford near Uckinghall (SO683375) and were either cut down as they ran or drowned in the Severn.

The area of the battle is still open farmland to the north of Ripple, little changed since the seventeenth century

Ross on Wye (SO5924)   The border town changed hands several times in the course of the Civil War as the Gloucester Parliamentarians repeatedly pushed west and then fell back in the face of Royalist pressure. In summer 1644, during one of his longer occupations of Ross, Massey established a fortified position in and around St Mary's Church, surrounding the churchyard with a circuit of ditch and bank.

Spetchley (SO8953)   According to a plausible tradition, Cromwell was based at Spetchley before the Battle of Worcester and lodged at Spetchley House, the home of Mr Justice Berkeley, on 30 August–2 September. The house, which no longer exists, stood a little south of the present nineteenth-century great house in Spetchley Park.

Strensham (SO9140)   Strensham House or Court was a small but important base in the south of the county, guarding the road north from Gloucester via Tewkesbury. Sir William Russell's fortified mansion was held by Parliament in 1644–45; although there is no record of fighting here, it must have changed hands at some point, for Strensham is listed as one of the minor outposts to be surrendered to Parliament in 1646 at the same time as Worcester. The old fortified mansion has been demolished, though its site is probably marked by the remains of a moat near the centre of the village. A later Strensham Court, which stood to the south-west, has also been demolished and its site obliterated under the M5.

Upton upon Severn (SO8540)   Before attacking the Royalists in Worcester, Cromwell wanted to gain free access to the west bank of the Severn, thus permitting him to assault the city from the south-west and breaking the possible Royalist line of retreat into Wales. To this end Lambert and a troop of dragoons were despatched to Upton on 28 August with orders to take the bridge. Arriving around dawn on the 29th, Lambert found that the Royalists had demolished the central arch of the bridge but that a plank had been left in place across the breach. Massey's 300-strong Royalist guard was nowhere to be seen – many of the Scots were allegedly sleeping off the night's excesses in the taproom of the Anchor Inn. A dozen or so Parliamentary volunteers managed to crawl across the plank and reach the west bank before the guard was roused. The Royalists quickly turned out, preventing anyone else getting across the bridge and surrounding the Church of St Peter and St Paul, in which the small party of

west bank Parliamentarians had hastily taken refuge. It seemed that they were doomed and that the mission had failed. However, Lambert saw that the river was unusually low and his main force were able to part ford part swim the Severn at a spot called Fishers' Row, just below the bridge. The Royalists were taken by surprise when further Parliamentarians appeared, fell back from the church and were driven off towards Worcester with heavy losses; Massey, the former Parliamentarian and hero of the siege of Gloucester, was badly wounded but lived. Cromwell visited Upton later on the 29th to inspect the bridge and to thank Lambert's men for their efforts. According to tradition he exchanged greetings with an old woman in a cottage near the church, on the strength of which a modern restaurant within the building was named 'Cromwell's'.

The old bridge at Upton has long gone and the present span is modern. The old parish church of St Peter and St Paul was largely demolished in the eighteenth century, though the fourteenth-century tower survives, now topped by a Georgian cupola. The adjoining information and heritage centre includes a display on Upton in the Civil War.

Walford Court (SO586206)   Walford Court Manor, a sixteenth-century castellated mansion, was the seat of the Kyrle family during the seventeenth century. Robert Kyrle (b1613) saw service on the Continent during the 1630s and at the outbreak of the Civil War he became an officer in the Parliamentary army. He later defected to the King's army, only to return to Parliament once again, helping to betray Monmouth to Massey's Parliamentarians in 1644. His house was garrisoned for the King until 1645–46, but in summer 1646 it became the base for Birch's Parliamentarians during their operation against Goodrich. Kyrle himself returned here after the war and lies beneath an inscribed tablet in the Kyrle Chapel of St Leonard's Church.

Weobley (SO4051)   In May 1691 John Birch was laid to rest in the Church of St Peter and St Paul in Weobley. Half a century before, Birch had joined the Parliamentary army and risen rapidly through the ranks. Severely wounded and left for dead during the attack on Arundel Castle, he survived to become one of the most active commanders in Herefordshire during the latter stages of the first Civil War, capturing Hereford in December 1645 and remaining there as governor. He fell from favour during the 1650s and actively supported the Restoration. Thereafter he enjoyed a long and rewarding political career and acquired considerable property in the Hereford area. A white marble statue in St Peter's and St Paul's shows Birch dressed in armour and carrying a baton.

White Ladies Aston (SO9252)   According to tradition Cromwell lodged on 29 August 1651 at George Symonds's half-timbered house at White Ladies Aston. The building was demolished in the nineteenth century.

Wigmore (SO4169)   Both sides established minor outposts at Wigmore at various stages of the war. The Harleys' medieval castle was ruinous by the seventeenth century and probably served as nothing more than a surveillance or artillery post. The main stronghold was probably St James's Church. Wigmore was one of the largest of the border castles but is now poorly preserved. The remains of an oval shell keep crown the high motte, below which the inner bailey is protected by fragments of the wall, mural towers and gatehouse which once encircled the area.

Wilton Castle (SO590243)   Wilton Castle, a medieval quadrangular fortress with corner towers and a south-western gatehouse, stands outside the village of Bridstow. The castle, which had been partly converted into a more comfortable Elizabethan mansion during the late sixteenth century, was garrisoned for the King in 1643–44 but fell to Massey's Parliamentarians in May 1644 when they forded the river and surprised the King's men. It was soon reoccupied by the Royalists. The late Tudor bridge which the garrison was protecting still spans the Wye.

Worcester (SO8555)   Having changed hands several times during the opening months of the Civil War, the city was secured for the King at the end of 1642 and thereafter became one of the principal Royalist strongholds and a base for operations over a wide area of the West Midlands and the Welsh Marches. The medieval town walls and the seven town gates were repaired and strengthened and several earthwork banks and bastions were added. The city endured occasional Parliamentary raids – on 29 May 1643, for instance, 3,000 men under Waller tried unsuccessfully to storm the place – but not until 1646 was Worcester seriously threatened. By spring of that year most of the surrounding region had fallen to Parliament and on 23 July the Worcester garrison abandoned the struggle and surrendered to the Parliamenta-

rians who had besieged and bombarded the city for nearly two months.

The region was fairly quiet during 1648 but three years later Worcester again became the Royalist HQ. On 22 August the small Parliamentary garrison here fell back at the approach of the main Royalist army and Prince Charles entered the city unopposed on the following day. He halted at Worcester, established his court at a house in the Corn Market and set about repairing the city's defences in preparation for the expected attack. Earthworks were thrown up beyond the walls, particularly around the gates and across the London road to cover the southern approaches to the city; a large, star-shaped fort, Fort Royal, was built south-east of the city and was linked to the walls by earth ramparts.

Cromwell appeared before Worcester at the end of August and laid careful plans for the final attack. His main force was stationed on Red Hill, south-east of the city, and from here Parliamentary cannon maintained a heavy bombardment to soften up the Royalists within. At the same time he secured the west bank of the Severn and stationed a secondary force under Fleetwood around Powick. To ensure easy communication between the two halves of his army, Cromwell constructed bridges of boats across the Severn and the Teme near the junction of the two rivers.

The two-pronged attack was launched on 3 September. On the west bank, Fleetwood advanced through Powick, throwing back the Scottish outposts – the bullet marks on Powick Church may have been made during this skirmish – and eventually carried Powick Bridge, though the Scots abandoned the crossing only after a fierce fight and the arrival of Parliamentary reinforcements from the east bank. The Royalist right eventually broke and fell back into Worcester. Watching from the tower of the cathedral, Charles had seen the Parliamentary redeployment and ordered his men to engage the depleted Parliamentary force on Red Hill. The Parliamentarians were initially pushed back by this Royalist attack, but Cromwell hurriedly returned with his troops from the now secured west bank, rallied his forces and countercharged. The Scots were routed and fell back into the city, closely pursued by the Parliamentarians who took Fort Royal and then burst into Worcester itself. Charles slipped away through St Martin's Gate as the final Royalist resistance on Castle Mound was being overcome. By the end of the day 3,000 Royalists were dead and up to 10,000 captured – many prisoners were temporarily held in the cathedral – the Royalist cause was shattered and Prince Charles was a fugitive fleeing for his life. The 'crowning mercy' of Worcester was also the triumphant finale of Cromwell's distinguished military career. He remained Lord General of the Army until his death but never again would he lead his soldiers into battle.

The battle raged over a large area, but there were two distinct centres of fighting. One, north of Powick Bridge and the Teme, remains open land, the Ordnance Survey battle symbol at SO846535 accurately indicating the position around which Fleetwood's men clashed with the Scots. Two slight depressions on Powick Ham, still visible at the beginning of this century, supposedly marked the position of large pits in which the dead were buried after the battle. The other centre of fighting, Red Hill, has since been built over and is now a south-eastern suburb of Worcester. The subsequent expansion of the city has also obliterated both the medieval stone walls and the Civil War earthworks, including Fort Royal.

As the city fell, Prince Charles briefly took refuge in Rowland Berkeley's town house, a Tudor half-timbered building in New Street, now known as King Charles's House. The Commandery off Sidbury Street, a Tudor building incorporating parts of an earlier hospital, became the Royalist HQ during the battle; recently restored, it is now a museum and contains displays on Worcester during the Civil War, including arms and armour, a copy of Cromwell's death mask and an excellent film presentation of the Battle of Worcester. The City Museum in Foregate Street also contains several relics from the war and the battle. The façade of the Georgian Guildhall in High Street incorporates statues of Charles I and II and Cromwell's head appears above the doorway, nailed by the ears to the wall behind.

The Cromwell Association has a memorial tablet in an alcove at the city end of Sidbury Bridge, adjoining St Peter's Church, on the site of the former Sidbury Gate through which Parliamentary troops first entered Worcester.

HERTFORDSHIRE

The county was held securely for Parliament throughout the period and saw no significant fighting during the Civil War. The Parliamentary army and its high command were frequently stationed in Hertfordshire and were in the area for much of spring and summer 1647 during their dispute with Parliament. Cromwell was certainly in Hertfordshire with the army in June and July 1647 but he must have passed through the county on many other occasions on his way between London and Cambridgeshire.

Berkhamsted (SP9907) Cromwell and the Parliamentary army were stationed here on 25 June 1647. The soldiers probably quartered in the grounds of the medieval castle; derelict by the early seventeenth century it had played no part in the Civil War. Berkhamsted or Castle Place, an Elizabethan mansion on Castle Hill, was owned by the Parliamentarian soldier and regicide Col. Daniel Axtell and Cromwell and the other senior officers may well have lodged here for the night. Little remains of the old house, a victim of late seventeenth-century fires and modern rebuilding.

Cheshunt (TL3402) Richard Cromwell spent his last years in quiet retirement in this small Hertfordshire village, now overshadowed by the extensive modern developments to the east. On his return to England in 1680 Richard lodged with the Pengelly family in Finchley, north London. At the death of Thomas Pengelly in 1700, his widow moved to a house in Churchgate, Cheshunt, left to her by her late uncle Arthur Otway, and Richard spent the last twelve years of his life here. The house, which was destroyed by fire in the nineteenth century, stood next to the present, much later Pengelly House.

By coincidence, another Cromwell came to Cheshunt a century after Richard's death. Oliver Cromwell, great-great-grandson of Lord Protector Oliver through his fourth son, Lord Deputy Henry, inherited Cheshunt Park and other parts of the former royal estate of Theobalds. Oliver, a London-based solicitor and author of a rather muddled biography of his illustrious forefather and namesake, used Cheshunt as his country retreat. He died here in 1821 and lies buried beneath an inscribed slab in the north-west corner of St Mary's churchyard. He left only

Cheshunt, Herts. Two descendants of Oliver Cromwell ended their days here. The Protector's eldest surviving son and successor as Lord Protector, Richard (*left*), enjoyed a mere nine months in power followed by half a century in exile or retirement. From 1680 he lived very quietly in England, calling himself John Clark but otherwise adopting little disguise. The sad life of 'Richard IV' – or 'Queen Dick' as the army officers had cruelly called him – ended in Cheshunt in 1712.

A brick table tomb in St Mary's churchyard (*above*) marks the resting place of Oliver Cromwell of London and Cheshunt. The lawyer and biographer was Cromwell's last male heir through the male line and the direct line died with him in 1821. According to tradition, King George had been approached sometime before to sanction the preservation of the name in the female line but had refused, allegedly declaring that there had been quite enough Cromwells already and that there should be no more!

daughters – a son had died in infancy forty years before – and at Oliver's death the Protector's direct male line became extinct. The Lord Protector has many descendants through the female line, but his namesake lying in St Mary's churchyard was his last male descendant through the male line.

Hatfield (TL236085)   During summer 1647 Charles I was lodged by the Parliamentary army at several points in Hertfordshire in order that he be kept close to the peripatetic army HQ. On 26–27 June he was held at Hatfield House, the magnificent Jacobean mansion built for the Earl of Salisbury in 1607–12. Hatfield House is open daily except Mondays throughout the summer.

Hertford (TL3212)   Cromwell and Fairfax stayed here in mid-November 1647 while negotiating with the discontented and semi-mutinous troops drawn up on Cockbush or Corkbush Fields, open ground to the east of the town. Some accounts claim that the two commanders lodged at the Bell, now the Salisbury Arms, a late sixteenth- and early seventeenth-century coaching inn which stands on the corner of Fore and Church Streets. Other reports have it that they stayed in Hertford Castle, a medieval fortress remodelled and modernised in the sixteenth century; most of the castle has since been demolished and the three storey turreted gatehouse is the only part to survive intact.

On 15 November Cromwell and Fairfax confronted the troops at Cockbush, crushing the half-hearted mutiny and arresting the ringleaders, who were tried by a hasty court martial and sentenced to death. They were forced to draw lots and the loser, Richard Arnold, was executed on the spot. The area is now covered by a modern housing estate, 1½ miles east-north-east of Hertford town centre; the street name Cockbush Avenue is the only reminder of the events of 1647.

Hitchin (TL1829)   According to tradition, Cromwell, Pym, Hampden and other prominent figures used to meet and confer at the Sun Inn, Hitchin, during the late 1630s and early 1640s. During the war it certainly became a meeting place for soldiers and officers. The Tudor inn, remodelled and refronted during the eighteenth century, still stands in Sun Street; a low, half-timbered range off the courtyard incorporates the former Tudor gallery.

Royston (TL3540)   Cromwell stayed here in early June 1647 while conferring with the discontented Parliamentary troops quartered around Thriplow (Cambs). A fortnight later, on 25 June, Charles I was lodged overnight in King James's Palace, his father's hunting lodge, a ramshackle collection of mostly Jacobean buildings which stood in the area between Kneesworth Street, Dog Kennel Lane and Melbourne Street. Most of the complex has disappeared, but several buildings in Kneesworth Street once belonged to the palace, including the former buttery, kitchen, guardhouse and the so-called 'Palace', a two storey brick house with large chimneys, much of which dates from the eighteenth century.

St Albans (TL1407)   Cromwell probably passed through the town on many occasions in the early 1640s as it lay on one of the routes – though not the most direct – between London and Cambridgeshire. According to tradition, he often broke his journey here and stayed with Col. Alban Cox. Moreover, Cromwell was probably with Essex's army as it marched through St Albans on the way to and from Edgehill in autumn 1642. He was certainly here on 14 January 1643, for he and his men broke up a pro-Royalist meeting in the Market Place – after a brief mêlée around the gateway of the Great Red Lion, the Parliamentarians arrested Sir Thomas Coningsby, the High Sheriff of Hertfordshire, who had been attempting to read a Royal proclamation.

St Albans was a convenient base for the Parliamentary army, and both the soldiers and the high command were frequently stationed here. Part of the abbey, now the cathedral, was requisitioned by the military and used as prison, conference hall and army court – it was here that Nathaniel Fiennes was tried, convicted and sentenced to death for the loss of Bristol. In mid-November 1648 Fairfax, Ireton and other senior officers – though not Cromwell, who was absent in Yorkshire – met in the Abbey to discuss the future settlement of the country. Despite opposition from Fairfax and others, the St Albans meeting ratified *The Remonstrance of the Army,* calling for the trial and punishment of the King.

Stanstead St Margarets (TL380116)   In St Margaret's Church lie several members of the Lawrence family, including Henry Lawrence, friend and sometime landlord of Cromwell during the 1630s, a leading supporter of the Protectorate twenty years later, a Member of the Protectorate Parliaments and President of the Protectoral Council. Lawrence retired to Stanstead at the Restoration and died here four years later. He lies beneath an inscribed slab in the chancel, near the altar.

Stevenage (TL2325)   The former Cromwell Hotel, now the Stevenage Moat Hotel, in the High Street was built around a sixteenth-century farmhouse supposedly owned at one time by John Thurloe, Cromwell's Secretary of State and Secretary of the Protectoral Council. Above the fireplace in what is now the Cromwell Bar is a stone bearing the date 1667 and the initials 'THF'; it has been suggested that they stand for Thurloe Home Farm.

Ware (TL3514)   Ware stood on the most direct road between London and Cambridge and Cromwell must have passed through the town on many occasions during the 1640s. He was certainly here on 4 June 1647, for he stopped at Ware for refreshment on his flight from London to the army. Three years later, on 28 June 1650, he lodged here for the night at the beginning of his journey north from London to Scotland.

HUMBERSIDE

Although most of Humberside was secured for Parliament at the outbreak of war, the area saw considerable fighting during 1643 as the Royalists advanced to the gates and ditches of Hull. The Royalist threat receded during the opening months of 1644 and disappeared altogether after Marston Moor. In September 1643 Cromwell visited the besieged garrison at Hull, his only recorded visit to the area covered by the modern county of Humberside.

Beverley (TA0339)   The town was held by Parliament in 1642–43 to defend the northern approaches to Hull and the garrison hastily repaired the medieval town walls. In June 1643 Sir John Hotham senior, former Parliamentary governor of Hull turned Royalist, was captured here as he fled north to join the King's forces. In the following month the garrison abandoned the town without a fight at the approach of Newcastle's 15,000-strong army. Of Beverley's medieval and Civil War defences nothing now survives except a single gateway, the fourteenth-century North Bar.

Boynton (TA138678)   Boynton Hall, a late Tudor brick hall with projecting wings, extensively remodelled in the eighteenth century, stands amid private parkland and plantations at the southern end of the village. The hall was the principal seat of the Strickland family, including Sir William (d1673), a prominent Parliamentarian and member of all the parliaments of the period, and his younger brother Walter, Parliament's agent in Holland in 1642–51, one of Cromwell's leading supporters during the 1650s, a member of the Protectorate Parliaments and a Protectoral Councillor.

Bridlington (TA1766)   Bridlington was secured by Newcastle in early February 1643 and on the 22nd Queen Henrietta Maria landed here with cash and plate collected on the Continent.

Parliamentary ships under Batten were in pursuit of the Queen's convoy and bombarded the town that night; according to tradition the Queen rushed back to her ship to rescue her dog and then sought refuge in a ditch while shot flew overhead. Some accounts indicate that after the incident the Royalists threw up batteries to overlook and defend the harbour, but there is no record of further fighting here and no trace remains of any Civil War earthworks.

Brigg (TA0007)   Seventeenth-century Brigg possessed neither walls nor a castle and the weakly defended town changed hands several times during 1643. It was not formally garrisoned until the end of the year, by which time the area had been secured for Parliament. Lord Willoughby's garrison threw up earthworks around the town early in 1644 but they were not put to the test for the Royalists never returned. No trace of the Civil War defences survives.

Burton upon Stather (SE8618)   The village guarded the lowest safe ferry crossing on the Trent before it joined the Humber estuary, control of which was vital to anyone seeking to defend or attack what was then north Lincolnshire, now south Humberside. In consequence, the village and ferry changed hands several times during 1643 before the Parliamentarians secured the area at the end of the year and established a large garrison at Burton to guard against further attack. The Civil War earthworks, thrown up during 1643 on both banks of the Trent, have been obliterated by repeated floods and by the growth of a small hamlet, The Ferry, on the east bank.

Flamborough (TA226702)
Walter Strickland, Parliamentary diplomat, politician and Protectoral Councillor, lies buried beneath an inscribed tombstone within the Church of St Oswald.

Kingston-upon-Hull (TA1028)
A vital east coast port and magazine during the mid-seventeenth century, Hull was one of the first towns in England openly to defy Charles I in 1642. It was a Parliamentary stronghold throughout the Civil War, one of the very few bases in the area to resist the Royalist tide of summer and autumn 1643.

Secure behind newly renovated medieval walls, governor John Hotham refused to admit the King on 23 April 1642 and continued to resist throughout the summer, enduring a Royalist blockade organised by Lord Lindsey from his base in Anlaby. The Royalists departed in August and over the following months Hotham made further repairs and additions to the town's defences. The Parliamentarians piled earth behind the fourteenth-century stone and brick walls which enclosed the old town to the west of the river Hull. As a second, outer line of defence, Hotham added a bank and ditch beyond the wall, with half-moon batteries covering each of the four principal town gates. The east bank of the Hull was defended by three blockhouses linked by a Tudor wall. During the early months of 1643 Hotham demolished most of the extra-mural suburbs to prevent them being used for shelter by a besieging army.

The feared assault began on 2 September 1643 when the Earl of Newcastle and 15,000 Royalists appeared before Hull and settled down for a long, formal siege, building their own earth forts and ditches around the town. Lord Fairfax, governor of Hull in place of turncoat Hotham, opened the sluices along the north bank of the Humber estuary, flooding not only the town ditch but also a large area of low ground around Hull, greatly disrupting Royalist operations. Moreover, Newcastle had curiously made no attempt to secure the south bank of the Humber estuary, which remained in Parliamentary hands throughout, and so was powerless to prevent supplies and reinforcements reaching Hull by sea or ferry. The position is well-illustrated by the ease with which Cromwell and Willoughby crossed the Humber unopposed and entered Hull on or around 22 September to confer with Sir Thomas Fairfax, who had himself arrived during the early stages of the ineffectual siege. Newcastle's position was hopeless and increasingly vigorous sallies induced the Royalists to abandon the effort and march away on 12 October.

Sadly the medieval and Civil War defences of Hull have been largely destroyed, and little remains of the walls and gates, the banks and the earthwork forts. A modern plaque in Whitefriargate shopping precinct marks the site of Beverley Gate, the town gate from which Hotham defied the King in 1642. Ye Old White Harte, off Silver Street, is a Tudor inn, extended in the sixteenth century and restored in the nineteenth. Sir John Hotham was dining here in April 1642 when he received word that King Charles was approaching. He retired to a back room, later dubbed the Plotting Room, to consult with Pelham and others about granting or refusing admission to the town.

Scorborough (TA017452)
A decayed moat south of the church and near the later great house is the only surviving trace of the late medieval moated hall which once stood here. In the seventeenth century the hall was the seat of the Hotham family, including Sir John senior and junior, the leading Parliamentarians in the county during the opening year of the Civil War who later attempted to defect to the King and were executed by Parliament in 1645.

Winestead (TA3024)
Andrew Marvell, the poet and Latin Secretary to the Protectoral Council, was born in Winestead in 1621. The Tudor rectory in which he was born and brought up has long since disappeared; it stood north of the towerless Church of St German, where Marvell was baptised on 5 April.

Wressle (SE707316)
Wressle Castle was one of the very few defensible fortresses within seventeenth-century Humberside. It was held for Parliament during most of the first Civil War and again in 1648 to block the road from Pontefract to Hull. The moated quadrangular castle with massive corner towers was built by the Percies in the fourteenth century. Partially slighted by Parliament after the Civil War, the ruined sections were incorporated within a later farmhouse, itself destroyed by fire in 1796. The extensive remains of two corner towers survive, together with the linking hall range.

ISLE OF MAN

The Isle of Man was dominated during the 1640s by the Earl of Derby, and his retainers crushed all opposition and held the island for the King. Derby's capture and execution in 1651 sparked an anti-Stanley rebellion here, which was fanned by the landing of Parliamentary troops. By the end of the year all the Royalist strongholds had fallen and the island was controlled by Parliament for the remainder of the decade.

The Royalists garrisoned a number of medieval strongpoints, including Peel Castle (SC242845), the thirteenth–fourteenth century cathedral-cum-fortress on St Patrick's Isle; the outer walls of Peel Castle were damaged by artillery in 1651 during its capture by Parliament. The Stanleys also built or refortified several earthwork defences around the island, most of which, includ- ing the fort at Point of Ayre (NX466052), have completely disappeared. However, one such earthwork, Fort Loyal, survived intact and has recently been restored. Built in 1648–9, the large rectangular fort with bank and ditch defences and corner bastions stands south-east of Ker- roogarroo (SC406970), and is freely accessible to the public.

ISLE OF WIGHT

In August 1642 the Royalist Countess of Portland surrendered Carisbrooke Castle, the only real strongpoint on the island, to the Parliamentary governor of Newport, and thereafter the Isle of Wight was held for Parliament without serious challenge. The island was a potential landing spot for foreign invaders and both during and after the war Parliament kept a tight grip on the Isle, with a large and well equipped garrison at Carisbrooke and a string of lesser bases around the coast, particularly on the northern shore, facing the mainland. There is no clear evidence that Cromwell ever visited the island.

Carisbrooke Castle (SZ486878) From November 1647 to autumn 1648 Charles I was held here as a prisoner of the Parliamentary army, watched over by the governor of the castle, Col. Hammond. The King was lodged either in the Governor's House itself or in adjoining rooms within the range of domestic buildings which runs from the foot of the motte to the north curtain wall. Charles passed much of the time playing bowls on the Old Barbican, an open space at the eastern end of the inner bailey. The Governor's House is now a museum, containing many items associated with the King's captivity here. The modern chapel within the grounds was built as a memorial to Charles I. The castle is open daily.

Cowes Castle (SZ495966) The small Henri- cian coastal fort served as a small Parliamentary outpost throughout the period. It now serves as the clubhouse of the Royal Yacht Squadron.

Newport (SZ4989) In September 1648 a de- legation from both Houses of Parliament, in- cluding Holles, Vane, Salisbury and Pembroke, arrived on the island to confer with the King at Newport. Talks aimed at reaching a political settlement were held in the old town hall, long since demolished, which stood on the site of the present guildhall. During the conference Charles was lodged at the old grammar school, a much renovated Jacobean building, which survives at the corner of St James and Lugley Street.

Yarmouth Castle (SZ354897) The Henrician coastal fort, completed in 1547, was garrisoned for Parliament throughout the period, but never saw action. The castle is square with a single arrowhead bastion commanding the water be- low. The garrison was housed in the southern range; the second floor gun platform is on the other side of the irregular courtyard. Yarmouth Castle is open daily.

ISLES OF SCILLY

The Isles of Scilly were nominally Royalist throughout the first Civil War, but played no part in the conflict beyond sheltering the Prince of Wales for six weeks in spring 1646 after he had fled the mainland. In the late 1640s St Mary's and Tresco became the base of Sir John Grenville and his force of pro-Royalist pirates, and their increasingly disruptive operation against Parliamentary shipping prompted Blake to lead a full-scale invasion of the islands in 1651. A fleet of 20 ships landed nine companies of Foot on the Scillies and combined land and sea operations quickly secured Tresco. Star Castle on St Mary's was then besieged and bombarded into submission. The islands were held peacefully by Parliament for the rest of the 1650s.

St Mary's Above Hugh Town stands Star Castle (SV899107), a late Elizabethan artillery fort in the shape of an eight pointed star surrounded by a rock cut ditch and earthwork ramparts. The castle has been converted into an hotel.

Tresco On high ground in the north-west of the island stand the fragmentary remains of King Charles's Castle (SV883162), a two storey artillery fort built by Henry VIII to cover the channel below. In the late 1640s the Royalists strengthened the place by adding a semi-pentagonal earthwork fort on the landward side.

Cromwell's Castle, a 60 foot high circular tower on a granite platform, stands on an isthmus a little to the south of King Charles's Castle (SV882159). Now entered at ground level through an eighteenth-century doorway, marks on the outer wall indicate where an external stairway originally led to the first floor, where the garrison was quartered. The guns were mounted on the roof and six gun ports pierce the low parapet. The castle was probably garrisoned for Parliament during the 1650s and was almost certainly built by Blake's troops immediately after the 1651 invasion. The well-preserved castle stands on land freely accessible to the public.

KENT

In August 1642 Cols Sandys and Livesey and their force of 2,300 troops secured the county for Parliament in the face of little serious resistance. Despite occasional plots and minor risings, the county remained firmly Parliamentarian throughout the first Civil War and saw no significant action until 1648, when Kent became one of the centres of Royalist rebellion. Cromwell made only one recorded visit to the area, in May 1652, long after order had been restored.

Canterbury (TR1457) On Christmas Day 1647 the Royalist elements within Canterbury rose up in rebellion and expelled the small Parliamentary garrison stationed here. 3,000 men, drawn largely from the London Trained Bands, invested the town in January and the rebels surrendered without a fight. The ringleaders were imprisoned in Leeds Castle and the town defences slighted to prevent further trouble – all the gates were broken down and a stretch of wall on the west side of the town demolished. Long stretches of the medieval flint walls remain, particularly around the south and east of the town. The fourteenth-century Westgate also survives and is now a museum, open daily.

Deal (TR378522) Deal Castle was one of a string of Henrician forts built along the south coast in the late 1530s and early 1540s. It saw no action during the first Civil War but in June 1648 it was seized and garrisoned by the Royalist rebels. Deal was promptly besieged by Parliamentary forces and endured a heavy bombardment by land and sea. The garrison surrendered on 25 August after a small relieving force had been scattered by the Parliamentarians. The castle, open daily, comprises a central circular keep surrounded by six semicircular bastions linked by an outer wall.

Dover (TR324420) Dover Castle was held by a

Above: Fort Loyal, Isle of Man. The Royalists' earthwork fort is typical of Civil War artillery works. The huge arrowhead corner bastions, which carried the principal artillery, were linked and surrounded by a bank, ditch and outer parapet.

Right: Tresco, Isles of Scilly. Cromwell's Castle, built by Parliament in 1651, was designed as an artillery point to cover the channel below.

Below: Carisbrooke Castle, Isle of Wight. On the far side of the courtyard stands the Governor's House, a domestic block renovated and enlarged in the sixteenth century. It was here that the King was held prisoner in 1647–8 and it was through one of its windows that he tried to escape.

small Royalist garrison during summer 1642 but on 21 August the fortress was siezed by Capt. Richard Dawkes and ten companions in a daring night raid. Dover remained in Parliament's hands througout the first Civil War. At the beginning of June 1648 the castle was besieged by Royalist forces under Sir Richard Hardress, but Governor Bradfield and his garrison held out until a relieving force arrived and drove off the King's men. Cromwell visited town and castle in May 1652 to enquire into naval business. The magnificent clifftop fortress, with a twelfth-century keep standing amid concentric circuits of walls, gatehouses and mural towers, is open daily.

East Farleigh (TQ7353)

On 1 June 1648 Fairfax and his army crossed the Medway at East Farleigh, avoiding the main Royalist outposts and thus approaching Maidstone from the south. The bridge he crossed still spans the river, a five-arched ragstone construction, one of the finest medieval bridges in southern England. In the nineteenth century a number of bodies were discovered in ground adjoining the bridge, probably members of the small Royalist guard who fell as Fairfax swept through.

The Parliamentarian and local M.P. Augustine Skinner owned East Farleigh Hall, since demolished. Skinner lies beneath a monument in St Mary's Church.

East Malling (TQ7057)

Matthew Tomlinson lived in retirement at East Malling after the Restoration. A colonel in the Parliamentary army, Tomlinson saw action throughout England during the 1640s and later served under Fleetwood and Henry Cromwell in Ireland. He is best remembered, however, as the commanding officer of the troop which guarded Charles I from December 1648 until his execution. His courteous treatment of his prisoner earned praises from the doomed King and saved his own head eleven years later. Tomlinson lies beneath an inscribed slab in the chancel of St James's Church.

Lullingstone Castle (TQ528645)

The castle, really a fortified manor-house, was captured in April 1645 in the course of a minor Royalist rebellion but was immediately retaken by two Parliamentary troops under Col. Blount. Most of the Tudor house was subsequently demolished and the present 'castle' dates from the eighteenth century. In the grounds, however, stands the original sixteenth-century gatehouse, a three storey embattled building in red brick.

The castle and grounds are open to the public during the summer.

Maidstone (TQ7656)

The Battle of Maidstone of 1 June 1648 was the only major engagement of the Civil War in Kent. At the end of May the Earl of Norwich and his 7–8,000 Royalists established themselves at Maidstone, throwing up barricades across the streets and sending out units to guard the approach roads. In response, Fairfax mustered his forces on Blackheath and marched on the town via Farleigh and Loose, thus avoiding the 1,000 Royalists posted at Aylesford to defend the Medway crossing (TQ7258); Fairfax had no difficulty in sweeping aside the much smaller force guarding Farleigh bridge. The Parliamentarians arrived before Maidstone at around 7 p.m. on 1 June and when their advanced units under Hewson were engaged by Royalist forces on the outskirts of the town Fairfax ordered a general assault. The fighting was very fierce, but the Parliamentarians eventually carried the barricades and then made their way up the High Street, pushing the rebels into St Faith's churchyard. Despite further stubborn resistance the Royalists were at last overwhelmed and by 11 p.m. the battle was over; 300 rebels were dead, over 1,000 were captured and the remainder were fleeing northwards.

In Earl Street stands the seventeenth-century town house of Andrew Broughton, sometime Mayor of Maidstone, who acted as Clerk of the High Court which tried the King. A plaque on the outside of the building records the association.

Penshurst (TQ528440)

Penshurst Place in the centre of the village was the family home of the Sidneys, Earls of Leicester. The fourteenth-century manor-house was largely destroyed 200 years later, when the present Tudor mansion was built, though parts of the original house survive, including the magnificent Barons Hall. Best known for its association with the Elizabethan poet and courtier Sir Philip Sidney (d1586), in the seventeenth century Penshurst was the home of the 2nd Earl of Leicester and his eldest son, Philip Sidney, Viscount Lisle, later the 3rd Earl. Lisle was one of Cromwell's leading supporters during the 1650s and became a member of the Protectoral Councils and Parliaments. Penshurst is open daily except Mondays during the summer.

Plaxtol (TQ602537)

The village church, which has no dedication, was begun in 1649 and was thus one of the very few churches built during the Civil War and Interregnum. The present building is far from pure seventeenth-century, for it incorporates parts of an earlier chapel which stood on the site and was later renovated and enlarged by the Victorians. The interior of the nave, however, with its great hammer-beam roof, is thought to date from 1649.

Rochester (TQ7468) A port and fortified town on the Medway, Rochester was secured for Parliament in autumn 1642 by Col. Sandys, who scattered a group of local Royalists trying to hold the bridge. In early June 1648 many Royalist rebels fled here after the Battle of Maidstone, but surrendered to Fairfax without further resistance. Cromwell visited the town in May 1652 on naval business.

Sevenoaks (TQ5255) In July 1643 around 1,000 anti-Parliamentarian or pro-Royalist pro-testers gathered at Sevenoaks, though many scattered on hearing that Parliamentary troops were approaching to restore order. On the 23rd Col. Browne's man entered the town and dis-persed the 700 rebels who remained, expelling them from the town and pursuing them south towards Tonbridge.

Shipbourne (TQ592522) The remains of Sir Henry Vane junior, the leading Parliamentarian executed in June 1662, were buried in St Giles's Church near those of his wife and parents.

Stone (TQ5774) In June 1648 Major Hub-bard's Parliamentarians caught a party of Royalist rebels here, killing 20 and scattering the rest.

Tonbridge (TQ5845) On 23 July 1643 a party of Royalist rebels, driven from Sevenoaks by Col. Browne, fled to Tonbridge, breaking down the bridge over the swollen Hilden Brook behind

them (TQ585474) in an effort to hinder the pursuing Parliamentarians. Five hundred rebels attempted to hold the town and castle but were expelled after a fierce exchange with Browne's troops. It was probably this episode which prompted Parliament to order the castle slight-ed. The ruins, including a fourteenth-century gatehouse with massive flanking towers, curtain walls and a twelfth-century shell keep, stand in the town centre; they are open daily.

Upnor Castle (TQ758708) Upnor Castle was built in 1561 to guard the entrance to the Medway and the shipping moored just inside the river mouth. Extended and strengthened in the late sixteenth and early seventeenth century, the fortress comprises a blockhouse with a large pointed bastion facing the river and a gatehouse on the landward side. It was held uneventfully for Parliament throughout the first Civil War and occasionally served as a prison for captured Royalist officers. The castle was seized by the Kentish rebels in May 1648 but was swiftly retaken by Parliamentary forces. Upnor Castle remained in military use until the nineteenth century but is now a scheduled monument, open to the public daily.

Walmer Castle (TR377501) The Henrician coastal fort, comprising a central circular keep surrounded by four semicircular towers enclos-ing a small courtyard, survives intact and re-mains one of the official residences of the Lord Warden of the Cinque Ports. Walmer was siezed by Royalist rebels in June 1648 but was soon under close siege. Royalist ships tried to relieve the garrison by sea but attempts to land stores and reinforcements on 5 and 9 July were beaten back by heavy fire. The 60 rebels within aban-doned the struggle soon after and surrendered Walmer on 12 July. The castle is open daily, unless the Lord Warden is in residence.

LANCASHIRE

Much of the county is fairly bleak upland and was neither garrisoned nor fought over during the Civil War. The conflict in Lancashire focussed on control of the road which ran from Warrington via Preston and Lancaster to Carlisle and thence to Scotland. There were few engagements in the field, and barely half a dozen important garrisons. Although most of the county was secured for the King by the Earl of Derby in 1642, from the outbreak of war the southern fringes of Lancashire fell under the influence of Parliamentarian Greater Manchester and during the first half of 1643 much of the county was captured by Assheton. The scattering of Derby's army at Whalley and the departure of the Earl himself crippled the Royalist cause in the area and by the end of the year the King's men were restricted to a handful of strongholds. Scottish Royalist armies marched through in 1648 and 1651; in August 1648 Cromwell pursued them to Preston and beyond, his only recorded visit to Lancashire.

Not THE Philip Sidney died 1580s

Right: Penshurst Place, Kent. In the 1650s this fine manor-house was the country seat of Philip Sidney, Viscount Lisle, heir to the earldom of Leicester. One of the few members of the old aristocracy actively to support Cromwell and a Protectoral Councillor, he left money in his will to a couple of his bastards, apparently sired during the 1650s.

Below: Astley Hall, Lancs. The richly carved and canopied oak four-poster is reputed to be the bed upon which Cromwell slept when he stopped here sometime after the battle of Preston. His riding boots, too wet to wear, were left at Astley when he continued his journey south.

Astley Hall (SD574184)

Astley Hall, Chorley, a richly plastered half-timbered hall, was built by the Charnock family in the sixteenth century. It was subsequently renovated and extended on several occasions – the front was redesigned in the 1660s – but much of the Elizabethan building survives. It is now an art gallery and museum, open daily. According to tradition Cromwell spent a night here in August 1648 after the Battle of Preston; his boots and the large oak bed in which he slept are on display within the hall.

Cromwell's movements at this time are well-documented and seem to rule out a night halt at Astley. On 17 August he fought the Scots outside Preston and then entered the town late in the day; if he had any sleep that night, it was probably in a building in or very near Preston (see Walton le Dale). On the 18th he marched south from Preston and spent the night quartered in open ground to the north of Wigan. If there is any truth in the tradition, it is more likely that Cromwell and the other senior officers stopped at Astley sometime around midday on the 18th to shelter from the driving rain and to snatch a few hours sleep before continuing their journey towards Wigan.

Blackburn (SD6827)

Houghton's Royalists occupied Blackburn unopposed in November 1642 but were expelled later in the month by a night attack led by Shuttleworth and Starkie. Thereafter neither side garrisoned the weakly defended town.

Clitheroe (SD743417)

The medieval hilltop castle housed a Royalist garrison in 1643–44 but was evacuated in August 1644 following the defeat of the northern Royalists at Marston Moor. It was slighted by Parliament some years later. The remains of the small twelfth-century square keep and the inner bailey wall stand on a limestone knoll above the town.

On 16 August 1648 the advanced guard of the Parliamentary army skirmished in the town with the rear of the retreating Scottish Royalists. Cromwell himself passed through Clitheroe later in the day.

Gawthorpe Hall (SD806341)

Restored by Barry in the nineteenth century, Gawthorpe Hall is a compact three storey fortified hall built in 1600 around an earlier square tower. It was owned by the Shuttleworth family in the seventeenth century and although some Shuttleworths fought for the King in the Civil War, the family home was garrisoned for Parliament by Col. Richard Shuttleworth. It saw little action. The well-preserved hall is open on Wednesdays and at weekends during the summer.

Greenhalgh Castle (SD500452)

Greenhalgh Castle outside Garstang is a rectangular fortified hall with corner towers. Built by a Stanley Earls of Derby at the end of the fifteenth century, it was garrisoned for the King by their descendant 150 years later. The Royalist garrison withstood one siege in summer 1644 but fell later in the year, a victim of the general demise of the Royalist cause in the area after Marston Moor. The castle was demolished by Parliament in 1649 and only fragments of walls and of one of the corner towers now remain. The ruins stand on private land but can be viewed from a public footpath which runs close by.

Hodder Bridge (SD705392)

The medieval three arched bridge, still sometimes called 'Cromwell's Bridge', stands next to the present modern road bridge across the Hodder. Cromwell held an impromptu Council of War here on 16 August 1648 to discuss the movement of the Scottish Royalists and the Parliamentary response. It was decided to march straight for Preston and the Parliamentary army immediately crossed the bridge and headed south-west towards the Scottish position.

Hoghton or Houghton Tower (SO622265)

Hoghton Tower was built by Thomas Hoghton in the 1560s, a fortified hilltop mansion in the form of a double quadrangle, with a cross wing and gatehouse separating the outer and inner courts. Sir Gilbert Hoghton garrisoned the place for the King at the end of 1642. The Royalist tenure was brief, however, for the garrison was attacked by Col. Starkie in February 1643 and surrendered almost immediately. By accident or design, the Royalist powder stored in the central gatehouse exploded as the hall was being handed over, wrecking that part of the building and killing Capt. Starkie and at least sixty other men. Hoghton Tower was restored after the war and has been remodelled on several occasions since. It is open to the public on summer weekends.

Hornby Castle (SD587687)

There was a castle on the site by the twelfth century, but the present remains date from the fourteenth and fifteenth centuries, when the fortress was rebuilt by Lord Conyers. Hornby passed to the Stanleys in the late fifteenth century and was garrisoned for the King by the Earl of Derby in 1642. Col. Assheton's Parliamentarians attacked the place in June 1643; as one party diverted the Royalists by assaulting the gatehouse, their colleagues forced an entry to the east and set fire to the castle. The King's men were smoked out and the castle was gutted. The remains, including part of the keep and curtain wall, stand behind the present 'castle', a spectacular Victorian pile incorporating fragments of its Tudor predecessor. Neither castle nor grounds are open to the public.

Lancaster (SD4761) Lancaster's involvement in the Civil War was brief but bloody. Neither side initially garrisoned the place and the Parliamentarians were able to occupy the town without serious opposition in February 1643. They were almost immediately attacked by the Earl of Derby, who overran and violently sacked the town and laid siege to the castle, in which up to 600 Parliamentary troops had taken refuge; the approach of a relieving force compelled Derby to fall back. A second siege in May was equally unsuccessful. Thereafter the Parliamentarians held town and castle almost unchallenged and Lancaster became the centre for operations throughout the north of the county. The Scottish Royalist army marched through in 1648 and 1651, but on both occasions it soon moved on without seriously attempting to capture the castle and its large Parliamentary garrison.

Only part of the fortress which saw action in the Civil War survives today. Much of the castle has been completely demolished and other sections were remodelled beyond recognition in the eighteenth and nineteenth century. Most of the site is now covered by the county court and gaol, both post-Civil War. The main medieval survival is John of Gaunt's great gatehouse, a large late fourteenth-century building, the gateway flanked by two octagonal towers. Slight earthworks on the south-west side may date from the Civil War.

Lathom House (SD4609) The present eighteenth-century Lathom House stands on or near the site of the medieval fortress of the Earls of Derby, a massive fortified mansion in red sandstone built around a great tower, the Eagle Tower. The house was defended by a moat and an outer curtain wall with nine mural towers and a gatehouse. A major Royalist stronghold from the outbreak of the Civil War, Lathom held out long after the collapse of the King's cause throughout the surrounding region. In January 1644 Fairfax summoned and invested Lathom with 2,500 Parliamentarians. Lady Derby and her 350-strong garrison endured a three month siege, lifted on 27 May at the approach of Prince Rupert. Col. Egerton resumed the siege later in the year, but not until 2 December 1645

did the defenders, then under the command of Col. Rosthorn, finally surrender Lathom. By holding out for so long, the Royalist garrison had tied down large numbers of Parliamentary troops and thus hampered the war effort. In revenge, Parliament ordered the mansion razed in 1646. So complete was the destruction that the position of the medieval fortress cannot now be located with certainty. Although the present Lathom House may stand on the site (SD459091), its surroundings seem inconsistent with contemporary descriptions of the Civil War stronghold. Extensive earthworks ½ mile south east, on a slight rise above a stream and amid post-seventeenth-century woods, may mark the site of the medieval fortress (SD466085).

Longridge (SD6037) Early on 17 August 1648 the rear guard of the Scottish Royalist army under Langdale was surprised here by units of the Parliamentary army led by Cols Hodgson and Smithson. The Royalists briefly attempted to hold the main street through the town but soon turned and fell back south-west, towards Preston. The main Parliamentary army under Cromwell passed through Longridge later in the morning.

Preston (SD5429) The town changed hands several times during the first Civil War but was, for the most part, under Parliamentary control. Johan Rosworm designed a circuit of earthwork defences.

The decisive battle of the second Civil War was fought at Preston on 17 August 1648 when the Parlimentry army under Cromwell caught and scattered part of the Scottish Royalist invasion force led by Hamilton, Callendar and Langdale. The Royalist force of 20,000 men was far larger than the Parliamentary army, but Cromwell skillfully exploited his enemy's disunity and never engaged the whole Royalist army.

By 17 August the King's men had reached the Preston area on their march south, but they had become dangerously strung out, with much of their Foot still approaching Preston as their Horse left Wigan, several miles to the south. The Royalist rear fell back from Longridge in the early morning, pursued all the way by advanced units of the Parliamentary army. Langdale halted his men two miles north-east of Preston and attempted to hold the sunken lane from Longridge to Preston at the point where it left the open space of Ribbleton Moor and ran through an area of hedges and enclosures. The Royalist high command in Preston was probably unaware that its rear was faced by the whole weight of the Parliamentary army and Hamilton refused to send Langdale any reinforcements. Thus Langdale's men were heavily outnumbered when Cromwell attacked at around 4 p.m., his main force charging down the road as flanking units set off to cut their way through the enclosures on each side of the lane. The fight was long and fierce but Langdale's men were pushed back, at first slowly, then in rout, and by evening Cromwell had entered Preston.

The Scottish Foot had hurriedly departed by this time, leaving units to guard the two vital bridges over the Ribble and the Darwen (SD552287 and SD557280 respectively) to the south of the town. But after further fighting, the heavily outnumbered Royalist guards were pushed back and the bridges captured.

Cromwell had faced only part of the Scottish Royalist army at Preston but had nonetheless scored a decisive victory. By the end of the day roughly a quarter of the original invasion force had been killed or captured and the remainder were fleeing south in disorder.

The area to the north-east of the town around which fighting was fiercest has since been built over and absorbed into Preston; the sunken lane of 1648 is now the main road through the north-eastern suburb of Ribbleton (SD5631).

Stonyhurst College (SD690392)

Despite many later alterations and extensions, Stonyhurst remains at heart the late Elizabethan quadrangular house built for Sir Robert Sherburne in the 1590s. Cromwell stayed here overnight on 16–17 August while on his way south-west to intercept the Scottish Royalists around Preston. The table on which he supposedly slept is in the Great Hall. Stonyhurst is now a Roman Catholic College and is not usually open to the public.

Thurland Castle (SD610730)

The medieval castle was garrisoned for the King at the outbreak of the Civil War but changed hands three times in the following year. In June 1643 local Parliamentarians captured the castle but did not garrison it and Sir John Girlington's Royalists quickly returned. In August a second Parliamentary force under Col. Rigby appeared before the castle, which surrendered two months later following a prolonged siege and a heavy bombardment. The old fortress was destroyed by fire in

the nineteenth century and the present 'castle' is a late Victorian mock-Tudor fortified mansion surrounded by the restored and remodelled moat which once protected its medieval predecessor.

Walton le Dale (SD5528)

According to tradition, a thatched seventeenth-century inn, the Unicorn (now a restaurant), in the lane leading from Darwen Bridge became Cromwell's HQ after the Battle of Preston. From here he directed the mopping-up operations around the town and despatched units south to pursue the fleeing Royalists; he may have spent the night of 17–18 August here. A Cromwell Association plaque on the outer wall records the building's link with Cromwell.

Whalley (SD7336)

In April 1643 Col. Ralph Assheton sent a Parliamentary force north from Rochdale to draw Derby's men away from the towns in the north and west of the county. The Earl called together his forces and stationed them around Whalley in the hope of blocking and intercepting the Parliamentarians; Derby himself quartered in the abbey. A detachment of Horse and Foot sent off south-east along the Padiham road to look for Assheton's men stumbled straight into an ambush and were put to flight by Parliamentary musketeers lying in wait by the road where it crossed the Sabden Brook. The Parliamentarians then swept down into Whalley and the main Royalist army, drawn up on low ground around the river Calder, made no attempt to stand and fight and instead turned and fled westwards in disorder. A partial stand at Lango Green (SD7034) was ineffective and the panic-stricken Royalists continued their disorderly flight along the Ribble valley.

The action at Whalley by no means finished the Royalist cause in the area – Derby escaped to the Isle of Man, several Royalist strongholds held out for another year or more and not until the destruction of the King's northern army at Marston Moor fifteen months later was the area finally secure for Parliament. Nonetheless the victory at Whalley lifted the immediate Royalist threat to much of Lancashire and permanently altered the balance of power in the area in favour of Parliament.

LEICESTERSHIRE

Lords Stamford and Grey secured Leicestershire for Parliament in autumn 1642 and most of the county remained under Parliamentary control throughout the Civil War. The King's men established a number of bases on the fringes of the county, chiefly Ashby de la Zouch in the north-west and Belvoir in the north-east, major centres of Royalist operations; both held out until early 1646. The county town was brutally sacked by Rupert's men in 1645, but otherwise Leicestershire suffered little more than fairly minor Royalist raids. Cromwell passed through the county on several occasions in 1643 and 1644 and was briefly based here in June 1645 after the Battle of Naseby. He passed through the county again in 1648 and 1650–51 on his way to and from Scotland.

Ashby de la Zouch (SK361166) A Royalist stronghold throughout the Civil War, the fifteenth-century castle was garrisoned for the King by Henry Hastings at the outbreak of war and became a centre for Royalist activities over a wide area of north-west Leicestershire and the adjoining counties. Town and castle were occasionally raided by Parliamentary units from Leicester, but not until autumn 1645 were the Parliamentarians strong enough to launch a sustained campaign against Ashby. The town was quickly overrun and the castle invested; it surrendered in the following February after a long siege. The fortress was slighted in 1648 and the south wall of the Hastings Tower and much of the outer defences were brought down by mines. The present extensive ruins, including the massive four storey tower added by Lord Hastings in the 1470s, are open daily.

Belvoir Castle (SK820337) The spectacular Gothic pile overlooking the Vale of Belvoir is the latest in a succession of buildings on the site stretching back to the eleventh century. Robert de Todeni's Norman castle was repeatedly strengthened and partially rebuilt over the succeeding centuries and was extensively modernised by the Earl of Rutland in the sixteenth. The castle changed hands several times during the opening year of the Civil War but by the latter half of 1643 the Royalists had secured the place and installed a large garrison. Like Ashby to the west, Belvoir became a major Royalist stronghold and a base for operations over a wide area; it, too, survived long after the general collapse of the King's cause in the East Midlands. Cromwell was around Belvoir in late April 1644 but apparently made no real attempt to take the fortress, and not until autumn 1645 did the Parliamentarians mount a prolonged campaign against the Royalist outpost. Col. Poyntz arrived before the castle in October and over the following months he gradually tightened his grip, overrunning the outer earthworks

and cutting the garrison's external water supply. The King's men surrendered in January 1646. The castle was slighted three years later and has been rebuilt several times since. In consequence very little of the fortress which saw action in the Civil War is now visible. The lower part of the Stainton Tower is believed to date from the sixteenth century and odd fragments of masonry elsewhere are probably late medieval or Tudor. Belvoir Castle is open to the public during the summer.

Bosworth Field (SK402002) The open ground above Market Bosworth is famous for its role in deciding an earlier conflict. On 1 July 1644 it was the scene of a much smaller engagement, when a Royalist raiding party from Ashby was surprised here and scattered by Col. Babbington's Parliamentarians.

Bradgate (SK534102) Bradgate was the principal country seat of the Parliamentarian Henry Grey, 1st Earl of Stamford. Built by his predecessor Thomas Grey, Marquis of Dorset, at the end of the fifteenth century, Stamford's fortified home was attacked and sacked by local Royalists at the outbreak of the Civil War. The Earl returned here after an inglorious war – he occupied Hereford in September 1642 but abandoned the place in December, he was heavily defeated by Hopton at Stratton (Cornwall) in the following May and he surrendered Exeter to the besieging Royalists later in the year. He declared for the King in 1659, survived the Restoration unmolested, and lived quietly at Bradgate until his death in 1673. The house was abandoned in the 1730s and rapidly fell to ruin; parts of three towers and of the adjoining walls remain standing. The chapel alone survives in good order, restored and reroofed this century; the 1st Earl and his wife lie inside, beneath a large table tomb bearing recumbent effigies of the couple.

Right: Ashby de la Zouch Castle, Leics. The Royalist strongpoint and centre of operations fell to Parliament in 1646 and was slighted two years later. The early medieval castle had passed to Edward IV's Chamberlain, Lord Hastings, in 1464 and he completely overhauled its defences, adding the huge tower which still bears his name.

Below: Staunton Harold Church, Leics. One of the very few churches built during the Interregnum, Holy Trinity was begun in 1653. As the inscription has it: 'When all things Sacred were throughout ye nation Either demollisht or profaned Sir Robert Shirley, Barronet, Founded this church, whose singular praise it is To have done ye best things in ye worst times, and hoped them in the most callamitous. The righteous shall be had in everlasting remembrance.' Shirley himself died in the Tower in 1656, aged 29. Holy Trinity survives almost unaltered, a curious mixture of Gothic architecture and Jacobean furnishings, the box pews still complete with their brass candlesticks. The rather poor ceiling of assorted clouds and swirls was painted by Samuel Kyrk in 1655 and probably represents the theme of order out of chaos.

Burley (SK885102) Burley House, built by the
1st Duke of Buckingham in the 1620s, served
for much of the Civil War as the Parliamentary
HQ for the old county of Rutland. It was hastily
evacuated in June 1645 when the Royalist capture of Leicester instilled near panic in the
surrounding area. The Royalists marched
through later in the month and breached the
outer defences of the house to prevent its reoccupation. Parliament completed the destruction
by slighting the house in the following year. No
trace of Buckingham's mansion survives and the
present Burley House dates from the very end of
the seventeenth century.

Coleorton (SK4017) Coleorton served as a
Parliamentary garrison for most of the war,
enduring frequent raids and evacuated from
time to time – for instance, the troops temporarily pulled out in May 1645 after the fall of
Leicester. The garrison was housed in the
sixteenth-century manor-house of the Beaumont
family, of which nothing remains. The present
hall on the site, a Gothic ashlar mansion, dates
from the early nineteenth century.

Cotes (SK5520) The decayed medieval village
of Cotes stood at an important crossing of the
river Soar and was the scene of several skirmishes. In March 1644, for instance, a Parliamentary force under Hartop engaged a party
of Royalists, moving to relieve Newark, around
the bridge; Hartop fell back on the approach of
Royalist reinforcements under Loughborough.

After the war Sir Christopher Packe acquired
Cotes Hall, the Tudor seat of the Skipwith
family, and he spent the last years of his life in
retirement here. The hall was destroyed by fire
in the eighteenth century.

Hemington Hall (SK4528) Medieval Hemington Hall served as a minor Royalist base during
the Civil War, defended by trenches and earthworks on the slope above. There is no record
of fighting here and the hall was probably
abandoned as Royalist fortunes waned. The
weathered earthworks survive and below them,
to the west of the church, stand the remains of
the hall, two stone ranges at right angles to each
other.

Hinckley (SP4293) In March 1644 a fierce but
indecisive skirmish developed around St Mary's
as a Parliamentary unit arrived at Hinckley and
attempted to rescue some of their colleagues,
held prisoner within the village church.

Kirby Bellars (SK7117) The early seventeenth-
century great house in Kirby Park was garrisoned for Parliament throughout the Civil War;
it was one of the bases hastily evacuated in June
1645 following the fall of Leicester, but seems to
have escaped Royalist attention. The old iron-
stone manor-house still stands, but it was dras-
tically altered and remodelled in the nineteenth
century. Neither house nor park is open to the
public.

Leicester (SK5804) After 2½ uneventful years
as the Parliamentary HQ for the county, Leicester was seriously threatened for the first time on
29 May 1645 by the arrival of Prince Rupert
and 5,000 Royalist troops. The King's men
surrounded the town and established a battery
on Raw Dykes, the decayed banks of the Roman
aqueduct beside the Aylestone Road. The walls
and banks which defended the town were
breached in several places on 30 May and
Rupert's men stormed the place in the early
hours of the 31st. The 2,000-strong Parliamentary garrison fiercely resisted, but despite heavy
fighting around West Bridge, East Gate, the
Newarke and St Margaret's churchyard, Leicester fell to the Royalists. Although pro-
Parliamentary accounts probably exaggerated
the ensuing massacre, there is little doubt that
Rupert exacted a bloody and violent revenge on
the town. The Prince and most of his men soon
marched on, leaving a small garrison to hold the
town. A fortnight later Fairfax and the main
Parliamentary army appeared before Leicester,
and Governor Hastings surrendered the town on
18 June after a two day siege and bombardment.

The Roman and medieval walls and the Civil
War earthworks have largely disappeared, the
victims of neglect and urban expansion. Parts of
the castle – the Parliamentarians' HQ and magazine – still stand, including the Norman motte
and the twelfth-century Great Hall, extensively
renovated in the eighteenth century and now the
county court. Two gates into the fifteenth-
century outer bailey, which was known as the
'New Work' or 'Newarke', also survive.

Cromwell was in and around Leicester on
several occasions during the Civil War and was
with Fairfax's forces on 16–20 June 1645 during the siege and capture of the town. He usually
stopped for the night in Leicester on his way to
and from Scotland in 1648–51 and contemporary accounts talk of him being feasted by the
Mayor on such occasions. The banquets may
have been held in the Old Guildhall in Guildhall
Lane, a fourteenth-century building with an
early Stuart Mayor's Parlour. The Guildhall is
open daily.

Lowesby Hall (SK7207) Although Col. Hutchinson, the Parliamentary soldier and republican, possessed considerable property in the north of Nottinghamshire, he also acquired the early Stuart mansion of Lowesby Hall. It was there that his widow wrote her account of Hutchinson after the Restoration. The present hall, a two storey brick mansion, is early Georgian, but it incorporates parts of the seventeenth-century stone mansion. Many of the woods, fishponds and terraces which Hutchinson laid out in the grounds of Lowesby Hall are still to be seen.

Market Harborough (SP7387) The Church of St Dionysius served as a temporary prison for some of the many Royalists captured or wounded at Naseby. This seems to be the origin of lurid and probably unfounded tales of massacre here after the battle.

Melton Mowbray (SK7519) Melton Mowbray was a Parliamentary base throughout the Civil War, its garrison enduring repeated Royalist raids from Belvoir and other centres. The worst attack took place in November 1643 when Col. Lucas and a party from Belvoir and Newark surprised the garrison and carried off 300 prisoners. Fifteen months later, in February 1645, Langdale's Horse surprised and scattered Rossiter's Parliamentary force just outside the town.

North Luffenham (SK928033) In autumn 1642 a 200-strong Royalist garrison was established in Henry Noel's fortified house, Luffenham House, which stood immediately west of the village church. In the following spring 1,200 Parliamentarians under Grey and Wray swooped down on the garrison, which surrendered after a brief bombardment. The hall was then plundered and burnt and today nothing survives except a dry ditch, the remains of the former moat, just west of the churchyard. (The large house to the east of the church now known as Luffenham Hall is a completely different building on a different site.)

A small circular mound surrounded by a ditch and bank stands nearby to the south of the river Chater and west of the road from North Luffenham to Morcott. Probably prehistoric in origin, it is said to be the spot on which Parliamentary guns were planted during the bombardment of the old hall.

Noseley (SP737985) Sir Arthur Hesilrige was born, brought up and spent much of his life at Noseley Hall, the family's Leicestershire seat. A prominent opponent of the King from the beginning of the Long Parliament, Hesilrige was one of the five Members whom Charles I attempted to arrest in January 1642. Hesilrige and his distinctively armoured troop of 'lobsters' saw service in southern England throughout the first Civil War; in 1648–51 he served in northern England and Scotland. Hesilrige returned to politics during the 1650s and became an increasingly outspoken opponent of the Protectorate. He was not a regicide, but he was arrested at the Restoration and held in the Tower, where he died in 1661. Although his house was later demolished – the present Noseley Hall is eighteenth-century – the adjoining thirteenth-century Chapel of St Mary survives intact. Hesilrige and his two wives lie buried here beneath an ornate marble monument. Sir Arthur rests in effigy on a table tomb, watched over by his second wife, who lies on her side next to him; beneath them kneel their twelve children.

Prestwold Hall (SK578215) Sir Christopher Packe, Parliamentarian, City politician and sometime Lord Mayor of London, acquired extensive property in Leicestershire during the 1650s and 1660s, including a mansion at Cotes and Prestwold Hall. He was barred from holding further public office at the Restoration but otherwise escaped unmolested and continued to live quietly here and at his other properties in London and Cambridgeshire until his death at Cotes in 1682. His house at Prestwold has disappeared – the present hall is eighteenth-century – but the medieval Chapel of St Andrew next to the hall escaped demolition and survives intact. Packe lies buried near the impressive mural monument in the chancel which shows a semi-reclining effigy of Sir Christopher dressed in his mayoral robes, with the Arms of the City of London, the City mace and other insignia by his side.

Staunton Harold (SK380209) As the inscription over the west door relates, Holy Trinity Church was begun by the Royalist Sir Richard Shirley in 1653, and although not completed until 1665, it is substantially an Interregnum church, one of very few built. It has been little altered and remains a mid-seventeenth-century church inside and out, with a short aisled nave, chancel, west tower, west gallery and screen and box pews.

LINCOLNSHIRE

Although the county was secured for Parliament at the outbreak of the Civil War, the Royalists soon began making inroads into the region and by autumn 1643 much of Lincolnshire had fallen to the King. The Royalist threat receded thereafter but fighting continued well into 1645 and the area was frequently raided by Prince Rupert and by troops from the bases at Belvoir and Newark. A party of Royalist rebels marched through the area in 1648. Cromwell was frequently in Lincolnshire during the 1640s and spent much of 1643 on campaign within the county. He had been present during the Edgehill campaign and had worked hard in 1642–43 to secure East Anglia and to organise the defence of Cambridgeshire, but it was in Lincolnshire during summer 1643 that Cromwell first experienced prolonged military action and began to rise to national prominence.

Ancaster Heath (SK9843) In March 1643 a large Royalist force led by Charles Cavendish and including men from the Belvoir and Newark garrisons advanced into southern Lincolnshire in the hope of cutting the county in two and breaking the lines of communication to Cambridgeshire and the south. The Royalists took Grantham and pushed on towards Boston. On 11 April 1643 their path was blocked at Ancaster by 1,500 Parliamentarians under Lord Willoughby and the younger Hotham. In a brief engagement on heathland just outside the town, the Parliamentarians were brushed aside by the larger and better organised Royalist army.

Belleau (TL4078) The old manor-house at Belleau was owned by Lord Willoughby during the 1640s and was acquired by Sir Henry Vane junior after the Civil War. Vane lived here and at Raby (Durham) until the Restoration. Sections of the sixteenth-century moated manor-house survive and are now incorporated within a later farmhouse and outbuildings; an octagonal dovecote, once part of the Tudor estate, stands near the Church of St John the Baptist. Within the largely nineteenth-century church (TL402785) is a modern memorial to Sir Henry Vane.

Belton (SK9339) On 13 May 1643 Belton was the scene of a confused skirmish between Parliamentarians under Cromwell and Willoughby and 1,200 Royalists from Newark and Gainsborough led by Cavendish and Henderson. Our knowledge of the engagement rests largely on a brief and sometimes dubious account given in one of Cromwell's letters. The Parliamentarians had just retaken Grantham and early on the 13th Cromwell led his troops out of the town towards Newark in a fruitless attempt to find the Royalist forces known to be in the area. In fact, Cavendish's men were already very close to Grantham and in the morning they attacked and scattered a Parliamentary outpost stationed around Belton. The main engagement took place

that evening, when Willoughby and Cromwell faced Cavendish's army on flat land between the river Witham and the present park gates of Belton House (which was built forty years after the Civil War), south-east of Tolthorp. After the dragoons had exchanged fire, Cromwell launched a Cavalry attack which seems to have surprised and shaken the Royalists – possibly they were off-guard, not expecting their opponents to give battle at 10 p.m. A brief mêlée in failing light left 100 Royalists dead or wounded, 45 captured and the rest falling back northwards in disorder.

Bolingbroke Castle (TF349648) The Norman motte and bailey castle in Old Bolingbroke, enlarged and strengthened by John of Gaunt in the fourteenth century, was occupied and garrisoned for the King in summer 1643. The Royalists were under siege by September and surrendered to the Earl of Manchester in the following month. It was then garrisoned for Parliament, but the troops were soon withdrawn for service elsewhere and the castle slighted to prevent its reoccupation. Some sections, including the gatehouse, survived until the nineteenth century, but very little now remains. Recent excavations have revealed extensive foundations, but nothing more than odd fragments of masonry are now visible on and around the motte.

Boston (TF3244) Boston was the principal Parliamentary stronghold and magazine in the south-east of the county, held for Parliament without serious challenge throughout the war. Cromwell passed through the town on many occasions in 1643 and was based here for much of September and early October.

Cressey Hall (TF225304) In one of the earliest engagements of the Civil War in Lincolnshire, Sir Anthony Irby surprised and scattered a party of local Royalists before Cressey Hall. A small Parliamentary garrison was established in the late medieval moated hall, but the troops were

Right: Crowland, Lincs. The carved figure on fourteenth-century Trinity Bridge, sometimes jokingly identified as Cromwell, is in reality Christ or the Virgin and almost certainly came from the medieval abbey.

Below: It was in Lincolnshire during 1643 that Cromwell first saw serious action and his capture in April of Crowland Abbey marks perhaps the true beginning of his military career. Robert Walker's much-copied portrait of Cromwell, executed sometime in the mid to late 1640s, shows the still relatively youthful and active soldier; subsequent service in Ireland and Scotland in 1649–51 broke his health and markedly aged him.

Below right: Tattershall Castle, Lincs. The huge fifteenth-century keep, which dominates the surrounding countryside, was built by Ralph, Lord Cromwell, from nearly one million bricks in local red clay.

soon withdrawn to serve in more important bases in the region and Cressey played no further part in the conflict. The hall thus survived the Civil War intact, but it was burnt to the ground in 1791 and nothing survives except the remains of the moat near the road and the present nineteenth-century hall.

Crowland (TF242105)

The medieval Abbey of Crowland and the village which grew up around it stood on an island of rising ground surrounded by low marshland. Most of the monastic buildings were demolished at or soon after the Dissolution, though parts of the great abbey church were retained and converted into a secular church. On 25 March 1643 a pro-Royalist faction within Crowland secured the village for the King and occupied and fortified the village church and other surviving sections of the abbey. Local Parliamentarians under Hobart and Irby soon surrounded Crowland, and operations were stepped up when Cromwell and his troops joined the siege on 25 April. Their heavy artillery pounded Royalist positions for three days until the King's men surrendered on the 28th.

The village saw further action in 1644. The Parliamentary garrison was temporarily evacuated in March as Royalists passed through. It was evacuated again in October when the Royalist army returned and on this occasion the King's men left a garrison to hold Crowland. Fairfax and Rossiter laid siege to the place as soon as the main Royalist force had marched on, but heavy autumn rains flooded the surrounding land and saved the garrison from direct attack. The Royalists were eventually starved into surrender at the end of the year.

Parts of the abbey church, including the north aisle and tower, still serve as the village church, incorporated within the largely nineteenth-century building; nearby are the remains of the nave and other sections of the medieval church.

By one of the flights of steps of the triangular bridge in Crowland is a seated figure holding a sphere. Despite suggestions that it is Oliver Cromwell with a bun, it is almost certainly an effigy of Christ or the Virgin Mary, crowned and holding an orb.

Denton (SK8632)

On 29 October 1644 Col. Rossiter intercepted and captured a Royalist troop at Denton. They were *en route* to Crowland to relieve the Parliamentary siege of the newly-established garrison.

Donington (TF2035)

Donington was the scene of several skirmishes 1643–44, the most important of which took place on 13 June 1643 when Royalists from Belvoir (Leics) surprised and routed a party of Parliamentarians from Boston. Cromwell himself had passed through the village just three days before.

Gainsborough (SK8189)

Gainsborough was an attractive and vulnerable target during the Civil War, a prosperous port and commercial centre defended by nothing more than earthwork banks and ditches and standing in an area which, though controlled by Parliament for much of the war, was dangerously close to Newark and other Royalist bases. Gainsborough was captured by a raiding party from Newark in January 1643 and remained in Royalist hands for six months. On 20 July Willoughby launched a surprise attack and overwhelmed the Earl of Kingston's men, retaking the town for Parliament. He was, however, almost immediately besieged by Charles Cavendish's Royalist army and summoned assistance.

On 28 July a 1,200-strong relieving force under Cromwell and Meldrum approached Gainsborough. They engaged and overcame Cavendish's advanced guard near the village of Lea (SK8286) and then pressed on over steep and difficult ground towards Cavendish's main force, drawn up on the hill immediately east of Gainsborough. The ensuing fight was fierce but brief, for the Parliamentarians soon broke the enemy Horse and began to push the Royalists from the field. Cavendish, however, had kept some troops in reserve, and at this point he charged the flank of the now disorganised and careless Parliamentarians. Cromwell, too, had held back three troops from the chase and with these he swooped down on the rear of Cavendish's reserve, breaking the last surviving element of the Royalist army and completing the rout. Cavendish was fatally wounded as he and his men were pursued downhill into the marshland beside the Trent. Long afterwards, the names of fields and other features in this area recalled the battle and ensuing slaughter – Redcoats Field, Graves Close and Cavendish Bog.

Cromwell had relieved Gainsborough and spent the night in the town but the respite was short-lived. On the following morning Newcastle and the main Royalist army were spotted approaching from the north and although Cromwell managed to get his troops away and back to Grantham, the garrison was left in a hopeless position; Willoughby surrendered on 31 July. The town changed hands twice more – it was retaken by Meldrum in December but evacuated in March 1644 at the approach of Prince Rupert – before it was finally secured for

Parliament by the Earl of Manchester in summer 1644.

Grantham (SK9135)

Although the town was held for Parliament for most of the war, it was vulnerable to attack from nearby Belvoir and Newark and changed hands several times in 1643. Royalists took the town in January but were promptly ejected. Two months later, on 23 March, a much larger force under Charles Cavendish stormed and captured Grantham and, although they did not garrison the place, their presence in the vicinity severed the main road between London and York and seemed to herald a full-scale invasion of Lincolnshire. In response, Willoughby, Hotham and Cromwell rendezvoused at Sleaford on 9 May and re-entered Grantham two days later. Although they had retaken the town without opposition, Cavendish's forces were still in the area and soon moved to expel them. On 13 May the armies clashed 2½ miles north-east of the town (see Belton).

Grimsthorpe Castle (TF045228)

Gilbert de Gant's thirteenth-century quadrangular fortress was extensively modernised during the sixteenth century when a fine south front was added. In the seventeenth century the castle was owned by the Berties, Earls of Lindsey, and they garrisoned the place for the King late in 1643. Grimsthorpe was captured in the following April by the Earl of Manchester, whose men proceeded to sack and partly demolish the place. It was repaired and remodelled by Vanbrugh and much of the present building dates from the eighteenth and nineteenth century. Of the fortress which saw action in the Civil War, there survive the four medieval corner towers, the Elizabethan south front and several early modern interiors. Grimsthorpe is open daily during August.

Horncastle (TF2669)

According to a strong and plausible tradition, Cromwell stayed in Horncastle after the Battle of Winceby, lodging at a house in West Street, now demolished, which stood next to the present Cromwell House. On 11 October he supposedly supervised the burial of Sir Ingram Hopton, a Royalist officer killed at Winceby as he was about to attack the unhorsed Cromwell. Hopton lies in St Mary's Church, near a later monument which describes Cromwell as an 'arch rebel'. The church also contains a number of relics found on the battlefield.

Hougham House (SK888442)

The medieval moated manor-house of the Bussey and Brundell families was garrisoned for Parliament during the Civil War. Near the western border of Lincolnshire, Hougham was always vulnerable to raids from Newark. In one such attack, a party of Newark Royalists surprised and captured Hougham in an early morning raid on 10 June 1645, only to fall themselves to Col. Rossiter in the course of a fierce counter-attack launched later the same day. The present stone mansion east of the church is Georgian, but it incorporates sections of its medieval and Jacobean predecessor; nearby are the remains of the medieval moat which surrounded the old house. The house and grounds are private but a public footpath runs close by.

Lincoln (SK9771)

By the seventeenth century the Roman and medieval defences at Lincoln were semi-ruinous and the town could put up little resistance to a determined attack. Thus although Lincoln was held for Parliament for much of the war, it never became a major base and it repeatedly fell to Royalist raids from Newark and, in 1644, from Prince Rupert's forces. The county town was plundered again in summer 1648 as Royalist rebels marched through. Cromwell was here in July 1643 and May 1644 and he spent most of August 1644 at Lincoln, kicking his heels while Manchester did nothing.

The extensive ruins of the Norman castle, open daily, stand in the north-west corner of the old town. Fragments of the Roman and medieval walls survive, together with Eastgate, Newport Arch and the foundations of Lower Westgate.

Mablethorpe Hall (TF492846)

In August 1643, at the height of their fortunes in Lincolnshire, the King's men established an outpost at Mablethorpe. The garrison fell to Parliamentary forces towards the end of the year. The Royalists garrisoned Mablethorpe Hall, the moated mansion of the Fitzwilliam family, one mile west of the village. The old house has been largely demolished, though fragments were incorporated in the modern farm buildings, still called Mablethorpe Hall, which stand amid the remains of the moat.

Saltfleet (TF4593)

Tradition has it that Cromwell spent the night after the Battle of Winceby – 11 October 1643 – in Saltfleet, sleeping in the seventeenth-century red brick manor-house opposite New Inn. There is, however, no contemporary evidence to place Cromwell here and the story conflicts with another unconfirmed but much more plausible tradition that he spent the night at Horncastle. Cromwell was certainly recalled to Cambridgeshire soon after the battle, and Saltfleet is hardly on the way. All that can be said in favour of the town is that Cromwell was in the general area east of Lincoln on several occasions in 1643–44 and was in Louth, about 11 miles away, on 8 October 1643, three days before the battle.

Sleaford (TF0645)   A small town in the centre of the county, Sleaford was garrisoned for Parliament for much of the war and served as a convenient base for operations over a wide area. The twelfth-century castle was very ruinous by this time and the garrison established a base in Sir Robert Carr's late medieval fortified house, the Old Place, in Boston Road about ½ mile east of the town centre. Cromwell probably lodged here on his frequent visits to the town in 1643 and 1644. A nineteenth-century 'L'-shaped house now stands on the site, though fragments of medieval masonry from the original hall show up in the garden walls. Town and garrison suffered repeated Royalist raids in 1643–44 and in March and October 1644 Sleaford fell to Prince Rupert, though on both occasions the Prince's army soon moved on and the returning Parliamentarians swiftly expelled the small garrisons left behind.

Stamford (TF0307)   The southern gateway to Lincolnshire, Civil War Stamford was defended by a medieval castle and town walls, though by the seventeenth century both were in some disrepair. The town was held for Parliament for most of the war and Cromwell was a frequent visitor, particularly during July and August 1643. However, the town lies in the very southwest of the county and was vulnerable to Royalist raids from east Leicestershire; it was captured by the King's men in April 1643 and October 1644, though on both occasions the Royalists soon departed. In summer 1648 a party of Royalists entered the town in search of arms and recruits but instead found a Parliamentary unit under Col. Waite, who attacked and dispersed the rebels.

Little now remains of the medieval defences repaired and reused during the Civil War. The castle has completely disappeared and although fragments of masonry survive, particularly around West Street and Wharf Road, most of the town walls and gates were destroyed in the eighteenth and nineteenth centuries.

Syston Park (SK9240)   Cromwell's letter of 13 May 1643 describing the capture of Grantham and the Battle of Belton was written from Syston Park, less than a mile from the scene of the engagement. Presumably Cromwell lodged in the great house after the battle while his troops quartered in the surrounding park. The private park still lies on the outskirts of the village, though the house in which Cromwell stayed has been demolished; the present Old Hall dates from the nineteenth century.

Tattershall Castle (TF211575)   Robert Tattershall's thirteenth-century castle was rebuilt by Ralph, Lord Cromwell two centuries later. Two moats and baileys surrounded the great red brick keep, four storeys high with crenellated parapets and octagonal corner towers. Tattershall was garrisoned for Parliament during most of the Civil War; it was captured and briefly held by the King's men in summer 1643. Although little now remains of the outer defences and of the domestic buildings which once stood within the baileys, the keep survives in good order, restored and consolidated at the beginning of the twentieth century, and is one of the most spectacular complete medieval brick buildings in England. Tattershall Castle is open daily.

Thorganby Hall (TF209982)   The late medieval and Tudor hall was sacked and damaged by Royalist rebels as they marched through the county in summer 1648. Although the hall was remodelled in the eighteenth century, the post-Civil War repairs are still apparent in the south and east faces of the building. Thorganby Hall is private but the exterior can be viewed from the public footpath which runs close by.

Torksey Castle (SK837788)   The Elizabethan fortified manor-house of the Jermyn family was held by Parliament during the Civil War to guard the Trent and the approach roads to Lincoln and Gainsborough. It was captured and briefly occupied by the King's men in October 1644. In the following August the Newark Royalists returned and this time they destroyed the castle before falling back at the approach of Parliamentary forces. The badly damaged fortress played no further part in the war. Torksey Castle is now a spectacular ruin, its stone and red brick west front, three storeys high and incorporating four octagonal towers, standing in a field near the church.

Wainfleet All Saints (TF4959)   The village grew up around an important crossing of the river Steeping on the main coast road north of Boston. Wainfleet was occupied by Royalist forces in August 1643 and the King's men began to construct earthwork defences around the bridge. They hastily evacuated the place in early October at the approach of part of Manchester's Parliamentary army. No trace of these Civil War earthworks survives.

Winceby (TF3168)   On 11 October 1643 the Parliamentary army under Manchester and Cromwell engaged and defeated a large Royalist force on open ground about ¾ mile north-west of Winceby. The armies drew up on parallel ridges which ran east–west but which curved round and met to the east, thus forming a horseshoe of high ground enclosing a natural amphitheatre. Manchester deployed along the southern ridge, with Cromwell in the van, the Royalists along the northern. The battle opened with the Dragoons charging forward and clashing in the low ground between the two armies. Both front lines then charged, exchanging fire at close range and engaging. In the course of the hand-to-hand fighting, Cromwell had his horse shot from under him and was attacked by Sir Ingram Hopton, who was himself cut down. Cromwell escaped unhurt but apparently played little further part in the battle. With a fierce but confused fight raging below him, Sir Thomas Fairfax led the second Par-

liamentary line along the ridge and round to the east and then charged down into the Royalist left flank, quickly breaking the enemy line. The Royalist Cavalry fled south-west, where they were trapped by high hedges and a narrow gateway and were cut down by the pursuing Parliamentary Horse; the spot was afterwards known as Slash Hollow. Although fairly small numbers had been involved, Winceby was a decisive and important Parliamentary victory, for it halted the Royalist advance south and east through Lincolnshire.

The battlefield is still open farmland to the east of the A115 near its junction with the A158. The battle symbol on Ordnance Survey maps is placed at TF315689, near the centre of the hollow.

Woolsthorpe (SK835338)   The medieval church at Woolsthorpe was held by the Royalists for much of the Civil War as an outpost of Belvoir. At the beginning of 1646, as part of the Parliamentary operation against the castle, Woolsthorpe was attacked and the church captured after a heavy bombardment which wrecked the building. It was never repaired and today the ruins still stand in the old graveyard about ¼ mile from the post-Restoration Church of St James which replaced it.

MERSEYSIDE

There was very little action within Merseyside during the Civil War. The Wirral played no part in the conflict and the only town and stronghold in the area was Liverpool, a small but prosperous port and a possible landing point for reinforcements from Ireland. Cromwell never visited the area.

Liverpool (SJ3490)   Garrisoned for Parliament in spring 1643, Liverpool was strongly defended by a medieval wall and ditch which ran in an arc round the landward side of the town; a thirteenth-century castle stood at the southern point. Rupert approached the town in June 1644 and began bombarding the stronghold with heavy artillery on the 7th. The defences held for five days, enabling Col. Moore to send men and ammunition away by sea, but on the 12th Rupert's guns finally demolished a section of wall near the northern end of the town and

the Royalists rushed in. Liverpool was then garrisoned for the King, but the town was soon isolated in a solidly Parliamentarian area and the Royalists surrendered in November after a long if half-hearted siege.

Seventeenth-century Liverpool covered the area now crossed by Duke, Water, Tithebarn, Chapel, Old Hall and Castle Streets. Sadly, the medieval walls and ditches which defended the old town have completely disappeared, as has the castle, the foundations of which lie somewhere beneath Derby Square.

NORFOLK

The county was held for Parliament without serious challenge throughout the Civil War and saw very little fighting. Minor Royalist intrigues were legion, but only at King's Lynn did their efforts bear fruit, provoking the one outbreak of major violence within Norfolk during the first Civil War. There were several pro-Royalist riots in the area in 1648, including a bloody outburst in Norwich. Cromwell toured the county in March 1643 investigating reports of Royalist activity and was present at King's Lynn later in the year, but he seems never to have returned to Norfolk after October 1643.

Great Yarmouth (TG5207) Cromwell passed through the town on 13 or 14 March 1643 on his way from Norwich to Lowestoft and he may have stopped here overnight, lodging in the house in South Quay belonging to John Carter, the leading Parliamentarian in Great Yarmouth. According to a later, rather unlikely story, Carter's house was the venue for a meeting of senior officers in 1648 at which it was decided to bring the King to trial. The house, No. 4 South Quay, was extensively altered in the eighteenth century but retains its late Tudor and Jacobean interiors. It is now a museum of domestic life.

Cromwell's granddaughter, Bridget Ireton and her husband Thomas Bandysh lived at Southtown, on the other side of the Yare, during the late seventeenth century. Both lie buried in the medieval Church of St Nicholas by St Nicholas Road, which was gutted by fire in 1942 and has since been rebuilt.

King's Lynn (TF6119) Cromwell visited King's Lynn on 20–21 March 1643 to investigate rumours of a Royalist plot and to ensure the town's loyalty to Parliament. The rumours were eventually matched by action, for on 13 August 1643 the governor, Sir Hammond L'Estrange, declared for the King, the first and only stronghold within the county to do so. The Royalists hastily repaired the town's defences, adding earthworks and bastions beyond the medieval stone walls. Local Parliamentary troops were refused admission and in late August Manchester arrived before the town, establishing his base at Setch Bridge to the south. Cromwell visited the siege in early September and reportedly supervised the placing of guns at West Lynn. The town was bombarded and St Margaret's Church hit, though little or no damage was caused. A

Civil War cannon-ball now hangs above the entrance to Hampton Court, a late medieval house and warehouse in Nelson Street. King's Lynn surrendered to Parliament on 16 September and a fortnight later, on 2 October, Cromwell visited the newly-secured town to confer with Manchester.

The Royalists' earthworks have long since disappeared but parts of the medieval stone walls survive, chiefly on the east side of the town, along Kettlewell Lane, Wyatt Street and the Walls. One gateway also remains, the South Gate, an early Tudor brick and stone building with angle turrets and battlements.

Norwich (TG2308) Cromwell was here on 12–13 and 17–19 March 1643 on his tour around the county. The town had a quiet Civil War and peace was shattered only once, in May 1648, when a series of pro-Royalist riots broke out and threatened Parliament's control of Norwich. Fleetwood's troops, stationed nearby, quickly put down the disturbances, but in the course of the troubles the magazine in the Committee House was ignited – whether by accident or design is unclear – and the resulting explosion killed 40 people, demolished the Committee House and badly damaged many buildings in the area, including St Peters Mancroft. Fairfax visited Norwich in July to survey the damage and to ensure that everything was quiet. Over 100 rioters were subsequently tried and seven or eight were shot by firing-squad in the castle grounds on 2 January 1649. The medieval castle itself played no recorded part in the war; the restored keep is now a museum of local history and possesses many relics from the period, including Civil War armour and Cromwell's death mask.

NORTHAMPTONSHIRE

Despite its size and central position, Northamptonshire saw surprisingly little action during the Civil War. Although the south-west of the county fell under the influence of Royalist Oxfordshire, most of the region was held for Parliament without serious challenge and suffered little more than minor and isolated raids. The exception was the Battle of Naseby, one of the largest and most decisive engagements of the Civil War. Cromwell was present for the battle but otherwise played no part in the war in Northamptonshire and rarely visited the county.

Althorp (SP682651) The early Tudor house, extensively rebuilt in 1790, played no significant part in the war. It does, however, contain many fine portraits from the period, including a representation of Oliver Cromwell thought to be by Walker.

Canons Ashby (SP577508) In the mid-sixteenth century the Dryden family built a quadrangular stone and brick house here on the site of the former guesthouse of the medieval priory. Extended in the early seventeenth century, Sir John Dryden's house became a base for Parliamentary units operating in the south-west of the county during the Civil War. One such unit was surprised by Royalists on the night of 18–19 August 1644 and took shelter, not in the house but in the nearby Church of St Mary, which was quickly surrounded. As the Royalists blew the doors with a petard, the Parliamentarians took refuge in the tower, but they emerged when the King's men threatened to burn the building down. The house itself survived the war intact and is now open to the public at weekends and on certain weekdays in summer. Amongst the furnishings and other relics on display is a small collection of Civil War arms and armour.

Daventry (SP5762) The final military action of the Interregnum took place just outside Daventry on 22 April 1660, when a motley Republican force under Lambert, Okey, Axtell and others was attacked by troops sent by Monck and commanded by Col. Ingoldsby, a former Parliamentarian and regicide out to earn a Royal Pardon. The engagement to the north of the town was brief and one-sided and after an exchange of fire and a short mêlée the Republican force disintegrated and Lambert was captured; he was never to know freedom again. A fortnight later the Convention Parliament declared Charles Stuart King of England.

East Farndon (SP716851) Although there is no record of fighting here, the village may have been garrisoned at some stage during the conflict, for earthworks here are sometimes described as Civil War defences. Other sources, however, suggest that they are part of the decayed medieval village.

Grafton Regis (SP7646) Although the south-west fringes of the county fell under the influence of Royalist Oxfordshire, the King's men established very few formal garrisons in the area. From time to time they attempted to garrison Henry VIII's palace at Grafton Regis, but the base was very vulnerable to Parliamentary attack and the Royalist tenure was usually brief. Eventually Skippon and 3,000 men from Newport Pagnell put an end to the outpost once and for all, capturing the garrison and then plundering and burning the house to prevent its reoccupation. A later manor-house now occupies the main site and the only part of the Tudor palace to survive is a rectangular outbuilding which stands by the road near St Mary's Church.

Holdenby House (SP693678) In spring 1647 King Charles was held by Parliament at the royal mansion at Holdenby while MPs discussed his own and the country's future. Suspicious of Parliament's intentions, an army unit under Cornet Joyce marched to Holdenby on 2 June and secured the place; two days later the King was removed to the army base in Cambridgeshire. Sir Christopher Hatton's double-warded Elizabethan mansion had been acquired by James I in 1607. After his son's execution, the house was bought by Col. Adam Baynes, a Parliamentary officer and close associate of Lambert, who proceeded to demolish most of the Tudor house. The present Holdenby House was built in the nineteenth century and incorporated odd fragments of the earlier, much larger mansion. Three of the original archways stand in the grounds, two on the lawn and the third, which bears the date 1659 and a defaced coat of arms, to the north of the modern house. The gardens are open to the public during the summer.

Kelmarsh (SP728801) After excavation in the 1960s, several earthworks in Kelmarsh were ascribed to the mid-seventeenth century and described as Civil War defences. However, there is no record of any action here and it seems likely that the earthworks, which have largely been destroyed, formed part of the decayed medieval village.

Lamport Hall (SP7574)

Although Lamport Hall was begun in the sixteenth century, much of the present building dates from the 1650s and is one of the very few country houses of the Interregnum to survive in something like its original condition. Now flanked by late seventeenth and eighteenth-century extensions, the five bay two storey block designed by John Webb in 1654–57 remains the central feature of the hall. The richly furnished hall is open on Thursdays and Sundays during the summer.

Naseby (SP6878)

Naseby was one of the largest and most decisive battles of the Civil War and the Parliamentary victory here on 14 June 1645 marked the beginning of the end of the Royalist cause in England.

Stung by the fall of Leicester, Fairfax abandoned the siege of Oxford on 5 June and marched north, determined to retake the town and engage the main Royalist army, then stationed around Daventry. Cromwell and his men joined Fairfax at Kislingbury early on 13 June. Surprised by Fairfax's approach, the King's army began marching away towards Market Harborough, closely pursued by the Parliamentarians. On the evening of the 13th Fairfax's main army was around Guilsborough, but the advanced guard entered Naseby, four miles to the north, surprising the Royalist rear lingering in and around the village. With Fairfax now so close, the King decided to turn and face his pursuers.

Both armies were on the move by the early hours of the 14th, stumbling around in the gloom and the fog, looking for each other and for a good position to give battle. Eventually the two forces drew up on either side of a slight valley, one mile to the north of Naseby; a track from Naseby to Sibbertoft – now a minor road – ran through the middle of both lines. The armies deployed in east–west lines, with the Foot in the centre and Horse on the wings. The Royalists drew up on the edge of Dust Hill, the Parliamentarians along the edge of Mill Hill, and the battle was fought in Broad Moor Valley, the wide and gently sloping valley between the two.

The Royalists moved first, advancing into the valley at around 10 a.m., but were soon met by the general Parliamentarian charge. The Parliamentary left was quickly broken by Rupert but the indisciplined Royalist Horse then careered off to Naseby to loot the Parliamentary baggage. In the centre, the fighting was fierce but the Royalists began to gain the upper hand. On the Parliamentary right, however, Cromwell had charged into the enemy line at speed, shattered the King's left wing and then held his men together to swing round and attack the Royalist centre from behind. Cromwell's manoeuvre changed the course of the battle, for the Royalist Foot, now surrounded and outnumbered, lost their initial advantage and were soon routed and surrendered *en masse*. Rupert and his Horse returned to the battlefield to find that all was lost and although he managed to ride round and rejoin the King behind his crumbling army, the surviving Royalists refused to charge and instead turned and fled northwards. Of the Royalist army of 8–9,000, over 1,000 were killed in battle and up to 5,000 captured.

Although currently threatened by a major road scheme, the battlefield is still open ground little changed since the 1640s. Part of the area is now hedged and cultivated but nothing more than a handful of farmbuildings impinge upon the scene. Two monuments commemorate the battle; a nineteenth-century obelisk bearing a pro-Royalist inscription, which stands away from the battlefield by the village (SP694784), and a Cromwell Association memorial by the Naseby to Sibbertoft road on the edge of Broad Moor Valley, near the centre of the battle where the Infantries clashed (the monument is at SP684800, the Ordnance Survey battle symbol at SP684803). The monument records that 'from near this site Oliver Cromwell led the cavalry charge which decided the issue of the battle and ultimately that of the Great Civil War'. There is a rather improbable story that Cromwell's body was secretly carried to Naseby in September 1658 and buried somewhere on the battlefield. His ghost supposedly still stalks the area.

To the west of the battlefield, near Sulby (SP66978013), is a depression in the hillside with a slight mound in the centre, reportedly a communal grave for those who fell in the battle. Nineteenth-century excavations uncovered many human bodies here.

According to tradition 'Cromwell's Table', now in All Saints Church, Naseby, once stood at an inn in the village and was the table around which Royalist officers were eating and drinking on the evening of the 13th when disturbed by the Parliamentary advanced guard.

Naseby Battle and Farm Museum, immediately south of the village, contains several Civil War relics found on the battlefield, together with a large model of the battle itself.

Naseby, Northants. Sprigge's plan of the battle of Naseby (*above*) is stylized and possibly exaggerates the size of the Royalist army, but it remains of great value as one of the very few contemporary illustrations of Civil War engagements with any claim to accuracy. A modern obelisk (*right*) commemorates the decisive battle fought here in June 1645. *Below:* Rockingham Castle, Northants. The great thirteenth-century gatehouse, with its twin drum towers, dominates the collection of Elizabethan and later buildings of the present 'castle'. Many of the medieval buildings, including the keep, were destroyed during or immediately after the Civil War.

Northampton (SP7560) Secure for Parliament throughout the Civil War, the county town frequently served as a rendezvous and rallying point. Essex gathered his army at Northampton in September 1642 and it was probably here that Cromwell and the Cambridgeshire contingent joined him. Cromwell certainly passed through the town on several occasions later in the war.

The only real fighting here took place in May 1649, when mutinous Leveller troops under William Thompson occupied the town. On 17 May Colonel Reynolds and a Parliamentary force burst into Northampton, pushing the Levellers into Holy Sepulchre Church in Sheep Street where they were captured after further fighting; the walls still bear bullet marks from the brief exchange. Thompson lies buried in an unmarked grave in All Saints Church, George Row.

The town was the centre for the manufacture of leather goods during the seventeenth century, and throughout the war the Parliamentary army marched in Northampton boots and rode in Northampton saddles. The Museum of Leathercraft in Bridge Street contains many examples of Civil War leatherwork.

Rockingham Castle (SP867914) Rockingham was one of the few fortresses in the county still defensible in the mid-seventeenth century, though by then most of the Norman motte and bailey stronghold had disappeared and the 'castle' which saw action in the Civil War was an Elizabethan fortified house, comprising the restored Great Hall and additional sixteenth-century ranges. Rockingham was secured for Parliament by Lord Grey in 1643 and garrisoned thereafter. The buildings were badly damaged at this time, though it is not clear whether by a Royalist attack during the war or by Parliamentary slighting after it. Parts of the castle were restored or rebuilt during the 1650s, including the three bay Walker's House to the north of the gatehouse. The building was remodelled and extended in the eighteenth and nineteenth century and the present castle is a confusing mixture of several ages, medieval – the gatehouse and parts of the Great Hall – early

modern – the restoration work to the Great Hall, the east and west ranges, Walker's House and the Laundry – and modern – the square south tower, the roof and most of the interior. The castle is open on Sundays and certain weekdays during the summer.

Titchmarsh (TL021800) Sir Gilbert Pickering, a close associate and distant relative of Oliver Cromwell, was born, brought up and lived at the late Tudor manor house in Titchmarsh. A man of adaptable religious and political views, he managed to survive most of the pitfalls of the period to remain at or near the centres of power. A member of every parliament 1640–60, he also served on numerous councils and committees, including the powerful Protectorate Councils of Oliver and Richard Cromwell. Barred from office at the Restoration, he retired to his extensive estates in Northamptonshire. His principal seat, which had been built for his father John in 1591, was demolished at the end of the eighteenth century and today nothing remains except extensive if poorly preserved earthworks on the north-west outskirts of the village.

Weedon Bec (SP6258) On 26 February 1645 a Royalist force attacked 400 Parliamentary Horse as they were moving through Weedon on their way from Daventry to Northampton. The Parliamentarians retreated westwards, harried all the way from Weedon to Borough Hill, and lost over 150 killed or injured before they reached the relative safety of Daventry.

Wellingborough (SP8968) There is a tradition that Cromwell spent the night before the Battle of Naseby, 13 June 1645, at the Hind Inn, now the Hind Hotel, in the centre of the town. However, Cromwell's movements immediately before and after the battle are fairly well documented and at no point does a night halt in Wellingborough appear plausible.

Four years later, in May 1649, William Thompson, the leader of the Leveller-inspired army mutiny, was shot by pursuing Parliamentary troops in Wellingborough Woods. Thompson managed to hit two of his pursuers before being cut down by carbine.

NORTHUMBERLAND

The county was held for the King without challenge during 1642–43 and the first real fighting occurred in January and February 1644 as the Scottish Parliamentarians marched through, throwing back the Earl of Newcastle's army and capturing most of the strongholds en route. With their departure southwards in March the King's cause in Northumberland made a brief recovery, encouraged by the short-lived presence of Montrose's Scottish Royalists. Their Parliamentary compatriots reappeared after Marston Moor and Royalism in Northumberland was effectively ended. Cromwell passed through the county in 1648 and 1650–51 on his way to and from Scotland.

Alnwick Castle (NU187136) The medieval border castle was taken by the Scots as they marched through in January 1644 and served as a minor Parliamentary outpost thereafter. Cromwell probably lodged here when he halted at Alnwick on 12–15 September 1648 and again on 17 July 1650. By the eighteenth century the former Percy stronghold was derelict and much of the present building dates from the eighteenth and nineteenth century, when the castle was restored and modernised. The shell keep, bailey walls, some of the mural towers, and the outer gatehouse and barbican are largely medieval. Alnwick Castle is open daily except Saturdays during the summer.

Bamburgh Castle (NU183352) The stunning clifftop castle occupies a site fortified since Roman times. The defences have been repeatedly strengthened and rebuilt and the present castle, though basically medieval, owes much to over-zealous restoration work of 1894–1905. The castle played no serious part in the Civil War, but the armoury contains a good selection of weapons and armour of the period. Bamburgh is open during the summer.

Berwick upon Tweed (NT9953) The most northerly town and stronghold of England, Berwick was in something of a military backwater in the seventeenth century and, despite its strong defences, saw no serious action during the first Civil War. In 1648, however, Berwick became one of the northern centres of the second Civil War, taken by Langdale's Royalists on 28 April and held by them throughout the summer. After the disintegration of the King's Scottish army around Preston, the Royalist elements in Berwick melted away and Cromwell entered the town unopposed in the latter half of September. He was in the area for nearly a fortnight before moving into Scotland on 3 October, and returned here in late July 1650 prior to his second Scottish campaign. On both occasions, however, he seems to have spent most of the time lodging outside Berwick, either at Norham to the west or Mordington just across the border to the north.

The town's rather unexciting Civil War history is one of the reasons why its defences survive in such good condition. The twelfth-century castle has gone, flattened by the Victorians to make way for the railway station, but the town walls remain almost complete. Begun by Edward I, they were remodelled and strengthened in the latter half of the sixteenth century, when several towers, bastions and gun platforms were added.

Holy Trinity Church, off the Parade, is of interest as one of only a handful of churches built during the Civil War and Interregnum. Designed by John Young of London and constructed 1648–52 under the supervision of Governor George Fenwick, Holy Trinity is a curious mixture of classical and gothic designs. It is rather heavy and squat, with no tower of any kind – according to tradition, plans for a tower were vetoed by Cromwell, who inspected the works on his visit to the town. The chancel and western turrets were added in the nineteenth century. Originally galleried on all four sides, only the west gallery now remains; the pulpit dates from 1652.

Chillingham Castle (NU062258) Cromwell's army quartered in the grounds of Chillingham Castle on 19 July 1650 and Cromwell himself probably lodged within the fortress. Built in the fourteenth century and extended over the following 200 years, Chillingham had been converted into a more comfortable, domestic residence during the second quarter of the seventeenth century. It was modernised again in the mid-eighteenth century, when the surrounding park was laid out. The quadrangular castle, with four three-storey ranges linked by square angle towers, is not usually open to the public.

Coquet Island (NU2904) The tiny North Sea island off the mouth of the river Coquet was held for the King during the opening year of the war, one of several off-shore strongholds secured as potential naval bases. It was overrun by Scottish forces on their way south in January 1644. No Civil War military works survive, and it is possible that the Royalists occupied and fortified the medieval monastic buildings on the island.

Corbridge (NY9864) At the beginning of 1644 Newcastle led 8,000 men north from Yorkshire in an attempt to halt the 20,000 Scottish Parliamentarians advancing through Northumberland. On 19 February the two forces approached each other at Corbridge, where Newcastle hoped to hold the bridge over the Tyne. After a brief skirmish, possibly involving only part of the two armies, the outnumbered Royalists fell back and the road south was open. Much of the Scottish army, however, halted here for six weeks while their colleagues tried unsuccessfully to capture the town of Newcastle, and the Earl of Newcastle and Sir Marmaduke Langdale were able to mount many destructive raids on the Scottish quarters in and around Corbridge.

Eglingham Hall (NU104194) The present hall, still a private residence, is largely eighteenth century but incorporates at the west end a section of the earlier Tudor house which stood on the site. Owned during the 1640s by the local Parliamentary leader Henry Ogle, Cromwell lodged here on 9 August 1651.

Ford Castle (NT945374) Odinel de Forde's medieval quadrangular castle at Ford was rebuilt in the sixteenth century in the form of an 'E'-shaped fortified manor; the original north-east and north-west corner towers were incorporated within the Tudor mansion, though the former was all but lost under Elizabethan reworking. Ford Castle was held by the Royalists from the outbreak of the Civil War until early 1644, when it fell to the Scots. It played no further part in the conflict. The Tudor house survives intact and nearby stands the now ruined and isolated south-west tower of the medieval castle.

Lindisfarne (NU137417) Much of the medieval monastery on Lindisfarne was demolished after the Dissolution and the stone carted off to build a Tudor artillery fort high above the sea at the southern point of the island. The fort was secured for the King at the outbreak of the Civil War and served as a base for land and sea operations along the north-east coast until besieged and taken by Parliamentary forces in 1645. The fortress remained in military use until the early nineteenth century, when it rapidly fell into disrepair. It was rebuilt as a grand and romantic house by Sir Edward Lutyens at the

beginning of this century. The house is open daily except Tuesdays during the summer, tides permitting.

Morpeth Castle (NZ197856) The Norman motte and bailey castle, extended and strengthened during the fifteenth century, changed hands no less than five times in 1644. Captured by the Scots on their way south in January, it was retaken by Newcastle's forces in the following month. The Scots returned to Morpeth in March, recaptured the castle, and installed a 500-strong garrison under Lt.-Col. Somerville. The departure of the main Scottish army into Yorkshire left the castle vulnerable to attack and in May Montrose swooped on Morpeth and besieged and bombarded his compatriots into surrender on the 30th. Within weeks the Battle of Marston Moor and the departure of Montrose had altered the balance of power once more, this time permanently, and Morpeth was reoccupied by Parliamentary troops without opposition later in the summer. Cromwell stayed here on 11 September 1648 and on 16 July 1650. Morpeth Castle is now ruinous.

Norham (NT8947) Despite its mighty castle and its position at a crossing of the Tweed, Norham apparently played little part in the Civil War. The medieval castle had been repaired and modernised in the sixteenth century but may have fallen ruinous once more by the mid-seventeenth century, for neither side seems to have garrisoned the place. Cromwell stayed at Norham on 19–21 September 1648, possibly lodging in the Tudor domestic range within the castle, possibly in a humbler building in the village.

Prudhoe Castle (NZ092635) The medieval Percy stronghold housed a small Royalist garrison 1642–44 and became an important base for harassing the Scottish Parliamentarians as they attempted to cross the Tyne here in February and March 1644. When the Scots pushed south, Prudhoe was evacuated and played no further part in the war. The castle, which stands on high ground south of the Tyne, comprises a free-standing keep and an inner and outer bailey, both protected by well preserved walls, mural towers and gatehouses. The remains, part of which have been incorporated within a late Georgian house, have recently been opened to the public.

Rock (NU2020) On 18 July 1650 Cromwell reviewed his troops on Rock Moor, to the west of the village, before marching to Chillingham

Top: Alnwick Castle, Northumberland. The medieval stronghold, restored in the eighteenth and nineteenth centuries, contains a large display of arms and armour, including a few items from the Civil War. *Above:* Berwick upon Tweed, Northumberland. The extensive Elizabethan defences, an elaborate system of ditches and bastions, artillery points and earth and masonry ramparts, were designed to sweep every approach with heavy gunfire.

and on to Scotland. It is not clear whether Cromwell stayed somewhere in Rock overnight – Rock Tower, the remains of which have been incorporated within the Youth Hostel seems a possible venue – or whether he pressed on to Chillingham on the 18th.

Warkworth Castle (NU247058) The impressive remains of Warkworth Castle stand above the town in a loop of the river Coquet. Warkworth was one of the strongest and most important English bases in the North, a simple twelfth-century motte and bailey castle later converted by the Percies into a complex and formidable stronghold. The castle played a surprisingly small part in the Civil War – possibly it was already semi-ruinous by the mid-seventeenth century – garrisoned by the Royalists at the beginning of the war but surrendered to the Scots with little or no resistance in January 1644. Parts of the keep are still habitable, but for the most part Warkworth is now a dramatic ruin, open daily.

NORTH YORKSHIRE

Most of North Yorkshire was secured for the King at the outbreak of the Civil War and remained firmly Royalist until the latter half of 1644. York quickly became a major Royalist stronghold, the King's northern capital in all but name. Only the very south of the county saw action in 1642–44, when the area around and to the south of York was repeatedly raided from Parliamentary bases in West Yorkshire and Humberside. The arrival of the Scots, the crushing defeat at Marston Moor and the fall of York in summer 1644 dramatically altered the situation and the whole region rapidly fell to Parliament with little opposition. Nothing more than a scattering of isolated bases remained in the King's hands by the end of 1644. Cromwell campaigned in the area in summer 1644: he fought at Marston Moor, was present during the siege and capture of York and then probably saw action nearby during the rest of July. He passed through the area again in 1648 and 1650–51 on his way to and from Scotland.

Bilbrough (SE530465) The Parliamentary Lord General Sir Thomas Fairfax, later the 3rd Lord Fairfax (d1671), lies buried in St James's Church, a nineteenth-century neo-Norman building incorporating parts of its medieval predecessor. Fairfax lies beneath a black marble tomb chest, richly decorated with foliage, shields and trophies. There is no effigy.

Bolton Percy (SE532413)   Ferdinando, 2nd Lord Fairfax (d1648), the father of the Lord General and himself one of the leaders of the Parliamentary war effort in the north during the first half of the Civil War, was buried in All Saints Church. He lies near a large railed mural monument with a sarcophagus and pediment.

Buttercrambe Castle (SE7358) The remains of the medieval castle served as a minor outpost of York, guarding the bridge across the Derwent. The small Royalist garrison was overpowered by the Scottish Parliamentarians as they pushed south in May 1644. No trace remains of the motte and bailey stronghold, which stood west of the bridge in what is now Aldby Park.

Byram House (SE4926)   Cromwell halted in Yorkshire during November 1648 to oversee the siege of Pontefract Castle. Although he spent most of the month at Knottingley, he lodged during the first week of November at Byram House, 1½ miles north of the town. The Tudor manor-house has since been demolished and the ruins of a later, eighteenth-century great house now stand in the private park.

Calton (SD9059)   Major General John Lambert was born and brought up at Calton Hall. The late medieval house was gutted by fire at the end of the seventeenth century and, although restored in the eighteenth century, it was then abandoned and fell to ruin and little or nothing of Lambert's home survives; what may be the west end of the original hall is now incorporated in a much later private house. Cromwell and Lambert passed within a few miles of Calton in August 1648 and it is possible that the two made a slight detour to visit the hall. If so, it was one of the last times Lambert saw his old home – he lived in London and Wimbledon during the 1650s and then spent the rest of his life a prisoner.

Top: Bilbrough, North Yorks. Sir Thomas Fairfax (*right*), Lord General of the army from 1645, effectively retired five years later. He lived quietly in Yorkshire after the Restoration and lies beneath a decorated and recently restored tomb (*left*).

Above: Calton, North Yorks. John Lambert (*right*), soldier, politician, and Cromwell's principal backer until he broke from him over the question of kingship, was brought up at Calton Hall. He was imprisoned after the Restoration and buried in Devon, but a modern plaque in Kirkby Malham church (*left*) commemorates his association with St Michael's.

Castle Bolton (SE033918)   Bolton Castle was built by the Scrope family in the fourteenth and fifteenth century, a quadrangular stronghold with corner towers and a large south-eastern gatehouse. It was garrisoned for the King throughout the Civil War and held out until 5 November 1645, when Col. John Scrope and his garrison were finally starved into surrender. The castle is open daily.

Cawood Castle (SE574376)   The medieval fortified palace of the Archbishops of York was secured for the King by Capt. Grey at the outbreak of the Civil War. On 4 October 1642 Hotham junior and 600 Parliamentary Foot from Hull stormed the castle and established a garrison of their own. Cawood changed hands at least twice more during 1643 as fortunes ebbed and flowed in the area south of York. The Parliamentarians recaptured the castle for the final time in May 1644 and with the collapse of the King's cause in the region two months later, peace returned to Cawood. Little now survives except the mid-fifteenth-century gatehouse built by Archbishop Kempe, an embattled block with corner turrets and a courtroom above the arched entrance.

Coxwold (SE533772)   Within the fifteenth-century Church of St Michael lie many members of the Bellasys family, including Thomas, Viscount or Earl of Falconberg (d1700), who married Cromwell's third daughter Mary in 1657. The elaborate white marble monument features an effigy of Falconberg dressed in Roman garb.

Crayke Castle (SE560707)   In the fifteenth century the Bishops of Durham built a small fortified palace here on the site of a Norman motte and bailey castle. Briefly garrisoned by both sides in 1643–44, Crayke played only a minor role in the war. It was, nonetheless, slighted by Parliament in 1647. One of the ruined ranges was rebuilt in the nineteenth century and remains a private residence; nearby is a very ruinous fifteenth-century tower house.

Denton Hall (SE147487)   Nothing remains of the late medieval hall owned by the Fairfax family in the sixteenth and seventeenth century in which the Parliamentary Lord General Sir Thomas Fairfax was born and brought up. The present Denton Hall dates from the 1770s.

Fort Airmyn (SE7225)   The Royalists established an earthwork strongpoint here, at the junction of the Aire and the Ouse, to guard the waterborne approaches to York and Selby. The outpost fell to the Scots in May 1644. No trace remains of the earthwork defences but the name 'Fort Hill' may commemorate the Civil War or earlier stronghold.

Helmsley Castle (SE612836)   The medieval castle above the river was begun by Robert de Rood, Lord of Helmsley and by the fifteenth century comprised a keep, great hall, chapel and domestic ranges standing within an enclosure defended by a curtain wall, mural towers and a gatehouse and southern barbican. The castle was held without challenge for the King by Sir Jordan Crossland in 1642–44. Sir Thomas Fairfax laid siege to Helmsley in August 1644 and although the King's men held out for over three months, they were eventually starved into submission and surrendered on 22 November. Fairfax was shot and badly wounded in the course of the long siege. Parliament ordered the castle slighted after the war and one side of the keep and several sections of the curtain wall were brought down by mines. The extensive ruins are open daily.

Kirkby Malham (SD893610)   Many members of the Lambert family of nearby Calton Hall are buried within St Michael's Church; most lie beneath the south chapel, otherwise known as the Calton Chapel. The Parliamentary Major General and politician, John Lambert, was baptised here and although he was buried in Plymouth (Devon), a modern plaque within the church commemorates his association with Kirkby Malham. There are contemporary monuments to many of his relatives, including a large tablet in memory of his son John.

Cromwell's signature in the parish records witnessing a marriage here in the mid-1650s is undoubtedly a forgery for at no time during the Protectorate was he anywhere near Yorkshire.

Knaresborough (SE348570)   The fourteenth-century double bailey castle was held for the King in 1642–44 but fell to Parliament in 1644 following a brief siege. Some accounts suggest that Cromwell was present during the operation in July 1644 and lodged in a house in the High Street, demolished in the eighteenth century, which stood near the Crown Inn. He was certainly here on 1 September 1648 *en route* to Scotland. The extensive remains of the castle are open daily during the summer.

Marston Moor (SE4952)   The Battle of Marston Moor was one of the largest and most decisive engagements of the Civil War and the Royalist defeat effectively ended the King's cause in northern England.

Marston Moor, North Yorks. According to tradition, Cromwell spent the night before battle in Long Marston Hall or Manor (*top*), a Tudor mansion, extended and refaced in the eighteenth century. To the west lies Marston Moor itself, the open ground where the Royalists' northern army was destroyed in July 1644. An inscribed memorial to the battle (*left*), erected by the Cromwell Association, stands by the Long Marston to Tockwith road near the probable centre of the conflict. In the late 1950s a commemorative service was held around the memorial (*above*), attended by the Rt. Hon. Isaac Foot, the founder of the Cromwell Association, and other historians and members of the Association.

Throughout June 1644 a 28,000-strong Parliamentary army had besieged York, creating increasing distress within the city. At the end of the month Rupert led 18,000 Royalists to relieve York and the Parliamentarians drew off and deployed to the west of the city, intending to engage the Prince head-on as he approached York. Rupert, however, swung north, avoided the main Parliamentary army and entered York unopposed on 1 July. Despite Newcastle's objections, the Prince determined to give battle, looking for justification to an ambiguously-worded letter from the King.

The two armies approached each other on 2 July on open moorland to the west of Long Marston. The Parliamentarians deployed in an east–west line south of and parallel to the Long Marston to Tockwith road, with the Foot in the centre and the Horse on the wings; Fairfax led the right wing, Cromwell the left. The Parliamentary command point was established on Cromwell's Plump, a small, tree-covered hillock to the rear of the Foot. The Royalists drew up between Kendal and Atterwith Lane in a line parallel to and north of the Parliamentarians. Their precise position is unclear: according to some historians they deployed on the far side of a broad and deep ditch well north of the Long Marston to Tockwith road, whilst other accounts suggest that they lined a hedge and small ditch which ran beside the road itself.

Both sides deployed very slowly during the afternoon and Rupert probably planned to stay in the field overnight and give battle on the 3rd. But the Parliamentary commander noticed that the Royalists appeared both outnumbered and unprepared and decided to attack at once. At 7 p.m. amid a heavy shower, the Parliamentary front line charged forward. The right, under Fairfax, crossed the Tockwith to Long Marston road and then began moving down Atterwith Lane, but here they met heavy fire and were thrown back. Elsewhere, however, everything went Parliament's way. The left, under Cromwell, smashed the Royalist right and then tore into the flank of the King's Foot, which began retreating and swinging round to meet the Cavalry attack. Repeated Parliamentary Cavalry and Infantry charges broke the Royalist Foot, which gave way and fled. The exception was Newcastle's troop of Whitecoats, who resisted to the end and were cut down almost to a man either in White Syke Close or in a hedged enclosure to the south-east. By 9 p.m. the battle was over; 4,500 Royalists had been killed or captured and the rest were fleeing eastwards.

Marston Moor is still open ground, covered with scrub and gorse and dotted with farm-houses and enclosures. The Tockwith to Long Marston road crosses the centre of the battlefield and several tracks still run off to the north, including Kendal, Moor and Atterwith Lane; the latter now kinks east before joining the road but in the seventeenth century it ran straight and thus met the road west of the present junction. The remains of the large ditch behind which the Royalists may have deployed can still be traced to the north of the road. The dead were buried in mass graves in White Syke Close and Wilstrop Wood. A Cromwell Association memorial stands by the junction of Moor Lane and the Long Marston to Tockwith road at SE490521; the obelisk bears inscriptions describing the battle and the parts played by Cromwell and Fairfax. Cromwell's Plump survives to the south of the road and is a good vantage-point for viewing the battlefield.

Cromwell supposedly spent the night before the battle at Marston Hall in Long Marston; the hall, which still stands, is reputedly haunted by his ghost. Cromwell was wounded during the initial charge and temporarily left the field; the house in Tockwith where, according to tradition, he had his injuries tended was destroyed during the Second World War.

On 8 March 1655 around 100 Royalists gathered on Marston Moor as part of the planned nationwide rising, but they panicked and dispersed without incident, leaving four cartloads of arms on the moor.

Middleham Castle (SE127875)

The extensive and spectacular remains of the former Neville fortress dwarf the surrounding village at the head of Wensleydale. The massive square keep, chapel and domestic ranges stand in an enclosure defended by a curtain wall, mural towers and a gatehouse. Despite its size, Middleham had a quiet Civil War, held without challenge for the King in 1642–44 and then abandoned without a fight after Marston Moor. It was slighted by Parliament in 1646. The ruins are open daily.

Mulgrave Castle (NZ839117)

Mulgrave Castle, the principal seat of the Sheffield family in the seventeenth century, was garrisoned for the King at the outbreak of the Civil War and held without challenge for three years. Capt. Steward and his garrison surrendered after a brief siege in 1645 and the castle was slighted two years later. Edmund Sheffield, 2nd Earl of Mulgrave, was one of the few members of the old nobility actively to support Cromwell in the 1650s and was nominated to the Protectoral Council. Mulgrave petitioned for and was

awarded £1,000 compensation for the demolition of his castle. The remains of the fourteenth-
century fortress – a rectangular keep with corner
towers and a double-towered gatehouse – stand
¾ mile south-west of the new 'castle', built in
the eighteenth century.

Newburgh Priory (SE543765)   The twelfth-
century Augustinian Priory was largely demolished by the Bellasys family after the Dissolution and a large sixteenth- and seventeenth-
century house, called Newburgh Priory, was
built on the site. Thomas Bellasys, Lord Falconberg, was born and brought up here and he lived
at Newburgh with his wife Mary Cromwell, the
Protector's third daughter, during the latter half
of the seventeenth century. The present house is
largely eighteenth century, but parts of the
earlier building survive, including a fine Jacobean porch. According to a rather implausible
tradition, Oliver Cromwell lies buried here in a
stone vault near the main staircase, his body
secretly carried from London to Newburgh by
his daughter in September 1658 or January
1661. Newburgh Priory is open on certain days
during the summer.

Nun Appleton (SE556400)   During the 1650s
Sir Thomas Fairfax lived in quiet retirement at
Nun Appleton Hall, one of several properties in
the area owned by the family. The old building
has completely disappeared and the present hall
dates from the late seventeenth and eighteenth
century. A modern plaque records Nun Appleton's association with Fairfax and Marvell,
poet, politician and Milton's assistant as Latin
Secretary to the Protectoral Council, who was at
one time employed and patronised by the family.

Old Malton (SE7972)   In winter 1642–43 a
Parliamentary force from Scarborough led by Sir
Hugh Cholmley raided Old Malton, capturing
the town and expelling the Earl of Newport's
Royalist garrison.

Poppleton (SE5655)   There was no stone bridge
over the Ouse here in the seventeenth century and
instead the Parliamentary forces besieging York
in summer 1644 constructed a bridge of boats at
Poppleton to facilitate movement around the
beleaguered city. On 1 July a detachment of
Parliamentary Dragoons guarding the bridge
was surprised by Prince Rupert and the main
Royalist army, who had unexpectedly swung
north as they neared York. The small guard was
quickly overcome and the crossing captured
intact.

Ripley Castle (SE283606)   The present 'cas-
tle', really an eighteenth-century mansion, incorporates a fifteenth-century gatehouse tower
and other parts of the late medieval fortified
home of the Ingilby family. According to tradition, Cromwell stayed in the old house on the
night after the Battle of Marston Moor, the
unwelcome guest of a gun-toting Lady Ingilby.
Despite the implausible frills, the story may have
a basis in truth for Cromwell was certainly in
the general area after the battle and a visit to
Ripley would tie in with accounts of him being
present at the siege of Knaresborough around
the same time. Ripley Castle now houses a fine
collection of furnishings, arms and armour and
is open to the public at weekends and on certain
weekdays during the summer.

Bullet marks in the east wall of All Saints
Church are believed to be a grim relic of the
execution of Royalists here during the Civil
War.

Scarborough Castle (TA050890)   The high
headland dominating the town has been the site
of defensive works since the Roman period, if
not earlier. The present medieval castle has seen
a great deal of action, from the capture of Piers
Gaveston to an attack by two German cruisers
in 1914. Scarborough was secured for Parliament at the outbreak of the Civil War and a
1,700 man garrison installed. In March 1643,
however, governor Sir Hugh Cholmley defected
and betrayed town and castle to the King. The
Parliamentarians raided the place several times
over the following year but not until summer
1644 did they mount a prolonged campaign to
retake Scarborough. The town was quickly
overrun but the castle held out for almost a year
of close siege and heavy bombardment from
Parliamentary batteries at Peasholm, on North
Cliff and in St Mary's Church. The Parliamentarians launched several unsuccessful attacks, during one of which their commander, Sir John
Meldrum, was fatally wounded. Starvation and
disease eventually forced Cholmley to surrender
on 22 July 1645.

Three years later history repeated itself, for
Governor Matthew Boynton declared for the
King and Scarborough became one of the Royal-
ist centres of the 2nd Civil War. Besieged by
early August, the garrison surrendered to Col.
Bethel on 19 December 1648.

The impressive ruins include the remains of
the massive Norman keep (the west wall was
largely destroyed during the bombardment of
1645), the thirteenth-century curtain walls and
mural towers of the two baileys, and a narrow
barbican. The castle is open daily.

St Mary's Church in Castle Road served as a Parliamentary battery in 1644–45 and in consequence sustained considerable damage during the Royalist counter-bombardment. The two west towers and the north transept were destroyed and it was probably Civil War damage which caused the main crossing tower to collapse in the 1650s.

Selby (SE6132)

Seventeenth-century Selby was a small town, possessing neither stone walls nor a castle, but it occupied an important position on the southern road and river approaches to York. The town was held for Parliament in 1642 and became the Fairfaxes' HQ from December 1642, when they fell back from Tadcaster, until March 1643, when the loss of Scarborough and the uncertain loyalty of Hull forced them to retreat into West Yorkshire. In May 1643 Sir Thomas clashed with a small Royalist force at Selby but successfully cut his way through and reached Hull. On 11 April 1644, as a preliminary to the siege of York, the Fairfaxes swooped down on Selby with the main Parliamentary army and captured the town and its large Royalist garrison.

Sherburn in Elmet (SE4933)

Sherburn lay in the very south of the county, near the Parliamentary strongholds of West Yorkshire and in an area which was fiercely contested during the opening year of the war. The town had no walls or castle and could not be defended against determined attack and thus it usually changed hands with little or no bloodshed. On 14 December 1642, however, Sir Thomas Fairfax attacked a Royalist unit temporarily quartered here and inflicted heavy losses. Three years later, on 15 October 1645, Digby and 1,500 Royalist Horse heading north, contrived to win and then lose a skirmish here. On entering Sherburn, Digby's advanced guard surprised and captured a small Parliamentary unit, but confusion and panic then spread amongst the main Royalist force who somehow believed that it was their colleagues who had been captured by a much larger force; the Royalists turned and fled in disorder.

Skipton Castle (SD994519)

The thirteenth- and fourteenth-century Clifford stronghold was garrisoned for the King throughout the Civil War. It was held without challenge until 1644, but after Marston Moor it was subject to repeated Parliamentary attacks. In 1645 Lambert arrived to take charge of the siege and brought with him heavy guns, which he placed on top of Cockhill to bombard the south side of the castle.

One of the last bases in the area to hold out for the King, Skipton was finally surrendered by Sir John Mallory on 21 December 1645. Cromwell may have lodged in the castle when he stayed at Skipton on 14 and 27–28 August 1648 on his way to and from meeting the Scottish Royalists in Lancashire. The fortress was slighted by Parliament at the end of the 1640s but was restored by Lady Ann Clifford in the following decade and has been remodelled several times since. The castle, which is still in good condition, comprises a fourteenth-century double-towered gateway, sixteenth- and seventeenth-century ranges of domestic buildings, a long banqueting hall and a Tudor octagonal tower. The extent of the damage caused by the Civil War bombardment and post-war slighting is still clear in the Watch Tower and Muniment Tower, where the lower levels of walling are much darker than Lady Clifford's repair work above. Parts of the castle are open daily.

Tadcaster (SE4843)

In late November 1642 Lord Fairfax occupied Tadcaster as part of his campaign to threaten York and set about defending the town with earthworks and barricades. These were put to the test on 6 December when Newcastle's 4,000 Foot attacked the town, but the 1,500 Parliamentarians within held off their opponents throughout the day and then slipped away to Selby under cover of darkness. On 29 March 1643 the small Royalist garrison fell back at the approach of Sir Thomas Fairfax but on the following day the Parliamentarians, in turn, were compelled to evacuate the place when a large force from York marched on Tadcaster. No trace of the Civil War defences survives.

York (SE6051)

The ancient stronghold on the Ouse became the Royalists' capital in the north of England from the outbreak of war until the city's fall in July 1644. York was defended by a near continuous circuit of Roman and medieval walls and two medieval castles. They had become rather dilapidated during the first half of the seventeenth century but were repaired and strengthened by the garrison during 1643. A number of earthworks and fortified churches and manor-houses outside the walls gave further protection.

In spring 1644 the northern Parliamentarians felt sufficiently strong to mount a sustained campaign against York. On 22 April Fairfax and Leven arrived at the head of 22,000 men and surrounded the city in an arc around the east, south and west sides. Manchester and Cromwell appeared on 3 June and their 6,000

Top: Newburgh Priory, North Yorks. An improbable
tradition has it that Cromwell lies buried in this stone
vault, his remains carried to Yorkshire in 1658 or
1661 by his daughter Mary (*above*), wife of Lord
Falconberg of Newburgh Priory. *Left:* Clifford's
Tower, York. A Royalist artillery point during the
siege of the city, the thirteenth-century tower was
badly damaged by the Parliamentary counter-
bombardment.

men were stationed to the north of the city, completing the encirclement. Manchester had his HQ at Clifton, then a village to the north-west of the city, now a suburb of York itself. Governor Sir Thomas Glemham had prepared for the expected siege by blocking the postern gates of the city walls, setting up cannon on the four principal gates and on Clifford's Tower, and occupying further outlying strongholds. During May Fairfax and Leven captured many of these outposts, including the churches of St Nicholas and St Lawrence beyond Walmgate. On 5 June Fairfax erected a five gun battery on Lamel Hill, south-east of the city, to cover Walmgate and established a second battery in St Lawrence's churchyard. Royalist fortlets on Holgate and Nun Mill Hills were captured, but the Scots failed to take the main Royalist fort, a huge four-bastioned earthwork called 'The Mount', which lay on the Tadcaster road south-west of Micklegate Bar. The bombardment of the city continued throughout June but to no great effect and an attempt to mine Walmgate was thwarted. On 16 June, however, St Mary's Tower was successfully brought down and a Parliamentary raiding party entered the city, only to be halted around King's Manor and expelled with heavy losses. The besieging forces marched away at the end of June to face Rupert's army but promptly returned after Marston Moor and resumed operations. Glemham's position was now hopeless and he surrendered on 16 July. Thereafter the city was held without serious challenge for Parliament. The walls and gates were repaired and the earthworks beyond largely demolished. Cromwell passed through the city in July 1650 and was greeted with volleys from Clifford's Tower. In 1655 York became the HQ of Deputy Major General Robert Lilburne, who established his offices in King's Manor.

Despite the subsequent urban development, much of Civil War York survives. The circuit of walls and gates is almost complete and shows many signs of the Parliamentary bombardment; Bootham Bar was repaired and refaced in the late 1640s; Walmgate Bar sustained very heavy damage in 1644 and was extensively rebuilt in 1646–48 (the barbican bears the date 1648) but still carries many scars where hit by cannon-balls; the outer half of St Mary's Tower was destroyed by a mine in 1644 and was subsequently rebuilt with noticeably thinner walls; and Toft's Tower at the north-west angle of the walls near Micklegate Bar was almost totally rebuilt in 1645 after the original tower had been demolished by cannon-fire. Several other parts of the wall, including sections near Micklegate

and Abbey Precinct Wall, bear marks where struck by cannon-balls.

The Norman castle in the south-west corner of the old city had largely disappeared by the seventeenth century and Glemham mounted guns on the bare motte, Baile Hill, which still stands off Cromwell Road. Its twin on the east bank of the Ouse, Clifford's Tower, had fared better and the thirteenth-century quatrefoil keep was still defensible in the seventeenth century. It was garrisoned in 1642 and the forebuilding was repaired and new floors and a gun platform added. Bombarded and badly damaged in 1644, it was repaired after the war. It is open daily.

King's Manor, off St Leonard's Street, was originally the home of the Abbot of St Mary's, but was converted for secular use after the Dissolution; the residence of the Earl of Stafford and the meeting place for the Council of the North in the decades before the Civil War, it survived the conflict with only minor damage and now belongs to the University of York. It is open daily.

The fourteenth-century Merchant Taylor's Hall in Aldwork served as a hospital during the siege. Although the Guildhall in Lendal Street was badly damaged in the Second World War and extensively rebuilt since, parts of the original fifteenth-century mansion survive, including the Inner Chamber in which part of the money owed to the Scots for their help in the first Civil War was counted before being handed over. Modern stained glass in the east window of the main hall includes a representation of Sir Thomas Fairfax and the siege of York. The City Art Gallery contains a fine lead bust of Fairfax.

Within the city walls, the churches of St Denys, St Sampson and St Olave sustained slight damage during the war, either from the Parliamentary bombardment or from the explosion of Royalist cannon mounted in or on them; all were subsequently repaired. Churches beyond the city walls were not so fortunate and St Maurice's, St Lawrence's and St Nicholas's were all wrecked during the siege and, with the exception of the tower of St Lawrence's, none now survive. The Minster was not damaged during the siege and was saved from sacking after the capture of the city by Sir Thomas Fairfax; there is a modern tablet in the Chapter House in memory of the Lord General.

The earthworks beyond the city walls have disappeared. Holgate Hill Fort (SE58955133) was destroyed by a housing estate in the 1930s; Nun Mill Hill Fort (SE60135074) lies under Southlands Methodist Church; Lamel Hill (SE61455095) is now a flat-topped mound in the grounds of The Friends' Retreat; The Mount

(SE59385107) stood on the Tadcaster road and gradually disappeared under successive widenings of the road and now survives only in the street name 'Mount Road'.

The York Heritage Centre, housed in the former Church of St Mary in Castlegate, traces the history of the city, including its role during the Civil War. The Yorkshire Museum in Museum Gardens has other items of the period, notably a model of the Battle of Marston Moor.

NOTTINGHAMSHIRE

The Civil War in Nottinghamshire was dominated by two towns, Nottingham and Newark. From his base in the county town, Col. John Hutchinson secured most of the region for Parliament in 1642 and oversaw military operations throughout the war. Newark, in contrast, became a major Royalist stronghold surrounded by an arc of lesser garrisons, a centre for frequent raids in the area; it survived until May 1646. Despite repeated scares during 1643–44, the expected Royalist invasion from Yorkshire never materialised and most of the county remained in Parliament's hands throughout the war and suffered nothing more than occasional raids. The eastern fringes, however, were controlled by the Newark Royalists until 1645–46. Cromwell's Lincolnshire campaign of 1643 frequently brought him into Nottinghamshire and he passed through the area on several occasions later in the war and in 1648 and 1650–51 on his way to and from Scotland.

Attenborough (SK5134)   The farmhouse next to the village church incorporates parts of the earlier seventeenth-century farmbuildings on the site, once owned by the Ireton family. The brothers John and Henry Ireton were born and brought up here. John left to pursue a commercial and political career in London and in time became Lord Mayor of London and a leading City politician during the Civil War and Interregnum. Henry, on the other hand, stayed at Attenborough until the outbreak of the Civil War, when he enlisted in the Parliamentary army and rose rapidly through the ranks to become not only a senior officer but also, by the latter half of the 1640s, the army's foremost political theorist. He married Cromwell's eldest daughter Bridget in 1646 and served under Cromwell in Ireland in 1649. He stayed there as Lord Deputy but the appointment soon killed him and he died of Irish swamp fever in 1651. A Cromwell Association plaque on the outer wall of the present house records its connection with the Ireton family.

East Retford (SK7080)   On Castle Hill, two miles south-east of the village, stand the remains of a prehistoric earthwork fort (SK7380). It was reoccupied and restored during the Civil War by Parliamentary troops who heightened the banks and dug or redug the outer ditch. The garrison was probably intended to oversee the main London to York road and to watch for movements from Newark and other Royalist bases in Lincolnshire.

Felley Priory (SK4851)   The present, modern building known as Felley Priory incorporates fragments of the elaborate brick and stone mansion built by the Millingtons during the sixteenth century; this house, in turn, incorporated parts of the twelfth-century Augustinian friary which stood here until the Dissolution. The Tudor house served as a minor Royalist outpost during 1643 but there is no record of fighting here and the garrison was probably evacuated sometime in 1643–44.

Newark (SK7953)   The small town of Newark lay on the Fosse Way and the Great North Road at the point where the latter crossed the Trent, and was thus a vital centre of road and river communications during the Civil War. Newark was secured for the King in December 1642 and became one of the most important and strongly defended Royalist bases in the country and a centre for operations over a very large area of the East Midlands. The garrison resisted repeated attacks and prolonged sieges and held out until May 1646, finally surrendering on the orders of the King.

Newark's medieval defences – a twelfth-century castle immediately south of the Trent Bridge and stone walls enclosing the town centre – were dilapidated and outdated by the mid-seventeenth century and the Royalist garrison set about rebuilding them. The castle was repaired and in 1643–44 a new defensive circuit of ditches and banks with interval bastions was constructed around the town, beyond the out-

grown medieval walls. Further earthworks defended the three main gates, North Gate, Balderton Gate and Mill Gate. In 1644 still more
earthworks were erected, this time well outside
Newark, including two large, square forts with
angle bastions – the Queen's and King's Sconce
– on the south bank of the Trent covering the
south-west and north-east approaches respectively. Royalist earthworks also protected the
bridge across the northern loop of the Trent
onto the 'Island', a roughly rectangular island of
flat land to the north of Newark created by the
dividing and rejoining of the Trent.

These defences were repeatedly put to the test.
In February 1643 Major General Ballard led
6,000 men to Newark, drove in the Royalist
outpost on Beacon Hill but was then repulsed
when he launched a conspicuously feeble attack
on Newark itself – collusion was suspected.
Several Parliamentary forces approached the
town later in 1643 – Cromwell was here around
12 June and again in early November – but no
serious assault was launched until the following
year.

Meldrum   and   Willoughby   approached
Newark at the end of February and by 6 March
they had driven in the Royalist outposts, swept
into the Island via Muskham Bridge and laid
siege to the town. A direct assault on the 8th was
repulsed but the siege continued. Early on the
21st a relieving force under Prince Rupert
appeared on Beacon Hill. His 6,400 men
charged down onto the 7,000 Parliamentarians
hastily drawn up below, forcing most of Meldrum's men back into the Spittal, an area of flat
land north-west of the town and south of the
Trent. The Royalists in Newark sallied out and
retook Muskham Bridge, cutting Meldrum's line
of retreat into the Island and away north. The
Parliamentarians were surrounded and short of
supplies and surrendered on terms on the following day. Rupert had won a tremendous victory.

Not until the end of 1645 was Newark again
under serious threat. A combined Scottish and
English force under Leven and Poyntz appeared
in November and laid siege to the town. The
operation proceeded very slowly, the Parliamentarians first establishing bases in and fortifying a ring of villages around Newark, included
Winthorpe, Coddington, Balderton, Hawton
and Farndon. In March and April 1646 they
built lines of banks and ditches with interval
forts in an arc around the south and east of
Newark; to the north, the Scots pushed into the
Island and threw up their own earthworks. In
the end, however, it was the King's command
rather than the Parliamentary siege which induced the garrison to surrender on 6 May.

The expansion and redevelopment of Newark
and the repeated ploughing and flooding of the
surrounding land has destroyed many of the
military works but the surviving earthworks are
still by far the most extensive in the country and
Newark remains the mecca for Civil War enthu-
siasts.

(I) *Royal defences.* The twelfth–fifteenth-
century castle, a rectangular stronghold with
square or hexagonal corner towers and a northern gatehouse, was garrisoned throughout the
war, suffered repeated bombardments – the
outer walls bear innumerable scars where struck
by cannon-balls – and was slighted after the
war; the ruins are open daily. The successive
governors of Newark lived in the Governor's
House, by the Market Place, a late medieval
timber-framed building with projecting upper
storeys. The museum in Appletongate Street
contains many relics of the Civil War, including
arms, armour, siege money and contemporary
maps of the defences and siege works. The
circuit of earth banks thrown up around the
town in 1643 has almost totally disappeared; a
single short stretch of bank at the north-east
angle survives in gardens along Friary Road and
by the junction of Sleaford Road with Appleton
Gate (around SK80285412).

Several of the outlying Royalist defences also
survive. The King's Sconce was destroyed in the
nineteenth century but the Queen's Sconce survives in good order in open land to the south-
west (SK79055305). A battery in the form of a
pear-shaped mound surrounded by a ditch
stands by Crankley Lane on the Island, just west
of the present A6065 (SK78965585). The main
entry to the Island in the seventeenth century
was over Muskham Bridge, which stood around
100 yards west of the present modern span
carrying the A6065; despite flood damage,
traces remain of the polygonal three-bastioned
earthwork fort which stood at the southern end
of the long-destroyed bridge (SK78655622).

(II) *Parliamentary   earthworks.* Although
the line of ditches and banks dug in 1646 has
completely perished, traces of two earthwork
forts which stood near the end of the line remain
– the northern rampart and bastions of Col.
Grey's Sconce, originally a square fort by the
Trent, largely destroyed by modern sewage
works (SK80255605), and parts of the ditches
and banks of the flood-damaged square redoubt
by   the   river   Devon,   west   of   Hawton
(SK78545130), adapted from the earthworks of
a long-demolished medieval hall.

Several earthworks built in 1646 by the Scottish forces on the Island survive, including the
south bastion of 'Edinburgh', a huge enclosed

Newark, Notts. Despite the impressive riverside frontage (*top*), the medieval castle is a gutted shell, its internal apartments and landward ranges demolished after the war and the surviving walls pitted with cannon scars. The Queen's Sconce (*bottom*), defending the flat land south-west of the town, is probably the best surviving Civil War earthwork in the country. Covering more than three acres, the sconce comprises a square embankment with large angle bastions, each designed to carry two guns.

camp north-east of the A617 (SK78325500), Sandhills Sconce, a four-bastioned fort north-west of Tolney Lane (SK78655382), a small square enclosure in a field east of the A6065 and near a sports ground (SK79505477) and a square enclosure with two bastions at Stoke Lodge (SK78705445) and marked 'redoubt' on Ordnance Survey maps. (The 'earthwork' immediately to the north-west is the square platform of the now demolished Red or Stoke Lodge and is not part of the Civil War defences.)

Although the villages occupied by the besieging army in autumn 1645 were all protected by earthworks, little of the defences now survives. Short stretches of decayed banks can be seen around Balderton and Coddington, and at Farndon the eastern angle bastion and adjoining banks stand in a field to the east of the village (around SK77075166).

St Mary Magdalene's Church, off Market Place, was badly damaged during the siege and was extensively repaired and refurbished in the 1650s and 1660s. The font bowl dates from 1660; an inscription on an adjoining pillar records that it was given to replace that 'demolish[ed] by ye rebels May 9th 1646'.

Newstead Abbey (SK5453)

The Augustinian priory was acquired by Sir John Byron at the Dissolution and converted into a secular house. It was garrisoned for the King during 1643 but was soon abandoned and evacuated without a fight. The house is now open to the public as a museum in honour of a later Byron, the nineteenth-century poet. The west front of the demolished priory church stands nearby amongst the fine, landscaped grounds.

Norwell (SK776617)

Gervase Lee's moated mansion at Norwell was hastily garrisoned for the King at the beginning of 1645 to protect the northern approaches to Newark. The 60-strong garrison was almost immediately besieged and quickly fell to Parliament. The Tudor and Jacobean mansion has been demolished but the moat which once defended it survives almost complete by St Lawrence's Church.

Nottingham (SK5740)

The Civil War formally began here on 22 August 1642 when Charles I raised his Standard on the spot in Standard Hill now marked by a small tablet in the road. On 13 September he marched away and by the end of the year the town was in Parliament's hands, secured by Col. John Hutchinson, who served as Governor of Nottingham for the rest of the war. Under him, the town became the main Parliamentary base and magazine in the county. In

September 1643 Sir John Byron attacked Nottingham, overcame the decayed medieval town walls and captured the town. He established his base in old St Nicholas's Church, mounted guns in the tower, and bombarded the castle, in which Hutchinson and his garrison had taken refuge. The fortress proved impregnable and Byron retreated four days later. In July 1644 Newark Royalists again captured the town in a dawn raid but once more the castle held out and the King's men fell back under heavy fire.

Cromwell entered Nottingham sometime around the middle of May 1643 and remained here for 2–3 weeks. He stayed here again on 3 August 1648 and early July 1650.

Little survives of Civil War Nottingham. The thirteenth- and fourteenth-century town walls, semi-ruinous by the seventeenth, have completely disappeared. The Norman castle was demolished after the war and the post-Restoration mansion built on the site was itself gutted by fire in 1831. Old St Nicholas's Church, east of the castle, was badly damaged by Hutchinson's counter-bombardment during the Royalist attack of September 1643 and the ruined building was then demolished to prevent it being used again as a base to attack the castle; the present St Nicholas's dates from the 1670s. In the seventeenth century the vital bridge across the Trent stood outside the town. There were frequent skirmishes here and both sides built earthwork defences at or near both ends of the bridge. All trace of these Civil War earthworks has been destroyed by the southward expansion of the city.

Owthorpe (SK6733)

During the 1650s Col. Hutchinson and his wife lived in semi-retirement at Owthorpe Hall, a Tudor manor-house completely demolished in the nineteenth century. John Hutchinson had secured most of Nottinghamshire for Parliament in 1642, served as Governor of Nottingham during the first Civil War, and throughout the 1640s was the most prominent and active Parliamentarian in the area. He became an MP and a regicide but withdrew from public life in 1653 and escaped with his head, though not his freedom, at the Restoration. He was imprisoned in the Tower and then Sandown Castle (Kent), where he died in September 1664. His body was brought back to Nottinghamshire for burial and rests beneath a monument in St Margaret's Church, Owthorpe; it incorrectly gives the year of death as 1663. In the fields around the church can be seen traces of canals, terraces and plantations, remnants of the extensive and elaborate gardens which Hutchinson laid out around the hall.

Left: Henry Ireton was born and brought up at Attenborough, Notts. A rather grave and stiff character, he fought with distinction during the first Civil War, but really came to the fore after 1646 as the army's leading political and constitutional theorist, prominent in debate and frequently in print. On campaign in Ireland from 1649, he died of fever or plague, and perhaps over-work too, in November 1651.

Below: Southwell, Notts. The Saracen's Head, a medieval hostelry rebuilt in the seventeenth century, has had a string of royal visitors, including Charles I at the beginning and the end of the first Civil War. An archway gives access from the road to a long coaching yard.

Rufford Abbey (SK646647) After the Dissolution, the twelfth-century Cistercian abbey at Rufford was bought by the Earl of Shrewsbury, who had most of the monastic buildings demolished and an Elizabethan mansion, Rufford Abbey House, erected on the site. Cromwell lodged here on 22 August 1651 on his way to Worcester. The house was remodelled and extended in the eighteenth century, fell ruinous in the nineteenth and was partly demolished in the twentieth. Parts of the sixteenth- and early seventeenth-century house survive, together with fragments of earlier monastic buildings.

On 8 March 1655 Rufford Abbey was the Nottinghamshire rendezvous for the projected nationwide Royalist rising. Up to 3,000 Royalists gathered here overnight but dispersed without incident on the following day.

Screveton (SK7343) Kirketon Hall was the home of the Whalley family of Nottinghamshire and the birthplace of Edmund Whalley. Edmund served in the Parliamentary army during the 1640s, signed Charles I's death warrant and became a senior officer, a Major General and a close colleague of Cromwell – his cousin – during the Protectorate. He fled the country at the Restoration and died in America. His old home, a late medieval manor-house, was extensively redesigned in the eighteenth century and completely demolished in the nineteenth. Ancient trees and slight earthworks west of the church mark the site of Kirketon Hall. Many of the family lie beneath monuments in St Wilfrid's Church.

Shelford House (SK673434) The medieval priory at Shelford was acquired by the Stanhope family after the Dissolution and partly converted into a Tudor mansion, Shelford House or Manor. The house was secured for the King in December 1642 and held throughout the war by Sir Philip Stanhope's 200-strong garrison. An existing ditch and rampart protected the house but the Royalists strengthened the defences by throwing up half-moon earthworks to guard the main approaches; a further wet ditch, probably part of the medieval drainage system, ran in a long circuit around house and gardens. Shelford House survived until November 1645. On the 1st Col. Poyntz and his 2,000 men occupied the village, expelling a small party of Royalists from the church. Two days later the house itself was stormed and captured, though not without a fierce fight in the course of which Stanhope and 140 of his men were killed. The house was then plundered and burnt to the ground. The present private house was built on the site in 1676;

slight traces of the medieval and Civil War earthworks survive in the grounds.

Southwell (SK7053) Although the itinerary of the King during 1642–46 lies beyond the scope of this work, an exception may perhaps be made for the Saracen's Head in Southwell. This early seventeenth-century coaching inn, which survives in good condition, saw the beginning and the end of the first Civil War: Charles I stayed here in August 1642 shortly before marching to Nottingham to raise the Royal Standard, and he returned nearly four years later to pass his last night of freedom before surrendering to the Scots around Newark.

Staunton Hall (SK805433) The Tudor house by the church was owned by the Royalist, William Staunton, and was raided and looted by Parliamentary troops in 1645. The bullet marks in the door are thought to date from the Civil War. Staunton Hall was extended during the eighteenth century and remains a private residence.

Thurgarton Priory (SK692492) Although much of the medieval priory at Thurgarton was demolished at or soon after the Dissolution, some parts, chiefly the priory church and outbuildings, were retained and converted for secular use. The church and stables were occupied for the King in December 1642 as an outpost of Newark and were held by a 40-man garrison under Sir Roger Cooper. Thurgarton remained in Royalist hands until December 1644, when a raiding party from Nottingham led by Col. Thornhaugh stormed and captured the building. The stables and other surviving sections of the medieval monastery were demolished in the eighteenth century when the present Priory Manor House was built. All that remains today is a section of the thirteenth-century monastic church, incorporated within the largely nineteenth-century Priory Church of St Peter.

Welbeck Abbey (SK5674) Welbeck Abbey was a fortified Tudor and Jacobean mansion built on the site of a medieval abbey and incorporating sections of the monastic cloister. It was owned in the seventeenth century by the Earl of Newcastle, the Royalist commander in the north, and was garrisoned for the King in December 1642. Welbeck was attacked and taken by Manchester in August 1644 after Marston Moor and then garrisoned for Parliament as a check on Newark. However, the 200-strong garrison was repeatedly raided by the Newark Royalists over the following year and the house was finally captured by them in July 1645.

Welbeck seems to have remained under Royalist control until early 1646, when the soldiers were withdrawn to defend Newark. Although sections of medieval and Jacobean work remain, the present rambling mansion largely dates from the eighteenth and nineteenth century.

Willoughby in the Wolds (SK6325) In summer 1648 a detachment of Royalist rebels marched south from Yorkshire, plundered their way through Lincolnshire and entered Nottinghamshire via Newark. They hurried south, pursued by a Parliamentary force under Col. Rossiter, but were first caught as they marched through Widmerpool. After moving a little further south, Sir Philip Monckton and his fellow Royalists turned and faced Rossiter outside Willoughby. According to tradition, the fight took place in a beanfield near the church; most of the villagers watched the spectacle from the church tower. The exhausted and inexperienced Royalists were routed by the professional soldiers and the second Civil War in Nottinghamshire was over.

Wiverton Hall (SK713364) Secured for the King in December 1642, Sir Thomas Chaworth's moated manor-house served as an outpost of Newark throughout the Civil War. The Parliamentarians made no serious attempt to take the hall until November 1645, when Col. Poyntz and his 2,000-strong force marched on Wiverton. Sir Robert Thervill surrendered without a fight and the Parliamentarians sacked and then completely destroyed the old hall. The medieval gatehouse alone survived and is now incorporated within the present Wiverton Hall, a private mansion built in the nineteenth century a little to the south of the site of the old hall. Seventeenth-century Wiverton was approached from the south, along a now disused road; the Royalist garrison threw up two half-moon batteries to flank this road as it neared the hall. The western earthwork has been ploughed out but the eastern survives in good condition, and stands in the grounds about 60 yards south-east of the present hall (SK71383634).

OXFORDSHIRE

After his failure to capture London in autumn 1642, the King withdrew to Oxford and the city became his capital and military HQ for the rest of the Civil War. The city was protected by a circle of garrisons guarding the approach roads, and the county was firmly Royalist during the opening years of the war. The Parliamentarians began attacking the fringes of Oxfordshire in late 1644 and slowly pushed the King's men back into an ever decreasing area around Oxford. The city itself held out until June 1646. Cromwell was frequently in the area between September 1644 and June 1646; he campaigned here during spring 1645 and was present throughout the siege of Oxford in the following year.

Abingdon (SU5097) Abingdon was held for the King from December 1642 until 25 May 1644, when the garrison was withdrawn as part of the operation to find troops for the summer campaign. Essex and Waller promptly occupied the town unopposed and Abingdon remained in Parliamentary hands thereafter and served as a base for the campaign against Oxford in 1645–46. The Royalists launched several unsuccessful attacks on their old base – on 11 January 1645 1,800 men under Rupert were halted and driven off just outside the town and in March 1646 a surprise attack reached the Abbey Gate before a Parliamentary counter-charge and the general congestion of men and carts around the gate halted the Royalist advance.

The commanders of the Parliamentary and Royalist garrisons probably established their HQ in the King's Head and Bell in East St Helen's Street. St Helen's Church, nearby, is the resting place of Thomas Trapham, Cromwell's military surgeon and the man who embalmed Charles I's body and sewed back the head after execution.

Banbury (SP4540) Banbury was held by Parliamentary forces during the first weeks of the Civil War, but fell to the Earl of Northampton on 29 October 1642; town and castle served as a Royalist base for the rest of the war. Parliamentary troops under John Fiennes overran the town in August 1644 but, despite a three month siege, were unable to take the castle – the Parliamentarians established their HQ in St Mary's Church and their battery in the churchyard – and were driven off by the Earl of Northampton on 26 October. Col. Whalley captured the town without difficulty in January 1646 but his initial assault on the castle was fiercely repulsed and the 3,000 Parliamentarians settled down for a long siege. Sir William Compton and his 400-strong garrison surrendered five months later on 8 May. The large, double bailey castle was slighted after the war and today nothing survives except a section of the moat and fragments of curtain wall. Medieval St Mary's Church has also disappeared and the present building dates from 1800. Banbury museum contains many relics from the Civil War in the area.

Besselsleigh (SP4501)   William Lenthall, Speaker of the Long Parliament and of the 1st Protectorate Parliament, owned the manor-house adjoining the church here. It was seized and fortified by Oxford Royalists at the end of 1644 but quickly retaken. The Parliamentarians, however, made no attempt to hold Besselsleigh and immediately withdrew, slighting the manor-house as they left. Nothing now remains of Lenthall's house except the seventeenth-century gatepier near the churchyard. In happier days during the 1630s Lenthall had financed the restoration of the medieval church, including the addition of the twin bellcote. St Lawrence's contains the tombs of many of the family, including Col. John Lenthall, the Speaker's son, himself a Parliamentary officer and politician, sometime Governor of Windsor. An inscription in the chancel records Speaker Lenthall's association with the church.

Bletchingdon House (SP5018)   The old manor-house, of which no trace now remains, served as a minor Royalist outpost throughout the war. It was surrounded by Cromwell's troops on 24 April 1645 and surrendered without a fight in the early hours of the 25th. Col. Windebank later protested that he had surrendered the house in this fashion because his young wife and her female friends were there, but the officers in Oxford were not impressed; Windebank was condemned to death by court martial and shot outside Oxford castle on 3 May.

Broughton Castle (SP419382)   The fourteenth–sixteenth-century fortified mansion was owned by Lord Saye and Sele during the 1630s and became a meeting place for leading opponents of the King's government in the pre-war years. Hampden, Pym, Brooke and others held secret conferences in the Council Chamber. During the war, Broughton was garrisoned for Parliament by Saye and Sele and his sons, John and Nathaniel Fiennes. It suffered frequent Royalist raids and was briefly taken by the King's men in December 1642.

The building survived the war intact and remains one of the finest and most complete medieval houses in England. Open to the public on Sundays and certain weekdays in the summer, Broughton Castle contains many relics of the Civil War, including arms and armour and portraits of Oliver and Richard Cromwell and John Hampden.

Burford (SP2512)   In May 1649 Burford became the centre of a Leveller-inspired mutiny in the Parliamentary army. The military leaders in London moved quickly to quell the outbreak and on 14 May Fairfax and Cromwell swept into Burford, surprising the soldiers, overcoming brief resistance around the Crown in Sheep Street and promptly crushing the mutiny. Three hundred and fifty rebellious troops were captured and spent an uncomfortable night locked in the church. On the following day they were all sentenced to death by court martial. In fact, only three ringleaders – Thompson, Church and Perkins – were executed, shot by the churchyard wall. Their colleagues were forced to watch the executions from the church roof and were then taken down to suffer a lecture on loyalty and Godliness from Cromwell. The Church of St John the Baptist (SP253124) has been little altered since the mid-seventeenth century. The font still bears faint traces of an inscription – 'Anthony Sedley 1649 Prisner' – carved by one of the Leveller soldiers on the night of 14 May. In 1979 a memorial to the three executed Leveller soldiers was placed on the outer wall of the Lady Chapel. The three lie in unmarked graves somewhere in the churchyard.

In 1637 William Lenthall acquired Priory House, a late Tudor building which stood on the site of a medieval Augustinian hospital. By the twentieth century the old house had been largely demolished and the remaining sections were in decay; it was restored and returned to the church. Lenthall retired to Burford after the Restoration and died in Priory House in September 1662. He was buried in the north transept of St John's Church, but no contemporary monument survives; a much later tablet on the north wall of the Tanfield Chapel commemorates Speaker Lenthall and his descendants.

Burford Church, Oxon. St John's (*top*) became a prison in May 1649, when Cromwell and Fairfax quelled a half-hearted mutiny and held the 350 rebellious troops in the church. Three ringleaders were subsequently shot in the churchyard and their colleagues forced to watch from the roof of the Lady Chapel (far left); a modern plaque on the outside wall of the Lady Chapel commemorates the three (*above*).

Right: Swinbrooke Church, Oxon. In the chancel stands a three tier monument to the Fettiplace family erected by Sir Edmund Fettiplace in 1686; it carries effigies of Sir Edmund at the top, his father beneath him and, at the bottom with straight hair, his Parliamentarian uncle who had served at Cirencester and elsewhere during the Civil War.

Chalgrove (SU6396) In the early hours of 18 June 1643 a party of Oxford Royalists under Prince Rupert raided Sir Samuel Luke's quarters at Chinnor, killing 50 Parliamentary soldiers and capturing 120. The Royalists pressed on in search of a Parliamentary convoy, which they knew to be travelling through the area, carrying £21,000 cash to pay Essex's troops. Rupert failed to locate the convoy – forewarned of the Prince's approach, it had taken cover – and turned back towards Oxford, pursued by a force of local Parliamentarians under John Hampden. After being harried for several miles, Rupert halted on Chalgrove Field and charged his pursuers, quickly routing and scattering them. The otherwise minor skirmish is memorable for the death of the Parliamentary commander. At some stage Hampden was badly injured – whether he was shot in the shoulder by a Royalist or lost a hand and arm when his own pistol burst is not clear – and died soon afterwards of his wounds. A large obelisk, erected in 1843 by the Old Watlington Road (SU645972), commemorates John Hampden and the Battle of Chalgrove Field.

Clanfield (SP285020) According to tradition, Cromwell stayed in Clanfield in spring 1645 while campaigning around Radcot, and lodged at the Plough Hotel, a seventeenth-century inn which stands at the centre of the village.

Coleshill (SU2393) One of the greatest houses of Interregnum England stood at Coleshill, a grand 2½ storey mansion built in 1650–52 and designed by Roger Pratt, possibly in consultation with Inigo Jones. Sadly the house was gutted by fire in 1952 and has been completely demolished. Today nothing remains but four pairs of gatepiers dating from the mid-seventeenth century.

Cornbury (SP357183) Although Cornbury House played no known part in the conflict, the remains of a Civil War earthwork stand ½ mile east of the house, near the river Evenlode. A double bank and ditch running around 2½ sides of a square enclosure, the earthwork was probably a gun emplacement thrown up by the Royalist Danvers family to protect their home against possible attack.

Cropredy (SP4646) On 29 June 1644 the King and his 8,500-strong army were travelling north through Oxfordshire, marching along the Daventry road on the east bank of the Cherwell. Waller's 9,000 Parliamentarians were shadowing the King, following a parallel road to the west of the river. The two roads were linked by a short lane running from Great Bourton to Williamscote and crossing the Cherwell by a bridge at Cropredy. Fearing attack, the King posted Dragoons to guard the bridge and attempted to hurry his men north and away across Hay's bridge. He succeeded only in dangerously stretching his line and so encouraging the Parliamentarians to attack. Waller led one party towards the ford at Slat Mill, one mile south of Cropredy, while Middleton and the rest of the army set out to capture Cropredy bridge. Both attacks were initially successful – Waller forded the river and threw part of the Royalist line into confusion and Middleton swept across the bridge and pursued the surprised Royalists north. However, the King's men regrouped and counter-charged and both the Parliamentary units were pushed back across the river with heavy losses. The armies stayed in position overnight but drew away on the 30th.

The area around the village is still open farmland, little changed since 1644. The present bridge at Cropredy (SP469465) was built in 1937 but an inscribed plaque on the south side commemorates the earlier bridge and the battle and prays 'From Civil War Good Lord Deliver Us'. The nearby Oxford Canal takes water from the Cherwell and thus the river today is not the obstacle that it must have been in the 1640s. Several pieces of Civil War arms and armour found on the battlefield are displayed within St Mary's Church.

Cuddesdon (SP6003) Cuddesdon Palace, an early Stuart bishop's palace, housed a small Royalist garrison for most of the war. The King's men were withdrawn in 1645, destroying the building as they left to deny it to Parliament. The palace was rebuilt after the Restoration but this building, in turn, was destroyed by fire in the 1960s.

Deddington (SP4631) The minor Royalist garrison here saw little action and was evacuated in 1645. The medieval castle, south-east of the village, was very ruinous by the seventeenth century and the King's men were probably based in Castle House, north of the church, a sixteenth- and seventeenth-century mansion in two-tone stone, incorporating part of a medieval manor-house which stood on the site.

Faringdon (SU2895) A Royalist base throughout the latter half of the war, the garrison survived a siege by Cromwell in late April and early May 1645 and held out for another year. On 24 June 1646 George Lisle and his men finally surrendered to Robert Pye and the besieging Parliamentarians. The Norman castle at Faringdon was very ruinous by the seventeenth century and the Royalist garrison was based in Faringdon House, the late medieval and Tudor seat of the Pye family. The house, which has been completely demolished, stood near the present Faringdon House, the late Georgian mansion north of the church. The mid-seventeenth-century gatepiers of the old house survive near the church.

The tower of All Saints Church was destroyed at some point during the war and was rebuilt in 1646. The earthworks on Faringdon Hill are sometimes described as Civil War siege works and may have been thrown up by Cromwell in spring 1645 or by Pye the following year.

Gaunt House (SP408033) The late medieval house, ½ mile east of Standlake, served as a minor Royalist outpost during the Civil War. Besieged and bombarded by Col. Rainsborough's troops during May 1645, the garrison surrendered on the last day of the month. Gaunt House survives as a private residence, but the present building appears to date from the 1660s; presumably the medieval house was largely destroyed during or after the Civil War.

Godstow House (SP477093) Most of the twelfth-century Benedictine nunnery of Godstow, near Wolvercote, was demolished soon after the Dissolution, but some of the cloisteral buildings were retained and converted into a secular residence, Godstow House. The house was held for the King from the outbreak of war until May 1645, when the garrison was withdrawn and the house slighted to prevent its reoccupation. Today little remains except a walled enclosure and scattered fragments of masonry. Parts of the medieval hospice may also have survived and been incorporated in a later inn, the Trout.

Great Milton (SP6302) Secretary of State John Thurloe leased the Priory at Great Milton for many years and lived here from time to time, particularly after the Restoration when he had lost much of his other property. There are colourful but unlikely stories of Cromwell and Milton visiting Thurloe here. The Priory survives in good order, a Tudor hall with projecting seventeenth-century wings, and stands north of the church near the village green. It is not open to the public.

Henley on Thames (SU7682) The town was frequently raided by Royalists during the Civil

War but remained a Parliamentary base throughout the conflict. Bulstrode Whitelock was governor of Henley for a time and established his HQ at Phillis Court, the late medieval hall which he owned just outside the town (SU765830); Whitelock's house was later demolished to make way for the present nineteenth-century Phillis Court.

William Lenthall was born and brought up in Henley, in the sixteenth-century gabled house in Hart Street now known as The Speaker's House.

Hinton Waldrist (SU3799) Hinton Manor, an early seventeenth-century manor-house on the site of an earlier castle, was owned during the 1630s and 1640s by Henry Marten, a member of the Long Parliament, one of the most outspoken opponents of Charles I and, later, a regicide. According to tradition, Cromwell and his troops quartered in and around Hinton Manor during their Oxfordshire campaign. Marten's old house survives in good order, an early eighteenth-century five bay front now concealing the early Stuart house behind; nearby are the remains of the moat and motte of the thirteenth-century castle.

Holton (SP6006) Cromwell probably lodged at Lady Whorewood's house at Holton during May and June 1646 while attending the siege of Oxford. On 15 June Henry Ireton married Cromwell's eldest daughter, Bridget, in St Bartholomew's Church. The Tudor and early Stuart mansion was completely demolished in the nineteenth century, but its moat survives within the former park. According to tradition, Cromwell himself planted the cherry tree which stood in the park.

Little Wittenham (SU567935) Cromwell's aunt Mary (d1617) and her husband Sir William Dunch (d1612) spent their married lives at the long-demolished manor-house at Little Wittenham. Both lie buried in the village church beneath an elaborate tomb in the tower. Mary is portrayed in alabaster, wearing a ruff and a stiff dress and her husband appears in rich armour; their nine children kneel around the base of the tomb. Several descendants lie nearby, including Ann Dunch (d1683), whose tomb is covered by a monumental brass.

Mapledurham House (SU671766) The fine Tudor house served as a minor Royalist outpost during the early stages of the war to guard the south-east of the county and the road north from Reading. As part of the operation to isolate and surround Reading, Parliamentary troops quickly overran the base in April 1643 and proceeded to loot the house. Mapledurham survived the war intact and remains one of the finest Elizabethan houses in the country. The richly decorated and furnished house is open on summer weekends.

Marston (SP5309) Marston was one of the Parliamentary bases in May and June 1646 during the siege of Oxford. Fairfax and Cromwell established their HQ in Unton Croke's manor-house. A slightly later building, known as Cromwell's House, stands on the site in Pond's Lane. Cromwell and Fairfax probably viewed the city from the tower of St Nicholas's Church.

Oxford (SP5305) For 3½ years Oxford served as the King's capital, the seat of the Royal Court, the Privy Council, Parliament and Courts of Justice, and as a military base and stronghold. It was not seriously threatened until 1645 and held out until 24 June 1646, when it surrendered on the King's orders.

The defence of Oxford lay primarily in a circle of outlying garrisons, designed to halt aggressors and prevent a direct attack on the city. Nonetheless, the Royalists quickly set about fortifying Oxford itself, building a circuit of banks, ditches and interval towers around the city to replace the outdated medieval defences — by the seventeenth century the castle was semiruinous and the town walls had been outgrown. The new earthworks were particularly strong to the north of Oxford, across the area of high ground between the Thames and the Cherwell; on the other sides, the rivers and adjoining low ground, which could be flooded, provided additional defence.

Oxford had a fairly peaceful Civil War and for much of the time the only Parliamentarians to be seen were the prisoners-of-war held in the castle. In spring 1643 Whitelock and other Parliamentary commissioners arrived in Oxford for abortive peace negotiations; they were lodged at the Katherine Wheel Inn, long demolished, which stood near St John's College. Waller and Essex were around Oxford in May 1644 and skirmished with Rupert in Headington, but not until 1645 did the Parliamentarians mount a serious attack on the city. In May 1645 Fairfax laid siege to Oxford, but vigorous Royalist raiding persuaded him to abandon the hopeless attempt in early June. In May 1646 Parliamentary troops returned in force, established an HQ and battery on Headington Hill, and closely invested the city. The garrison surrendered seven weeks later at the King's command.

The subsequent expansion of Oxford has destroyed almost all the Civil War defences. A section of the earthwork bank survives to the east of Mansfield Road, running between Merton's and Balliol's sportsgrounds, and with its north-west end near a Victorian house in Mansfield Road known as King's Mount House; a further fragment of the bank stands in the Warden's garden at Wadham College. The Norman castle in New Road, derelict by the seventeenth century and used during the Civil War as nothing more than a prison, was subsequently destroyed and little remains today except the motte and a single mural tower, the twelfth-century St George's Tower.

Most of the college buildings requisitioned by the Court during the war still exist. The King and Court were based at Christ Church, where the Privy Council met and the Oxford Parliament assembled for formal ceremonies; the Great Hall was struck by cannon in 1645 and in the following year articles of surrender were signed in the Audit Room. The Queen lived at Merton College, and New Inn Hall, on the site of the present St Peter's College, became the Royal Mint. The Commons and courts of law usually met in Convocation House by the Divinity School. New College Cloister and Quadrangle became the principal Royalist magazine and the troops mustered and exercised all around the town, particularly in Merton Park and Christ Church Meadows.

Cromwell was present throughout the siege of Oxford in May and June 1646 and returned with Fairfax and other senior officers in May 1649. They entered the city to an official welcome on 17 May and stayed for three days, lodging in the warden's rooms of All Souls College — the present Warden's Lodgings are later. They dined at Magdalen on the 19th and were awarded honorary degrees.

Oxford Museum in St Aldate's contains many relics of the Civil War, including arms, armour and plans and paintings of the siege of Oxford. The Ashmolean, off St Giles's, possesses Cromwell's death mask, watch and Great Seal, a later bust of the Lord Protector, and many other items from the period.

Radcot (SU285994) Radcot was important during the Civil War because of the bridge over the Thames here. The crossing was held by Royalist troops for most of the war, but the village was frequently raided by Parliamentarians and there were repeated skirmishes in open land near the bridge, still known as Garrison Fields. Cromwell supposedly clashed with Royalists here sometime during spring 1645.

The Royalist garrison here finally surrendered to Fairfax on 24 May 1646. The fourteenth-century three-arched bridge at Radcot is probably the oldest surviving span over the Thames.

Rousham House (SP479242)

Sir Robert Dormer's early seventeenth-century house was garrisoned for the King during the latter half of the Civil War, at which time the shooting holes, still to be seen, were made in the oak doorway of the Great Hall. There is, in fact, no record of fighting here and the house survived intact. Remodelled by Kent in the eighteenth century, the richly-decorated building is still owned by the Dormer family and is open on Sundays and Wednesdays during the summer.

Shirburn House or Castle (SU696960)

In the late fourteenth century the Lisle family built a fortified manor-house at Shirburn, a quadrangular mansion in brick and stone with round corner towers, a moat and a western gatehouse. The house was held for the King throughout the war but the garrison was small and inactive and there is no record of any fighting here. The house was surrendered to Fairfax in May 1646 after a brief siege and survived the war intact. In the following century, however, much of the medieval building was demolished and the remainder, including the south-west and south-east towers, the gatehouse and part of two ranges, incorporated within a Georgian mansion. The latter survives as a private residence.

Shrivenham (SU241891)

In St Andrew's Church is the tomb of John Wildman (d1693), whose long and colourful career included periods serving in the Parliamentary army in England and Ireland, gathering intelligence for Cromwell and plotting against him during the Protectorate. He lies beneath an inscribed slab in the chancel, alongside the altar.

Stanford (SU3493)

Cromwell supposedly lodged at Penstone or Penistone Farm, Stanford, during his Oxfordshire campaign of spring 1645. The early seventeenth-century building, restored and extended in the eighteenth century, is one of many in the area traditionally linked with Cromwell.

Swinbrooke (SP2812)

St Mary's Church contains many monuments to the Fettiplace family. The north wall of the chancel is covered by a series of ornate effigies, including the reclining figure of Col. Fettiplace, the Parliamentary officer and governor of Cirencester in February 1643 when the town fell to Rupert.

Thame (SP7005)

Despite frequent raids from Oxford Royalists, Thame was held by Parliament throughout the Civil War. In June 1643 John Hampden died in the Greyhound Inn of wounds received on Chalgrove Field. An eighteenth-century building, known as Hampden House, stands on the site of the demolished inn on the north side of Market Square; a plaque on the outer wall tells the story of Hampden's death.

Wallingford (SU609898)

Town and castle were held for the King throughout the Civil War to guard the south-east approaches to Oxford. Parliamentary raids occasionally progressed as far as Wallingford, but not until 1646 did the Parliamentarians mount a sustained operation against the stronghold. Fairfax invested Wallingford on 11 May and six weeks later, on 27 June, Col. Blagge surrendered the castle, one of the last bases in the county to fall to Parliament. The mighty Norman castle was demolished in 1652 and the stone carted off, and little now remains except fragments of masonry on and around the motte.

Woodstock (SP4416)

Woodstock was a Royalist base for most of the Civil War, one of the many strongholds protecting the approaches to Oxford. The town was captured and briefly held by Fairfax in summer 1644, but was quickly retaken by the King's men and held out until April 1646, when the garrison surrendered after a three week siege and bombardment. The King's forces had occupied the magnificent royal palace at Woodstock, begun by Henry I and enlarged by Henry II, a massive complex including the great hall, chapel, cloistered courts and extensive gardens. Semi-derelict by the seventeenth century, the buildings were badly damaged during the Parliamentary bombardment of 1646. In the early eighteenth century the 1st Duke of Marlborough acquired and demolished the ruins and nothing now survives above ground. The site of the medieval palace is marked by a stone and inscribed plaque in the grounds of Blenheim Palace, on the north-east side of the Great or Grand Bridge.

Wytham Abbey (SP4708)

The sixteenth-century house in which Cromwell lodged on 23–25 May 1645 no longer exists. The present house by the church is a mock-Tudor edifice built in the nineteenth century, possibly incorporating part of the earlier mansion known to Cromwell.

SHROPSHIRE

The Civil War in Shropshire quickly developed into a conflict of garrisons and raiding. There were no major battles and few significant skirmishes in the region; instead each side set about securing and manning towns and villages, medieval castles and Tudor manor-houses. There were a very large number of garrisons within Shropshire – the Royalists alone had at least 31 bases here. The King's men held almost the whole county in 1642 but they were slowly driven out by Parliamentary forces advancing from the north and east, though not until 1645–46 did the last Royalist bases fall. There is no evidence that Cromwell ever visited Shropshire.

Albright Hussey (SJ502176)   The isolated house served as a Royalist garrison, established by Rupert to cover Wem, but later withdrawn as the area fell under Parliamentary control. The Tudor half-timbered hall, extended in brick in 1601, survives as a private residence. A public footpath runs past the building.

Apley House (SO7198)   The Elizabethan house of Sir William Whitmore, garrisoned for the King for most of the war, was destroyed during or soon after the conflict. A succession of houses have stood on the site, and the present grand mansion dates from the nineteenth century, though it incorporates part of a Georgian predecessor. No trace survives of the building which saw action in the Civil War.

Atcham (SJ541093)   St Eata's Church housed a small Royalist garrison from 1643 until 1645, when it was hastily withdrawn after the fall of Shrewsbury. At some stage there was fighting here, for the church bears marks of gun- and cannon-fire inside and out. The garrison had been placed at Atcham to cover the bridge across the Severn; the present span is eighteenth-century.

Benthall (SJ656026)   Benthall Hall was garrisoned for the King from the outbreak of war until summer 1645, when it fell to Parliamentary forces pushing south-west from Staffordshire. The Parliamentarians then garrisoned the place to cover the Severn and the south-east approaches to Shrewsbury. The building survived the war intact and has been little altered since. The finely decorated hall is now owned by the National Trust and is open on Saturdays and certain weekdays during the summer. St Bartholomew's Church served as an outpost of the main garrison; the building was badly damaged during the war and was rebuilt after the Restoration.

Bridgnorth (SO7193)   The hilltop town above the Severn was held for the King without serious challenge throughout the war and became an important base for operations in the West Midlands and southern Staffordshire. On 31 March 1646 the town was stormed by Parliamentary troops who forced an entry through the north gate via St Leonard's churchyard. The Royalists hastily retreated into the castle, setting fire to the town behind them; the flames reached their powder, stored in St Leonard's, and the resulting explosion demolished the medieval church and wrecked many other buildings in the area. The King's men held out in the castle for almost a month, but heavy bombardment and mining persuaded them to surrender on 26 April. The Norman fortress, badly damaged during the bombardment, was slighted after the war. The ruins of the leaning keep, its crazy angle caused by Parliamentary mines and later subsidence, stand in a public park at the south end of High Town. St Leonard's was rebuilt soon after the war, but the present church is almost entirely Victorian.

Broncroft Castle (SO545867)   The picturesque red brick building, with several towers and a decorated hall, owes much to nineteenth-century restoration, but the great tower near the entrance is mostly fourteenth-century work, one of the few sections of the late medieval stronghold to survive. The fortress was garrisoned by Royalists for much of the war but was evacuated in spring 1645. The King's men slighted the defences as they left. It was occupied and restored by Parliamentary troops in June and a Royalist counter-attack on 4 July was fiercely repulsed.

Caus Castle (SJ337078)   The twelfth-century border castle at Caus was held for the King from the outbreak of war until summer 1645, when it was besieged and bombarded by Col. Mackworth's Parliamentarians; the small garrison surrendered on 23 June. The castle originally comprised a large shell keep, surrounded by curtain walls and mural towers protecting a double bailey, but is now very ruinous.

Clun Castle (SO299809)   Bicton Ditches, two

parallel ditches running across the isthmus between the river junction, ¾ mile north-west of Clun, have frequently been described as Civil War earthworks, constructed or reused by the Parliamentary troops besieging the castle in 1644. The fortress itself had been held for the King since the outbreak of war but the small garrison saw little action and surrendered in 1644 on the threat of bombardment. Much of the Norman castle has been demolished but the banks and ditches which surrounded the two baileys still survive, together with fragments of the curtain wall and two semicircular mural towers.

High Ercall (SJ595174)
In the seventeenth century High Ercall Hall comprised four ranges around a central courtyard protected by a gatehouse, drawbridge and moat. It was garrisoned for the King in 1644–45 and survived several Parliamentary attacks, including brief sieges in February, March and July 1645. The garrison finally surrendered on 28 March 1646 after a prolonged siege and heavy bombardment which badly damaged the hall – two of the four ranges were subsequently demolished. The now 'L'-shaped Jacobean hall, with an impressive brick and red sandstone north front, stands by the road near the village church. St Michael's and All Angels' was itself badly damaged during the Parliamentary bombardment and was largely rebuilt in the 1670s using the original stone.

Holgate Castle (SO562897)
Holgate housed a minor Parliamentary garrison, designed to cover Corve Dale and any northern movement from the Ludlow Royalists. Of the thirteenth- and fourteenth-century castle, little now survives except a semicircular tower in fine ashlar north of the church and behind a modern farmhouse.

Hopton Castle (SO367780)
Hopton Castle was the scene of one of the most notorious massacres of the English Civil War. In mid-February 1644 the medieval castle was fortified and garrisoned for Parliament but was almost immediately besieged by Royalist forces. On 13 March Sir Michael Woodhouse stormed the castle and then cold-bloodedly killed the 31 captured Parliamentarians. Their bodies were dumped in a pool, possibly the remains of a moat. The fragmentary ruins of the Norman castle stand in a field on the outskirts of the village of Hopton Castle.

Lea Hall or Castle (SJ333036)
The late medieval and Tudor fortified hall was garrisoned for the King during the Civil War but the garrison was evacuated in February 1645; they slighted and burnt the place as they left. The old house has completely gone but the moat which defended it survives around the modern, private building.

Lea Castle (SO3589)
The medieval castle and its small Royalist garrison fell to Middleton in October 1645. A single tall fragment of the fourteenth-century keep survives, adjoining a nineteenth-century house.

Lilleshall Abbey (SJ738142)
Much of the abbey, particularly the church, was converted into a secular residence after the Dissolution and was still in good order in the mid-seventeenth century. It housed a Royalist garrison for much of the Civil War. In March 1644 a Parliamentary force sent to capture the place was intercepted and repulsed *en route* (see 'Longford') and Col. Leveson's garrison survived for another 17 months. Not until 23 August 1645 did Lilleshall fall, bombarded and then stormed by a large Parliamentary force under Col. Braine. The Parliamentary cannon had brought down much of the central tower, north transept and Lady Chapel. The impressive ruins of the twelfth- and thirteenth-century Augustinian abbey are open daily.

Longford (SJ7218)
On 25 March 1644 a unit of 500 Parliamentary Foot led by Col. Mytton bound for Lilleshall was caught and routed at Longford by Royalist forces under Vaughan and Ellis. The King's men went on to besiege the small Parliamentary garrison in Longford House, which surrendered on 2 April. The present hall dates from the late eighteenth century.

Longnor Hall (SJ4800)
The present hall, a Stuart red brick and stone edifice, was built after the Civil War. The Royalist garrison of 1643–45 was based in the medieval hall, completely demolished in the eighteenth century, the position of which is indicated by decayed earthworks and broken ground.

Loppington (SJ472293)·
In autumn 1643 a troop of Parliamentarians under Capt. Bromhall was surprised at Loppington and hastily retreated into St Michael's. The King's men fired the church, forcing the Parliamentarians out. A fight developed, but the arrival of reinforcements from Wem compelled the Royalists to fall back. The timber south porch was destroyed in the course of the action and was rebuilt in the 1650s.

Ludlow (SO5174) Town and castle served as
an important Royalist base throughout the war
and a centre for operations in the south of the
county. Occasional Parliamentary raids during
1644–45 were turned back outside the town and
Ludlow held out until spring 1646, one of the
last important bases in the county to remain in
the King's hands. Col. Birch and a large force of
Hereford Parliamentarians attacked and quickly
overran the town on 24 April 1646, but their
initial assault on the castle failed and Birch was
compelled to lay siege to the fortress. The
garrison finally surrendered on 29 May. The
massive red sandstone castle was slighted in
1652, but large parts of the eleventh- to
sixteenth-century fortress remain, including the
outer walls, gatehouse and mural towers, the
Great Hall and a separate twelfth-century round
chapel; the ruins are open daily. The town's
defences have fared less well and of the circuit of
medieval walls and gates, little but the
fourteenth-century Broadgate survives.

Madeley Court (SJ6905) Madeley Court, a
Tudor mansion incorporating parts of an earlier
priory grange, was garrisoned for the King until
the fall of Shrewsbury led to its hasty evacuation. The gatehouse survives intact, a striking
ashlar pile with two large polygonal towers
topped by pyramidal roofs. Of the main house,
however, only part remains, including the Elizabethan hall range with a projecting side wing.

Montford Bridge (SJ432152) The important
bridge over the Severn to the west of Shrewsbury
was protected by a Royalist garrison from early
1643 until June 1644, when the crossing fell to
Denbigh's Parliamentarians. Although the present span is eighteenth-century, slight earthworks on the north-west side may be the remains of Civil War defence works.

Moreton Corbet Castle (SJ560231) The early thirteenth-century castle, modified and extended by the Corbet family in the sixteenth
century, was garrisoned for the King in 1643–
44. It fell to a surprise night attack on 8
September 1644, but the Parliamentary garrison
soon retreated in the face of Royalist pressure.
The King's men, in turn, evacuated the place in
1645 following the fall of Shrewsbury, and they
probably slighted the castle as they left to prevent its reoccupation by Parliamentary troops.
The ruins, which are open daily, include an early
thirteenth-century keep standing amid the ruins
of Sir Andrew Corbet's Elizabethan domestic
buildings and a northern gateway, originally
medieval but heavily remodelled in 1579.

Oswestry (SJ2929) In June 1644 a large Parliamentary force attacked Oswestry, which had
been garrisoned for the King by Lord Capel in
the previous year. St Oswald's Church was
taken and used as a battery from which cannon
bombarded the Royalist defences in and around
the castle. In the end, however, it was a petard
which blew the castle gates and compelled the
garrison to surrender. A Royalist attempt to
retake the town in July ended when their forces
were intercepted and scattered at Whittington,
three miles east of the town. The medieval castle
was badly damaged during the bombardment of
June 1644 and was slighted after the war; today
only fragments of the shell keep survive on a
mound behind Bailey Head. St Oswald's
Church, damaged by the Royalist counter-
bombardment, was repaired after the war and
survives intact.

Rowton Castle (SJ3712) The medieval castle, slighted in the late fourteenth century and
very dilapidated by the seventeenth, housed a
small Royalist garrison in 1643–45. Parliament
ordered the castle demolished after the war and
nothing survives. A red brick Queen Anne
house, with a Victorian round tower, stands on
or near the site.

Shrawardine Castle (SJ401153) The medieval castle was garrisoned for the King by Sir
William Vaughan in spring 1644 and became a
base for attacks on the many Parliamentary
outposts in the area; Vaughan soon became
known amongst the Shropshire Parliamentarians as 'the Devil of Shrawardine'. In October
1644 Mytton moved to eliminate the troublesome base and he surprised and captured
Vaughan and other officers in St Mary's Church.
Nonetheless, the garrison resisted fiercely, and
Mytton was compelled to fall back. The fortress
finally surrendered on 29 June 1645 after a long
siege. Little survives of Shrawardine Castle except three crags of masonry, the remains of the
keep, on a low mound, north-east of the towerless church.

Shrewsbury (SJ4912) Charles I entered the
town in September 1642 and thereafter Shrewsbury was a major Royalist base and the centre
for operations over the surrounding region. It
was also Prince Rupert's HQ for much of the
war. The medieval castle and town walls were
repaired and strengthened and the four town
gates put in order. Occasional Parliamentary
attacks during 1644 were strongly repulsed by
the large garrison, but on 22 February 1645
town and castle fell with surprising ease to Col.

Above: Ludlow, Salop. Two buildings dominate the town's skyline. In the foreground stands the massive border castle which served as a major Royalist base throughout the Civil War. Beyond rises the mighty tower of St Laurence's.

Right: Hopton Castle, Salop. The peaceful rural setting of the ruined Norman keep belies its bloody past. In one of the most notorious incidents of the Civil War, the 31 members of Col. More's Parliamentary garrison were put to death after the castle fell to Woodhouse's Royalists.

Below: Stokesay Church and Castle, Salop. The fortified manor-house with its adjoining church offers a view of medieval England almost without equal. The castle was a Royalist base until captured by Parliament in 1645, but it survived unscathed and remains perfectly preserved. The church was not so lucky – it took the brunt of the parliamentary bombardment and was extensively damaged.

Mytton. The night attack appears to have caught the King's men unprepared and although they put up some resistance in and around the castle, the Parliamentarians swept all before them.

A thirteenth-century mural tower and adjoining sections of the wall survive along the south side of Town Walls Street, but the rest of the town's defences, including the four gates, have completely disappeared. The castle, built in the eleventh and twelfth centuries but heavily restored and remodelled by Telford and others in the late eighteenth and nineteenth centuries, comprises a medieval keep and later domestic ranges encircled by curtain walls and a gatehouse; it is open daily during the summer. An early seventeenth-century two-storey timber-framed building off Church Street, now the Prince Rupert Hotel, was reputedly Rupert's HQ during the war.

Sir Thomas Mytton (d1656) was buried in Old St Chad's Church. Mytton was the leading Parliamentarian in Shropshire and worked with Sir Thomas Middleton, a relation by marriage, to clear the county of Royalists. He was appointed governor of Wem, the first important Parliamentary base in the county, and went on to become governor of Oswestry and captor of Shrewsbury. In 1645 he was appointed Commander-in-Chief of North Wales and captured the surviving royal bases in the area during 1646–47. In 1648 he led operations to contain and crush the renewed Royalist rebellion in North Wales. Sir Thomas lies somewhere beneath the present rather sad and decayed church, a shadow of its former glory – large parts of the medieval building collapsed in 1788.

Stokesay Castle (SO435817)

The beautiful thirteenth-century fortified manor-house was garrisoned for the King at the outbreak of war and remained in Royalist hands until 1645. Contemporary and later sources give conflicting accounts of the precise dates and sequence of events in 1645, but it is clear that the castle was taken by Parliament in the early summer after a siege and that Royalist attempts to retake it a little later in the year were defeated. The castle was neither damaged during the war nor slighted after it and survives intact, a perfect example of a late medieval fortified manor-house, with a thirteenth-century great tower and adjoining chambers ranged around a courtyard protected by a curtain wall, an Elizabethan timber gatehouse and a moat. Stokesay Castle is open daily except Tuesdays.

The adjoining Church of St John the Baptist, originally the castle chapel, was also garrisoned for the King as an outpost of the castle. It was badly damaged during the Parliamentary bombardment of 1645 and the north wall of the nave was completely destroyed. St John's was extensively rebuilt in 1654 and remains a largely Interregnum church.

Tong (SJ7907)

The castle and church to the south changed hands several times in the course of the Civil War until finally secured for Parliament in spring 1645. The medieval castle or fortified house has long since disappeared; the eighteenth-century mansion which stood on the site was itself demolished in 1954. St Bartholomew's, however, still bears evidence of Civil War conflicts – the north wall of the church is pitted with musket shot and the scar of a cannon is visible near the blocked doorway.

Wem (SJ5128)

The town was occupied by Parliamentarians in September 1643, one of their first bases within the area, and despite repeated Royalist raids and occasional sieges, it remained in Parliamentary hands for the rest of the war.

Wrockwardine (SJ6212)

The village was garrisoned for Parliament in 1644–45 and served as a base for operations against High Ercall. The Parliamentarians resisted several counterattacks from Vaughan and others. The garrison was probably based in St Peter's Church and in Wrockwardine Hall to the north-east, a two-storey Jacobean building, which was remodelled and extended in the eighteenth century.

SOMERSET

The county was initially controlled by Parliament but in June 1643 Hertford and Hopton invaded from the west and quickly carried all before them. By the end of July Waller had departed and for a year Somerset was secure for the King. Fighting began again in summer 1644 as Parliamentary forces began the gradual reconquest of Somerset, but not until 1645 were the Royalists dislodged from most of the county. Cromwell was frequently here during his southern campaigns of 1645 and he played an active part in the reconquest of the county.

Babylon Hill (ST588158) Babylon Hill, east of Yeovil, was the scene of a brief but fierce skirmish on 7 September 1642. The Marquis of Hertford, marching west from Sherborne, sent Hopton and 350 men ahead to secure the road for the main army. They halted on Babylon Hill to keep watch over the surrounding area, particularly the Parliamentary units in Yeovil below. There was minor skirmishing throughout the day, but the Parliamentarians appeared few in number and unwilling to risk a major engagement. However, at the end of the day, as Hopton was preparing to march east and rejoin Hertford, the Parliamentary forces launched a surprise attack which created confusion and near-panic in the unprepared Royalist ranks. Hopton hurried away into the gathering darkness, but he lost over 20 dead. Babylon Hill is now crossed by the main A30.

Bridgwater (ST2937) A Parliamentary stronghold during the first year of the war, the town was evacuated in June 1643 at the approach of Hopton's 6,000 Royalists, who occupied Bridgwater unopposed on the 6th. It remained a Royalist base for two uneventful years. The Parliamentarians returned in July 1645 and for ten days the main army under Cromwell and Fairfax laid siege to the town. Bridgwater was defended by a medieval tidal ditch, newly renovated and deepened by the Royalists, stretches of stone walls and earth banks and a medieval castle. The Royalist garrison under Col. Sir Hugh Wyndham had been bolstered by the arrival of that part of Goring's army which had survived Langport. The Parliamentary high command established a base at Chedzoy, three miles east of the town, and Cromwell probably lodged here during the early part of the operation. Royalist outposts were attacked and driven in, including a unit at Sydenham House, one mile north-east of the town. Massey led a detachment over the Hamp to threaten Bridgwater from the south-west. By the 20th, the Parliamentary deployment was complete and Fairfax and Cromwell formally summoned the town; according to tradition the reply was issued by Lady Wyndham who took a pot-shot at Cromwell. The assault began that night and the Parliamentary troops soon breached the East Gate and took Eastover, the area east of the Parrett. The Royalists, however, withdrew into the western half of the town, either destroying the bridge or lifting the drawbridge spanning the already demolished arches as they went. They held out for a further three days, during which much of the town was wrecked by a heavy bombardment, before surrendering on 23 July.

Little survives of the Civil War defences. The ditch, bank and walls have all long gone and the present town bridge is Victorian. The medieval castle, which occupied the area between Fore Street, Kings Square and Chandos Street, was slighted after the war and the site was redeveloped in the following century; the principal survival is Water Gate, a simple arched postern in West Quay.

Bridgwater has close links with Robert Blake, the Parliamentary soldier and admiral. Blake was born here in 1599, spent much of his early life at Knowle, three miles to the north-east (ST3340) and was elected MP for Bridgwater in 1640. He had a distinguished Civil War, conspicuous in operations at Bristol, Lyme Regis and Taunton, and then as a General-at-Sea he embarked upon a very successful naval career during the 1650s. He died on campaign in 1657 and was buried in Westminster Abbey. He was probably born in the Tudor house in Blake Street, now the Admiral Blake Museum, which includes a permanent Blake exhibition. A fine bronze statue of the Admiral stands in Cornhill.

Burrow Mount or Mump (ST358305) The curious hill rises abruptly above Burrow Bridge, the last passage over the Parrett before Bridgwater. A ruined fifteenth-century church on top of the mound served from time to time during the Civil War as a lookout and base for troops guarding the bridge. In July 1645 150 Royalists took refuge here after the Battle of Langport but surrendered on the 13th at the approach of a Parliamentary detachment. The present hilltop church, begun in 1793 but never completed, stands above the scattered village which has grown up around the bridge. Hill and church are now owned by the National Trust.

Cannington (ST2539) John Pym – leader of the Parliamentary party in the Long Parliament until his death in December 1643 and one of the five Members whom Charles I had tried to arrest in January 1642 – was born and brought up at Brymore House, near Cannington.

Chewton Mendip (ST5953) The first serious engagement in summer 1643 between the Royalist invasion force and the Somerset Parliamentarians took place on the evening of 10 June, when Waller clashed with the Royalist Cavalry around Chewton Mendip. Waller's Horse drew up on Nedge Hill (around ST585512), 1½ miles south-west of the village. The Royalists charged and pushed their opponents into Chewton Mendip and beyond, but here they ran into the main Parliamentary army and were repulsed. It was probably at this point that Prince Maurice was wounded and temporarily captured. A more general skirmish developed around Chewton but evening mist and then nightfall soon brought proceedings to a close and the two forces disengaged.

Dunster Castle (SS992434) Dunster Castle was secured for Parliament at the outbreak of war but was evacuated in May 1643 at the approach of Hopton's forces. It remained in Royalist hands for the rest of the war, finally surrendering in summer 1646 after a five month siege, the last stronghold in Somerset to fall to Parliament. Much of the medieval and Tudor fortress was demolished in the eighteenth century, when the castle was extensively remodelled and rebuilt. One of the Norman towers and sections of Tudor work were incorporated in the new castle and nearby stands the thirteenth-century gateway and flanking towers guarding the entry to the former bailey, now the terrace; a Civil War bullet is embedded in one of the gateway's medieval, iron-bound doors. Dunster Castle is open from Saturday to Wednesday during the summer.

Farleigh Hungerford (ST801576) Farleigh Hungerford Castle was begun by Sir Thomas Hungerford in the 1370s and extended by his son Walter, who moved the village away from the castle walls to a new position further up the hill. The former village church, St Leonard's, became the castle chapel. Hungerfords fought on both sides during the Civil War and their castle changed hands several times, finally falling to Parliamentary troops in September 1645. Derelict by the eighteenth century and now very ruinous, the castle comprises a square central block with corner towers and a southern gate-

house, and an inner and outer bailey defended by curtain walls, mural towers and gatehouses. The ruins are open daily. Parts of St Leonard's Church now serve as a museum and contain armour and other relics from the Civil War. St Ann's Chapel contains fine white marble effigies of Sir Edward Hungerford (d1648) and his wife. Sir Edward was one of the leading Parliamentary officers in west Wiltshire and east Somerset during the first Civil War and it was he who retook the castle from his Royalist half-brother in September 1645.

Isle Moor (ST3722) In early July 1645 George Porter and a detachment of Royalist Horse were sent west from Langport in the hope of deceiving Fairfax and Cromwell into thinking that the Royalists were about to attack Taunton and thus distracting them while the main army retreated into Bridgwater. The plan worked all too well, for Fairfax sent Massey and 4,000 men to oppose the Royalist force. Failing to set a proper watch, Porter was caught by surprise on 8 July as he and his men were relaxing on Isle Moor. The unprepared Royalists were quickly routed by Massey, 500 falling prisoner and the remainder fleeing in confusion.

Langport (ST4226) At the approach of Fairfax, Cromwell, and a 14,000-strong army in late June 1645, Goring hastily abandoned the siege of Taunton and marched east to meet the threat. Failing to hold the area around Yeovil, the Royalists turned north-west and began marching along the Yeo valley toward Bridgwater. On 10 July Goring took up a strong defensive position to the east of Langport in the hope of holding off his pursuers while his guns and baggage were taken to Bridgwater. His men drew up along the west bank of the Wagg Rhyne, a large stream which ran south through a distinct valley and into the Yeo. His position, east and north east of the village of Huish Episcopi, was well chosen, defended by the Yeo to the south, areas of marshy ground and the steep valley of the Wagg. Advancing from the east, Fairfax had little option but to attempt a direct frontal assault on Goring's line, probably where the Somerton to Langport road (now the B3153) forded the Wagg near the centre of the Royalist line (around ST441276). After Rainsborough dislodged Royalist Musketeers lining the hedges, the Parliamentary front line under Bethel charged across the stream, throwing the Royalists back towards Langport. When Goring's reserve halted the initial attack, Disbrowe led the second wave across the ford, swinging round across the now cleared ground west of the Wagg

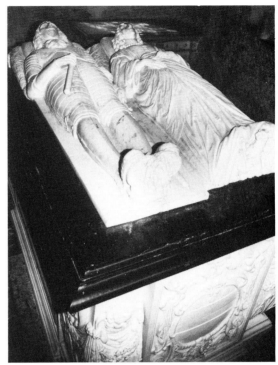

Above: Bridgwater, Somerset, Robert Blake, Parliamentary soldier during the Civil War turned Cromwell's most successful Admiral at Sea during the Interregnum, towers over his native town. Pomeroy's statue was completed at the very end of the nineteenth century.

Top right: Farleigh Hungerford Castle, Somerset. Sir Edward Hungerford and his wife, Margaret, lie beneath a fine marble monument in St Ann's Chapel. Sir Edward, an energetic and forthright character, given to quarrelling with his Parliamentary allies just as fiercely as with his Royalist foes, is portrayed in full armour.

Right: Nunney Castle, Somerset. The huge corner towers, high walls and deep moat which made de la Mare's castle so formidable in the fourteenth century proved less of an obstacle in the seventeenth and the deployment of heavy artillery soon opened the walls and brought Royalist opposition to an end. The far wall of the castle was then brought down by mines, so rendering the place indefensible.

and falling on the Royalist flank. Goring's line soon broke and the Royalists fled in confusion towards Bridgwater, pursued by Cromwell for several miles. Three hundred Royalists died in battle and many more fell along the Bridgwater road.

The area of the battle has changed little since the seventeenth century. The main A372 now skirts the southern edge of the battlefield, crossing the Wagg at ST433265, and a certain amount of modern ribbon development has taken place along the road, but the area to the north is still open land.

Marshall's Elm (ST4834)

The first blood of the Civil War in Somerset was spilt near this tiny scattered village on 4 August 1642. A newly raised body of 80 Royalist Horse under Sir John Stawell and Lt.-Col. Lunsford, drawn up on Walton Hill, saw 600 Parliamentary troops marching through the cornfields below. Lunsford decided to attack and sent his Dragoons to take up positions in quarry pits on the lower slopes of the hill. Their fire halted the inexperienced Parliamentarians and Stawell then charged down into the stationary and bewildered force. Sixty Parliamentarians were captured, seven were killed on the spot and 20 died later of their wounds. Thus did the Civil War begin in Somerset.

Norton St Philip (ST7755)

The George Inn is a fine early fifteenth-century stone house with a Tudor half-timbered upper storey. According to tradition, Cromwell lodged here at some point during his Somerset campaign of 1645.

Nunney (ST736458)

The ruined shell of Sir John de la Mare's fourteenth-century castle stands in the village, a small rectangular keep dwarfed by massive cylindrical corner towers, surrounded by a moat and an outer bank. Held for the King by Col. Richard Prater in 1643–45, the castle was attacked by Parliamentarians in summer 1645 but endured a prolonged siege and surrendered on 20 August only when heavy artillery, brought to Nunney two days before, had opened several breaches in the walls. According to tradition, during the siege the starving Royalists had daily tortured their one and only pig in the hope that its squealing would convince the Parliamentarians that the garrison was well-supplied and encourage them to abandon the siege. The castle was slighted by Parliament after the war, when mines brought down a large section of the north wall; more walling on the north side collapsed early this century. The otherwise extensive ruins are open daily.

Taunton (ST2324)

Despite the general Parliamentary sympathies of its inhabitants, Taunton changed hands several times during the Civil War as the two sides fought for control of southern Somerset. The town was garrisoned for Parliament at the outbreak of the war, but surrendered to Hopton's 6,000-strong Royalist army on 5 June 1643. The Royalist garrison enjoyed a year of peace until July 1644, when a Parliamentary force under Blake and Pye pushed west, overran the outer earthwork defences and laid siege to the 80-man garrison which had sought refuge in the castle. Reeve surrendered a week later on 10 July. Taunton was the first stronghold in Somerset to be recaptured by Parliament in 1644 and for many months stood in peril in a largely Royalist area. Three times the King's men tried to recapture the town and only heroic efforts by Robert Blake and his garrison preserved the town for Parliament. In autumn 1644 Col. Wyndham besieged Taunton but was driven off on 14 December by a relieving force under Cols Holborne and Ashley Cooper. A larger force under Grenville and Berkeley returned in April 1645, surrounding the town with their own earthworks and overrunning the outer suburbs in early May. In fierce street fighting on 8 and 9 May Blake and his men were pushed back into the town centre, an area between the castle and St Mary's Church protected by earthworks. This, too, fell on the 10th and Blake took refuge in the castle, but on the following day the approach of a large relieving force under Col. Weldon compelled Berkeley to withdraw. The Royalists tried again in June, but Goring's forces marched off at the end of the month to meet the main Parliamentary army.

The Civil War earthworks around the town and in the town centre have long disappeared but much of Henry of Blois's medieval castle survives, including the thirteenth-century outer gateway, remains of the twelfth-century keep, and other towers and ranges, medieval and later, parts of which house a library and local museum, open daily.

Wells (ST5445)

In August 1642 the Marquis of Hertford secured Wells for the King and established his HQ in the Bishop's Palace. The expected Royalist support in the area did not materialise and instead several thousand local Parliamentarians gathered on Prior's Hill, 1½ miles to the north. Negotiations and occasional exchanges of cannon-fire ended when Hertford and his small force broke out of Wells and fled to Dorset. The town was retaken by Royalist forces without opposition in July 1643 and was held by them for two uneventful years. They evacuated the place in 1645 and Wells changed

hands for the third and final time, again without bloodshed.

SOUTH YORKSHIRE

The area covered by the small modern county contained few important strongholds in the seventeenth century and saw very little action during the Civil War. Sir John Gell secured much of the county in autumn 1642, but the Parliamentarians pulled back at the approach of Newcastle's army in the following spring and the region fell to the King with little or no fighting. It returned to Parliament in summer 1644 in an equally unspectacular fashion after the Royalist troops were withdrawn to defend York. Cromwell was here in July and early August 1644 during his brief Yorkshire campaign and passed through the area again in 1648 and 1650–51.

Bramhope (SE2543) The chapel in the grounds of Bramhope Hall was built in 1649 and retains much of its mid-seventeenth-century appearance inside and out. It is a fairly plain and simple rectangular building; inside, a three-decker pulpit stands in the middle of the north side, with box pews arranged to focus upon it.

Doncaster (SE5703) On 29 October 1648 a party of Royalist rebels from Pontefract burst into Doncaster and attempted to sieze Col. Rainsborough who was lodging at an inn. They probably intended to take him prisoner, but in the ensuing struggle Rainsborough was killed and the Royalists returned to Pontefract empty-handed.

Cromwell stayed at Doncaster on 25 July–5 August 1644 at the end of his Yorkshire campaign and again on 9 August 1648 and 21 August 1651 on his way to intercept Scottish Royalist armies.

Great Houghton (SE4306) The chapel of the former Old Hall was built in 1650 and survives almost unaltered, a rare example of an Interregnum church. It comprises a single, undivided nave and chancel, with box pews and a pulpit opposite the entrance. The Elizabethan mansion to which it was originally attached has recently been demolished.

Houndshill (SE3304) Houndshill manor-house, an early seventeenth-century 'H'-plan mansion in stone and timber, stands ½ mile south-south-west of Barnsley. It was built for the Elmhirst family and garrisoned for the King by Col. Richard Elmhirst at the outbreak of the Civil War. Sir Thomas Fairfax besieged and bombarded Houndshill in the following summer and the 40-man garrison within surrendered when

the Parliamentarians threatened to storm the place.

Rotherham (SK4292) Rotherham was secured for Parliament by Sir John Gell during the opening months of the Civil War but was evacuated in March 1643 at the approach of Newcastle's Royalists. The town was retaken without opposition in the latter half of 1644. Cromwell stayed in Rotherham on 8 August 1648 on his way to intercept the Scottish invasion force.

Sheffield (SK3587) Sheffield was taken unopposed by Sir John Gell in November 1642 and a small Parliamentary garrison installed in the medieval castle. The town was evacuated in the following March as Newcastle approached, and town and castle were then held for the King for over a year. In late July 1644 the town quickly fell to Crawford's Parliamentarians but the Royalist garrison in the castle put up greater resistance. Attempts to drain the moat and bring down the walls by tunnelling were unsuccessful and not until heavy artillery arrived and pounded the fortress did the Royalists abandon the struggle; Major Thomas Beaumont surrendered on 11 August. The castle was slighted in 1648 and today nothing survives except odd fragments of masonry around the Cattle Market, which covers the site of the former bailey.

Skellow Hall (SE5310) According to tradition Cromwell once lodged at Skellow Hall, Old Skellow, while on his way through the area travelling to or from Scotland. The building no longer exists.

Tickhill Castle (SK593928) The Norman motte and bailey castle, repaired and modernised in the sixteenth century, was held for the

King throughout 1643–44. Col. Monckton's mutinous garrison surrendered to Col. John Lilburne on or around 26 July 1644 after a brief siege. Cromwell had travelled over from Doncaster to supervise the surrender and evacuation of the castle. In fact, all was not well in the Parliamentary army, for Manchester had slipped into characteristic inactivity and was far from

happy to learn that his subordinates had resumed hostilities without his approval.

Tickhill Castle was slighted after the war and today the fragmentary remains stand on private land by the road. The twelfth-century gatehouse, reconstructed in the sixteenth, survives in fairly good order but the shell keep and curtain walls have largely disappeared.

STAFFORDSHIRE

The Civil War in Staffordshire was a conflict of garrisons and raiding, not of field armies and set battles. In the opening year of the war the two sides garrisoned a large number of towns and villages, castles and manor-houses, so many that only a selection can be mentioned below. In the main, the Royalists initially held the south and west of the county, the Parliamentarians the north and east, though from the start of the war each side had outposts in territory largely controlled by the other. In an unspectacular manner the Parliamentarians slowly extended their control, though not until 1645–46 did the last Royalist strongholds fall. Cromwell played no part in the Civil War in Staffordshire and seems never to have set foot in the county during the 1640s. He may have visited the area in August 1651, travelling through Burton and Tamworth on his way to Worcester, but even that is in doubt, for other sources suggest that he followed a more easterly route through Leicestershire.

Alton Castle (SK073425) The fragmentary remains of Alton Castle stand in the forecourt of a Victorian great house, now a school. Built in the twelfth century, the small fortress lay in an area of Staffordshire fiercely disputed during the first half of the Civil War and it changed hands several times. Its eventful Civil War history is probably one of the causes of its present, very ruinous condition and little remains above ground except a single corner tower. (Alton Towers, nearby, is an entirely separate post-Civil War building.)

Barton under Needlewood (SK1818) Barton House, a late medieval and Tudor mansion, served as a Royalist outpost of Burton for much of the Civil War. In June 1645 the garrison was evacuated and the hall burnt to the ground to prevent it being used by the Parliamentarians. The present Barton Hall was built in the eighteenth century on or close to the site of the old house.

Biddulph (SJ8856) Biddulph Old Hall, an Elizabethan mansion of four ranges round a central courtyard, was garrisoned for the King by Lord Brereton throughout the opening year of the Civil War. In February 1644 a Parliamentary unit led by the governor's own uncle, Sir William Brereton, arrived before the hall. Three days of close siege and the arrival of heavy

artillery, particularly 'Roaring Meg', persuaded Lord Brereton that further resistance would be both futile and costly and the Royalists surrendered on 22 February. The ruins of the Tudor Old Hall or of a later seventeenth-century rebuilding stand in the grounds of a farm.

Burton upon Trent (SK2423) A combination of factors conspired to ensure Burton an eventful and unhappy Civil War. The town stood at a major crossroads and controlled an important crossing over the Trent, it lay in a hotly contested frontier zone between Parliamentarians to the north and Royalists to the south and west, and it possessed very weak defences, probably nothing more than a circuit of earth banks and barricades. Burton could not be held against a serious attack and the town changed hands at least eight times during the war as fortunes ebbed and flowed in the surrounding area. No trace of the Civil War defences survives.

Caverswall Hall or Castle (SJ950429) Walter de Caverswall built a castle here in the thirteenth century, a quadrangular fortress with polygonal corner towers. In 1615 Matthew Craddock demolished parts of the medieval castle and converted the rest into a more comfortable domestic dwelling, with a three-storey embattled hall and a mock-medieval tower. The hall was garrisoned for Parliament for most of the Civil War

Above: Bramhope, South Yorks. A simple, plain rectangular hall, Bramhope is the only surviving example of the handful of new chapels built in the area during the Interregnum.

Left: Tamworth Castle, Staffs. The Norman and Jacobean castle, which was garrisoned by both sides during the Civil War, stands on a site fortified since the Saxon period.

Below: Lichfield Cathedral, Staffs. The cathedral was the focus of action in 1643 and 1646 as troops fought their way into the Close and sustained heavy damage. Parts of the central and western spires were brought down and had to be rebuilt after the Restoration.

but apparently never saw serious fighting. It survived the war intact and is now a convent and guesthouse.

Chillington Hall or Castle (SJ862069)

Although Chillington has been the seat of the Gifford family for over 800 years, the present building on the site is no earlier than the sixteenth century, and most of it is later still. John Gifford's Tudor fortified hall, occasionally referred to as Chillington Castle in deference to the earlier fortress which it replaced, was garrisoned for the King at the outbreak of the Civil War. It was captured by Brereton in August 1643 and seems to have played no further part in the war. The Tudor hall was extensively rebuilt and remodelled in the eighteenth and nineteenth centuries and the house which saw action in the Civil War is all but lost amid the present Georgian mansion. Chillington Hall is open to the public on Sundays and certain weekdays during the summer.

Colwich (SK011211)

Many members of the local Wolseley family lie within the medieval village Church of St Michael. Most of the family sided with the King during the Civil War, but young Sir Charles Wolseley became a strong supporter and close friend of Cromwell during the 1650s. He was named a Protectoral Councillor in December 1653 and thus at just 23 or 24 became one of the most powerful politicians in the country. He served as a Councillor and MP throughout the Protectorate and then spent over fifty years in semi-retirement in Staffordshire. At the death of his former master, Richard Cromwell, in 1712, Wolseley became the last senior Protectoral politician left alive and survived to see a Hanoverian on the throne. He was buried in St Michael's, Colwich, in November 1714. Wolseley Hall, the family seat and still a private residence, lies south-east of the village by the main road to Rugeley (SK025203).

Eccleshall Castle (SJ828295)

The early fourteenth-century castle originally comprised four corner towers linked by blank walling or domestic ranges and surrounded by a moat. It was garrisoned for the King by Lord Capel at the beginning of the war to protect the eastern approaches to Shropshire. Eccleshall was besieged by Brereton and Middleton at the beginning of August 1643 and the Parliamentarians established their HQ in nearby Holy Trinity Church, mounting guns on the tower and in the churchyard to bombard the recalcitrant garrison. Hastings temporarily relieved the garrison, but the Parliamentarians soon returned and

resumed the bombardment. The Royalists within refused to serve the Dutch mercenary whom Hastings had left behind as governor and the unhappy garrison surrendered the badly damaged castle on 29 August. The remains of the castle were incorporated within later farm buildings on the site. One of the nine-sided corner towers survives in fairly good order, together with a fourteenth-century bridge across the remains of the moat.

Hopton Heath (SJ953263)

The minor battle fought on open land to the north-east of Stafford was the only serious field engagement in Staffordshire during the Civil War. On 19 March 1643 a combined Parliamentary force under Brereton and Gell approached Stafford in the hope of surprising and capturing the Royalist base. The attack was expected, however, and the Parliamentary advance was halted three miles north-east of the town by a Royalist force under Northampton and Hastings which had been stationed in the area to protect Stafford. The Parliamentarians deployed across a slight moorland ridge immediately east of the village of Hopton; Gell's men, approaching from Weston, formed the centre and left of the Parliamentary line while Brereton's forces, who had marched south from Salt, made up the right wing. Although the area was largely open land, the extended Parliamentary line was protected in places by stone walls or hedges. The Royalist army, advancing from Stafford, threw back an advanced party of Parliamentary Dragoons and then halted while their cannon bombarded the enemy line. Northampton charged forward, broke the Parliamentary Horse and pushed them from the field. Gell's Foot proved more robust and, in failing light, the battle degenerated into a series of increasingly confused Royalist attacks on the Parliamentary Infantry. Brereton and Gell retreated under cover of darkness, having lost 500 men and most of their artillery. The Royalist victory was an expensive one for they, too, had suffered heavy casualties – the Earl of Northampton and many officers were dead and Byron and Hastings were among the wounded.

Hopton Heath is still open ground beyond the village and can have changed little since 1643. The track across the top of the ridge around which the Parliamentarians deployed survives as a minor road and runs down into the village. Many of the dead lie in mass graves somewhere on the field; others were carried to Sandon and Weston for church burial.

Keele Hall (SJ8145)

The Tudor hall, built for the Sneyd family around 1580, was fortified and garrisoned for the King from the beginning of the war. It saw little action and was probably evacuated sometime during 1644–45. The building which was garrisoned in the Civil War has gone and the present hall, a large 'L'-shaped building in red sandstone, was built in the early nineteenth century. It is now owned by the university.

Lapley (SJ8712) Lapley House or Hall, a sixteenth-century fortified mansion, changed hands several times during the opening 18 months of the war. Initially secured for Parliament, it fell in spring 1643 to a daring night raid launched from Chillington: a handful of volunteers scaled the outer wall and, undetected by the garrison, opened the main gates to admit their colleagues, who quickly overpowered the 70 Parliamentarians. Lapley was recaptured by Parliament at the end of 1643 and garrisoned for a further two years. In 1645 the troops were withdrawn and the outer wall and gatehouse demolished to render Lapley indefensible. The Elizabethan house itself escaped slighting and survived intact; it was enlarged and remodelled in the nineteenth century and remains a private residence.

All Saints Church nearby was frequently held as an outpost by the garrison and in consequence suffered repeated bombardments. Civil War cannon-fire may have been responsible for the demolition of the medieval transepts – they both disappeared in the mid-seventeenth century – and for damage to the north-west corner of the nave.

Lichfield (SK1109) The Royalists entered the town unopposed at the beginning of 1643 and hastily set about securing Lichfield against possible attack. Seventeenth-century Lichfield possessed neither town walls nor a castle and instead the King's men established their base in the Cathedral Close, the area immediately around the cathedral, encircled by a high wall; Minster Pool afforded additional protection on the southern side. The Royalists stored their ammunition within the cathedral and mounted cannon at strategic points on, in and around the building.

The expected onslaught began at the end of February 1643 with the arrival of a Parliamentary force under Lord Brooke. The Parliamentarians besieged the Close and bombarded the Royalist positions, badly damaging the towers and spires of the cathedral. Although Lord Brooke was killed by a Royalist sniper – a modern plaque in Dam Street marks the spot

where he fell – the attack continued under Sir John Gell and the small Royalist force surrendered in March. The Parliamentary troops sacked the cathedral and garrisoned the Close themselves, thus blocking the main north–south road through the county.

Prince Rupert moved quickly to recover the town and arrived on 10 April at the head of 4,000 men. He overran the town without difficulty but the Close again proved a greater obstacle and a ten day siege, enlivened by repeated attempts to scale the walls, achieved little. On 20 April, however, the Royalists used mines to open up a huge breach in the wall and the Parliamentarians inside promptly surrendered.

Lichfield remained in Royalist hands for nearly three years and served as a centre for operations throughout the south of the county. It held out long after the collapse of the King's cause in the surrounding area and not until 6 March 1646 did Brereton finally recapture the Close.

The cathedral towers and spires and St Chad's Chapel were very badly damaged during the Civil War and had to be almost completely rebuilt after the Restoration. The defensive wall around the Close has disappeared, but many medieval and early modern buildings remain within the area it once enclosed. Minster Pool lies in a small public park south of the cathedral.

Patshull (SJ800006) The late medieval and Tudor manor-house was garrisoned for the King by Walter Astley from 1642 until its capture by Parliamentarians in summer 1645. Ruinous by the end of the seventeenth century, the old hall has been completely demolished; it stood on low ground below the present eighteenth- and nineteenth-century hall. The archway into the forecourt of the hall contains the figures of two civil war soldiers in military dress. St Mary's church nearby contains an elaborate monument to a Royalist officer, Captain Richard Astley (d1688), who is depicted riding at the head of his troop of Cavalry.

Paynsley Hall (SJ897380) The isolated late medieval and Tudor manor-house served as a minor Royalist outpost for much of the war; it was stormed and taken by Parliamentary troops in 1645. The hall has been demolished and the present Paynsley is modern. However, remains of the old moat and associated earthworks which defended the Civil War stronghold are still visible around the house. A track and several footpaths run past the site.

Stafford (SJ9223)   Civil War Stafford was protected by a rather dilapidated system of medieval defences, including a circuit of walls and two castles, one within the town and the other near Castle Bank, on a hill to the west. The county town was secured for the King at the end of 1642 but immediately became the target of repeated Parliamentary raids. Although the garrison turned back several attacks in February and March 1643, the town fell on 15 May to a surprise dawn raid led by Brereton. It remained in Parliament's hands for the rest of the war.

Most of the Civil War defences have disappeared. The town walls and castle have long gone and the town gates are nothing more than a memory preserved in the street names. The castle to the west of the town was slighted by Parliament after the war and the remains were later incorporated within a nineteenth-century Gothic pile, which has itself been largely demolished; recent excavations have investigated the remains of the Norman-cum-Victorian fortress. The only building with clear Civil War associations which still stands intact is High House, a very large four storey timber-framed building on the west side of Greengate Street; Charles I and Prince Rupert stayed in the late Tudor house in 1642 and from 1643 it served as a gaol for captured Royalists.

Stourton Castle (SO8685)   This small medieval castle, two miles west-north-west of Stourbridge, was occupied by Col. Fox at the beginning of 1644 to disrupt Royalist lines of communication between Shropshire and the West Midlands. On 24 March a large body of Royalists under Gerrard marched towards Stourton, defeated a 300-strong Parliamentary force drawn up on Stourbridge Heath and went on to expel the small garrison remaining in the castle. Stourton fell derelict in the late seventeenth and eighteenth century and the fragmentary ruins were incorporated within the private mansion, still known as the castle, which was built on the site in the nineteenth century.

Swynnerton Hall (SJ8535)   The Tudor seat of the Fitzherberts was garrisoned for the King during 1643–44. The old hall was demolished in the early eighteenth century and the present hall, a severe 2½-storey mansion which dominates the village, was built in 1725.

Tamworth Castle (SK2004)   Tamworth Castle was secured for the King at the outbreak of the Civil War, but it lay too close to the Parliamentary strongholds in the West Midlands to survive for long. It was captured and garrisoned by Parliament early in 1643 and although it stood in an area which continued to be disputed until 1644–45, Tamworth apparently remained under Parliament's control for the rest of the war. The Norman shell keep stood on a motte originally raised and fortified by the Saxons; a number of early modern buildings were added within the walls, including a sixteenth-century banqueting hall, now a museum. The castle ruins are open daily except Fridays.

Trentham (SJ8641)   The twelfth-century Augustinian priory at Trentham was acquired by the Leveson family at the Dissolution. Much was demolished, but the remainder was converted into a grand secular house, remodelled and extended in the 1630s. It was garrisoned for the King for much of the war. The house survived the Civil War intact, but was completely demolished in the early eighteenth century and replaced with a much grander edifice, itself repeatedly extended and remodelled over the succeeding century. The house was demolished in 1910; its extensive grounds are now a public park.

Tutbury Castle (SK209291)   Tutbury Castle was held for the King throughout the Civil War, its small garrison frequently reinforced by troops from the nearby bases of Lichfield and Ashby to help repel the repeated Parliamentary attacks and sieges. Not until early 1646 did the then isolated stronghold surrender to the besieging forces. The castle was slighted after the war and little now survives of the eleventh–fifteenth-century fortress. The medieval keep has completely disappeared – a much later building stands on the site – but fragments of the outer bailey wall survive, together with the remains of a gatehouse, a mural tower and late medieval domestic ranges. The ruins are open daily.

Uttoxeter (SK0933)   Although armies frequently passed through the area during the Civil War, Uttoxeter was not fortified or garrisoned until 1645, when the Parliamentarians threw up earthworks and erected street barricades and turned the town into a military base for operations against Tutbury and Lichfield.

In late August 1648 the remnant of the Scottish Royalist Horse which had survived Preston and fled from Warrington was trapped here by Lambert and Grey. Hamilton surrendered without a fight and large numbers of prisoners were temporarily held in churches at Uttoxeter, Bramshall and other villages in the area.

Wootton Lodge SK098438)   Sir Richard Fleetwood's early seventeenth-century house was garrisoned for the King in 1642 but fell to local Parliamentarians in the following summer after a two day bombardment. The Parliamentary guns were sited on rising ground nearby, still known as 'Cromwell's Battery', though Cromwell himself was over 100 miles away at the time. The lodge was repaired after the war and has been repeatedly renovated since, but it still retains much of its original Jacobean appearance.

Wrottesley Hall (SJ8501)   Wrottesley Hall was garrisoned for the King during the opening years of the war, but by 1645 the Royalists had been expelled and Wrottesley became a base for Parliamentary operations in the area. The building which saw action in the Civil War was probably Tudor in origin, extended and strengthened in the early seventeenth century; it comprised a two storey central block with cross wings defended by a moat and gatehouse. The old hall was demolished in 1690 and a new house built a little to the south-west. This house, in turn, was gutted by fire and the present hall largely dates from the 1920s.

SUFFOLK

Suffolk was secure for Parliament throughout the period and saw no significant fighting during the Civil War. Cromwell payed a brief visit to the county in March 1643 to secure Lowestoft and he returned in spring 1647 when the discontented Parliamentary army was temporarily based in north-west Suffolk.

Bury St Edmunds (TL8564)   Part of the Parliamentary army was stationed around Bury during spring and summer 1647. Although Cromwell was ill in London for much of March, some contemporary reports suggest that he travelled to Bury on or around the 20th to meet the disaffected troops. He was, however, almost certainly absent when the Council of the Army met in Bury St Edmunds on 29 May 1647 to discuss military and political grievances and the army's response to them.

Kentford (TL7066)   The Parliamentary army held a general rendezvous on the open heathland around Kentford on 4–5 June 1647 before moving closer to London to pursue their grievances with Parliament. Cromwell had spent most of the previous months in London attending Parliament, but he was also a senior officer and had – and was known to have – considerable sympathy for the army in its growing rift with Parliament and was accordingly viewed with increasing suspicion by many MPs. Cromwell hurriedly left London early on 4 June and travelled north to join the army here.

Lowestoft (TM5593)   Cromwell arrived in Lowestoft on 14 March 1643, surprising and overpowering a party of local Royalists who had hoped to deliver the town to the King. The King's men were in the process of securing the town with barricades and chains stretched across the streets, but they put up no resistance to Cromwell and his troops. Cromwell spent two days here and established his HQ in the Sun Inn, long since demolished, which stood on the east side of the High Street.

Newmarket (TL6463)   Charles I was lodged at Newmarket on 7–24 June 1647 as a prisoner of the Parliamentary army, quartered nearby in Cambridgeshire and Hertfordshire. The King stayed in the royal palace which stood on the south side of the High Street. The late fifteenth-century buildings, redesigned and extended by Inigo Jones in the seventeenth century, were acquired by Col. Okey after the King's death and he demolished much of the complex. Charles II completed the destruction, using the brick and stone to build a new palace slightly to the east. This, too, has largely perished and the only section still visible is part of the eastern block, preserved in the lower storeys of the later Palace House Mansion by Palace Street.

Somerleyton Hall (TM493978)   Cromwell lodged in the Tudor brick mansion on 14–16 March 1643 while securing Lowestoft from Royalist plots. The surviving estate accounts indicate that Cromwell's troops also took advantage of Somerleyton's hospitality and quartered in the hall or its grounds. The present hall, open on Sundays and on certain weekdays during the summer, dates very largely from the extensive rebuilding of the nineteenth century but fragments of the Tudor and Jacobean mansion survive.

SURREY

Surrey was secure for Parliament throughout the Civil War and saw very little fighting. The Royalists occasionally pushed as far as Farnham during the first Civil War and in 1648 the Earl of Holland's Royalists marched through the county, though the major engagement which ended the rebellion was fought just over the border in Greater London. Cromwell paid only one recorded visit to Surrey, to Farnham in March 1648, but in fact he probably passed through the north-west of the county on several occasions during the first Civil War while travelling between London and Hampshire.

Banstead Down (TQ2355)   On the downland to the east of Walton on the Hill stand the remains of four earthworks (TQ231552 and TQ236554), each comprising a rampart and ditch enclosing a roughly rectangular area with an entrance on one of the shorter sides. They have sometimes been described as Civil War earthworks, thrown up as defensive positions in preparation for a Royalist attack on London planned for spring 1643 but never executed. However, the account connecting these earthworks with a planned attack on London seems unconvincing and there is no satisfactory evidence to link them with the Civil War at all.

Cranleigh (TQ0639)   Near the altar of St Nicholas's Church is an inscribed plate marking the resting places of Sir Richard Onslow (d1664) and his wife Elizabeth (d1679). Sir Richard was a prominent Parliamentarian and colleague of Cromwell during the 1640s, but he became increasingly disillusioned with the Interregnum regimes and was an outspoken critic of the Protectorate. The family seat was at Knowle, ¾ mile south-west of Cranleigh; the Tudor mansion was demolished during the eighteenth century and only fragments survive within the modern buildings on the site. Despite a strong tradition that Cromwell once stayed here, there is no surviving evidence to show that he ever visited Knowle.

Ewell (TQ2263)   On 7 July 1648 the Earl of Holland's Royalists marched from Reigate back towards their original base at Kingston upon Thames, harried all the way by pursuing Parliamentary forces under Livesey and Audley. A fierce skirmish took place 'in a pass' between Ewell and Nonsuch – possibly the track now known as Ox Lane – before both forces continued their troubled march north out of Surrey.

Farnham (SU8446)   Farnham Castle (SU837473) occupied a strategic position roughly half way between Winchester and London and as such was in something of a frontier zone: the castle was the most westerly of an arc of Parliamentary bases protecting the approaches to

London, whilst Royalist campaigns in central southern England occasionally progressed as far east as the Farnham area. At the outbreak of war the castle was garrisoned for Parliament by George Wither, but he soon fell back before the approaching Royalists and Sir John Denham entered town and castle unopposed in early November. His 100-strong garrison did not survive for long, however, for on 30 November a large Parliamentary force under Waller arrived before the castle. Waller had no artillery but he managed to blow the main gates with a petard on 1 December. His men rushed in, demolishing the hastily erected barricades in the courtyard and overwhelming the garrison. Thereafter Farnham Castle served as a Parliamentary stronghold, suffering occasional raids from Rupert, Hopton and Goring, but rarely under serious threat. The now ruinous medieval castle, open daily, comprises a shell keep with mural towers and a gatehouse enclosing a circular ward which contains the remains of an earlier great tower. The adjoining Bishop's Palace, which was used by the garrison as an additional storeroom and living quarters, survives intact but is not open to the public.

Farnham had two distinguished visitors in 1648. On 19 December Charles I stayed here overnight on his way from the Isle of Wight to London; he was lodged in Vernon House, West Street, now a public library. Cromwell visited the town earlier in the year, on 27–28 March, to discuss with Richard Maijor the terms of the planned marriage between Cromwell's son Richard and Maijor's daughter Dorothy; Cromwell may have lodged at the Goat's Head Inn on the corner of Borough and Castle Street.

Nonsuch (TQ2363)   Although the outline of Henry VIII's favourite palace was recovered by excavations in the late 1950s, almost nothing now survives above ground. The double quadrangular palace was demolished in the 1680s and only a section of the garden wall and a rectangular platform – probably the base of the Banqueting House – remain in the south-west corner of the park. The palace was acquired after the Civil War by Thomas Pride, the Parliamentary soldier and later an MP and a Major General, best known for his prominent role in purging the Long Parliament in December 1648. He lived here until his death in October 1658, after which the palace was briefly owned by John Lambert before returning to the Crown at the Restoration.

Pride was buried in 1658 in the palace church, which stood within the inner courtyard. Although he was attainted two years later and his body ordered exhumed, hung, drawn and quartered, his remains escaped the indignity, presumably because they could not then be located. Pride still lies undisturbed somewhere beneath the parkland.

Redhill (TQ2850)   On 6 July 1648 Holland's Royalists marched from Kingston upon Thames, though north Surrey via Ewell, Leatherhead and Dorking to Reigate, where they halted for the night.

Cavalry units posted on Redhill Common to guard against an attack from Kent were soon put to the test, for Audley's Parliamentarians fell upon them in the evening, driving the Royalists from the common and back into Reigate. Holland avoided a major engagement by hastily evacuating Reigate in the early hours of the 7th and retracing his steps towards Dorking and Kingston.

TYNE AND WEAR

Firmly Royalist at the outbreak of the Civil War, the county remained in the King's hands until 1644 and saw no serious fighting until the Scottish Parliamentarians arrived in February and March of that year. The Scots halted here for several weeks and overran many of the smaller towns and garrisons but they failed in their main objective, the capture of Newcastle. They moved on in early April and the King's cause survived for a few months longer, but the disaster at Marston Moor and the reappearance of the Parliamentarians at the end of July soon marked the end of Royalism in Tyne and Wear. Cromwell passed through the county in 1648 and 1650–51 on his way to and from Scotland.

Gateshead (NZ2563) Seventeenth-century Gateshead was a small ribbon development strung out along the road south of the Tyne Bridge. With neither a castle nor stone walls the town could not withstand determined assault and the Scots had little difficulty in expelling the heavily outnumbered Royalist garrison on 27 July 1644.

Newcastle upon Tyne (NZ2464) Seventeenth-century Newcastle was one of the principal centres of trade and commerce in the north-east and was an important Royalist asset during the first half of the war. The King's hold on Newcastle was first challenged in February 1644, when the Scottish Parliamentarians approached the town and quickly overran the outlying Royalist bases. Newcastle itself proved a far more difficult obstacle and after a fruitless month-long siege the Scots abandoned the operation and moved on south. Governor Sir John Morley took the opportunity to strengthen the walls and ditches which surrounded the town. His work was soon put to the test, for the Scots reappeared in early autumn and attacked the town with renewed vigour. On 19 October mines were sprung under several sections of the town

wall and opened large breaches around Westgate and White Friars Tower. The Scots poured in and by the following day the town had fallen. The King's men sought refuge in the castle but their position was hopeless and they surrendered a week later.

Civil War Newcastle was defended by a hastily repaired circuit of fourteenth-century town walls, originally containing 7 gates and 19 mural towers. Only fragments of the medieval defences remain, including lengths of ruined walling around Forth Street, Bath Lane and Stowell Street on the west side of the town and the Plummer and Sallyport Towers on the east side. The Normans' motte and bailey 'new' castle, which stood at the south entrance to the town guarding the bridge across the Tyne, was replaced in the twelfth–thirteenth century by a great square keep and adjoining defensive and domestic buildings. The keep was repaired in the nineteenth century and is open daily.

Cromwell may have lodged within the domestic ranges of the castle during his visits to Newcastle. He was here on 9–10 September and 17–19 October 1648 and again on 10–15 July 1650.

South Shields (NZ3667) South Shields was garrisoned for the King in 1643 but fell to the Scots at the second attempt on 20 March 1644. The town was retaken by Montrose's Scottish Royalists in May but evacuated after Marston Moor.

Stella Hall (NZ1763)   The Elizabethan and Georgian hall in which Cromwell lodged on 12 August 1651, *en route* from Scotland to Worcester, has recently been demolished. Only the roofless summer-house remains, an octagonal brick structure on Summerhouse Hill.

Sunderland (NZ3956) The small and generally pro-Parliamentary port of Sunderland was secured by the Scots in early March 1644 and served as a base during their operations against Newcastle over the following weeks. Although heavily outnumbered, the Earl of Newcastle decided to offer battle in an effort to halt the Scottish advance and relieve the pressure on Newcastle, and during March he repeatedly approached Sunderland, harrying outposts. A series of limited and rather confused engagements took place on 23 March around Hylton (NZ3557), then a separate village, now a western suburb of Sunderland. The armies clashed on the lower slopes of Bedwich Hill on the north bank of the Wear. The enclosed nature of the ground precluded the use of Horse, but the two

Infantries engaged in a series of running fights which began in the afternoon and continued well into the night. Neither side emerged victorious: the Scots sustained heavy losses and drew back into Sunderland but the Earl had insufficient men to attack the town and instead returned to Durham, leaving the Parliamentarians free to continue the siege of Newcastle and resume their march south.

Tynemouth (NZ372693) The remains of the medieval priory and castle occupy the same clifftop promontory above the North Sea. The dual nature of the site ended at the Dissolution, when the outer defences were strengthened and many of the former monastic buildings taken over by the military. Tynemouth Castle was garrisoned for the King in 1643; it resisted a brief siege in March 1644 but fell to the Scots upon their return to the area in October. Four years later, in October 1648, the Parliamentary garrison within the castle declared for the King but Hesilrige acted quickly to stifle the rebellion. He arrived before Tynemouth with a large force and promptly stormed town and castle. Most of the rebellious garrison, including the governor, Col. Henry Lilburne, were killed during the attack. The ruins of the priory and castle, including the remains of the fourteenth-century curtain wall, gatehouse and barbican, are open daily.

WARWICKSHIRE

With the exception of the southern fringes of the county, which lay within the orbit of Royalist Oxfordshire, Warwickshire was held for Parliament throughout the war. The Battle of Edgehill, the first major engagement of the war, was fought in Warwickshire but thereafter the county saw nothing more than isolated raids and minor skirmishes. Cromwell was with the Parliamentary army on the Edgehill campaign but he rarely returned to Warwickshire and was involved in no further fighting within the county.

Astley House or Castle (SP312895) The medieval castle at Astley was derelict by the mid-seventeenth century and it was the Tudor house standing within the ruins and also known as the 'castle' which was garrisoned by Parliament in 1642 and held throughout the war. The house was raided by Lord Loughborough's Royalists in January 1646. The Elizabethan house survives in good order, a long, embattled, rectangular block; beyond are the fragmentary remains of the gatehouse and the curtain walls of the medieval fortress. The castle is private.

Bascot Heath (SP4063) On 23 August 1642 the first serious confrontation of the Civil War in Warwickshire took place on Bascot Heath. A Parliamentary troop from Warwick Castle under Lord Brooke clashed with a party of Royalists, killing up to 50 of the King's men and putting the rest to flight.

Caldecote Hall (SP3595) The Tudor hall was the seat of the Purefoy family, including the prominent Parliamentarians William and George. The hall was attacked by Rupert on 28

Above: Farnham Castle, Surrey. The original castle gatehouse survives beneath the nineteenth-century roof and clock tower and modern plaster rendering which completely conceal the medieval work. It was this gatehouse, comprising two rectangular towers with semi-octagonal outer projections, which Waller's men blew and overwhelmed as they retook the castle at the end of November or 1 December 1642.

Right: Newcastle Castle, Tyne and Wear. The great square keep, which replaced the Norman's 'new' castle by the bridge, was held by the King's men until 1644. Cromwell may have lodged in the keep or in adjoining domestic buildings (which do not survive) when he visited Newcastle in 1648 and 1650.

August 1642 but the motley band within, Mrs Purefoy, her son-in-law George Abbot and a small group of servants, managed to repulse the first assault. Rupert returned in the evening, firing the outbuildings and then overpowering the defenders. The old hall was completely demolished in the eighteenth century and the present Caldecote Hall on the site dates from the nineteenth century.

The bullet-marked oak door of the old hall was rescued prior to demolition and now stands in the porch of St Theobald and St Chad. Within the church is an alabaster mural monument to George Abbot (d1649) which mentions his defence of the hall.

Compton Wynyates (SP330419)

A perfect Tudor mansion in a hillside setting, Compton Wynyates was built by Sir William Compton in the early sixteenth century and incorporated sections of an earlier moated hall which stood on the site. The Comptons were staunch Royalists during the Civil War and their house was garrisoned for the King; the soldiers were quartered in a seventeenth-century barrack-room which still survives. A Parliamentary force under Col. Purefoy captured the house in June 1644 after a brief siege and Compton served as a Parliamentary base thereafter. At the end of the war the moat was drained and the outer fortifications demolished but otherwise the hall was undamaged and survives in good order. The richly furnished and decorated quadrangular house in pink brick, with embattled towers and numerous ornate chimneys, has recently been closed to the public.

Coughton Court or Castle (SP083605)

The fortified house of the Royalist and Catholic Throckmorton family, Coughton Court was seized by Parliamentary troops in 1643 and held by them for the rest of the war, resisting occasional raids launched from Royalist bases in Hereford and Worcester. Much of the building which saw action in the Civil War survives in good order, including the imposing sixteenth-century gatehouse – now incorporated within the Georgian west front – and two Tudor ranges at the rear with timber-framed upper storeys resting on brick and stone ground floors. Coughton Court is open from Wednesday to Sunday during the summer.

Edgehill (SP3747)

The first major battle of the Civil War was fought on 23 October 1642 on what was then an open plain between Edgehill and Kineton. On the morning of the 23rd the King's army gathered on Edgehill itself before descending and drawing up at the foot of the hill. The Royalist line faced north-west and had its centre just north of the village of Radway. Essex, meanwhile, had deployed his army 1½ miles south-east of Kineton in a line stretching from the present B4086 to Oak's Wood. Battle commenced with the Royalist Cavalry on both wings charging the Parliamentary flanks, breaking Essex's Horse and chasing them from the field. There followed a long, fierce and ultimately indecisive Infantry engagement in the centre of the plain. The two forces disengaged at nightfall, slept in the field and then drew off and marched away on the 24th. Both sides had lost around 700 men apiece and the battle was effectively a draw. Cromwell had marched with Essex's army and was certainly in the vicinity of Edgehill on 23 October, but what part, if any, he played in the battle itself is not clear.

If contemporary accounts leave many points uncertain, the present state of the battlefield only adds to the confusion. Although some parts of the plain were hedged by the seventeenth century, the battle was fought over largely open ground. Today, however, the area is dotted with woods – The Oaks stand where Essex's right would have been stationed and Battleton Holt where the Royalist guns were deployed. Moreover, large parts of the battlefield are now covered by an army ordnance depot and are strictly private. The ruins of King's Ley Barn, in which Charles I supposedly spent the night after the battle, lie ½ mile north of Radway. A modern monument to the battle stands by the B4086 at SP373473. The Ordnance Survey battle symbol at SP353492 accurately marks the centre of the battlefield. An eighteenth-century tower at Ratley Grange on Edgehill (SP373473), now the Castle Inn, serves as a good vantage-point for viewing the battlefield on the plain below. There is now an impressive battle museum by Farnborough Hall (SP432494).

Kenilworth Castle (SP278723)

The extensive medieval castle, begun in the twelfth century and greatly enlarged 200 years later, had been restored and modernised in the late sixteenth century and was in good order at the outbreak of the Civil War. It was occupied without opposition by Parliamentary forces in September 1642 and was garrisoned for a little over a year. With Coventry to the north and Warwick so close to the south, Kenilworth was found to be an unnecessary drain on money and manpower and the garrison was withdrawn at the end of 1643. The castle was then slighted – the north wall of the keep and parts of the north curtain wall were brought down and the Norman dam was breached to drain the sur-

Top: Compton Wynyates, Warks. One of the finest early modern mansions in England, the main house survived the Civil War undamaged and remains a perfect example of Tudor domestic architecture. A mass of red and orange brickwork, large mullion windows and ornate chimney stacks serving the numerous fireplaces, the whole house reflects the greater peace and prosperity of the sixteenth century. *Bottom:* Warwick Castle, Warks. A Parliamentary stronghold throughout the Civil War, the mighty castle overlooking the Avon stands on a site occupied since the Conquest. The present building is a mixture of severe medieval military work and rich domestic apartments.

rounding moat-cum-lake. The impressive ruins are open daily.

Maxstoke Castle (SP2386)

The medieval castle housed a small Parliamentary garrison throughout the war but saw little or no action and survived undamaged. Restored and extended in the nineteenth century, the castle is a spectacular combination of medieval and modern, comprising four ranges linked by polygonal corner towers and surrounded by a moat. Sadly, both the castle and surrounding land are private.

Milcote on Stour (SP1952)

The Grenville mansion at Milcote was sacked and burnt down by Purefoy's Parliamentarians in 1644. The remains of the old manor-house, including part of a Tudor chimney, stand in open land near the present modern Milcote Hall.

Offchurch (SP3666)

Pittings on the south face of the tower of St Gregory's Church are often attributed to Civil War bullets. There is, in fact, no record of fighting here.

Packwood House (SP173722)

Packwood is a Tudor and early Stuart timber-framed house with additional late seventeenth-century brickwork, standing in gardens which were originally laid out during the 1650s. According to tradition, Henry Ireton lodged here in October 1642 before the Battle of Edgehill. The whole house is richly furnished but the Ireton Room is particularly fine, with original seventeenth-century oak panelling and a decorated overmantle. Packwood is now owned by the National Trust and is open on Wednesdays and Saturdays during the summer.

Stratford upon Avon (SP2054)

Stratford was important during the Civil War because of its bridge across the Avon and its position at the crossing of the Oxford to Shrewsbury and Coventry to Gloucester roads. Thus when Col. Wagstaffe and his Oxfordshire Royalists attempted to establish a garrison in the town in 1643, Parliamentary forces under Lord Brooke were quick to meet the threat. Brooke marched to Stratford on 25 February and routed the Royalists in an engagement on Welcombe Hill, one mile north of the town. He then took Stratford itself, though in the process a stray spark ignited the Royalist magazine and the resulting explosion killed many Parliamentary troops and demolished the old town hall. Although the Oxfordshire Royalists remained active in the area until 1645, they never again established a formal garrison in Stratford.

Cromwell stopped overnight in Stratford in June 1645 and again in August 1651 when on his way to Worcester. There is no clear evidence to indicate where he lodged.

Warwick Castle (SP2865)

The massive castle above the river was a centre of royal and baronial government during the Middle Ages and of Parliamentary dominance during the Civil War. The fortress was secured for Parliament by Lord Brooke in August 1642 and was held for the rest of the war. The Earl of Northampton briefly besieged the castle during the opening fortnight of the war, but thereafter the only Royalist soldiers seen here were prisoners – Warwick Castle became one of the main prisons for the West Midlands and inscriptions on the walls of the dungeons below Caesar's Tower are thought to have been carved by captive Royalists. The castle served as the Parliamentary HQ for Warwickshire and housed a large garrison and magazine. Cromwell probably lodged in the castle during his visits to Warwick in June 1645, July 1648 and August 1651. The extensive buildings, open daily throughout the summer, contain a fine collection of arms and armour, including many items from the Civil War period. The Protector's death mask is on display, as is a Civil War helmet claimed to be Cromwell's own.

Wormleighton (SP448538)

John Spence's early Tudor manor-house at Wormleighton was probably similar in design to nearby Compton Wynyates. It stood in the south east of the county and fell under the control of Royalist Oxfordshire for much of the Civil War. Garrisoned for the King from early 1643, the outpost survived for 18 months until Warwick Parliamentarians moved against it in summer 1644. The manor-house was besieged and bombarded and the garrison within quickly surrendered. Only one range of the once quadrangular house now survives, a ruinous brick wing dating from the early sixteenth century; nearby are the remains of the stone gatehouse added in 1613.

WEST MIDLANDS

Now dominated by the Birmingham conurbation, this small modern county, comprising parts of former Warwickshire, Worcestershire and Staffordshire, covers an area which was strongly Parliamentarian in sympathy during the 1640s. Although most of the main centres were held for Parliament throughout the war, they suffered frequent raids from the King's Worcestershire bases. Cromwell was probably in the area during the first month of the war, marching with the Earl of Essex's army, and he returned nine years later, passing through Coventry in August 1651 en route for Worcester.

Aston Hall (SP079899)   Aston Hall is a fine red brick Jacobean mansion with a central hall and domed towers flanked by projecting wings. It was built in then open countryside to the north of Birmingham by Sir Thomas Holte, an ardent Royalist who entertained the King here in autumn 1642 and installed a Royalist garrison in December. The Birmingham Parliamentarians moved quickly to eliminate the threat; 1,200 troops arrived before the hall on 26 December and proceeded to bombard the place into submission. The hall, which had sustained only minor damage, remained in Parliamentary hands without serious challenge for the rest of the war. Now surrounded by the urban sprawl of Birmingham, Aston Hall stands in a small park 2½ miles north of the city centre. It is open to the public daily during the summer and on certain weekdays in winter.

Birmingham (SP0686)   A small but growing manufacturing centre in the seventeenth century, Birmingham was overwhelmingly Parliamentarian in sympathy throughout the war and supplied the army with arms and equipment. There was no formal garrison here – with no stone walls or natural defences, Birmingham would have been a very insecure base – but troops were often quartered in the town, afforded some protection by a circuit of earth banks and ditches around the town. The later massive expansion of the town has obliterated all trace of the Civil War defences.

In early April 1643 Rupert marched through the area and decided to punish the town for its disloyalty. Advancing from the south at the head of 1,200 Horse and 700 Foot, Rupert approached the town along the Stratford Road on 3 April. He found the road blocked beyond Springfield around Camp Hill, then an open track outside the town, now a main suburban road about one mile east-south-east of the city centre. Here a force of 200 Parliamentarians under Capt. Greaves had drawn up behind hastily erected barricades and earthworks. Rupert attacked the heavily outnumbered Parliamentary force, but his men were twice thrown back under heavy fire. Not until he sent out flanking parties through the adjoining fields did Greaves and his men abandon the struggle and fall back into Birmingham. The so-called Battle of Camp Hill was not one of Rupert's more illustrious victories. Even then, the fighting was not over, for as the Royalists advanced up High Street, Deritend, they came under renewed fire and as they entered the town itself they were surprised by a Parliamentary counter-charge which temporarily halted their advance and inflicted heavy casualties, including Lord Denbigh, who was severely wounded and died within a week. Rupert took a fearful revenge, expelling Greaves' force and then sacking Birmingham, plundering, killing and burning almost indiscriminately before marching on. Royalist armies under Rupert and Maurice passed through Birmingham again in 1644 and 1645, on these occasions meeting no serious resistance and confining their activities to minor looting.

The City Museum and Art Gallery contains a fine portrait of Oliver Cromwell, probably by Walker.

Coventry (SP3379)   Secure behind their well-maintained fourteenth-century walls and gates, the pro-Parliamentary citizens refused to admit Charles I's troops in August 1642. The Royalists bombarded the town and broke down New Gate but marched off at the approach of Lord Brooke and his troops. The town saw little serious action thereafter and was held for Parliament throughout the war. Coventry was one of the centres for holding Royalists captured in the Midlands – they were lodged within St John's Church and elsewhere – and the phrase 'sent to Coventry' may spring from this, though there are several alternative explanations. Retribution followed in 1660, for Charles II ordered the town's defences demolished. Today all that remain are parts of two medieval gates, the Swanswell and Cook Street Gates, and a fragment of the wall in Lady Herbert Garden off White Street.

Dudley Castle (SO945907)   The medieval hilltop castle was almost the only defensible fortress within the county during the seventeenth century. Secured for the King in the closing months of 1642, it remained a Royalist stronghold throughout the Civil War, an outpost and centre of operations in an otherwise Parliamentary region. Local Parliamentarians attempted several times to remove this thorn in their side. In May 1644 Lord Denbigh, Parliamentarian heir of the Royalist Lord Denbigh fatally wounded at Camp Hill, laid siege to the castle with a large force drawn from several garrisons in the region. Although he managed to repell Lord Wilmot's relieving force in a confused and bitter action around Tipton Green (SO9592) on 11 or 12 June, lack of ammunition and Waller's demands for reinforcements compelled Denbigh to abandon the operation soon after. The garrison held out until 14 May 1646 when its governor, Thomas Leveson, surrendered on terms to Brereton's besieging army. The fortifications were slighted on Parliament's orders and a fire in the eighteenth century reduced the domestic buildings within the bailey to a similarly ruinous state. The remains, including parts of the gatehouse, barbican and tower-house, now stand in the grounds of Dudley Zoo, which is open daily. Leveson supposedly still haunts the remains of his former stronghold.

Edgbaston (SP0584)

Edgbaston Hall, an early Georgian mansion standing in parkland south west of Birmingham city centre, was built on the site of an earlier medieval hall. The original hall, longtime home of the Gough family, was seized by Col. Fox in March 1644 and garrisoned for Parliament thereafter, a base for raids throughout northern Worcestershire. The hall survived the Civil War intact, but was completely destroyed by Birmingham rioters in 1688.

Hawkesley Hall (SP0478)

In 1644 Col. Fox siezed Hawkesley Hall, the home of the Catholic Royalist Middlemore family, and garrisoned the late medieval mansion for Parliament under Capt. Gouge. The hall and adjoining village of Kings Norton accordingly became targets of Royalist raids launched from Dudley, but the garrison held out until May 1645. On 13 May the main Royalist army under Rupert, Maurice and Astley appeared before Hawkesley and summoned the garrison to surrender. The 100 Parliamentarians refused and endured a three-day bombardment – the deep moat around the hall hindered Royalist operations and prevented a direct assault – before Gouge abandoned the struggle and surrendered on 16 May. The Royalists quickly sacked and burnt the hall before marching on. Nothing remains of the old hall beyond slight traces of the moat, preserved amid a modern housing estate.

Rushall (SK0201)

The fifteenth-century Rushall Hall and the adjoining medieval parish church changed hands several times during the Civil War. Held initially for Parliament by Col. Edward Leigh, the hall was attacked and taken by Prince Rupert in April 1643 and a Royalist garrison was installed. Col. Lane's garrison survived for a year and was a serious threat to Parliamentary communications in the area north of Birmingham. In late May 1644 Denbigh arrived before Rushall with a large force and heavy artillery and proceeded to bombard both the hall and adjoining Church of St Michael, held as an outpost and store. On the 29th the King's men abandoned the by then badly damaged buildings and surrendered. Old St Michael's has completely disappeared and the present church in Leigh Road is Victorian. Next to it stand the fragmentary remains of Rushall Hall, a ruined fifteenth-century gatehouse and parts of the once extensive curtain wall, the latter bearing numerous scars where struck by Civil War cannon-balls.

Willenhall (SO9899)

Bentley Hall, which stood by the main road between Willenhall and Walsall, was garrisoned for the King by Col. John Lane. The outpost was in a strongly Parliamentarian area and the garrison was quickly expelled by troops from Birmingham. The hall is better known as one of the places where Prince Charles stopped and was given aid after the Battle of Worcester. The main building perished long ago and the last surviving parts, the stables and other outbuildings, were demolished in 1927. Its site is marked by a cross, just off the main road, and commemorated in the name of a local pub, the Lane Arms. The suburb of Bentley now covers the area.

Wolverhampton (SO9198)

Wolverhampton was a small and unimportant town during the Middle Ages and never acquired stone walls. With nothing more than earthworks and street barricades for protection, the town could not be held against determined assault during the Civil War, was never formally garrisoned and changed hands frequently with the minimum of bloodshed. The Royalist army was based here briefly in October 1642 and the soldiers spent the night in St Peter's Church. In May 1643 Brereton launched an early morning raid on the town and surprised and captured a party of Royalists who were in Wolverhampton gather-

Left: Aston Hall, West Midlands. The Jacobean mansion, garrisoned for the King on the outbreak of war, quickly fell to a force of local Parliamentarians. Their siege and bombardment apparently did little damage, though scarring on the great wooden staircase was reputedly caused by a Civil War cannon.

Below: Arundel Castle, West Sussex. The massive castle, dramatically sited on the wooded slopes above the Arun, appears almost too perfect. Indeed, the medieval fortress which guarded the pass through the downs has largely disappeared, wrecked by Waller's guns in 1643–4 and left derelict thereafter; most of the present castle was built in the eighteenth and nineteenth centuries.

ing supplies. In May 1645 the King's army again passed through unopposed, but Capt. Stone's Parliamentarians then fell upon and scattered the Royalist rear, which had carelessly become detached from the main force.

WEST SUSSEX

West Sussex was held by Parliament for most of the Civil War and saw very little fighting. On two occasions – in December 1642 and November and December 1643 – Royalist forces invaded from southern Hampshire, pushing east in the hope of securing the whole south-east coast; on both occasions, however, they progressed no further than West Sussex and were quickly halted and expelled. It seems that Cromwell never visited the area.

Arundel Castle (TQ018074) The castle changed hands three times during the opening months of the Civil War but at the beginning of 1643 the Parliamentarians established control and the fortress served as a Parliamentary stronghold and garrison for the rest of the year. In December 1643 town and castle fell to Hopton's forces, the high-point of the Royalist invasion of the region. Waller retook the town on 20 December and settled down to besiege and bombard the castle and its 1,000-strong garrison. Heavy guns were hauled up the tower of St Nicholas's Church to pound the north and west sides of the castle. By early January the walls had been shattered and the Royalists opened negotiations which led to the castle's surrender on the 6th. The returning Parliamentary garrison carried out makeshift repairs but the castle fell derelict and ruinous after the war and much of the present fabric dates from the eighteenth and nineteenth century when the building was restored and largely rebuilt. Arundel Castle is open daily except Saturdays during the summer.

Bramber (TQ193106) Bramber was the furthest point reached by the Royalists during the invasion of December 1643. Hopton and Ford were making for Lewes Castle but found the bridge over the Adur at Bramber held by a Parliamentary force under Capt. Temple. A fierce engagement left 100 Royalists dead, many more injured and the remainder hurrying back westwards.

Chichester (SU8604) The walled town was seized by Sir Edward Ford's Royalists in November 1642 and garrisoned for the King. On 20 December Waller appeared before Chichester with 6,000 men and established his HQ on the Broyle, high ground to the north. The town was besieged and the extra-mural suburbs quickly overrun. Guns were mounted on the almshouses in Broyle Road to attack the north gate of the town, and on the tower of St Pancras's Church to bombard the east gate. The Royalists surrendered early on 27 December when the Parliamentarians threatened to storm the town. Chichester saw no further action during the Civil War and was by-passed by the Royalists in December 1643. Although the town gates have disappeared, the circuit of Roman and medieval walls around the town is almost complete and survives in good order.

Cowdray House (SU9021) The quadrangular fortified mansion was begun at the very end of the fifteenth century and completed by the Earl of Southampton in the 1530s. Hopton captured Cowdray House in late November 1643 and left a small garrison here when his main force moved east. It was retaken without serious resistance on 18 December. The house was gutted by fire in 1793 and although the three storey Tudor gatehouse in the west range survives in fairly good order, the rest is now very ruinous. The remains are open daily.

Haywards Heath (TQ3323) The efforts of Sir Edward Ford, the Royalist High Sheriff, to secure Sussex for the King in December 1642 came to an abrupt halt on Haywards Heath. Advancing east and making for Lewes, he and his forces were intercepted by local Parliamentarians on what was then heathland just outside the town; a church now stands on the site (TQ331239). The Royalists were outnumbered and routed and lost 200 dead or wounded.

Petworth House (SU976219) The medieval manor-house was captured by Hopton's Royalists in early December 1643, but the small garrison left here surrendered to Waller without a fight a fortnight later. The old manor-house was demolished in the late seventeenth century and the present Petworth House was built on the site. The thirteenth-century chapel is the only part of the medieval mansion to survive. House and gardens are now owned by the National Trust and are open at weekends and on certain weekdays during the summer.

Stansted House (SU760102) The late medieval and early Tudor royal hunting lodge in the very west of the county was captured by Hopton and Ford in late November 1643 and garrisoned for the King. A month later, after the main invasion force had been halted and expelled, Waller arrived before Stansted. Unlike most of the Royalist garrisons established in the area, Stansted resisted the initial summons and only when Waller bombarded the defences and threatened to storm the house did the Royalists emerge. The lodge was largely destroyed in the eighteenth century, though fragments of Tudor masonry survive in the west front and south porch of the largely nineteenth-century chapel, which stands to the south-west of the present modern house on the site.

WEST YORKSHIRE

The prosperous and vulnerable West Yorkshire woollen towns were an inviting target and changed hands several times during the opening nine months of the Civil War as both sides fought for control of the area. The townspeople were generally Parliamentarian in sympathy and the two Fairfaxes were active on behalf of Parliament, but the troops and civilians were heavily outnumbered by Newcastle's huge Royalist army. When the Earl left the region in March 1643 – he was under instructions to escort the Queen to Staffordshire – the Fairfaxes were able to take or retake several strongholds, but Newcastle's return in June and the ensuing Battle of Adwalton quickly extinguished the Parliamentarians and West Yorkshire was firmly Royalist throughout the latter half of 1643. The departure of Royalist troops to reinforce York in spring 1644 and their destruction at Marston Moor in July saw the region return to Parliament. There was little further fighting in the area until 1648, when Pontefract became one of the Royalist bases during the second Civil War. Cromwell oversaw operations here en route *to and from Scotland in 1648; he marched through West Yorkshire again in 1650–51, before and after his second Scottish campaign.*

Adwalton Moor (SE2228) On 30 June 1643 Newcastle's 10,000 Royalists met and defeated the Fairfaxes' 4,000 Parliamentarians on open moorland outside Bradford. Lord Fairfax had judged that his men stood no chance of holding Bradford itself against such numbers and had marched out east to engage the Royalists in the open, in the hope that a surprise attack might halt Newcastle's advance. However, the element of surprise was lost when the Parliamentarians stumbled into the Royalist advanced guard on Westgate Hill and as the Fairfaxes reached Adwalton Moor they found Newcastle's army already deployed. The Royalists had drawn up in a line running north–south across the top of the moorland ridge about ½ mile west of Adwalton. The Parliamentarians drew up a few hundred yards further west; the main force under Lord Fairfax deployed across the top of the ridge but Sir Thomas Fairfax and a small detachment were stationed to the south, below the ridge, around the point where Warren Lane branches off to the south. After a series of charge and counter-charges in which Lord Fairfax generally had the best of the fighting, a ferocious Royalist attack led by Col. Skirton broke the Parliamentary Infantry on the left wing and the line gave way. Lord Fairfax was compelled to fall back on Bradford but his son at the foot of the ridge did not see the general retreat and fought on against great odds. By the time he had realized the situation, his direct line of retreat to Bradford had been cut and instead he had to flee south and then swing round in a large arc back to the town. The battle had left 500 Parliamentarians dead and 1,500 captured and it effectively ended the Parliamentary cause in West Yorkshire for the rest of the year.

Much of the area of the battle, including the ridge on which Lord Fairfax drew up, has been built over and is covered by the suburbs of Adwalton, Drighlington and Moorside. Part of the battlefield, however, is still open common crossed by public footpaths, and Warren Lane, around which Sir Thomas Fairfax was stationed, still exists. The Ordnance Survey battle symbol is at SE222283.

Bradford (SE1633) Described by Fairfax as a 'very untenable place', Bradford had neither stone walls nor a castle and was very vulnerable to attack. The defending force usually made St Peter's Church – now the cathedral – their strongpoint, but cannon placed on and around the church could achieve little against a determined assault. Bradford changed hands at least four times during the opening year of the war as the Fairfaxes repeatedly captured but then evacuated the town. Newcastle attacked Bradford on 1 July 1643 after the Battle of Adwalton Moor and captured a large part of Fairfax's Infantry. Thereafter Bradford remained in Royalist hands until the general collapse of the King's cause in the region in summer 1644.

Howley House or Hall (SE253255) Howley

House or Hall, the Tudor seat of the Saville family, became a Parliamentary garrison under Sir John Saville at the end of 1642. Over the following months it served as a base for operations throughout the south of the county – Parliamentary forces rendezvoused here on 21 May 1643 before the attack on Wakefield. Despite strong resistance, Howley fell to Newcastle's Royalists on 22 June 1643 and thereafter played no part in the war. The ruins of the hall stand by a golf course in an area crossed by several public footpaths.

Kirkheaton (SE1818) In St John's Church is a

monumental brass to Adam Beaumont (d1655) and his wife. Beaumont was the son-in-law of Sir Ralph Assheton, the leading Lancashire Parliamentarian, and was himself active for Parliament in the north. He is portrayed wearing half armour of the period.

Leeds (SE2933) Like Bradford to the west,

Leeds changed hands repeatedly during the opening months of the war as the two armies vied for control of the region. By the end of 1642 the town was in the King's hands, but when Newcastle went into winter quarters, Fairfax took advantage of an unusually fine January to resume operations, storming Leeds on the 23rd and capturing the town and its 500-strong garrison after a two hour fight. The town was lost in June in the wake of Adwalton Moor and was not retaken until the Royalist evacuation of summer 1644.

Pontefract (SE461224) Secured for the King

by Sir Richard Lowther in 1642, Pontefract Castle became a major Royalist stronghold and survived long after the collapse of the King's cause elsewhere in the region. A base for attacks on Leeds and Bradford during 1643, the castle was itself under attack from the following sum-

mer and was almost continually besieged from August 1644 to July 1645 by Parliamentary forces under Fairfax, Lambert and Meldrum. By summer 1645 all hopes of relief had vanished, the castle had been badly damaged – Fairfax had brought down the Piper Tower at the north-west angle and had opened up several breaches in the outer walls – and the garrison within were short of food and ammunition; the Royalists surrendered to Col. Poyntz on 21 July.

In 1648 Pontefract became the scene of renewed fighting, for it was seized for the King by Cols Morris and Paulden on 8 June and served as one of the centres of the second Civil War. Over 500 Royalists joined the garrison before Parliamentary troops surrounded and besieged town and castle. Pontefract again proved a difficult obstacle and endured a nine month siege. Cromwell was here on 10 August and led an attack which overran the town and forced the Royalists to take refuge in the castle. He returned in early November and spent three weeks overseeing the rather uneventful siege of the castle from his base at Knottingley (SE5023). The castle finally surrendered on 22 March 1649, long after Cromwell's departure and the King's execution.

Pontefract Castle was slighted after the war and its outer bailey and defences have now completely disappeared. The ruins of the thirteenth-century shell keep, with a chapel, dungeons and adjoining towers, are open daily. The museum within the castle grounds contains several relics from the Civil War, including a collection of the siege money coined by the beleaguered Royalists.

Sandal Castle (SE337182) Only the moat,

motte and a few sections of ruined masonry remain of this early fourteenth-century shell keep castle. It was probably already semi-ruinous by the mid-seventeenth century and was not occupied until the later stages of the Civil War. Sandal was garrisoned for the King in 1645 as an outpost of Pontefract, but fell to Sir John Saville in early October following a brief siege.

Seacroft Moor (SE3635) The engagement be-

tween Fairfax and Goring on Seacroft Moor on 30 March 1643 was merely the final stage in a running fight which had begun over five miles away. The defection of Scarborough and the uncertain loyalty of the Hothams in Hull compelled Fairfax to fall back from his position near York. As Sir Thomas pulled out of Tadcaster on the morning of 30 March and began moving south-westwards he was approached by 500

Royalist Horse under Goring. A running battle developed along the road to Leeds as Goring harried the increasingly disorganized Parliamentary rear. Fairfax made a stand on Bramham Moor, where his Horse held Goring off while his Foot made for Leeds. A more serious clash took place on Seacroft Moor as Fairfax was nearing the town, when Goring fell upon the now tired and careless Parliamentarians. Many of Fairfax's troops panicked, tried to flee from the moor and were cut down, and although Fairfax managed to get his main force into Leeds, he lost up to 1,000 men killed or captured in the process. Goring had insufficient men or artillery to assault or besiege Leeds itself and turned back once Fairfax entered the town. Seacroft Moor has been completely built over and is now an eastern suburb of Leeds.

Wakefield (SE3320) In common with most towns in the area, Wakefield changed hands repeatedly during the opening year of the war. A small Royalist force had secured the town by the end of 1642 but the King's men hastily evacuated the place and fell back to York following the fall of Leeds on 23 January 1643. Wakefield was reoccupied in April after Fairfax's reverse at Seacroft Moor but the Parliamentarians, anxious for a victory to raise flagging morale and to obtain prisoners to exchange for captured colleagues, mounted a daring raid on Wakefield on 21 May. The town was held by Goring and his 3,000-strong garrison, but seventeenth-century Wakefield had no walls or castle and the Royalists relied on street barricades and rather feeble earthworks. The King's men may have been forewarned of Fairfax's plans and they certainly outnumbered the 1,200-strong Parliamentary force, but after fierce fighting around the barricades at Warrengate and Norgate, Fairfax's men overcame the resistance and entered the town. They then battled their way up the main street and into the Market Place; when they took the Royalist guns in the churchyard of All Saints, Goring's men lost heart and fled in disorder. Fairfax had achieved a tremendous victory and returned to Leeds with 400 prisoners, including Goring himself, plus captured guns and ammunition.

Wetherby (SE4048) The town was occupied by Fairfax at the end of 1642 as part of the Parliamentary operation to isolate York. Possession of Wetherby not only threatened York directly but also secured the bridge across the Wharfe, thus preventing a Royalist flanking attack on the main Parliamentary force at Tadcaster (North Yorks). Sir John Glemham led 800 Royalists out of York to clear these Parliamentary bases but Fairfax was forewarned of his plans and the Royalists were fiercely repulsed when they launched a night attack on Wetherby. Nonetheless, the general Royalist pressure compelled Fairfax to fall back from Wetherby and his other bases around York in February and March 1643.

WILTSHIRE

Although Wiltshire was largely Parliamentarian during the opening months of the Civil War, the Royalists quickly established several bases within the area and the north-eastern fringes of the county soon came under the control of Royalist Oxfordshire. During 1643–44 most of the county fell to the King's men, and it was now the Parliamentarians who were isolated in scattered outposts, particularly in the north-west of the county. Wiltshire was retaken by Parliament during 1645. Cromwell was frequently here during his southern campaigns of 1645 and saw action at Highworth, Devizes and Longford House. He travelled through Wiltshire in 1649 and 1650 on his way to and from Ireland.

Aldbourne (SU2675) On 18 September 1643 Prince Rupert fought a delaying action on the rolling downland of Aldbourne Chase. Having relieved Gloucester, the main Parliamentary army under Essex marched back towards London, pursued by the King, who hoped to block the road and force battle on favourable ground. On 18 September, with both armies making for Newbury, Prince Rupert launched a surprise attack on the Parliamentarians outside Aldbourne, inflicting heavy losses before being driven off. But his main purpose was to slow and divert Essex's advance and his action at Aldbourne, coupled with the Lord General's curiously dilatory movements, enabled the King to enter Newbury ahead of his opponents.

Amesbury (SU1541) The George Inn was originally part of the medieval abbey, converted to secular use at the Dissolution and remodelled in the eighteenth century. In 1645 it became the temporary HQ of Fairfax and the high command as the Parliamentary army campaigned in the area.

Bishopstrow (ST8943) Tradition has it that Cromwell breakfasted beneath a yew in Salisbury Road after the Battle of Newbury.

Broad Hinton (SU105763) In the Church of St Peter ad Vincula is a monument to Col. Glanville, a Royalist officer killed at Bridgwater in 1645; his armour, worn throughout the Civil War, is displayed above. Nearby is a memorial tablet to his kinsman, Sir John Glanville (d1661), Speaker of the Short Parliament.

Devizes (SU0061) Garrisoned by Sir Edward Hungerford for Parliament at the outbreak of war, Devizes was abandoned in February 1643 as the King's men advanced through Wiltshire and from then until September 1645 it served as a Royalist base. In July 1643 Waller tried to retake the town; advancing from the west, he brushed aside the Royalist outpost guarding the ford just north of Rowde and laid siege to the town on 9 July with his army of 4,500 men. The Royalist forces inside the town, including Goring's army, manned the barricades, ditches and earth banks which surrounded Devizes, enduring a heavy bombardment from Waller's batteries in Coatefield and the Jump to the east. The approach of Wilmot's relieving force and the destruction of Waller's army at Roundway Down saved the town, which was not seriously threatened again until September 1645.

On 15 September Cromwell arrived before Devizes and quickly overran the town, forcing Charles Lloyd's garrison to seek refuge in the castle gatehouse. This was bombarded from all sides – Cromwell's main cannon were sited in the Market Place – and on 22 or 23 September the garrison surrendered. The castle was subsequently slighted.

By the seventeenth century most of the medieval castle had been destroyed – the outer bailey had been built over and the twelfth-century shell keep was derelict and ruinous – and only the gatehouse remained intact. Whatever survived the Parliamentary slighting was removed in the nineteenth century when the present castellated mansion was built on the site. The medieval churches of St John and St Mary both suffered during the Civil War; in July 1643 Goring stripped the lead from the roofs to make bullets and Waller directed his cannon at the

Royalist look-out posts in the towers. St John's tower still bears the scars where it was struck by Parliamentary cannon-balls. No trace of the Civil War earthworks which encircled the town now survives.

Great Chalfield (ST860630) Great Chalfield Manor changed hands several times during the closing two years of the war. It was fortified and garrisoned for Parliament in spring 1644 but evacuated in September before the advancing Royalists. The King's men themselves withdrew shortly afterwards at the approach of Massey, who restored a Parliamentary garrison. Built by Thomas Tropenell in the late fifteenth century, the house survived both the Civil War and nineteenth-century restoration and remains one of the best preserved late medieval mansions in the region. Although the inner moat survives, an outer wall and moat which once surrounded both the manor-house and the adjoining church have disappeared. Great Chalfield Manor is open to the public on certain summer weekdays.

Highworth (SU202924) The Church of St Michael was fortified and garrisoned for the King in 1644. On 27 June 1645 Cromwell supervised the bombardment and storming of the place by a detachment from Fairfax's main Parliamentary army. Scars on the outside of the tower near the doorway are usually ascribed to Parliamentary cannon.

Lacock Abbey (ST919684) Sir William Sharington acquired the medieval Augustinian nunnery at Lacock after the Dissolution and converted it into a secular mansion, retaining much of the former cloister and cloisteral buildings and adding a polygonal tower in the south-east corner. Lacock Abbey was garrisoned for the King in 1644–45 but surrendered on 24 September 1645 following a brief Parliamentary siege. The house was neither damaged during the war nor slighted after it and survives intact. Famous for its association with Fox Talbot and the development of photography in the nineteenth century, Lacock Abbey is now owned by the National Trust and houses a permanent Fox Talbot display. It is open daily except Tuesdays during the summer.

Littlecote (SU3070) Littlecote House is a splendid brick and flint manor-house, largely Tudor but incorporating fragments of medieval masonry from an earlier house which stood on the site. It was owned by the Popham family in the seventeenth century, two members of which, Cols Edward and Alexander, fought for Parlia-

Top: Great Chalfield Manor, Wilts. Thomas Tropenell's manor-house, which survived the Civil War almost unscathed, was built on an 'E'-shaped plan, with a central range and projecting porch flanked by large gabled wings. *Bottom:* Littlecote House, Wilts. The arms and armour of Sir Alexander Popham's troops have recently been acquired by the Royal Armouries, but they remain on display in the Great Hall at Popham's country seat. The oustanding collection includes firearms, buff coats, swords, helmets and breastplates, several of which have been dented by bullets fired either in battle or to test the armour's strength.

ment during the Civil War and were active in north Wiltshire, Somerset and Avon. The house was garrisoned for Parliament – the soldiers were quartered in the long attic on the north side of the house – but there was no serious fighting here and the house survived intact. Open to the public on summer weekends and also on weekdays during August, Littlecote contains a superb collection of Civil War relics. A large equestrian portrait of Col. Alexander Popham hangs at the west end of the Great Hall, around which is displayed a large selection of Civil War arms and armour, including pistols, muskets, bandoliers, helmets, swords, Popham's own armour and the distinctive suits worn by Hesilrige's 'lobsters'. The chapel in the north-west range is also of interest, for it is one of the very few in the country to preserve its mid-seventeenth-century furnishings and arrangement, with an elevated wooden pulpit and reader's desk at the east end in place of an altar and a gallery around the other three sides. By the main entrance to the house is a small Civil War guardroom, with a flagstone floor, seventeenth-century furnishings and a standing effigy of a guard dressed in armour. Parliamentary troops supposedly still haunt their old garrison.

The future of Littlecote House is in some doubt and the collection of Civil War arms and armour, now owned by the National Armouries, may not stay there.

Longford House or Castle (SU172267)

Sir Thomas Gorges built the fortified house, sometimes called a castle, in the 1590s, a fantastic triangular mansion with three richly decorated and elaborately faced ranges linked by low, round corner towers; additional towers stand in the middle of two of the ranges. Longford was garrisoned for the King from 1643 until Lord Coleraine's Royalists surrendered on 17 or 18 October 1645. Cromwell was present to oversee the brief siege and surrender. The house was not slighted after the war but fell derelict and ruinous during the eighteenth century. It was restored and extensively rebuilt in the nineteenth century, though care was taken to preserve the original Tudor appearance.

Lydiard Tregoz (SU1084)

In the Church of St Mary there is a grand and gaudy monument to Capt. Edward St John, a Royalist officer killed in 1645. St John is portrayed in life-size effigy dressed in full military uniform of the Civil War – the armour is now in gilded gold – with pictures of his soldiers on either side. His

armour and pennants are also on display within the church.

Maiden Bradley (ST8038)

New Mead Farm, on the eastern outskirts of the village, was the birthplace of Edmund Ludlow, the Parliamentary officer and radical politician who fought with distinction in England and Ireland during the 1640s. A regicide and republican, he opposed the Protectorate and fled the country at the Restoration.

Malmesbury (ST9387)

The circuit of twelfth-century town walls was very dilapidated by the seventeenth century and, despite the additional earthworks and barricades, Malmesbury remained vulnerable, unable to resist determined assault. In consequence the town changed hands at least six times during the war, as control of north-west Wiltshire passed from one side to the other. At different times Hopton and Rupert took the town for the King, Waller and Massey for Parliament. No trace of the Civil War earthworks remains, though fragments of the medieval stone defences survive, including parts of the East Gate at Holloway and a section of wall by the Town Bridge. During the course of Waller's recapture of the town in March 1643, part of Abbey Row was demolished in an explosion and was not rebuilt. Bullet marks in the west wall of the Abbey Church supposedly date from the Civil War and are often described as the grim evidence of military executions.

Marlborough (SU1869)

Marlborough changed hands several times during the Civil War, usually with little or no fighting, the garrison evacuating the weakly held town at the approach of a larger force. On only one occasion was there serious bloodshed here, on 5 December 1642, when a Royalist force under Wilmot and Digby attacked the town in the early morning. The defenders were caught by surprise and the Royalists soon overcame the lightly defended barricades. However a fierce fight developed as the King's men slowly pushed their way up the High Street, clearing the side streets and buildings as they went. The town was eventually captured and sacked and many members of the Parliamentary garrison were taken prisoner and carted off to Oxford. Marks on the outer walls of St Mary's Church are usually attributed to Civil War gunfire.

Ramsbury Manor (SU256710)

Cromwell passed through the area in July 1649 *en route* to Ireland; according to tradition, he lodged on the 12th not in Marlborough itself but at Ramsbury

Manor, the Earl of Pembroke's seat three miles east of the town. The Pembrokes acquired the medieval palace of the Bishops of Salisbury in the sixteenth century and converted it into a grand Tudor mansion. The building in which Cromwell was reputedly entertained was completely demolished in 1680, when the present brick manor-house was built on the site. The house and its park are private.

Roundway Down (SU0165)
On 13 July 1643 Waller lifted the siege of Devizes and marched his 4,500 men north-east to meet a 1,800-strong relieving force under Wilmot which had been despatched from Oxford. Goring's 3,000 Royalists in Devizes possibly believed that Waller's departure was a ruse to draw them out of the town and they did not march out to assist Wilmot until the very end of the battle. Thus Wilmot was heavily outnumbered when the two armies clashed in the wide shallow valley between Roundway and Morgan's Hills, roughly one mile north-north-east of the village of Roundway. There was little coordinated strategy and the battle soon developed into a confused mêlée at close quarters. Despite their numerical disadvantage, the Royalists gained the upper hand and broke Waller's Horse, which then bolted west, where many of the horses and their riders fell to their deaths down the precipitous western slopes of Roundway Hill; the hollow at the bottom of the slope gained the nickname 'Bloody Ditch'. Without Cavalry cover, the Parliamentary Foot came under great pressure and was routed. Waller himself escaped but his army had been destroyed: 600 Parliamentarians were killed, over 800 captured and the remainder put to flight.

The area is still open farmland, encircled by a number of roads. The Ordnance Survey battle symbol is at SU016655 in the flat open valley, little changed since the seventeenth century. Despite its name, 'Oliver's Camp', an Iron Age hill-fort a little to the west (SU001647) has no connection with Oliver Cromwell or the Civil War.

Salisbury (SU1429)
With neither town walls nor a castle, Salisbury could offer little resistance to determined attack and the town changed hands several times during the Civil War, usually with little or no fighting. In December 1644, however, Salisbury witnessed considerable bloodshed as Ludlow first captured and then lost the town. At the beginning of the month his forces surprised and routed a party of Royalist Horse stationed in the Close, the fourteenth-century walled enclosure around the cathedral and the only easily defensible place within the town. Ludlow proceeded to garrison the Close for Parliament, establishing his HQ in the Belfry, a massive thirteenth-century tower, 200 feet high and with walls eight feet thick, which stood 70 yards north of the cathedral nave. Within a fortnight the Parliamentarians had gone, surprised and expelled by Langdale's Royalist Horse. There was fierce fighting as the Royalists burst into the town and the Parliamentarians lost at least 80 men as they tried to halt the attack in Endless Street and around the Market Place. The King's men held Salisbury for three months but then evacuated the place in March 1645. Cromwell stopped in Salisbury on several occasions later in the year during his Wiltshire campaign.

Two later rebellions started in Salisbury. At the beginning of May 1649 it was one of several rendezvous points for Leveller Parliamentary troops whose mutiny ended at Burford later in the month. On 12 March 1655 John Penruddock and his Royalist colleagues siezed the town and captured the High Sheriff, Chief Justice Rolle and Baron Nicholas, who were here on assize circuit; the rebels opened Fisherton Gaol and proclaimed Charles II in the Market Place before marching away westwards.

Much of the medieval Close survives, with well preserved lengths of fourteenth-century walling to the south and east along St Nicholas Road and St John and Exeter Street; the north wall is more fragmentary and is obscured by later houses and the west wall has largely disappeared. Several medieval town gates into the Close also survive, including the North Gate, St Ann's Gate, Bishop's Gate and Harnham Gate. The Belfry was completely demolished in the eighteenth century and in the following century Fisherton Gaol, which stood on the south side of Fisherton Street near the river, was destroyed during the general redevelopment of the area.

According to tradition, Cromwell lodged on 17 October 1645 at the George in the High Street, a late medieval inn. The building was gutted and partly demolished in the 1960s. The front survives, now the entrance façade of the Old George Shopping Mall, and the great hall was also preserved as The Old George Room of the adjoining restaurant.

Stockton (ST9838)
Stockton House, on the outskirts of the village, is a fine Elizabethan gabled hall decorated with bands of flint and stone. The adjoining chapel dates from the 1650s and is one of the few Interregnum churches to survive. House and chapel are private and should be viewed from the road.

Wardour Castle (ST938263) Old Wardour Castle, the principal seat of the Arundell family, was held for the King at the outbreak of the Civil War. The garrison was a small one — probably less than 30 men — but the mighty outer walls of the castle made Wardour a formidable stronghold. In late April 1643 Sir Edmund Hungerford laid siege to the place with his 1,300-strong force but neither a week-long bombardment nor the Parliamentarians' vast superiority in numbers had any impact on the Royalist defences. Tunnelling operations brought better results and when sections of the outer wall were breached on 8 May the Royalists surrendered on terms. The damage was quickly repaired and the castle garrisoned for Parliament by Edmund Ludlow. In the following December the Royalists returned to retake the fortress but Wardour again proved a formidable obstacle. The King's men besieged the castle for three months, throwing up earthworks and an earth and turf fort on the hillside above the outer gate, but not until March 1644 were the Royalists able to get close enough to the walls to lay mines an thus break the stalemate. The mines were sprung in mid-March and brought down two of the six angle turrets and opened large breaches in the walls. Although Ludlow repulsed one Royalist assault, the ruined castle was all but indefensible and the 75-man garrison surrendered to Sir Francis Doddington. Wardour had been damaged beyond repair and played no further part in the war. Indeed, the damage was never made good and when the Arundells returned to the area in the eighteenth century they lived not in the medieval castle but in New Wardour Castle, a Georgian mansion built for them nearby.

The fourteenth-century castle was built to a curious and probably unique plan. Within the walled bailey stood a large hexagonal keep, the six ranges enclosing a central courtyard. The exterior was not a perfect hexagon, for a very large rectangular gatehouse, extended in the sixteenth century, projected to the east. The extensive ruins are open daily.

Warminster (ST8745) By the churchyard path of the Minster Church is the weathered gravestone of Capt. Gourden, an officer fatally wounded at Edgehill.

Wilton House (SU099310) Wilton House, the Earl of Pembroke's Tudor mansion, stood on the site of a medieval nunnery. It was garrisoned for the King in 1643–44 but evacuated without a fight towards the end of 1644. Cromwell stayed here on 10 April 1645. The house was accidentally gutted by fire in 1647 and subsequently restored; it was again restored and extensively remodelled in the nineteenth century. With the exception of the Tudor Holbein Gate, which is detached from the main house and stands in the grounds, very little of the original sixteenth-century work is now visible. House and gardens are open from Tuesday to Saturday throughout the summer.

WALES

CLWYD

Although the county was secured for the King in 1642 and remained overwhelmingly Royalist throughout the war, it saw considerable action as the trio of Brereton, Middleton and Mytton launched repeated Parliamentary raids across the border from Cheshire and Shropshire. Brereton invaded north-east Clwyd in autumn 1643 but fell back in December when Royalist reinforcements from Ireland landed at Mostyn. Not until 1645–46 did most of the county finally fall to Mytton. Clwyd remained fairly quiet during the second Civil War. Cromwell was never in the area.

Chirk Castle (SJ269381) The Edwardian border castle was owned in the mid-seventeenth century by the Parliamentary politician and soldier Sir Thomas Middleton. He secured and garrisoned the fortress at the outbreak of war but on 15 January 1643 it fell to a Royalist raiding party under Col. Robert Ellis. Chirk remained in the King's hands until 23 February 1646, when Sir John Watts surrendered the castle to besieging Parliamentary forces, allegedly in return for a £200 bribe. Middleton declared for the King in summer 1659 but his castle was quickly bombarded into submission by Lambert's men.

The thirteenth–fourteenth-century fortress was quadrangular, with round corner towers and semicircular mural towers; the domestic ranges were grouped around a central courtyard. Although the medieval work survives in good order, parts of the exterior and most of the interior date from the eighteenth and nineteenth century, when Chirk was extensively renovated and modernised. Now owned by the National Trust and open during the summer, the castle contains many relics from the Civil War.

Sir Thomas Middleton was born in 1586 and served in several Parliaments during the 1620s. Despite his age, he was one of the most active and successful regional commanders during the Civil War and worked closely with Brereton and Mytton to retain or capture Shropshire, Cheshire and North Wales for Parliament. His efforts for the King in 1659 ensured his safety at the Restoration and he continued to live in retirement at Chirk. He was buried in 1666 in the parish church beneath an inscribed tablet; nearby are monuments to many other members of the family.

Denbigh (SJ0566) The hilltop castle, built by the Earl of Lincoln in the 1280s, was held by Col. William Salisbury and his Royalist garrison throughout the Civil War. Charles I visited the castle in 1645 and lodged in the tower which now bears his name. The castle and walled town were besieged by Mytton's Parliamentarians from late 1645 until 26 October 1646, when the garrison finally abandoned the hopeless struggle. The castle was then held for Parliament and in July 1648 Col. Twistleton beat off a Royalist attempt to free Sir John Owen, the leader of the North Wales rebellion, who had been lodged here after his capture at Aber. It was briefly held by the Royalist rebels in 1659.

The castle (SJ052658) was partly demolished after the Restoration and is not as well preserved as some of the Edwardian castles in the region. The remains comprise parts of the double curtain walls with round and octagonal mural towers, the three storey gatehouse and the domestic buildings within the roughly oval bailey. The ruins are open daily. The castle stood in the south-west angle of the thirteenth-century town walls, long stretches of which still stand. By the foot of the Goblin Tower are the remains of a crescent-shaped earthwork thrown up by the Royalists during the Civil War.

On 1 November 1645 Mytton and Brereton intercepted a unit of 2,000 Royalists just outside Denbigh. Sir William Vaughan and his men were moving north in the hope of relieving Chester but were caught by the pursuing Parliamentarians at Denbigh Green, ¾ mile north-east of the town centre, near Whitchurch. Mytton and Brereton quickly cleared the musketeers lining the road and then engaged Vaughan's main force in open ground around the ruins of the medieval friary (SJ060667). The Royalists were routed; 100 were killed and 400 captured and the remainder, including Vaughan, fled to Conway. Despite the subsequent expansion of Denbigh, the area of the main fighting around the friary ruins is still open ground.

Flint Castle (SJ246733) The medieval castle was garrisoned for the King from the beginning of the war. In mid-November 1643 Brereton besieged the fortress and may have taken it – contemporary accounts are rather vague – but he fell back into England in December when Royalist reinforcements landed at Mostyn, and the King's men held the castle without challenge for a further 2½ years. Mytton besieged Flint from spring 1646 until 24 August, when Col. Mostyn's garrison abandoned the struggle and surrendered on terms. The castle was subse-

Chirk Castle, Clwyd. Although the castle owes its present, decidedly non-medieval appearance to extensive eighteenth- and nineteenth-century restoration, it remains at heart the thirteenth–fourteenth century quadrangular fortress held for the King for much of the Civil War and recaptured by its Parliamentarian owner, Sir Thomas Middleton, in 1646.

quently slighted and is now very ruinous. The late thirteenth-century Edwardian fortress comprised a large outer bailey and a smaller square inner ward protected by curtain walls linked by three corner towers; at the fourth angle stood a detached round keep, quite separate from the two baileys and protected by its own moat. The ruins overlooking the Dee Estuary are open daily.

Hawarden Castle (SJ319654) The thirteenth-century castle was secured for the King at the outbreak of the Civil War but fell to Brereton on 16 March 1643. In the following November most of the Parliamentary troops evacuated the region on the landing of Royalist reinforcements and a skeleton garrison was left in the castle to try and hold the place or at least delay the Royalist advance. In the event, the Parliamentarians offered little resistance and surrendered on 4 December. In May 1645 Brereton tried and failed to retake the castle and it held out for the King for a further year until the collapse of the Royalist cause in Cheshire and the border area rendered further resistance futile. Sir William Neale surrendered to the besieging Parliamentarians on 16 March 1646 and the castle was slighted. The remains of the old fortress, including parts of the thirteenth-century round keep and banqueting hall and later round and square towers, stand in parkland south-east of the village and are open to the public during the summer. (The other 'castle' at Hawarden is, in fact, an eighteenth-century mansion.)

Holt (SJ4053) This small and undistinguished village was of crucial importance during the Civil War because it guarded one of the few crossings between England and North Wales. Indeed, in the mid-seventeenth century only two bridges spanned the lower reaches of the Dee – one, at Chester, was firmly under Royalist control for most of the war; the other was at Holt.

The Royalists secured the place at the outbreak of war, garrisoned the small medieval castle and established an outpost in St Chad's. They knocked down one of the arches of the bridge and replaced it with a movable drawbridge, defended by a gatehouse on the Welsh side. Brereton approached Holt in November 1643 and although heavy fire forced him to abandon an attempt to cross the river by boat, his troops managed to take the bridge itself, cutting the ropes and thus bringing the drawbridge section crashing down. After further fighting the Royalists were expelled from castle and church. This was but the first of several serious clashes here, for bridge and village

changed hands at least thrice more in 1644–45 before Mytton finally secured the passage for Parliament in spring 1646. Even then, the Royalist garrison within the castle held out and not until 13 January 1647 were Sir Richard Lloyd and his men starved into surrender.

The fifteenth-century eight-arched bridge still spans the Dee here (SJ412544); the missing arch was rebuilt after the war and no trace of the drawbridge or gatehouse survives. The late thirteenth-century castle stood on a rocky outcrop above the river, ⅓ mile south of the bridge (SJ412537); the curtain walls and angle towers which defended a pentagonal enclosure are now very ruinous and only odd fragments of masonry survive above ground. Marks on the aisle walls of St Chad's are usually attributed to Civil War bullets.

Rhuddlan Castle (SJ023779) In common with most of the Edwardian castles of North Wales, Rhuddlan had a rather uneventful Civil War. It was secured for the King unopposed in 1642 and held without serious challenge or incident until the very end of the war. In May 1646 Mytton appeared before Rhuddlan but did not attempt a direct attack, preferring to besiege the fortress and starve the garrison out. Col. Byron surrendered on terms at the end of July and the fortress was slighted. The thirteenth-century castle was laid out on a simple concentric plan, a square inner ward defended by a curtain wall, with round towers at the north and south angles and double-towered gateways at the east and west, all protected by an outer curtain wall. The outer wall has largely disappeared but the inner curtain and corner towers survive in good order. The castle is open daily.

Ruthin Castle (SJ124578) The late thirteenth-century castle was held for the King throughout the first Civil War. Col. Sword and his garrison resisted occasional Parliamentary raids, including an attack by Sir Thomas Middleton on 19 October 1644 which was repulsed with heavy losses. The Parliamentarians returned in strength in January 1646, quickly overran the town and laid siege to the fortress. Cols Trevor and Raingold and their garrison were eventually starved into submission on 12 April 1646. The castle, which was in the form of an irregular pentagon, with curtain walls linked by five angle towers and a double-towered gatehouse, was slighted after the war and by the eighteenth century was very ruinous. Most of the remains were incorporated within a grand castellated mansion, also known as the 'castle', which is now a hotel; further fragments of walling and towers stand in the hotel grounds.

Wrexham (SJ3349)   Although seventeenth-century Wrexham was the largest town in North Wales, it possessed neither stone walls nor a castle; street barricades and hastily erected earthworks afforded only limited protection and in consequence the town changed hands several times and never became a major base. The area was held by the King during the opening year of the war and Wrexham served as a recruiting and rendezvous point. In November 1643 Brereton occupied the town, but the Parliamentary garrison was later withdrawn and Sir John Owen reoccupied Wrexham for the King in February 1645. It was not formally secured for Parliament until late 1646.

DYFED

Much of this large modern county comprises bleak and mountainous territory which largely escaped bloodshed during the Civil War. With the exception of Aberystwyth, Kidwelly and the coastal plains, the conflict was confined to the south-west, particularly former Pembrokeshire. This area saw some of the most dramatic and frequent changes of fortune of the whole Civil War. Secured for Parliament at the outbreak of war, all but a handful of bases fell to Carbery's Royalists during 1643. In the following February and March the region was invaded by Laugharne's Parliamentarians, only to be retaken by Gerard's Royalists in June and July. It was gradually reconquered by Parliament once more from late 1644. Even then the process was far from smooth and repeated Royalist raids during 1645 caused several bases to change hands yet again and fighting continued well into 1646. Thus most strongholds in the area changed hands four times in the course of the first Civil War, and some as many as six. In 1648 Pembroke became one of the centres of the second Civil War and Cromwell was in the area from May to July to oversee the Parliamentary operation against the town; he passed through again in summer 1649 on his way to Ireland.

Aberystwyth Castle (SN579815)   The concentric, double-warded castle was built by Edward I in the 1270s to protect the newly-founded walled town which lay below it. Although semi-derelict by the early seventeenth century, the castle was still defensible and was garrisoned for the King by Col. Whiteley throughout the first Civil War. The mint was withdrawn but the castle remained an important bullion store as well as a base for Royalist raids in the surrounding area. One such attack, on a Parliamentary unit at Llanbadarn (SN6081), ended in disaster when the Royalists were fiercely repulsed and struggled back to Aberystwyth with heavy losses – 13 drowned in Mill Pond. Town and castle were attacked several times by Powell and Laugharne in the latter half of 1645 but the garrison held out for another winter, finally surrendering to Powell's besieging army on 14 April 1646. The castle was slighted in 1649 and, despite recent excavation and consolidation, is one of the most ruinous of Edward I's Welsh fortresses. The remains of the curtain walls, gatehouse and internal apartments stand in parkland freely accessible to the public.

Boulston (SM9712)   Boulston House, the seat of the Wogan family, was garrisoned for the King at the outbreak of the war but was evacuated without a fight in February 1644 at the approach of Laugharne. The ruined shell of the three storey fortified manor-house stands on the north bank of the Cleddau, a little south of the later, Georgian Boulston house; a public footpath runs past the ruins.

Cardigan Castle (SN177459)   The medieval castle overlooking the Teifi and guarding the town bridge changed hands several times in the course of the first Civil War. It was taken by Gerard's Royalists in summer 1644 and retaken by Laugharne's Parliamentarians in December, following a brief bombardment. Gerard attacked the newly returned garrison in January 1645 but was beaten off by a relieving party under Col. Laugharne. The Royalists returned five months later and succeeded in capturing the fortress, which was then held for the King until the end of the year, when it changed hands for the fourth and last time. Laugharne slighted the castle in 1646–47 and little remains today. The fragmentary ruins of the circular keep and curtain wall with two mural towers, all probably thirteenth-century, stand by the road; the interior is not open to the public.

Carew Castle (SN046037) Although the Normans erected a stronghold at Carew, the present spectacular remains above the tidal creek are probably no earlier than the thirteenth century. The medieval quadrangular stronghold, with round corner towers and an eastern gatehouse, was remodelled in the early sixteenth century, when the west front was largely rebuilt, and again towards the end of the century, when Sir John Perrott greatly extended the northern range in exuberant Tudor style. The Royalists established a garrison here sometime in 1643 but Carew surrendered to Col. Poyer in March of the following year. In summer 1644 and 1645 the castle was twice retaken and briefly garrisoned by Gerard's Royalists. Now a grand and extensive ruin, the castle is open to the public during the summer. The southern curtain is particularly ruinous, probably the result of Civil War bombardment. Traces of several earthworks around the castle, particularly the remains of a ravelin (a 'V'-shaped trench) beyond the eastern gateway, may date from the Civil War.

In 1643–44 the Royalists also garrisoned the Old Rectory at Carew, a fifteenth-century mansion which stood about 100 yards from the church. The house was largely rebuilt in the nineteenth century but a low square tower and part of the embattled outer wall escaped demolition and survive in fairly good order.

Carmarthen (SN4120) The town and its thirteenth-century castle changed hands repeatedly during the latter half of the Civil War as first Gerard, then Laugharne, gained the upper hand in the area. They were finally secured for Parliament by Laugharne on 12 October 1645; the castle was subsequently slighted.

The Norman motte and bailey on a high bluff overlooking the river was rebuilt in stone in 1223; the remains, including most of the motte and the ruins of a gatehouse and a tower with adjoining walls, are partly hidden by modern council offices. The site is not open to the public.

In 1643 the Royalists threw up earthwork defences around the town, a small section of which survives to the west of the town in the suburb of St Peter's. The bank and ditch, known as 'The Bulwarks', lie north of the Tywi and immediately north-west of the site of the medieval friary.

Cromwell passed through Carmarthen on 22 May 1648 *en route* to Pembroke, but according to tradition lodged for the night outside the town at Golden Grove (see below). He did, however, stay in Carmarthen on 31 July or 1 August 1649 on his way to Milford Haven and lodged at the Nag's Head in St Mary Street; the building does not survive.

Colby Moor (SN043174) On 1 August 1645 1,100 Royalist Foot and 450 Horse under Col. Stradling were routed by Laugharne's Parliamentarians on open ground to the east of Haverfordwest. The Royalists were marching from Haverfordwest towards Narberth but around 6 p.m. they were intercepted by the Parliamentarians at Colby. After a brief fight the King's men broke and fled back west, some occupying and trying to hold the Rath, an ancient earthwork three miles north-east of Haverfordwest (SM985188). One hundred and fifty Royalists perished and 700 were captured.

Colby Moor remains an area of flat, open high ground, now encircled by minor roads. Those who fell in battle supposedly lie beneath the field immediately north of the present Colby Moor Farm.

Golden Grove (SN5920) To the east of the village stood a large mansion, the seat of the Earl of Carbery, the Royalist commander in South Wales during the opening years of the Civil War who was later replaced by the more dynamic Gerard. According to tradition, Cromwell visited the place on 22 May 1648, was entertained by the Countess – the Earl was absent – and spent the night there. The great house was destroyed by fire and a post-seventeenth-century building, now an agricultural college, stands on the site.

Haverfordwest Castle (SM954158) In common with most of the strongholds in the area, the late thirteenth-century castle above the Cleddau changed hands several times during the first Civil War. A Parliamentary garrison in 1642, it was in the hands of Carbery by autumn 1643 but the nervous Royalists evacuated the place in the following February on seeing what they believed to be the Parliamentary army crossing a hilltop above the town. It was, in fact, a herd of cows and when Laugharne arrived in earnest a day or two later he was able to occupy the fortress unopposed. It was retaken by Gerard on 22 August 1644 and held for the King for a year; the small garrison surrendered to Laugharne immediately after Colby Moor. Although the shell of the castle appears very imposing and quite complete from most angles, one of the curtain walls has, in fact, almost completely disappeared and the internal ranges are very ruinous. The castle is currently closed to the public while excavations and restoration are in

Above: Carew Castle, Dyfed. Sir John Perrott's grand Tudor range overlooking the tidal creek survived the Civil War intact; the medieval ranges behind it were not so fortunate and the southern, in particular, was badly damaged in the bombardments of 1644–5.

Left: Laugharne Castle, Dyfed. The thirteenth-century castle above the Taf estuary was restored in the sixteenth century and survived a week-long Parliamentary siege in 1644 before a heavy bombardment compelled the garrison to submit.

Below: Pembroke Castle, Dyfed. The huge clifftop castle was a major Parliamentary base throughout the first Civil War and the centre of Royalist rebellion in South Wales during the second. Cromwell mounted a long and successful operation against the medieval stronghold from May to July 1648.

progress but the interior can be viewed from a point near the museum.

In a field one mile south of the town stand the remains of Haroldston, a thirteenth-century fortified manor-house garrisoned for the King in 1643 but abandoned without a fight in the following February. Parts of one tower and several sections of walling survive above ground.

Kidwelly Castle (SN409071)
Although still defensible in the seventeenth century, the medieval castle above the tidal estuary at Kidwelly lay well east of the area of bitterest fighting and played only a minor role in the Civil War. Laugharne took the fortress in April 1644 and left a small garrison here; in the following month, however, Gerard besieged and bombarded the Parliamentarians into submission. There is no record of further fighting here. The extensive ruins, open daily, comprise a fourteenth-century gatehouse opening onto a semicircular outer ward, protected by well-preserved curtain walls and mural towers; the rectangular inner ward contains the remains of a thirteenth- or fourteenth-century chapel.

Laugharne Castle (SN302107)
The medieval castle, extensively restored and modernised in the sixteenth century, was occupied by Gerard's Royalists in summer 1644. The Parliamentarians approached the castle in the following October and captured the outer ward after a week-long siege and bombardment; the Royalist garrison then surrendered on terms. Laugharne played little further part in the conflict. Sections of the medieval castle, including the thirteenth-century keep, a round tower and gatehouse and sections of the outer curtain, were retained when the building was converted into a grand fortified Tudor mansion. The interior of the castle is temporarily closed while a programme of excavation and consolidation is in progress, but the impressive shell can be viewed from several vantage-points, including the area of flat marshland by the estuary at the lower end of the town.

Llandeilo (SN6322)
In late April 1648 a Parliamentary unit under Col. Flemming, operating against Royalist rebels in the area, was ambushed just outside Llandeilo and took refuge in the town church. The Royalists proceeded to surround and attack the church and the Parliamentarians surrendered. Over 100 troops were captured but Col. Flemming was found dead from a bullet wound in the head – it is not clear whether he committed suicide or was murdered by the Royalists.

Manorbier Castle (SS064977)
The castle apparently played only a minor role in the Civil War, possibly because it was already semi-ruinous by the seventeenth-century. It may have changed hands several times as the conflict ebbed and flowed in the region but the only recorded action here took place in September 1645, when the castle fell to Laugharne's Parliamentarians. The extensive remains of the double-warded castle include parts of the original twelfth-century fortress – chiefly a hall, a small square tower and a gatehouse – but most of the present ruins date from the thirteenth–fourteenth century. Earthworks around the castle are sometimes ascribed to the Civil War. The castle is open daily.

Milford Haven (SM9006)
The natural harbour was one of the principal ports for passages to Ireland, south-west England and other points around the Welsh coast. Unlike most of the strongholds in the region, it remained under Parliamentary control throughout the Civil War: Parliament's almost unchallenged control of the sea and the support and protection afforded by the fleet made Milford almost impregnable. Cromwell spent the first two weeks of August 1649 here before boarding the *John* on 13 August and sailing for Dublin.

In January 1644 the Royalists had begun constructing a counter-stronghold at Pill, one mile east-north-east of the town. The Parliamentary garrison quickly launched a combined land and sea operation to crush the threat. Laugharne posted men in St Cewydd's Church at Steynton (SM918078) to cover any attempt by the Haverfordwest Royalists to come to the aid of their colleagues, while his main force and the fleet pounded the Royalist position at Pill. The King's men hastily abandoned their incomplete fort and fled east. The remains of the fort are still visible at the head of the inlet (SM919064), the foundations of the tower standing amid a small enclosure protected by a ditch to the east and an earth bank to the north.

Newcastle Emlyn (SN311407)
The thirteenth-century quadrangular castle within a loop of the Teifi was strengthened in the following century when a gatehouse and polygonal tower were added; it was again renovated and partly rebuilt in the fifteenth century. It was held for Parliament from the outbreak of the Civil War until its capture by Gerard in summer 1644. Laugharne besieged the castle in spring 1645 but was routed by Gerard's relieving force on 23 April in a fierce engagement below the castle walls. It was finally taken by Parliament in December 1645 after a

brief siege and was subsequently slighted. Now very ruinous, the crags of masonry standing on the weathered motte are freely accessible to the public.

Pembroke (SM9801) The clifftop castle and the walled town to the east were Parliamentary strongholds throughout the first Civil War, resisting attacks by Gerard's Royalists in summer 1644 and 1645 and remaining Parliamentarian even when the surrounding area had fallen to the King.

In marked contrast, Pembroke became one of the major Royalist bases during the second Civil War. In March 1648 the new governor, Col. Flemming, was denied access to the castle and he and his small Parliamentary unit were expelled from the town. Pembroke declared for the King under Col. John Poyer, a former Parliamentary officer, and he was soon joined by many other ex-Parliamentarians, including Cols Rice Powell and Rowland Laugharne. By mid-May, however, the South Wales rebellion had suffered a fatal reverse at St Fagans (South Glamorgan) and Pembroke was under siege. Cromwell arrived on 24 May to oversee operations in person and established his base just outside the town, on a hill overlooking Underdown. At first the Parliamentarians possessed only light artillery, which could make little impact on the well-maintained medieval walls. Attempts to storm the town on 4 and 24 June were equally unsuccessful. The stalemate was broken on 1 July when heavy cannon, brought by ship from Gloucester, were landed at Milford Haven and by the second week of July several breaches had been opened in the walls of the town and castle. By this stage the garrison was also very short of supplies and the King's men abandoned the struggle and surrendered on the 11th. (A later story that the garrison was forced to surrender through lack of drinking water after Cromwell had cut the external supply which ran via Monkton appears unfounded, and the remains of pipes in Monkton Bridge probably have no Civil War associations.) Cromwell immediately entered the town and gave orders for the defences to be slighted – parts of the Barbican Gate, Foss Bastion and the Bygate, Henry VII, Westgate and Northgate Towers were subsequently brought down by mines. He stayed in Pembroke for five days, lodging at the 'York Tavern' in Main Street and attending a Thanksgiving service in the church on Sunday the 16th. Later that day he left Pembroke and began the long journey north to meet the Scottish Royalists. Meanwhile Poyer, Laugharne and Powell were taken to London, where in due course they were court martialled and sentenced to death; two were reprieved, but Col. Poyer was shot in Covent Garden on 25 April 1649.

Pembroke Castle is now a spectacular and extensive ruin, open daily. Although the internal wall which divided the baileys has largely disappeared, the castle originally comprised a large outer ward, defended by a curtain wall, five round mural towers and a southern gatehouse, and a separate triangular inner ward to the north in which stood and stands an enormous round keep.

The town gates have all disappeared but long stretches of Pembroke's medieval walls survive, particularly along the southern side of the town.

Picton Castle (SN009134) The medieval castle was held for Parliament from the outbreak of war until 1645, with a short interlude in 1643 when it was captured and briefly garrisoned by Carbery. The fortress was stormed and taken by Gerard in summer 1645, only to be retaken by Laugharne three months later. Now an extensive ruin, the remains of the thirteenth- and early fourteenth-century quadrangular fortress with round angle towers and a doubled-towered gatehouse, stand in private parkland. The park, though not the castle, is occasionally open to the public during the early summer.

Pwllcrochan (SM921026) In late March 1648 Col. Read and 350 Parliamentary troops sailed from Bristol and landed on the peninsula west of Pembroke. They intended to attack the Royalist rebels in that town but were themselves surprised by Poyer's forces. On 29 March the King's men raided the temporary Parliamentary quarters in St Mary's Church, Pwllcrochan. After a brief skirmish the Parliamentarians escaped south-west and occupied Henllan House, which was, in turn, attacked and captured by Poyer. The old house has long since disappeared and a modern building, renamed Hentland, now stands on the site.

Roch Castle (SM880212) The medieval castle was held for the King from 1643 until 1645, excepting a few weeks in spring 1644 when it was taken and briefly garrisoned by Laugharne. The derelict and ruined fortress was restored and remodelled in the twentieth century and remains a private residence. The thirteenth-century 'D'-shaped tower survives in good order and is visible for miles around; the exterior can also be viewed from the road and public footpath which run close by.

Stackpole Court (SR977962) The Elizabethan

manor-house west of the village was held by a 60-strong Royalist garrison from 1643 until its capture by Laugharne in the following February. The Tudor building has been completely demolished and nothing remains except traces of the foundations and associated earthworks on private land.

Tenby (SN138005) The Norman fortress and the circuit of medieval town walls at Tenby were semi-derelict but still defensible in the mid-seventeenth century and town and castle changed hands several times during the Civil War. Royalist attempts to secure town and castle for the King at the outbreak of war were countered by a show of force and Tenby declared for Parliament. In August 1643 town and castle were taken by Carbery's Royalists, only to fall to Laugharne once more in the following March. They remained in Parliamentary hands for the rest of the first Civil War, despite two attempts by Gerard's men to take the town by siege and by storm.

In March 1648 Tenby Castle was secured by a unit of Royalist rebels. Col. Horton had the place surrounded and under siege by the end of the month but the King's men held out for over ten weeks. They were still resisting when Cromwell passed through the town on 23 May on his way to Pembroke; he may have returned during the following week to inspect progress. The Royalist garrison was finally starved into surrender on 31 May.

The ruins of the clifftop castle, including parts of the Norman keep, thirteenth-century 'D'-shaped barbican and a later watch-tower, stand in parkland freely accessible to the public. Several sections of Tenby's thirteenth-century town walls also survive.

Trefloyne House (SS106998) Only fragments of the late sixteenth- and early seventeenth-century mansion survive, now incorporated within a modern farm complex, visible from the road or public footpath which run close by. The old house was held for the King in 1643–44 and at one time a 200-strong garrison was based here. The main force was withdrawn at the approach of Laugharne in February 1644 and the small garrison which remained surrendered the house without a fight.

Welston Court (SN032022) In summer 1648 Cromwell established his base at Welston Court, the country house of Capt. Walter Coyney, while directing operations against Pembroke. Cromwell was here for much of the six weeks of the siege, reportedly suffering from gout. The house was completely demolished in the nineteenth century and the present Welston Court is a private nineteenth–twentieth-century building.

Wiston Castle (SN022182) In 1643 the Royalists established a small outpost at Wiston, presumably refortifying the substantial motte and the remains of the twelfth-century castle. They withdrew, however, without a fight when Laugharne renewed operations in the area in spring 1644.

When the Church of St Simon and St Jude, Wiston, was restored in 1864, many bodies were found in shallow graves beneath the floor of the nave. They were thought to be the remains of some of those who fell at Colby Moor.

GWENT

There was little major fighting in Gwent during the first Civil War and the conflict soon developed into a struggle for control of a handful of castles and castle towns. The area remained overwhelmingly Royalist until 1645–46. Chepstow figured briefly in the second Civil War and Cromwell oversaw the capture of the town in May 1648 while en route to Pembroke. He travelled through Gwent again in July 1649 on his way to embark for Ireland.

Abergavenny Castle (SO299140) The Norman motte and bailey castle at Abergavenny was strengthened in the thirteenth–fourteenth century when a curtain wall, mural towers and a gatehouse were added. It was garrisoned for the King from the outbreak of war until 1646, when it was bombarded into submission and then slighted. The fragmentary remains of four towers and of the gatehouse and barbican are open daily.

Chepstow (ST5394) Town and castle were se-

Chepstow Castle, Gwent. The medieval castle high above the Wye (*above*) was held for the King throughout the first Civil War and became a major Royalist outpost during the second. It was neither slighted nor abandoned after the war and instead became a garrison, prison and administrative centre during the Interregnum and after the Restoration. The regicide and republican Henry Marten spent twenty years of uncomfortable captivity in the round tower which now bears his name (*right*).

cured for the King in 1642 and, although briefly evacuated in April 1643 at the approach of Waller, were retained without serious incident until autumn 1645. In October a 1,300-strong Parliamentary force approached Chepstow, overran the town and besieged and bombarded the castle; the 64 Royalists within promptly surrendered.

In spring 1648 Sir Nicholas Kemeys seized Chepstow for the King and established a 120-strong garrison in the castle. Cromwell and his army arrived here on 11 May and took the town with minimal opposition. The Royalist force within the castle proved more troublesome and three days later Cromwell and most of his troops marched on, leaving a unit under Col. Ewer to continue the siege. A heavy bombardment eventually brought down parts of the curtain wall near Marten's Tower but the Royalists still refused to surrender. Ewer's men then took the castle by storm, in the course of which most of the garrison, including Kemeys, perished. The castle was not slighted but maintained as a garrison and prison throughout the Interregnum. It remained a prison after the Restoration and for 20 years Henry Marten was held in the tower which now bears his name.

One of the most radical and outspoken opponents of the King in the Long Parliament, Marten was briefly expelled from the House in the mid-1640s, during which time he served in the Parliamentary army and became governor of Aylesbury. Readmitted in 1646, he was prominent during the trial and execution of the King but fell from favour during the 1650s and spent much of the Protectorate in prison. He surrendered in 1660 and eventually escaped with his head, but spent the rest of his life in prison in Chepstow Castle, where he died in September 1680. He was originally buried in the chancel of St Mary's, but the remains were later moved into the nave and now lie beneath an inscribed slab near the west door.

The extensive castle ruins stand on a spectacular site, a rocky spur almost sheer above the Wye. Begun by the Normans – their Great Tower survives – and greatly extended over the following centuries, the present three bailey fortress is long and narrow, adapted to fit the irregularly shaped knoll. Marten's Tower stands on the east side of the lower bailey; to the west and north-east the curtain wall has been repaired where breached by Parliamentary cannon in 1648. The castle shows further signs of Interregnum renovation – the medieval battlements on most of the towers were replaced with stronger parapets designed for artillery and the southern curtain wall was thickened and the parapet looped for musketry. The castle is open daily and contains an important civil war display.

Much of the thirteenth-century wall, the Portwall, which encircled Chepstow still stands, together with a sixteenth-century town gate.

According to tradition Cromwell lodged on 11–14 May 1648 at 'Cromwell House' in Bridge Street; possibly fifteenth-century in origin but extensively restored and refurbished since, the building is now a leather and craft shop.

Llangibby (ST3797)

West of the village, beneath the ruins of the old castle, stands Llangibby House or Castle, the seat of the Williams family. The two storey house, built in the first half of the seventeenth century and possibly designed by Inigo Jones, was garrisoned by Sir Trevor Williams for Parliament at the start of the war. The area was overwhelmingly Royalist, however, and Williams soon switched allegiance to the King; Llangibby became a minor Royalist base, surviving several Parliamentary raids during the latter half of the war. Llangibby House survived the war intact and remains a private residence.

Monmouth (SO5113)

Town and castle changed hands at least four times during the first Civil War as Royalist troops fell back before raids led by Waller and Massey only to return a few days or weeks later when the Parliamentarians themselves retreated from an overwhelmingly hostile area. Monmouth was finally secured for Parliament in October 1645 when 3,000 troops besieged, captured and garrisoned the place. Its only part in the second Civil War was to play host to Cromwell and his troops on 10 May 1648 as they travelled through the region.

The twelfth–thirteenth-century castle was slighted and largely destroyed in 1647, though parts of the Great Tower and medieval domestic buildings remain, south-east of the Monnow near the post-Civil War Great Castle House; the ruins are open daily. Odd fragments of the medieval town wall also survive.

Raglan Castle (SO415083)

One of the last great castles of medieval Britain, Raglan served as the centre of Royalism in south-east Wales throughout the first Civil War. The Marquis of Worcester put his fortress and his fortune at Charles I's disposal and frequently played host to the King, particularly during the latter half of 1645, after Naseby. Not until 1646 was Raglan under serious threat. Throughout the spring and summer it was closely besieged by Col. Morgan's Parliamentarians, who dug trenches around the castle and threw up several gun

Raglan Castle, Gwent. A centre of Royalism throughout the area, Raglan held out for the King until 1646 and was the last principal stronghold in England and Wales to fall. The Pitched Stone Court (*above*) took the brunt of the Parliamentary bombardment of 1646 – most of the windows and battlements of the gatehouse were blown out and the outer wall was breached by the Closet Tower (left). The separate keep or great tower (*right*) was slighted after the war, the Parliamentarians soon abandoning attempts to demolish it with pickaxes and instead bringing down the whole of the eastern face by undermining.

positions. The bombardment did little damage – the battlements and windows were knocked out and a small breach opened in the wall of the Pitched Stone Court near the Closet Tower. The garrison eventually surrendered on terms to Sir Thomas Fairfax on 19 August, long after the submission of the King and the collapse of his cause. Raglan was not the last base in mainland Britain to hold out for the King – Harlech, for one, stood until 1647 – but it was the last major stronghold which posed a real threat to security and Parliament held a day of Thanksgiving for its fall. The castle was looted and then slighted. It played no part in the rebellion of 1648.

The extensive and picturesque ruins of the fifteenth-century fortress stand on high ground ¾ mile north-east of the village. They comprise two courts, separated by a great hall, each defended by its own gatehouse, curtain wall and mural and angle towers, with apartments ranged around the inside of the wall. The massive hexagonal keep stands in isolation on an island; its southern face was brought down by mines after the Civil War.

Traces of several offensive and defensive Civil War earthworks survive around the castle, parti-cularly to the north-east, on rising ground beyond Castle Farm, where there are substantial remains of an earthwork bastion and adjoining breastwork; probably built in 1642–43 to strengthen the defences, it was taken by the Parliamentarians during the siege and served as a battery. Nearer the castle, in a clump of trees adjoining the farmyard and at several points near the present car park, are slighter remains of earthwork defences.

Wonastow Court (SO485107)   The hilltop Tudor mansion occupied a strong site overlook-ing the road between Monmouth and Raglan. Garrisoned for the King at the outbreak of war by the Herberts, Wonastow was betrayed to Parliamentary forces in 1644. Thereafter it served from time to time as a minor Parliamen-tary outpost, covering any movements from the Royalist base at Raglan and withstanding sever-al raids by the King's men. The late fifteenth-century mansion has been largely demolished, though parts of the old house were incorporated in modern Wonastow Court, which stands by the small church overlooking the main road.

GWYNEDD

The county was secure for the King throughout the first Civil War and saw no significant action until the very end of the war, when the Royalist garrisons in the mighty Edwardian fortresses were slowly starved into surrender. Fighting broke out again in May and June 1648, when Sir John Owen led a short-lived Royalist rebellion in North Wales. Cromwell was never in the area.

Aber (SH6572)   The second Civil War on the North Wales mainland ended on the coastal plain to the west of Aber. In May 1648 Sir John Owen marched around North Wales, gathering forces for the King and skilfully eluding Par-liamentary troops. On 5 June, however, he was finally caught between Aber and Bangor at a site known locally as Y Dalar Hir. With 140 Horse and 120 Foot Owen outnumbered Twisleton's detachment and initially gained the upper hand in the fierce exchange, but a counter-charge by the professional and experienced troops sur-prised and broke Owen's motley army and the Royalists scattered. Thirty were killed and 60 more, including Owen, captured.

Anglesey   Anglesey was a Royalist strong-hold throughout the 1640s, secure for the King in 1642–46 and a centre of Royalist rebellion of 1648.

Holyhead (SH2482) on Holy Island was one of the principal ports for communications with Ireland. Defended by a small fort and garrison during the first Civil War, the town escaped major bloodshed.

Anglesey's main stronghold, however, stood in the south-east of the main island, overlooking the straits and the mainland. Beaumaris Castle (SH607763) was built by Edward I in the thir-teenth century and, although never completed, was one of the most perfect concentric castles in Britain. The roughly square inner bailey is de-fended by a double circuit of walls, each with mural towers and two gatehouses. Beaumaris was held for the King by Lord and Col. Bulkeley from 1642 until the garrison was starved into surrender on 14 June 1646. Col. Bulkeley re-turned in 1648 and the castle was again seized and held for the King. It surrendered without a fight in October 1648 when Mytton threatened to execute the prisoners taken at Red Hill (see below). The extensive and well-preserved remains are open daily.

On the western outskirts of Beaumaris, 300 yards west-south-west of the parish church, stood Bryn Britain, a triangular earthwork, probably of ancient date, refortified during the Civil War to defend the harbour and the approaches to the castle. The banks and ditches have been mutilated and largely destroyed by a modern housing estate.

To the west again (around SH5976) lies Red Hill Park, where the Royalist rebellion in North Wales was finally crushed. Mytton and Twistleton had defeated Sir John Owen's Royalists near Aber in June and had thus effectively ended the mainland rising, but the King's men held on to Anglesey for a further three months. At the end of September Mytton crossed the Menai Straits with 1,500 Horse and Foot and set about trying to bring the Anglesey Royalists to battle. The major engagement took place two weeks later, on 1 October, when Mytton clashed with Bulkeley's Royalists in parkland around Red Hill House. The rebels proved no match for Mytton's professional troops and although the casualties were fairly equal – around 30–40 killed on each side – the Royalists were routed; 400 were captured and the remainder scattered. Some, including Cols Bulkeley and Whitely, sought refuge in Beaumaris Castle but the fortress surrendered soon after without further bloodshed. The private parkland survives, though Tudor Red Hill House has long since disappeared and the present great house is post-seventeenth-century.

Two and a half miles north-north-east of Beaumaris, south-east of Llangoed, stands Castell Aberllienwag (SH616793). The weathered eleventh-century motte is surmounted by the remains of a later medieval defensive work, a square stone blockhouse with round corner towers. The place was garrisoned during the first Civil War as an outpost of Beaumaris, but apparently saw no fighting.

Barmouth (SH6115) On 23 May 1648 Twisleton and 80 Parliamentary Horse intercepted a detachment of Royalist rebels heading north along the coast road to join Owen's army around Caernarvon. After a brief fight outside Barmouth, Col. Lloyd and 40 of his men were captured and the rest of the Royalist force scattered.

Caernarvon (SH477627) Caernarvon Castle, the largest and most magnificent of Edward I's Welsh fortresses, had become rather dilapidated by the mid-seventeenth century but remained a

formidable stronghold. It was held for the King by Col. Byron throughout the first Civil War, excepting a short interlude in 1644 when the town and possibly the castle too may have briefly fallen to a naval attack under Col. Swanley. It was besieged by Mytton in spring 1646 and surrendered on 4 June. The castle was then garrisoned for Parliament and held out in spring 1648 against a brief siege by Owen's Royalist rebels. Although most of the buildings within the bailey were demolished during the Interregnum, an order for the destruction of the outer walls was not implemented. The mighty curtain wall, polygonal mural towers and northern gatehouse survive in fairly good order. The castle is open daily.

Conway (SH783774)   Edward I built the castle above the river Conway in the late thirteenth century to command and protect the adjoining walled town; eight almost identical round towers were linked by massive curtain walls enclosing two wards. In the mid-seventeenth century the derelict castle was owned by John Williams, Archbishop of York, and he paid for the place to be renovated and refortified in 1642–43. Town and castle were held for the King throughout the first Civil War. Col. Carter's Parliamentarians overran the town on 9 August 1646 but Sir John Owen and the Royalist garrison retreated into the castle and held out for a further three months. The beleaguered fortress surrendered on 18 November after a heavy bombardment.

The roofs and fittings of the internal apartments have disappeared, but otherwise the castle is almost intact; it is open daily. The thirteenth-century town walls, mural towers and town gates also survive in good order.

Gwydir Castle (SH799613)   The restored castle on the west bank of the Conway stands on the south-west outskirts of Llanrwst. The original sixteenth-century fortified mansion on the site was occupied by Vaughan's 900-strong Royalist force in November 1645 after the defeat at Denbigh. They evacuated the place and moved on at the approach of the Parliamentarians a few days later. The Tudor house was gutted by fire in the 1920s and most of the present 'castle' is modern restoration.

Harlech Castle (SH580313)   The rectangular concentric castle was built by Edward I on a rocky outcrop above the sea. The curtain walls are linked by large round corner towers and a massive gatehouse stands on the east side. It was held without challenge for the King throughout the first Civil War, its great distance from

Top: Harlech Castle, Gwynedd. The superb Edwardian castle on the west coast was far removed from the main theatres of action during the Civil War and its isolated Royalist garrison survived longer than any others on the English and Welsh mainland. It apparently escaped slighting after the war and survives as an extensive ruin. *Bottom:* Caernarvon Castle, Gwynedd. The largest, grandest and most expensive of Edward I's string of castles in North Wales, Caernarvon was hastily repaired in 1642 and garrisoned for the King. The jumble of domestic buildings within the bailey was swept away during the 1650s but a Parliamentary order for the slighting of the curtain walls and towers was never executed.

England and the poor roads in the area making it almost impossible to bring up heavy artillery. The garrison thus survived until March 1647, when John Jones and his men appeared before Harlech. They fought their way into the town and laid siege to the fortress; Col. William Owen and his 28-man garrison surrendered on 15 March. Harlech was thus the last base in England and Wales to hold out for the King during the first Civil War. The extensive remains of the castle are open daily.

Maes y Garnedd (SH6427) John Jones was born and brought up in this low, two storey farmhouse which still stands four miles east of Llanbedr beyond Pont Cerrig. Jones served in the Parliamentary army in Wales during the Civil War and was a colonel by 1646. He became MP for Merioneth in 1647 and a regicide two years later, and served in Ireland during the early 1650s. Despite his Republicanism and his opposition to the Protectorate, he married Cromwell's widowed sister, Catherine, in 1656. He was executed in London in October 1660, and thus it is most unlikely that the John Jones buried at Llanenddwyn church (SH5823) was Cromwell's brother-in-law and fellow regicide.

MID GLAMORGAN

The county played very little part in the Civil War. The valleys and mountains did not figure in the conflict and in the seventeenth century the coastal plain possessed no important town or castle to detain the armies which occasionally marched by. Cromwell travelled through in summer 1648, on his way to and from Pembroke, and again in the following year en route to Ireland, but apparently he never broke his journey here and no location within mid-Glamorgan is reliably linked with him.

Caerphilly (ST157871) The medieval castle was neither garrisoned nor attacked during the Civil War. The already ruinous defences may have been further slighted sometime during the 1640s, for around this time the dam was breached at the southern end and several mural towers mined, including the famous leaning tower.

A modern bridge leads between the lakes and across the north-west or outer moat to the site of a Roman fort. A Civil War artillery emplacement was thrown up here, presumably to guard against the possible occupation of the castle itself. The fortlet now comprises a square earth platform, eroded at the south-east, but with projecting bastions at the other corners, defended by a parapet. There is no record of any fighting here.

POWYS

Much of the huge modern county is bleak upland and mountains which escaped serious fighting during the Civil War. Although garrisons – usually Royalist – were established in most of the important towns in 1642–43, only those in the north-east of the county, part of old Montgomeryshire, saw major bloodshed. Most fell to Brereton, Middleton and Mytton in 1644. Cromwell never visited Powys.

Abbeycwmhir (SO055712) The Cistercians founded an abbey in this isolated, wooded valley in the twelfth century. It was laid out on a surprisingly grand scale – the abbey church possessed the longest nave in Wales – but the buildings were probably never completed and only excavation would reveal the precise plan. Parts of the church and adjoining buildings escaped demolition at the Dissolution and survived in sufficiently good order to house a Royalist garrison from autumn 1642. In December 1644 Cwmhir Abbey was attacked by Middleton's Parliamentarians, Col. Fowler's 70-strong garrison was overwhelmed and the outpost was lost. The fragmentary remains of the great abbey church stand ¼ mile south-east of

St Mary's; almost nothing of the cloisteral buildings is now visible.

Montgomery (SO2296)

Montgomery has long been a key border base guarding the main routes between England and mid-Wales, and a succession of strongholds have stood on the ridge above the town. The present ruins are the remains of the thirteenth-century castle which once covered the whole hilltop; curtain walls and numerous mural towers defended a string of five separate wards. The castle was secured for the King in 1642 but fell to Parliament on 7 September 1644 when Sir Thomas Middleton besieged the place and frightened its feeble governor, Lord Herbert, into surrender; in return, Herbert was assured that his London library would not be seized and sold, as Parliament had intended. Rupert immediately despatched Lord Byron and Col. Erneley from Shrewsbury to recover the castle and a Parliamentary force was hurriedly raised amongst local garrisons to counter the threat. By mid-September the two armies – Byron's 2,000 Royalists and a combined force of 3,000 Parliamentarians led by Brereton – were closing on Montgomery and on the 18th they clashed on rolling ground north of the town. Contemporary reports of the battle are rather vague and neither the precise location of the conflict nor its course can be discerned with certainty. It is clear, however, that the Royalists were routed and Byron's army effectively destroyed – 500 men were killed and over 1,000 captured. The threat to the castle had been lifted and it remained in Parliamentary hands until the end of the war. It was slighted very thoroughly in 1649 and most of the stone carted away. Today only one tower survives to any height, surrounded by several stretches of ruined curtain wall. The site is freely accessible to the public.

New Radnor (SO212610)

The thirteenth-century fortress at New Radnor was still defensible in the mid-seventeenth century and housed a small Royalist garrison from 1642. It fell to Parliament two years later after a heavy bombardment which caused extensive damage to the already derelict building. Although substantial earthworks remain – including the ditched motte and the bailey entrenchment – on the northern outskirts of the town, no masonry survives above ground.

Newtown (SO1091)

On 3 September 1644 Middleton and his troops left Oswestry (Shropshire) and marched into Wales overnight, taking care to avoid Royalist scouts. Early on the 4th they launched a dawn raid on Sir Thomas Gardiner's small garrison at Newtown, catching them completely by surprise and quickly overwhelming and capturing the ill-prepared Royalist force. More important, perhaps, for the Parliamentary cause was the large quantity of arms and ammunition found in the town.

Welshpool (SJ2207)

In August 1644 Middleton and Mytton led a combined party of over 500 Cavalry in a dawn raid on Welshpool, surprising Sir Thomas Dallison's troop of Royalist Horse temporarily stationed in the town. The Parliamentarians returned to Shropshire heavily loaded with booty.

Middleton returned in the following month to attack the Royalist garrison based just outside Welshpool. The town itself was weakly defended – the Norman motte and bailey on the eastern outskirts was derelict and indefensible by the seventeenth century – and the main stronghold stood one mile to the south. Powis Castle (SJ215064), too, began as a simple Norman motte and bailey, but the Powis family acquired the site in the late thirteenth century and built a double-warded castle in red sandstone, with curtain walls, gatehouses and a round keep in the inner ward. Extended and modernised in the sixteenth century, Powis Castle was garrisoned for the King from 1642 and became an important store for arms, ammunition and valuables. Middleton's 300 Horse and 100 Foot launched a surprise attack at 2 a.m. on 3 October, blowing – and largely destroying – the west gate with a petard and quickly overpowering the dazed garrison. The castle yielded a rich haul of prisoners, military supplies and treasure. Although Powis was not slighted, much of the present building is post-Civil War. The medieval and Tudor work survives but is now incorporated within the extensive late seventeenth–nineteenth-century remodelling and rebuilding. Powis Castle is owned by the National Trust and is open at weekends and on certain weekdays during the summer.

SOUTH GLAMORGAN

The small modern county possessed only one stronghold of any significance in the seventeenth century and thus largely escaped bloodshed during the first Civil War. In 1648, however, the decisive battle of the second Civil War in South Wales and one of the largest and bloodiest engagements of the whole conflict in the Principality was fought outside Cardiff. Cromwell passed through the county in 1648 and 1649 and usually broke his journey in Cardiff.

Cardiff (ST1877) Although town and castle changed hands several times in the course of the war, they were usually under Royalist control from 1642 until September 1645, when a large Parliamentary garrison was installed. Royalists returned once more and besieged the castle in January–February 1646 but on this occasion the Parliamentarians held out and were eventually relieved. Philip Jones was appointed governor of the castle and its garrison after the war.

The present castle, off Castle Street, is an amalgam of many periods. The Normans built a motte and bailey stronghold here in the corner of a Roman fort; the present shell keep on the mound is twelfth-century in origin, though it has been remodelled on many occasions since and owes much to large-scale nineteenth-century restorations. Charles I stayed here in 1645 and Cromwell may have lodged in the castle on 15–16 May 1648, when he stopped in Cardiff *en route* to Pembroke; he was here again in late July 1649. There is, however, an unconfirmed tradition linking Cromwell with the Griffin Inn at Lisvane (ST1983), on the north-east outskirts of Cardiff; the fifteenth-century buildings have recently been modernised and a plaque added recording the Cromwellian connection.

Fonmon Castle (ST047682) Philip Jones acquired Fonmon Castle after the Restoration and set about renovating the dilapidated thirteenth–fourteenth-century fortified house. He greatly extended the castle to the north and converted it into a grand mansion. He lived here until his death in 1674. The buildings survive in good order and remain a private residence.

Penmark (ST059689) Philip Jones was laid to rest in Penmark church in September 1674. From humble beginnings, Jones rose spectacu-larly during the 1640s and acquired not only political dominance in South Wales but also a large fortune. Appointed governor of Swansea and Cardiff, he became a close friend and political ally of Oliver Cromwell and in due course served as a Protectoral Councillor and MP and as Comptroller of Cromwell's Household. He survived the Restoration and several bitter lawsuits with his fortune more or less intact and spent the last years of his life in retirement at Fonmon. He lies buried near an inscribed tablet.

St Fagans (ST1177) One of the largest battles of the Civil War in Wales was fought at St Fagans on 8 May 1648, when Col. Horton's 3–4,000 Parliamentarians routed up to 8,000 Royalist rebels under Col. Laugharne. The two forces clashed in the early morning to the north-west of the village, the action centred on the bridge which carried the St Bride's to Fairwater Road over the Nant Dowlais brook (ST103779). The professional Parliamentarians overwhelmed their opponents, some of whom were experienced soliders but others raw recruits and all poorly disciplined. Many were killed – according to tradition the Ely flowed red – 3,000 were captured and the rest scattered in all directions; Laugharne and a few others struggled back to Pembroke.

St Fagans House or Castle (ST118772) is an Elizabethan manor-house, built on the site of a Norman castle and incorporating parts of its medieval predecessor; it is now the centre of the Welsh Folk Museum though, unlike the surrounding buildings, it remains *in situ*. The area to the north-west, where fighting was fiercest, is now crossed by a minor road, disused railway lines and their embankments and a new bypass, though most of the area remains open farmland.

WEST GLAMORGAN

West Glamorgan largely escaped bloodshed during the Civil War – there was little fighting in the hills and valleys, and of the towns and villages on the coastal plain, only Swansea was of any significance in the seventeenth century. Cromwell broke his journey there when travelling along the coast in 1648 and 1649.

Llangyfelach (SS6499)   Philip Jones, friend and councillor of Oliver Cromwell and the leading Parliamentarian in South Wales, was probably born and brought up at Pen y Waun farm, south-east of the village. The early seventeenth-century building, which stands near Clase House, survives in good order and remains a private residence.

Swansea (SS6593)   Seventeenth-century Swansea was a small and weakly defended town and it played a correspondingly limited role in the Civil War. The town was garrisoned for the King from the outbreak of war until August 1644, when it surrendered under threat of a combined land and sea attack. Thereafter it was held by Parliament without serious challenge. Governor Philip Jones entertained Cromwell in Swansea on 19 May 1648 and 30 July 1649. Jones probably owned and occupied property in the town centre, but almost nothing of seventeenth-century Swansea survives and no building in the modern city centre can be linked to Jones or Cromwell. Swansea Castle, a fourteenth-century fortified manor-house owned by the Bishops of St David's, was probably semi-derelict by the early seventeenth century and was largely demolished in 1647; a section of ruined masonry still stands in Castle Street.

SCOTLAND

BORDERS

Fast Castle (NT862710)   The fragmentary ruins of Fast Castle, the former stronghold of the Logans of Restalrig, stand on a promontory above the sea, protected on the landward side by a wide ditch. The small medieval fortress fell to Parliamentary troops in February 1651 after a brief siege and bombardment.

Hume Castle (NT705413)   Hume Castle, the principal seat of the Hume family, stood on high ground above the village and guarded one of the main inland routes between England and Edinburgh. In late January 1651 the castle and its 300-strong Royalist garrison were attacked by a Parliamentary detachment under Cols Fenwick and Slyer and Governor Cockburn surrendered the badly damaged fortress on 2 or 3 February, following a heavy bombardment. The ruins are incorporated within a private eighteenth-century mansion which now stands on the site.

Mordington House (NT950560)   Lord Mordington's mansion just over the border was Cromwell's usual base while waiting around Berwick for men and supplies. He was here in September 1648 and on 22–24 July 1650, prior to his two Scottish campaigns. The present Mordington House is largely post-seventeenth-century; it is not open to the public.

Neidpath Castle (NT236405)   The Fraser stronghold, begun in the fourteenth century and repeatedly extended and modernised over the following 200 years, stands above the river Tweed to the west of Peebles. It was held for the King by Lord Yester in the mid-seventeenth century and survived several sieges during summer and autumn 1650 before surrendering to Parliamentary forces in February 1651. The castle has recently been restored and is now open to the public during the summer.

Newark Castle (NT421294)   The roofless shell of the stark rectangular tower-house stands on a hill above the main A708. Built in the fifteenth century, the former royal hunting lodge became a slaughterhouse in September 1644 when over 200 Irish soldiers, members of Montrose's army captured at Philiphaugh, were shot in the castle courtyard and their bodies tipped into a mass grave, 'Slain Men's Lee'. Secured for the King at the end of the decade, Newark fell to Cromwell's troops in summer 1651.

Philiphaugh (NT4528)   On 13 September 1645 Montrose's brilliant Royalist campaign came to an end in a field by Ettrick Water, near Philiphaugh. He had marched south towards England during August but desertions reduced his army to less than 1,000 and he faced almost certain defeat at the hands of Leslie's experienced and far larger force which was marching north to intercept him. Montrose turned about and attempted to return to the Highlands, and by 12 September had reached Philiphaugh. The Marquis and his 200 Horse spent the night in Selkirk, his Foot camped in a meadow along the northern bank of Ettrick Water, just below the junction with the Yarrow, south of the village of Philiphaugh. Under cover of the dawn mist, Leslie fell upon the Infantry camp in the early hours of the 13th, surprising the Royalists and overrunning their weak earthwork defences. In the ensuing skirmish – 'battle' is hardly appropriate – some of the Foot were killed outright and many more captured, only to be executed soon after. By the time Montrose and his Cavalry arrived from Selkirk, all was lost and they were repelled and scattered by the victorious Parliamentarians.

The main A708 now skirts the northern edge of the site and industrial works have encroached to the south-east but most of the battlefield is still open, flat meadow. The Ordnance Survey battle symbol is at NT454282.

CENTRAL

Blackness Castle (NT056802)   The fifteenth-century rectangular tower-house dominates the village of Blackness, once a thriving port of the Forth. The royal castle frequently served as a prison and in the mid-seventeenth century was one of the principal gaols for captured Covenanters. Blackness was besieged by Parliamentary troops in late March 1651 as part of a wider operation to clear the south bank of the Forth; the garrison surrendered on 1 April. Maintained

Newark Castle, Borders. The stark tower house above the Yarrow was the scene of a bloody massacre in 1644 after the battle of Philiphaugh. Scores of Montrose's Irish troops, captured in battle – possibly on the offer of quarter – were systematically put to death in the castle courtyard.

long after as a military base and store, the castle is still in a good state of repair. It is open to the public throughout the year.

Callendar House (NS898794) Although Cromwell frequently marched through and quartered in Falkirk in autumn and winter 1650–51, a small and inactive garrison survived at Callendar House, just south-east of the town, until summer 1651. Cromwell summoned the place to surrender on 16 September 1650 but soon moved on and not until mid-July 1651 did he seriously attempt to oust the garrison. Governor Galbraith and most of his men perished when Cromwell bombarded and stormed the house on 15 July. The late medieval tower-house, comprising a square central block with round angle towers and a towered gateway, had been renovated and extended by the Livingstones in the early seventeenth century. It was extensively remodelled again after the Civil War and is now a long, thin, symmetrical range of several dates and incorporates the remains of the medieval castle near the west end. The restored house and surrounding park are open to the public.

Callander (NN6207) On 13 February 1646 Royalist troops surprised and scattered a Covenanter detachment under Campbell just outside Callander; over 500 Covenanters perished.

Castle Campbell (NS962993) The simple four storey tower-house built by the Earl of Argyll in the fifteenth century was repeatedly extended and strengthened over the following two centuries, when a walled enclosure, further ranges and a northern gateway flanked by gunports and gunrooms were added. Castle Campbell was one of the seats and an occasional residence of Archibald, 8th Earl and 1st Marquis of Argyll, and in consequence was repeatedly but unsuccessfully attacked by Montrose in 1644–45. Repaired and regarrisoned in 1648, it fell to Monck's Parliamentarians six years later. The castle and the surrounding glen are open daily throughout the year.

Castlecary (NS787876) Built in part from Roman stones robbed from the nearby fort, the castle was begun by the Livingstone family in the late fifteenth century; their tower-house was extended 200 years later when an east wing and outbuilding were added. The fortress was owned by the Baillie family in the mid-seventeenth century and was one of the residences of General William Baillie, a senior officer in the Scottish army who fought for Parliament at Marston Moor, was defeated by Montrose at Alford and

Kilsyth and took part in the Scottish Royalist invasion of 1648. The castle has been restored and is still a private residence.

Doune Castle (NN7301) Doune Castle was probably founded in the late fourteenth century by Robert Stewart, Duke of Albany, Regent of Scotland, but was never completed. The great tower in the north-east corner of the walled enclosure served as both gatehouse and principal residence and contained a hall, living quarters and a chapel. Although there were other buildings within the courtyard – a second hall to the south and a kitchen block nearby – the ranges planned to stand against the curtain walls were never, in fact, built. Restored in the sixteenth century, the incomplete castle was occupied by Montrose in 1645 and held for the King as one of the bases guarding communications to and from the Highlands. Restored again in the nineteenth century, Doune is one of the best-preserved late medieval castles in Scotland. It is open daily during the summer.

Larbert Bridge (NS859819) On 2 July 1651 Cromwell and the English army marched to Falkirk and faced the Scottish forces across the river Carron by Larbert Bridge. There was minor skirmishing and exchange of cannon- and musket-fire throughout the day, but the Scots refused to be drawn into a general engagement and Cromwell withdrew on the 3rd. The Parliamentary army approached the area again on 14 July, causing Scottish scouts to hurry north across the bridge, but once more Leslie refused to give battle. The present eighteenth-century bridge spans the Carron a little east of the demolished medieval crossing.

Loch Dochart Castle (NN406256) The ruins of the late sixteenth-century Campbell stronghold stand on a small island in Loch Dochart. The island fortress covered the main road west and in December 1644 heavy artillery fire from the castle temporarily halted the Royalist advance into Strathclyde and the Highlands. Montrose eventually overcame the obstacle by deceit: a party of Royalists approached the island by boat claiming to be carrying letters from Argyll himself and were admitted into the castle, whereupon they overpowered the small and gullible garrison. The castle was slighted and Montrose resumed his march west.

St Ninians (NS796918) On 17 September 1650 Cromwell and the English army approached the Scottish base at Stirling and established a temporary HQ at St Ninians. The troops quar-

Right: Doune Castle, Central. The Stewarts' fourteenth-century castle survived the Civil War intact but fell derelict during the nineteenth century. Carefully restored by the Earl of Moray in 1883–6, Doune is now one of the best preserved late medieval castles in the country.

Below: Stirling Castle, Central. The mighty fortress, which served as the Royalists' base from September 1650, was too strong for direct attack and Cromwell never seriously attempted to take it. Stirling was eventually starved into surrender by George Monck.

tered for the night in the village church and on the following day Cromwell viewed the Scottish defences from the church tower before abandoning the operation and marching back to Edinburgh. The old church was largely destroyed in 1746 when Jacobite powder stored there exploded; the early eighteenth-century tower survived intact but the rest of the building was wrecked. The ruined chancel and nave remained in use for some time for burials and still stand 50 yards west of the new church.

Stirling (NS7993) Following their defeat at Dunbar and evacuation of Edinburgh in September 1650, Leslie and the Scottish army established their base in the mighty royal castle and palace of Stirling. Cromwell approached the town on several occasions – he was in St Ninians in September 1650 and on 20 July 1651 pursued Leslie as far as Bannockburn – but was never

strong enough to attempt a direct assault and lacked the artillery and supplies necessary to maintain a prolonged siege. Town and castle eventually fell in the latter half of 1651, long after the main Scottish and Parliamentary armies had departed. Monck besieged the place with 5,000 troops and finally starved the small garrison into submission. The spectacular fortress, begun in the thirteenth century but dating mainly from the sixteenth and early seventeenth century, survives in good order and is open all year.

Torwood Castle (NS835843) Cromwell and his troops quartered in and around Torwood Castle on 17 July 1651 before pursuing Leslie's army back towards Stirling. The roofless shell of the sixteenth-century tower-house survives in fairly good condition but little remains of the quadrangular domestic ranges added in the seventeenth century.

FIFE

Burntisland (NT2385) On 29 July 1651 Cromwell crossed to Burntisland and rejoined his army, which had been ferried across the Forth during the previous week. A brief bombardment persuaded the small Scottish garrison in Rossend Castle to surrender and Cromwell spent the night within the fortress; the early seventeenth-century fortified house, overlooking the shipyards, has recently been restored.

Fordell Castle (NT146854) According to some accounts, Cromwell and Lambert spent the night of 30–31 July 1651 at Fordell Castle *en route* from Burntisland to Perth.

Inverkeithing (NT1383)   On 17 July 1651

Overton and Lambert were sent across the Firth of Forth at the head of 4,500 troops to cut Leslie's supply lines to Fife and the north-east and so lure him out of Stirling. Alive to the threat, the Scottish commander despatched 4,000 men under Browne and Holbourne to dislodge the Parliamentarians. The Scottish force approached Inverkeithing on 20 July but Browne attempted to fall back and await reinforcements before attacking the larger than expected English force. Okey, however, fell upon the retreating Scottish rear and compelled Browne to give battle. Lambert attacked and routed the Royalist army in a fierce and bloody battle just outside the town, killing 2,000, including Browne, and capturing 1,500.

GRAMPIAN

Aberdeen (NJ9406) Montrose and his growing Royalist army made for Aberdeen in September 1644, pursued by Argyll. The Royalists appeared before the town on 13 September and summoned the Covenanter garrison to surrender; in response, the Covenanters shot and killed Montrose's drummer and then marched out,

confident of defeating the outnumbered and inexperienced Royalists. The 3,000 Covenanters deployed just outside the town along the crest of a slight hill north of How Burn and straddling the road which ran away south. Montrose advanced towards the Covenanter line and drew up just north of the Burn. The Covenanter Cavalry charged the Royalist flanks but was repulsed by heavy fire. Montrose then charged up the slope, hitting his opponents' line at speed and quickly breaking the Covenanters, who fell back in disorder into the town. Aberdeen was secured without further opposition and there followed three days of plunder and mayhem before Montrose marched on. Argyll and his forces entered the shattered town unopposed two days later. Over 1,000 Covenanters had died in the battle and at least 100 more perished during the ensuing violence.

The area of the battle has been completely built over and lies under the urban sprawl, a little south-west of the town centre. Modern Hardgate and Holburn Street cross the Civil War battlefield.

Alford (NJ5717) On 2 July 1645 Montrose's Royalists engaged and routed a Covenanter army under Baillie on open ground one mile west of Alford. Montrose drew up in an east–west line along or just below the brow of a slight hill overlooking the Don valley to the north; the left wing lay in front of Gallows Hill, a little east of Leochel Burn. Baillie advanced from the north, crossing the river Don and the low, marshy ground beside it and then deployed along the rising ground a little north of the Royalist line. Both armies numbered around 2,500. Tactics and strategy played little part in the ensuing clash. Montrose threw his main line down the hill into the Covenanter army, which resisted fiercely but was forced to give ground, at first in a slow and orderly fashion. The retreat turned to rout, however, when the Royalist second line, kept in reserve behind the brow of the hill and thus concealed from Baillie, advanced and charged. Baillie's men fled back across the Don and away north as best they could, but over 1,500 fell in the battle and the retreat; the few Royalist casualties included Montrose's close friend and adviser Lord George Gordon.

Most of the battlefield is still open farmland and common outside Alford. The lane along which Baillie advanced is now a made up road, crossing the Don by a modern bridge, around which a small village, Bridge of Alford, has grown up. The Ordnance Survey battle symbol is at NJ562164.

Balvenie Castle (NJ326408) In the thirteenth century the Comyn family built a quadrangular stone fortress beside the Fiddich, just north of Dufftown. It was extended and modernised in the late fifteenth and sixteenth century and a three storey fortified block, the Atholl building,

was added. Balvenie was occupied by Montrose's Royalists at the beginning of November 1644, following the operation around Fyvie, but was later evacuated without a fight. The roofless remains are open daily.

Dunnottar Castle (NO882839) The ruins of Donnottar Castle stand in splendid isolation on a clifftop 160 feet above the North Sea. Although the great rectangular tower was built in 1392, most of the present fortress, including the massive gatehouse and four domestic ranges enclosing a courtyard, date from the fifteenth and sixteenth century. Montrose approached Dunnottar in March 1645, but the Earl Marischal refused to join his former ally and his garrison successfully resisted a brief Royalist siege and bombardment. Five years later the Earl changed allegiance once more and declared for the new king; the Scottish regalia were temporarily lodged here. Overton besieged the place from September 1651 and Sir George Ogilvy and his garrison were eventually starved into surrender on 24 May 1652. The castle was slighted in 1718 after the Jacobite rebellion. The ruins are open daily.

Fyvie Castle (NJ763393) Fyvie Castle was begun around 1400 by Sir Henry Preston and was repeatedly extended over the following 150 years. The river Ythan and adjoining water-meadow protected the fortress to the north and west; the southern and eastern approaches were defended by a high curtain wall with flanking towers and a huge central gatehouse. Montrose occupied Fyvie Castle unopposed on 27 October 1644 but on the following day Argyll and the Covenanter army approached the fortress – it is not clear whether Montrose was taken by surprise or whether he had deliberately lured Argyll into battle. For two days the rival armies skirmished inconclusively around Fyvie, with a series of attacks and counter-attacks on the hillside below the castle where the Royalists had dug several lines of defensive banks and trenches. After two days of futile manoeuvres, Argyll withdrew and Montrose resumed his march towards Huntly. Fyvie Castle has recently been opened to the public.

Huntly Castle (NJ532407) A succession of medieval castles stood on the site above the river Deveron, each grander and stronger than the last. Around 1600 the 1st Marquis of Huntly built the present 'castle', really a grand renaissance palace with round corner towers, elaborate doorways and windows, ornate chimneys and various heraldic embellishments. Montrose occupied Huntly several times in 1644–45, usually meeting little or no resistance. The Royalist garrison he left here was starved into submission by Covenanter forces towards the end of 1645. The roofless but otherwise well preserved shell of the palace is open to the public daily.

Kildrummy Castle (NJ455164) The thirteenth–sixteenth-century castle which replaced an earlier motte and bailey timber stronghold stands on a ridge covering the main road north from the Grampian mountains. It was occupied by Montrose in September 1644 and became his temporary HQ while he gathered reinforcements in the area; he left a small garrison here when he and his men marched on into the Highlands. Kildrummy was captured and slighted by Parliamentary troops in 1654. It was subsequently repaired, served as a Jacobite stronghold in 1715 and was slighted once more. The extensive ruins comprise a medieval curtain wall with mural towers and a double-towered gatehouse defending a bailey in which stand several domestic ranges. The remains are open daily.

Kincardine Castle (NO671751) William the Lion's twelfth-century fortress was garrisoned for the King by Napier in 1645–46. It was besieged by Middleton on 2 March 1646 and fell fifteen days later after the external water supply had been cut. The Royalist officers were promptly executed and the castle slighted. No trace of the medieval fortress remains and the small village which grew up in its shadow has also largely disappeared – the disused graveyard of the demolished Chapel of St Catherine is almost the only part of the former settlement to survive.

Rattray Head (NK1057) Little trace remains of the once flourishing medieval port and royal borough of Rattray; in the eighteenth century a storm sealed Loch Strathbeg from the sea and the land-locked town went into rapid decline. Montrose's spectacular campaign of 1644–46 formally ended here in August 1646 when he paraded and disbanded his few remaining troops outside the town before surrendering to General Middleton.

HIGHLAND

Ardvreck Castle (NC240236) Montrose sought refuge in this MacLeod stronghold in spring 1650 after the Battle of Carbisdale. The details of what followed are unclear and hotly disputed – did MacLeod simply arrest the Royalist leader or did he first welcome him as an honoured guest and then betray him for reward? Certainly, Montrose was handed over to a Covenanter patrol at Ardvreck on 4 May and taken to Edinburgh for execution. The ruins of the late sixteenth-century three storey towerhouse overlooking Loch Assynt are freely accessible to the public.

Auldearn (NH9155) On 9 May 1645 Montrose's Royalists engaged and routed Sir John Hurry's Covenanter army outside the village of Auldearn. Baillie had sent Hurry and 4,600 men to cover Montrose's movements around the south bank of the Moray Firth. After several days of minor skirmishing, they came upon Montrose's 2,700-strong army quartered at Auldearn. The village stands on a ridge running south from St John's Church, with a distinct hollow to the south and the motte of the long-demolished Norman castle to the north. Warned of the Covenanters' approach – Hurry had carelessly let his men fire off their muskets to clear them for battle – Montrose placed part of his army to the west of the village to attract the enemy, but kept large detachments in reserve, hidden from Hurry in the hollow to the south and in enclosures to the north. Advancing from the west along the south bank of a small burn and surrounding marsh, Hurry fell upon the small Royalist force stationed before the village. Montrose's plan seems to have been to let the Covenanters through the visible but small centre and then attack them on both flanks with the concealed units held in reserve. The plan went astray, however, for the northern Royalist unit of the Macdonalds moved too soon and Hurry was able to swing left and engage them head on. A fierce fight developed in which the Covenanters began to break up the outnumbered Royalist force. The appearance of the second Royalist force, previously concealed in the southern hollow, and the unexpected attack on the right flank and rear of Hurry's army saved the day and the Covenanter assault collapsed. Hurry

Dunnottar Castle, Grampian. The clifftop castle above the North Sea was one of the few major strongholds left in Royalist hands by summer 1651 and various items, including precious documents, money and the Scottish crown and sceptre, were moved here for safekeeping. By the autumn Dunnottar too was under threat, and it eventually fell after a nine month siege; the regalia, however, were smuggled out and eluded the Parliamentarians.

and most of his Horse got away but up to 3,000 Foot perished.

The village has grown considerably since the 1640s but the lie of the land is still clear. The old castle motte survives and is now topped by Boath Doocot, a late seventeenth-century circular dovecot (NH917556); motte and dovecot are owned by the National Trust. A plan and description of the battle are on display nearby. The Ordnance Survey battle symbol at NH916550 is, perhaps, a little south of the site of the main fighting.

Carbisdale (NH5795)

Montrose's brief second campaign ended on 27 April 1650 on the lower slopes of Carbisdale. He had halted in the valley to await reinforcements supposedly gathering in the surrounding area. A Covenanter army approached from the south, a small troop of Horse leading the way in the hope of luring Montrose from his camp, which had been protected with earthworks. The ploy worked and the main Covenanter army then fell upon the Royalists on the slopes around Culrain. Strachan's army heavily outnumbered the 1,200 Royalists and the battle was brief and one-sided. Montrose and his small Cavalry unit escaped but the Royalist Foot were routed and destroyed.

Dunbeath Castle (ND158283)

The clifftop castle, one mile south of the village, was attacked and captured by Montrose in 1650, the only significant success of his second campaign. The fortress was besieged on 17 April and surrendered four days later; a small garrison was installed but dispersed without further fighting after Carbisdale. The early seventeenth-century tower-house, which replaced a late medieval keep, was restored and extended in the nineteenth century and is still a private residence.

Inverlochy (NN1275)

In January 1645 Argyll and the Covenanter army gathered around Inverlochy in an attempt to block Montrose's expected line of advance north from Inverary. Montrose, however, turned into the Highlands and gathered reinforcements before doubling back unexpectedly. In deteriorating weather he surprised and fell upon Argyll's 3,500 men in Inverlochy before they could reunite with Baillie's forces, then stationed around Inverness. Montrose approached on the night of 1–2 February, driving in Covenanter outposts from the hills above the town. Argyll took to his galley in the loch, leaving Duncan Campbell to command the army. He deployed his troops along the slight ridge running north–south above the estuary flats; his left wing rested on Inverlochy Castle. The Royalists charged down from the foothills at dawn on the 2nd and threw themselves on to the Covenanters. Campbell's centre moved forward to meet the attack and initially held its own but the left and right wings were broken by the Royalist charge. Outflanked, surrounded and with their line of retreat into the castle broken, the Covenanter centre began to give ground and the rout was soon complete. Duncan Campbell and 1,500 of his clansmen perished; Montrose, in contrast, claimed to have lost less than 20 men. Argyll, watching the disaster on board ship, hurriedly set sail as the small garrison in Inverlochy Castle surrendered without further resistance.

The extensive remains of the thirteenth-century quadrangular castle have recently been restored and incorporated within a modern building, now a hotel (NN122755).

Inverness (NH6645)

In 1652 the Parliamentary forces in Scotland built a new stronghold at Inverness, a five sided star-shaped fort above the Ness. It was largely demolished after the Restoration but a single isolated tower, 'Cromwell's Clock Tower', survives off Shore Street. Stone from the demolished Interregnum fort was used to build Dunbar's Hospital, the late Stuart almshouse in Church Street.

Kinlochaline Castle (NM693477)

The fifteenth–sixteenth-century fortress at Kinlochaline was occupied in July 1644 by a force of Irish Royalists who had recently landed in Scotland; they soon marched on to join Montrose, firing the castle as they left. Partially restored in the nineteenth century, the extensive remains of the rectangular four storey block stand on a rocky crag overlooking the head of Loch Aline.

Mingary Castle (NM502632)

This small thirteenth-century castle on the Ardnamurchan peninsula was the scene of the first serious fighting of what became Montrose's first Scottish campaign. In July 1644 the newly arrived Irish army besieged the castle and starved the Covenanter garrison into submission. The small Irish Royalist force left to hold Mingary was itself besieged during the winter of 1644–45 but held out and eventually evacuated the place without further fighting in the latter half of 1645. The ruined castle is open all year.

Rhu of Ardnamurchan (NM4267)

The Rhu is the most westerly point of the Scottish mainland and affords fine views over the Western

Isles and the Atlantic. Alastair and his 1,100 Irish Royalist troops landed here on 5 July 1644 with their wives, children and cattle.

LOTHIAN

Bass Rock (NT6087)   The volcanic island rising dramatically from the North Sea served for many centuries as both religious centre and military base. The island and its castle were secured by the Royalists in 1650 as a naval base for operations in the Firth of Forth. They were taken by Monck in April 1652 following a long blockade. The ruins of the sixteenth-century fort stand above the sea on the gentle southern slope of the island and are visible from the mainland; partly restored in 1902, they are now dominated by a modern lighthouse.

Borthwick Castle (NT370597)   The fifteenth-century stronghold, comprising a massive five storey tower-house, a curtain wall and southern gatehouse, was held by Lord Borthwick's Royalists in 1650. It was besieged by Parliamentary troops in the autumn; Cromwell wrote to Lord Borthwick from Edinburgh on 18 November, demanding the prompt surrender of the fortress and warning that 'if you necessitate me to bend my cannon against you, you may expect what I doubt you will not be pleased with'. The cannon, indeed, opened fire – the large scar on the east wall is often attributed to Parliamentary artillery – but the garrison was short of supplies and, with little hope of relief, soon acceded to Cromwell's demand. Borthwick Castle survives in good order as a private residence.

Dalhousie Castle (NT3263)   Cromwell stayed at Dalhousie Castle on 8–9 October 1648 *en route* from Edinburgh back to England. The fortress was begun by the Ramsays in the fifteenth century as a simple 'L'-shaped tower-house with an adjoining enclosure defended by a curtain wall and mural towers. Several ranges were added within the bailey during the sixteenth and early seventeenth century and the fortress was remodelled and extended again in the following two centuries. Dalhousie was recently redesigned as a hotel, but much of the early modern work and the lower levels of the fifteenth-century tower-house were retained.

Dirleton Castle (NT517840)   The medieval castle, begun by John de Vaux around 1225, was held by Royalist forces in 1650. Besieged by Parliamentary troops in the autumn, the garrison was starved into submission on 8 November, whereupon several officers were executed and the castle slighted. The impressive ruins, including part of three drum towers, the shell of the sixteenth-century hall block, a dovecot and sections of curtain wall, are open daily.

Dunbar (NT6878)   Dunbar was one of Cromwell's bases during the early stages of his Scottish campaign and the site of the only major battle which he fought north of the border.

Cromwell and his troops were frequently stationed here during late July and August 1650 for Dunbar formed a convenient base on the main road to Edinburgh, well east of the Royalist positions; it also possessed a sheltered harbour where the Parliamentary fleet could safely land supplies. Cromwell garrisoned and usually lodged at Broxmouth House, the Earl of Roxburgh's mansion, which stood to the south of the town (NT697776); nothing remains of the old house and the present Broxmouth dates from the eighteenth and nineteenth century.

On 1 September Cromwell fell back on Dunbar, pursued by Leslie, whose troops occupied Cockburnspath and thus blocked the English line of retreat. Trapped in Dunbar, the 11,000 Parliamentarians had little choice but to stand and fight the 22,000 Royalists drawn up on Doon Hill. On the night of 2–3 September Cromwell deployed his army on flat ground around the Cockburnspath road, south-east of Dunbar and north of Broxburn. Soon after 4 a.m. the English attacked Leslie's right, which had drawn up on the narrow coastal strip. Leslie's Horse stood their ground and only when Cromwell himself led a third English charge did they collapse and scatter. The Parliamentary army then swung right or south-west and tore into the flank of the now undefended Scottish Infantry crowded onto the lower slopes of Doon Hill; surprised and demoralised, they surrendered *en masse*. Within three hours Leslie's army had effectively ceased to exist: 3,000 Scots were dead and up to 10,000 captured and Leslie struggled back to Edinburgh with less than

5,000 men. Dunbar was a stunning victory – not surprisingly Cromwell saw it as a miracle and described it as 'one of the most signal mercies God hath done for England and His people'. The Parliamentarians had not only destroyed a far larger army but also opened Edinburgh and most of the Lowlands to the English.

The battleground has changed little since 1650 and is still open ground outside Dunbar. The Ordnance Survey battle symbol is at NT696766. By the old A1 road nearby (NT705768) stands a Cromwell Association monument to the battle, bearing a quotation by Thomas Carlyle.

Dundas Castle (NT118767)

Cromwell visited the castle on two occasions during his Scottish campaign, on 20 September 1650 to confer with Deane, and on 24 July 1651, when he lodged here for one or two nights before returning to Leith. The fifteenth–sixteenth-century 'L'-shaped tower-house survives in good condition and now adjoins a massive nineteenth-century mansion. Both castle and mansion are private.

Dunglass (NT766718)

The Parliamentary army quartered at Dunglass on 25 July 1650 and Cromwell spent the night in Dunglass House. The seventeenth-century building has long gone and the present Dunglass House, the latest in a succession of great houses on the site, is largely nineteenth-century.

Edinburgh (NT2573)

Cromwell visited the Scottish capital on several occasions. He entered the city unopposed in autumn 1648 as the honoured guest of Argyll and the Covenanters and stayed here on 4–7 October, lodging in Moray House, Canongate, and attending a banquet in the castle.

His next visit was not so peaceful, for in summer 1650 he led a Parliamentary army north against Leslie's Royalist force based in Edinburgh. From late July to late August Cromwell marched backwards and forwards around the city, too weak to launch a direct attack and unable to lure the Scots out to give battle. On 29 July Cromwell advanced to Restalrig and skirmished with the Scottish garrison on St Leonard's Hill before falling back. He returned in August and established his HQ and camps on Braid and Blackford Hill, south of the city; on the 18th he took Colinton Castle and a week later he besieged, bombarded and then stormed Redhall Castle. Still Leslie refused to give battle and at the end of the month the Parliamentarians evacuated the newly won bases and returned to Dunbar. Lambert secured the city without serious resistance after the Battle of

Dunbar and Cromwell entered Edinburgh on 7 September; it became his base for the remainder of the Scottish campaign. A Royalist garrison in the castle held out for a further 2½ months, resisting a siege and bombardment, but on 24 December Cromwell's numerous letters to Governor Dundas, combining dire threats with generous offers and political propaganda, bore fruit and the well-supplied fortress was surrendered to the English.

Throughout his frequent and lengthy visits to the city Cromwell lodged at 174 Canongate, the Edinburgh residence of the Earls of Moray, often known as 'Moray House'. Cromwell spent much of winter 1650–51 here and lay seriously ill in Moray House in February–April and May–June 1651. The rather severe, two-storey rubble and ashlar house, built by Mary, Dowager Countess of Home in 1625, was originally quadrangular, but two of the seventeenth-century wings have been demolished. Of the house known to Cromwell only the north block, facing the road, and part of the west range survive; the southern sections of the present building are eighteenth-century and later. The once extensive gardens at the rear have also largely disappeared.

The present castle is a much larger and more imposing building than its seventeenth-century predecessor and owes much to extensions and rebuildings of the eighteenth and nineteenth century. Of the fortress which saw action in the Civil War, there survive the Great Hall, Royal Palace, and the Half Moon and Farewell Batteries. In November 1650 Cromwell tried to bring down the defences by driving tunnels into the crag below the southern walls, but the rock proved too hard and the operation was soon abandoned; several scars and indentations on the south side of the crag, visible from Johnston Terrace, were supposedly made during these tunnelling operations. The Half Moon and adjoining sections of the castle were damaged by fire from the battery which Cromwell established in Ramsay Gardens. Edinburgh Castle is open daily.

In mid-November 1650 fire badly damaged parts of the sixteenth- and seventeenth-century royal palace of Holyrood, one of the many buildings in Edinburgh used as winter quarters for the Parliamentary army. Repaired after the Restoration, Holyrood is open to the public daily unless the royal family or the Lord High Commissioner are in residence.

Restalrig (NT2874) has been built over and absorbed into Edinburgh. Blackford and Braid Hill (NT2570 and NT2569 respectively) remain open ground, though both are now surrounded

Below: Dunbar, Lothian. Carlyle's lyrical phrase adorns a Cromwell Association memorial to one of the most remarkable battles of the entire Civil War. *Right:* Tantallon Castle, Lothian. The spectacular castle above the Firth of Forth, defended by sheer cliffs and a huge landward wall, resisted repeated sieges in the fifteenth and sixteenth centuries but proved more vulnerable to Monck's heavy artillery in February 1651. *Bottom:* Edinburgh, Lothian. Skyline and city are dominated by the castle, a complex of medieval, early modern and modern buildings crowded onto the basalt outcrop. Cromwell was an honoured guest in 1648; two years later he returned and took the castle by force.

by the southern suburbs of the city. Colinton Castle (NT2169), a three storey 'L'-shaped fortified hall dating from the sixteenth and early seventeenth century, has been largely destroyed and is now but a fragmentary ruin above the Leith. Redhall Castle (NT2170), once the baronial stronghold of the Otterburn family, has fared no better; the remains of a single angle turret and of the adjoining walls survive northwest of the present, much later Redhall House.

Hailes Castle (NT576758)

Begun by the Earl of Dunbar and March in the thirteenth century, the fortified manor-house was strengthened 100 years later when high curtain walls and a square tower were added. The castle was captured by Parliamentary forces in 1650 and subsequently slighted. The extensive ruins on the south bank of the Tyne are open daily.

Leith (NT2776)

In summer 1650 Leslie prepared to face Cromwell behind a line of defensive earthworks running from Edinburgh to the then separate port of Leith. From September the town became one of Cromwell's bases and he was frequently in Leith, consulting with his naval commanders and overseeing the landing of supplies. In 1651–52 Monck erected a new fort here, a £10,000 pentagonal stronghold with angle bastions; it has long since disappeared under the docks and dockland redevelopments. The Royalist earthworks have similarly vanished, obliterated by the eastward and northward expansion of Edinburgh.

Linlithgow (NT0077)

Linlithgow served as a convenient base between Edinburgh and Glasgow to the west and Falkirk and Stirling to the north-west, and Cromwell and his troops frequently quartered here during 1650–51. The soldiers usually camped in the grounds of Linlithgow Palace, while Cromwell lodged in the royal palace itself. The fifteenth–sixteenth-century building, with its great rectangular central block and adjoining ancillary ranges, fell derelict in the eighteenth century and was gutted by fire. The roofless and ruined shell stands on a knoll overlooking the loch (NT002774) and is open daily.

Livingstone or Livingston Village (NT0366)

The old village, west of the large new town, was a favourite stopping place for Cromwell and the army on their journeys to and from Edinburgh. Cromwell was here on 15 October and 27 November 1650 and on 17 April 1651. The Lord General lodged in 'Livingston House', presumably the old hall which in the seventeenth century stood amid extensive gardens to the north of the village. It was demolished in the early nineteenth century and no trace of it now remains.

Musselburgh (NT3472)

Cromwell and the Parliamentary army were frequently based here in July and August 1650 during the operations around Edinburgh. Cromwell repaired the sixteenth-century defensive earthworks around the town and strengthened the rampart and battery at the west end of Musselburgh, around St Michael's churchyard, to protect his quarters against possible attack from Edinburgh. Detachments from Leslie's army did, indeed, attack the English camp on several occasions, but they were repulsed without serious incident. No trace of the sixteenth–seventeenth-century earthworks survives.

Niddry Castle (NT096744)

The Parliamentary army quartered in and around the castle on 14 September 1650 *en route* to face Leslie at Stirling. The officers probably lodged in the castle itself but Cromwell was not amongst them – he had returned to Leith to confer with Deane and rejoined his troops on the march on the 15th. The ruined shell of the four storey tower-house, built by the 4th Lord Seton around 1500, stands south-east of Winchburgh.

Tantallon Castle (NT596851)

The spectacular and extensive ruins of the fourteenth-century Douglas stronghold stand on the clifftop above the Firth of Forth. Garrisoned by Royalists in 1650, the castle was viewed by Monck and Lambert in the autumn but not until February 1651, when heavy cannon became available, was a serious attack launched. Tantallon was besieged and bombarded by Monck for twelve days until the Royalists surrendered the badly damaged fortress on 23 February. The castle was left derelict and fell into further decay in the eighteenth century. The ruins, which are open daily, include substantial remains of the massive curtain wall, with flanking towers and a central gatehouse, which defended the southern, landward approaches; little survives of the domestic buildings which stood within the clifftop enclosure.

ORKNEY

Noltland Castle (HY429487) In summer 1650 the remnant of Montrose's defeated army, including many senior officers, sought refuge in this fifteenth–sixteenth-century fortress in the north-west Orkneys. Although the massive outer walls and south-western tower offered considerable protection, the castle and its demoralized and outnumbered garrison were quickly captured by local Covenanters. The castle, parts of which are still in good order, is open at all reasonable times on application to the custodian.

STRATHCLYDE

Ayr (NS3321) In the early 1650s the Parliamentary army in Scotland built a new fort or citadel in Ayr; it stood on the site of the twelfth-century Church of St John the Baptist and incorporated parts of the medieval building. The tower of St John's still stands off Eglington Terrace but the Interregnum fort was demolished after the Restoration and today nothing more than odd fragments of masonry remain in parkland around the church tower.

Brodick Castle (NS015379) The principal stronghold on the Isle of Arran, Brodick Castle was built by the Hamiltons in the fourteenth century to command Brodick Bay and the sea route from the mainland. It was held by Royalist forces from 1650 until 6 April 1652, when it surrendered to besieging Parliamentary troops who had been shipped across from Ayr. Much of the present building is Victorian but the original north wing and tower survive in good order. Brodick Castle is now owned by the National Trust and is open during the summer.

Castle Sween (NR713788) Castle Sween was built in the mid-twelfth century and was thus one of the earliest stone castles in Scotland. Raided by Sir Alexander Macdonald's Royalists in 1647, it was plundered, burnt and left in ruins. The extensive remains of the great rectangular tower-house and adjoining keep are open daily.

Dumbarton (NS400744) A succession of strongholds, Roman, Celtic and medieval, have stood on the high volcanic plug above Dumbarton. The medieval royal castle, repaired and extended in the early seventeenth century, was garrisoned by Royalist troops in 1650 and fell to Monck on 29 December 1651 after a long siege. By the end of the century the building was in ruins and although fragments of the medieval Wallace Tower survive, most of the present castle is post-Civil War rebuilding. Dumbarton Castle is open all year.

Dunaverty Castle (NR6908) Dunaverty Castle was an early medieval stronghold of the Lord of the Isles and stood at the southern end of Kintyre on a rocky outcrop above the sea Secured for the King in 1645, it was captured by Leslie two years later and its garrison put to the sword. The castle is now very ruinous and only two small sections of the tower-house survive above ground. The remains stand on land freely accessible to the public.

Glasgow (NS5965) Cromwell visited Glasgow on three occasions during his Scottish campaign, on 11–14 October 1650 and 20–30 April and 6–12 July 1651. There is no contemporary evidence to indicate where he lodged, though several later traditions have sprung up, including one that he stayed at the former Silver Craigs House on the east side of the Salt Market. More reliably, Cromwell's letters show that he attended several services in the High Kirk.

Inverary (NN095092) In the seventeenth century the small fishing village was dominated by the whitewashed castle, the principal seat of the Campbells. In winter 1644–45 Montrose's Campbell-hating Scottish-Irish soldiers persuaded him to launch a daring raid on their enemy's base. Taking advantage of unseasonably mild weather, Montrose swooped on Inverary in December 1644, surprising Argyll and his colleagues who hastily withdrew into the castle. Without artillery, Montrose could do little to threaten the mighty fortress, but for over two weeks he and his men plundered the village and surrounding land while Argyll watched helplessly from the castle. The sixteenth-century fortified mansion was demolished in the 1770s when the present grand house, also known as the 'castle' was built on the site.

Kilsyth (NS7278)   On 15 August 1645 Montrose's Royalists routed a Covenanter army on open ground to the north-east of Kilsyth. Montrose had been marching south for several days, closely followed by Baillie's men. On 14 August the Royalists halted around Kilsyth and prepared to engage their pursuers before they had a chance to unite with a second Covenanter force to the south. On the following day Baillie approached the town from the east to find the Royalists deployed in a natural amphitheatre outside Kilsyth with hills rising to the north and east of their position. Baillie halted his advance and began flanking round to the right along the high ground in an effort to secure the northern ridge, but the manoeuvre was complex and poorly executed. Montrose sent a detachment up Banton Burn valley, effectively cutting Baillie's army in two, isolating the van, who had already crossed the burn and were on the northern ridge, from the main Covenanter force still lining the eastern hill. The northern Covenanters

were attacked and, despite fierce resistance, were eventually routed. Montrose then threw his main force against Baillie's position on the eastern ridge. The tired and indisciplined Horse quickly turned and fled leaving Baillie's Foot to their fate – up to 6,000 perished.

Most of the battlefield, including the low ground in which Montrose initially deployed and the hillsides on which much of the fighting took place, is now underwater, covered by a modern reservoir. The Ordnance Survey battle symbol at NS742787 lies amid the water. Many relics from the battle are on display at Colzium House nearby, open to the public on Sundays and certain weekdays throughout the year.

Five years later Kilsyth saw further fighting, for Cromwell's troops besieged and captured Kilsyth Castle, the sixteenth-century fortified hall of the Livingstone family. Cromwell and his troops quartered in and around the fortress on 10 October 1650 and again on 6 February 1651. Nothing now survives except odd fragments of wall standing in open ground on the outskirts of the town (NS717786).

TAYSIDE

Blair Atholl Castle (NN865662)   The present Blair Castle is a Georgian mansion, 'fortified' and given a medieval appearance in the nineteenth century; open during the summer, items on display include arms, armour and documents of the Covenanter period. The original thirteenth-century Atholl stronghold on the site was occupied by Montrose in summer 1644; on 30 August he unfurled the royal banner ½ mile away in a field near Tilt. Eight years later it was bombarded and captured by Parliamentary forces. The foundations and lower levels of Comyn's Tower survive but the rest of the medieval fortress was destroyed after the 1745 rebellion.

Dundee (NO4030)   On 4 April 1645 Montrose and his 750-strong Royalist force attacked Dundee, gained an entry through a breach in the sixteenth-century town walls near the north-west angle, swept aside the feeble resistance of the town militia under gouty Lt. Cockburn and proceeded to sack the town. They made a hasty exit that afternoon, leaving via the east gate as Baillie and his Covenanter army entered from the west. Baillie pursued the Royalists beyond

the town, but Montrose doubled back unexpectedly and escaped into the hills west of Dundee.

In 1651 Monck led 4,000 Parliamentarians to Dundee to crush Royalist unrest. The town was once more sacked and burnt – books and documents from the church library were used to smoke out a group of soldiers and civilians who had taken refuge in the tower of St Mary's.

Little remains of seventeenth-century Dundee. The town walls have been demolished, though one gateway, the Cowgate or East Port, survives in Cowgate Street. The fifteenth-century tower and steeple of St Mary's still stands in Overgate – it is now a local museum – but the rest of the church has completely disappeared.

Perth (NO1123)   Perth was taken without opposition by Montrose on 1 September 1644 after the Battle of Tibbermore. The Royalists remained here for four days, lodging their Covenanter prisoners in St John's Kirk.

The walled town was held by Royalists in 1650–51 and was the scene of Cromwell's last military operation in Scotland before heading south. On 1 August 1651 the Lord General

Castle Sween, Strathclyde. The ruined fortress on a rocky promontory above the waters of Loch Sween is probably the oldest medieval stone castle in Scotland of which substantial parts remain. Sween was sacked by Macdonald's Royalists in 1647 and they rendered the place indefensible before moving on.

arrived before Perth and summoned the garrison to surrender. The Royalists submitted on terms on the following day, and Cromwell and most of his army quickly marched off in pursuit of Prince Charles and the Scottish invasion force. Monck remained in Perth and supervised the erection of a new fort or citadel here, a quadrangular stronghold with corner bastions surrounded by a moat, which stood at South Inch on the site of the Grey Friars' medieval convent. Although fragments of the old town wall remain, the Parliamentary fort was demolished after the Restoration and has completely disappeared.

Tibbermore (NO0523)   On 1 September 1644 Montrose and his 2–3,000 Royalists engaged and routed Lord David Elcho's 7,000 Covenanters near Tibbermore (or Tippermuir). Marching east along the Strathearn valley and then swinging north towards Perth, Montrose found Elcho's army blocking his way, deployed in open, flat ground below Methven Hill, west of Tibbermore. Montrose drew up in a line south of and parallel to Elcho's army. Battle began around noon when the Irish Infantry on the Royalist right engaged the Cavalry on Elcho's left wing. The whole Royalist line then charged forward and although their opponents at first stood their ground, the Highlanders eventually broke the inexperienced Covenanter centre. Elcho's Infantry turned and fled towards Perth but were cut down in large numbers *en route*. The Covenanter right under Sir James Scott was still intact but was now isolated and surrounded and was quickly destroyed. Elcho had lost 2,000 dead and 1,000 captured; Montrose claimed to have lost just one man.

Weem Castle (NN837496)   In the sixteenth century the Menzies family established their principal seat at the newly built fortress of Weem. Alexander Menzies allied with Argyll in 1644 and harried Montrose as he marched past in August; the Royalists returned four months later in search of vengeance and successfully stormed and captured the castle and its garrison. Extended and renovated in the nineteenth century, the castle is still a centre for the Clan Menzies.

IRELAND

(The six-figure map references relate to the Irish National Grid, which is quite separate from the British Ordnance Survey's grid used elsewhere in this volume)

COUNTY CORK

Bandon (149055)   Bandon or Bandonbridge was a planted town of English Protestants, founded by the Earl of Cork in 1608 and defended by a circuit of well-maintained walls. Cromwell visited Bandon in late December 1649 or early January 1650 to inspect the defences and Ewer's Parliamentary garrison. Most of the walls and mural towers were destroyed in 1688–89 and only fragments of the early seventeenth-century defences now remain.

Cork (167072)   The main Parliamentary army quartered in and around Cork during winter 1649–50 and the town became one of Cromwell's bases for much of late December and January. According to tradition, he lodged at the house of a Mr Coppinger in South Main Street, where he spent Christmas; the house has long since disappeared.

Glengariff (092056)   There is an unsupported tradition that Cromwell visited Glengariff in January 1650 during his tour of southern bases and that 'Cromwell's Bridge', west of the village, was built by locals at an hour's notice when Cromwell threatened to hang them for destroying the old crossing; the bridge is now ruinous. However, no contemporary evidence confirms the colourful tale and it seems unlikely that Cromwell would have marched so far west for no pressing reason in the middle of winter.

Mallow (155098)   According to his report to Lenthall, Cromwell marched to Mallow on 29 January, at the beginning of his 1650 campaign, and visited the English garrison here. Parliamentary troops had secured and occupied Mallow Castle, a large late sixteenth-century fortified mansion which stood on the site of a medieval fortress, in the south-east corner of the old town. A four-storey rectangular block with polygonal towers at two corners and a projecting entrance tower in the west front, the extensive remains of the castle are open to the public. The later castle outbuildings, which stood nearby, have been extended and converted into a separate, mock-Tudor manor-house.

Youghal (210078)   Refortified as an English stronghold in the 1640s, Youghal became one of Cromwell's bases during winter 1649–50. He entered the town on 6 or 7 December and remained here until the 17th, when he moved on to Cork; he was here again during the latter half of January. He returned on 26 May to embark for England. During his visits, Cromwell lodged at the castle, known as the 'Magazine', which has been completely demolished, and at College House. The latter was built by Richard Boyle in 1608 on the site of an earlier building used as a residence and training centre for parish clergy; parts of Boyle's house, including the flanking towers and a chimney, survived the subsequent demolition and were incorporated in New College House, a later Georgian mansion which still stands on the site. Parts of the town walls survive, including the Water Gate, also known as Cromwell's Gate, because Cromwell passed through it when he left Ireland.

Two prominent Parliamentarians lie in St Mary's Church. Michael Jones fought for Parliament in Cheshire and North Wales during the latter stages of the first Civil War, was appointed virtual commander-in-chief in Ireland in 1647 and served as Cromwell's second-in-command in autumn 1649; he died of fever at Dungarvan in December and was buried in the Cork transept of St Mary's. Roger Boyle, Lord Broghill, 1st Earl of Orrery, was a Royalist who accepted Parliamentary service in Ireland in 1649–50 and actively supported Cromwell during the Protectorate; he was elected to Parliament in 1654 and 1656 and served as President of the Protector's Scottish Council. In 1660 he helped secure Ireland for the King, was rewarded with titles and land and spent most of the remainder of his life in southern Ireland. He died at Youghal in 1679.

COUNTY DUBLIN

Dublin (315234)   Cromwell landed at Ringsend, Dublin, on 15 August 1649 after a rough crossing from Milford Haven, and stayed in the city for a fortnight, awaiting the arrival of Ireton and the rest of the Parliamentary army. He returned to Dublin on 16 September after the capture of Drogheda and remained here for 1½ weeks before marching south. According to tradition he lodged in a house which stood on the corner of Castle and Werburgh Street; it was

Dublin, Co. Dublin. During the Protectorate, Ireland was administered by a Lord Lieutenant or Deputy based in Dublin, and the castle remained the official seat of government. Almost nothing remains of the quadrangular fortress known to Cromwell and his ministers and the present castle (*above*) is largely eighteenth century and later. Charles Fleetwood (*bottom left*) and his wife Bridget (*top left*) – the Protector's daughter and Ireton's widow – were based in Dublin during the opening years of the Protectorate. Fleetwood was rather weak and easily led and deceived, and his administration was marked by growing unrest amongst some elements of the Parliamentary army stationed in Ireland. Fleetwood was replaced in 1655 by Henry Cromwell (*bottom right*), the younger but abler of the Protector's two surviving sons. Despite his youth, he proved a skilled administrator and soon took a firm grasp on colonial government and army politics.

demolished in the early nineteenth century. It is clear from his letters, however, that Cromwell was using Dublin Castle as his official residence and HQ. He supposedly stabled his horses in St Patrick's Cathedral.

Throughout the 1650s Dublin served as the military and administrative base of the various commissioners and officers appointed to govern Ireland. Ireton was on campaign during most of his 18 months in office, but the more peaceful days of the mid and late 1650s enabled Charles Fleetwood and Henry Cromwell to spend most of the year in Dublin. The Lord Lieutenant or Deputy lived at Cork House in the city centre and used the adjoining castle for business and as the official seat of government; Phoenix House, a country residence west of the city, was also available and often served as a summer retreat. Cork House was completely destroyed during the redevelopment of the city in the eighteenth century and the street name Cork Hill alone preserves the memory. Phoenix Park survives, one of the largest parks in Europe, but the great house, a sixteenth-century mansion extended by

Henry Cromwell in the 1650s, fell derelict after the Restoration and was demolished at the end of the seventeenth century. Dublin Castle, begun in the thirteenth century as a simple quadrangular fortress with corner towers but repeatedly extended and rebuilt since, survives in good order. Although sections of the medieval and early modern stronghold survive – chiefly parts of the original south-east and south-west corner towers, now the Bermingham and Record Towers respectively – most of the present building is post-seventeenth-century. Parts of the castle are open daily for guided tours.

Rathfarnham (314229)   Retreat House, next to Rathfarnham Castle, incorporates a late sixteenth- or early seventeenth-century barn, now known as 'Cromwell's Barn', in which the Parliamentary commander supposedly held council during his Irish campaign. He was certainly in the area south of Dublin on several occasions during the early stages of the campaign, but no contemporary evidence links Cromwell to this building.

COUNTY KILKENNY

Callan (241143)   The medieval walled town was defended by three castles, an Anglo-Norman motte and bailey stronghold built by William the Marshall in the thirteenth century, a late fourteenth- and early fifteenth-century fortified hall built by the Butlers, and a western gatehouse known as Skerry's Castle. The town was held by Irish Royalists in 1649–50 but fell to Col. Reynolds's Parliamentarians on 7 or 8 February 1650. The west gate was bombarded by heavy artillery and Skerry's Castle fell after a fierce fight; the Royalists within were put to the sword. The motte and bailey castle to the northwest was then bombarded and stormed and the garrison again massacred. The troops in the adjoining Butler castle decided to abandon the struggle and surrendered on terms. Cromwell marched to Callan at the end of the first week of February but his letters do not make clear whether he reached the town in time to oversee the operation in person or whether Reynolds had already taken Callan in his absence. Parts of all three medieval and early modern strongholds survive – the remains of Skerry's Castle stand in West Street, fragments of masonry from William the Marshall's fortress lie on and around the great motte by the river and a Georgian mansion

in West Court incorporates the remains of Butler's medieval fortified house.

Castle Eve (247144)   To the west of Kells and north of King's River stand the remains of Castle Eve, the medieval and Tudor stronghold of the Swetman family. According to tradition, a sniper within the castle shot at Cromwell as he marched past in early February 1650 *en route* to Callan. The Parliamentary troops captured and plundered the fortress but the would-be assassin, a simpleton, was spared on Cromwell's orders.

Gowran (263153)   The plague-ridden town of Gowran fell to Hewson's Parliamentarians without serious resistance in early March 1650. The Royalists, however, retained control of the medieval castle which stood outside the town walls and were still holding out when Cromwell arrived here on 19 March. The siege was stepped up and when heavy cannon were placed before the castle on the 21st the Royalist garrison lost heart and surrendered. The soldiers, members of Ormonde's own regiment, were allowed to march away, but their officers were shot and the castle burnt. The shell of the fortified tower-house stands by a large motte in Pigeon Park.

Kilkenny (250156) Kilkenny had been the centre of the Catholic Confederacy during most of the 1640s and became one of Ormonde's principal bases in 1648–49. Cromwell approached the town in early February 1650 but did not attack the strongly defended base; instead Parliamentary troops spent the following six weeks campaigning in the surrounding region, overrunning outlying towns and castles in an attempt to isolate and encircle the place. By late March Cromwell felt strong enough to launch an attack on Kilkenny itself. He appeared before the town on 22 March, summoned the garrison to surrender and overran parts of the extra-mural suburbs. William Butler and his large Royalist garrison were protected by a circuit of medieval town walls and a twelfth–fifteenth-century castle and rejected the initial summons to surrender, though the governor did enter into prolonged negotiations with Cromwell. Fighting continued as the talks dragged on – Parliamentary cannon in St Patrick's Church bombarded the west gate, the suburb of Irish Town was taken and on 25 March a breach was opened in the town wall, though a subsequent attempt to enter the town was repulsed and the breach made good. On 27 March terms were agreed and the town was surrendered and garrisoned for Parliament by Col. Axtell. Cromwell did not lodge in Kilkenny for fear of the plague but stayed for several days at Dunmore, two miles north, before marching away at the end of the month.

The medieval castle, a quadrangular stronghold with massive cylindrical corner towers, stood in the south-east angle of the town walls, south of the Nore. Three of the towers attached to the present castle are original but the fourth and most of the three connecting ranges – the courtyard is now open to the east – are post-Restoration work, renovated or rebuilt again in the nineteenth century. The castle is open all year. Stretches of the medieval town wall survive on the east and west side of the town centre and one gateway, the Town Gate in Abbey Street, still stands.

Knocktopher (253137) Cromwell entered the town on 18 March 1650, marching south from plague-infested Thomastown. According to tradition, he met minor resistance from the small garrison in the Anglo-Norman castle, but the fortress and its Irish occupants were soon bombarded into submission. Today little survives of the former Butler stronghold except fragments of masonry on an earlier motte – 'Knocktopher Moat' or 'Garrison Castle' – by St David's churchyard. Cromwell's stay here was brief, for on the 19th he turned north once more and headed towards Kilkenny.

Thomastown (258141) Cromwell spent much of early March 1650 overseeing operations from Cashel but on the 16th or 17th he returned to the field, joining Col. Reynolds and his troops who had just taken Thomastown. Despite the town's formidable defences – a complete circuit of town walls and separate fortifications guarding the bridge over the Nore – the Royalist garrison had put up little resistance and quickly evacuated the town and fled across the bridge to Grenan Castle. The medieval fortress, south-east of the town on the west bank of the Nore, was promptly besieged and the garrison surrendered on terms on 18 March after two days of negotiation enlivened by occasional exchanges of fire. Cromwell had been present during the early stages of the siege but may have marched away south before its successful conclusion. The extensive ruins of the former Den stronghold still stand outside the town.

COUNTY LIMERICK

Kilbeheny (185116) On 31 January 1650 Cromwell took 'a castle called Kilbenny, upon the edge of the county of Limerick, where I left thirty Foot'. The ruins of the medieval fortress stand north-west of the village.

Limerick (158157) Cromwell made no attempt to take the county town and kept well away from the Royalist stronghold throughout his Irish campaign. In 1651 his son-in-law, Henry Ireton, laid siege to the walled town, which was betrayed to him in October, following a six-month investment. Many of the Irish officers and civilian leaders were immediately executed but the operation also cost Ireton his life for he fell ill with the plague during the latter stages of the siege and died on 26 November. His body was carried back to England.

COUNTY LOUTH

Drogheda (309275)   The ancient town at the mouth of the Boyne was one of Ormonde's principal strongholds; it occupied a vital position on the main road to Ulster and was a possible embarkation point for an invasion of the British mainland. In consequence, it became the first target of Cromwell's Irish campaign. Cromwell appeared before Drogheda on 2 September 1649 at the head of a 12,000-strong Parliamentary army. The town was held by the veteran Sir Arthur Aston and his 3,000 Royalists; they had hastily repaired and strengthened the circuit of medieval walls which protected Drogheda. Cromwell bombarded the town for a week, pounding the south-east angle of the walls near St Mary's Church. The church itself was used as a Royalist look-out point until Parliamentary cannon brought down the steeple. On 10 September two breaches appeared in the south wall and the Parliamentary army stormed the town on the following afternoon. Although the first two attacks were repulsed with heavy losses, a third charge, led by Cromwell himself, carried the earthworks which Aston had thrown up behind the breached wall and forced the Royalists back. Aston and some of his men sought refuge on Mill Mount, an artificial hillock protected by a bank and ditch and a timber pallisade, but the flimsy defences were soon broken down and the Royalists put to the sword; Aston was battered to death with his own wooden leg. The rest of the garrison fled across the Boyne into the northern half of the town but Parliamentary troops took the bridge before the movable sections could be raised and the slaughter continued up Ship Street and St Peter's Street. Many were cut down in and around St Peter's Church and those who took shelter in the church perished when Cromwell's men set fire to the building. Parties of Royalists sheltering in the mural towers were starved out on the following day. Over 2,000 people perished in Drogheda, including all the Royalist officers and most of their troops, Catholic priests and a few civilians; the surviving members of the garrison were transported to Barbados. Cromwell and his troops probably stayed in or around Drogheda for several days before returning to Dublin.

The medieval town gates of Drogheda have long since disappeared but the barbican of St Lawrence Gate, an embattled and double-towered foregate, survives at the junction of King and St Lawrence Street. Sections of the thirteenth-century walls still stand in several places around the old town, particularly to the south near Mill Mount. The latter, the motte of a long-demolished twelfth-century castle, lies off Barrack Street and is now surmounted by a cross. St Mary's Church in Mary Street incorporates parts of the medieval friary church badly damaged by Cromwell's bombardment. Protestant St Peter's Church by William Street, north of the Boyne, is an eighteenth-century and later successor to the medieval building in which so many Irish Royalists perished.

Dundalk (304307)   Col. Coote secured the town for Parliament without serious opposition in mid-September 1649 – Ormonde's men had fled on hearing news of the fall of Drogheda. Although Cromwell addressed a letter of summons to Dundalk, there is no evidence that he visited the place either during or after its capture.

COUNTY MEATH

Athboy (271264)   Persistent but unconfirmed traditions have Cromwell briefly campaigning in County Meath between the fall of Drogheda and his return to Dublin on 16 September. He and his troops supposedly camped on Hill of Ward, an ancient meeting place surmounted by the remains of a hill-fort, which stands one mile east of Athboy. Cromwell then besieged, bombarded and captured Rathmore Castle, the fifteenth-century Plunkett stronghold, the ruins of which stand three miles north-east of Athboy.

Bective (286259)   According to tradition, Cromwell and his troops were active in the area around Bective in the days after the fall of Drogheda. They allegedly captured Trubly Castle with little opposition – Ormonde's garrison had withdrawn on news of the fall of Drogheda

– and Cromwell lodged here for the night; he slighted the fortress and marched away on the following day. The remains of the square tower keep with round flanking towers stand on a crag east of the Boyne, 1¼ miles south-west of Bective.

Trim (280256)   Trim Castle on the banks of the Boyne was the largest Norman military construction in Ireland. A massive square keep with small projecting square towers in each face stands amid a large bailey defended by a curtain wall with interval and angle towers and two gatehouses and barbicans. According to tradition, Cromwell and his troops marched to Trim in mid-September 1649 and captured the fortress. The extensive remains are open to the public throughout the year.

COUNTY TIPPERARY

Burncourt (194117)   The ruins of Burncourt or Clogheen Castle stand to the south of the Mitchelstown to Caher road and north of the village of Burncourt. The great embattled house built for Sir Richard Everard in 1641 – the datestone is now incorporated within a wall near the entrance to the adjoining farmyard – was captured by Cromwell and the Parliamentary army as they marched past on 2 February 1650. Cromwell left a small garrison here but the troops were soon withdrawn and the house was burnt and gutted. The impressive shell of the three storey rectangular block with projecting square corner towers survives in fairly good condition.

Caher (205125)   The small market town and castle on the river Suir were held by Irish Royalists in 1649–50. In early February 1650 Cromwell and his troops marched through the area but they carefully avoided the town and crossed the Suir with difficulty a little to the south. They returned, however, on 24 February, and besieged the island fortress; Cromwell summoned the garrison and threatened that 'if I be necessitated to bend my cannon upon you, you must expect what is usual in such cases'. Governor Matthews initially ignored the summons and the Parliamentarians unsuccessfully tried to scale the outer walls, but when Cromwell brought up his cannon the garrison promptly surrendered on terms. The magnificent twelfth–thirteenth-century castle stands on an island formed by a loop of the Suir. The massive stronghold, one of the largest medieval castles in Ireland, was considered impregnable until the advent of gunpowder and cannon. Restored in the nineteenth century and now in good order, Caher comprises a massive keep overlooking three irregularly-shaped wards defended by curtain walls with mural towers and gatehouses. The castle is open to the public throughout the year.

Carrick on Suir (240122)   In November 1649 Parliamentary troops under Jones and Ireton captured the market town without serious resistance. Cromwell lodged here during the first half of April 1650 while overseeing negotiations for the surrender of minor Royalist bases in the surrounding area. He probably established his HQ in Carrick Castle, a late medieval quadrangular fortress partly rebuilt in the sixteenth century as a fine, two storey Elizabethan manor-house. The latter survives in good condition east of the town centre off Castle Street; beyond stand two ruined towers belonging to the medieval Ormonde fortress.

Cashel (207140)   Cashel had been attacked and taken by Parliamentary forces in 1647 and the inhabitants massacred, and when Cromwell approached the place two years later the residents were in no mood to risk a repetition. The town surrendered to Parliamentary troops without resistance on 3 or 4 February. Cromwell stayed here on 15–17 February and was based at Cashel for a week or more during the first half of March while overseeing operations in the area, including the capture of castles at Golden Bridge and Dundrum.

Clonmel (220122)   On 27 April 1650 Cromwell rejoined his troops besieging Clonmel and summoned the garrison to surrender. Hugh Duff O'Neill's garrison was running short of supplies but the summons was nonetheless rejected and the Royalists survived another three weeks of siege and bombardment. On 9 May the town wall was breached on the north side and Parliamentary troops rushed in, only to be repulsed with very heavy losses. O'Neill repaired the breach with stone and timber barricades. A second attempt to storm the town on 17 May was also fiercely repulsed. O'Neill realised that it was only a matter of time before town and garrison would fall to the far larger besieging army and he and his men slipped away that night under cover of darkness; on the 18th the Mayor and civilian authorities surrendered on terms. Several sections of the medieval town wall still stand, particularly to the north and west of St Mary's churchyard, where the north-west angle tower and two flanking towers also survive in fairly good order. The medieval town gates have all perished – the present West Gate is a nineteenth-century reconstruction.

Fethard (222134)   Cromwell described Fethard as 'most pleasantly seated, having a very good wall with round and square bulwarks'. His first view of the town was less pleasant, for he and his troops arrived in a downpour in the middle of the night of 2–3 February 1650. Despite the hour, the garrison was immediately summoned to surrender and after brief negotiations Governor Butler delivered Fethard to the Parliamentarians. Thereafter it became one of Cromwell's bases for operations in Tipperary and he was here on 3–4 and 9–14 February and on 23–26 April. He usually lodged in the former fourteenth-century Augustinian friary which stood to the east of the town centre, outside the walls; the cloisteral buildings are now very ruinous but the medieval church has been renovated and reroofed. Several sections of Fethard's fourteenth-century town walls also survive, complete with gates and mural towers.

Kiltinan Castle (223133)   The remains of Kiltinan Castle stand on a rocky outcrop above the Clashawley, three miles south-east of Fethard. Described by Cromwell as 'a very large and strong castle', the medieval Butler fortress comprised a rectangular tower-house with corner towers. Cromwell and his troops appeared before Kiltinan on 27 February 1650 and bombarded the small garrison into submission – scars and breaches supposedly made by the Parliamentary cannon are still visible. The ruined shell of the castle survives, though one of the angle towers has completely disappeared and two more have been incorporated within a modern private house.

Rehill Castle (200120)   The medieval Butler stronghold, known in the seventeenth century as Roghill or Raghill Castle, fell to Cromwell and the Parliamentary army as they marched past on 2 February 1650.

COUNTY WATERFORD

Dungarvan (226093)   On 4 December 1649 Cromwell and his troops marched south-west from Kilmacthomas and entered the small port of Dungarvan unopposed – the Irish Royalist force within the small Norman castle had surrendered to Broghill on the previous day. The thirteenth-century castle was later incorporated within a military barracks, wrecked in 1921, the remains of which still stand. The Parliamentary army was based here on 4–7 December while Cromwell rested and consulted with Broghill. Most of the troops moved on to Youghal on the 7th, but Cromwell's ailing Lieutenant-General, Michael Jones, was too ill to be moved; he died at Dungarvan on the 10th.

Kilmeadan (251110)   Cromwell and the army marched through the small village on 2 December 1649 *en route* from Waterford to Kilmacthomas. Kilmeadan Castle was captured and, according to tradition, its governor was immediately hanged. The ruins of the medieval fortress stand on the outskirts of the village.

Passage East (270110)   The small port on the west bank of Waterford harbour has long been a base for a ferry across the Suir Estuary. On 24 or 25 November, at the beginning of the siege of Waterford, Cromwell sent Jones and Ireton at the head of one troop of Horse and three of Dragoons to take the village. The fairly large but outnumbered Royalist garrison was routed – 100 were killed and 350 captured – and the village was secured for Parliament.

Two miles north-west, outside the village of Faithlegg, stand the ruins of the Ailwoods' medieval stronghold; the castle was held by Royalists in 1649 but it, too, fell to Cromwell's troop sometime in late November as part of the operation against Waterford.

Waterford (260112)   In late November 1649 Cromwell left his base at New Ross and moved against the Catholic Royalist stronghold of Waterford. He arrived before the walled town on 24 November and summoned the governor to surrender it; Lieutenant-General O'Farrel refused but opened prolonged and probably insin-

Top: Trim Castle, Co. Meath. Tradition has it that Cromwell captured Trim in September 1649, after the fall of Drogheda. The well-preserved keep is surrounded by the scattered remains of the walls, towers and gatehouses which defended the bailey.

Middle: Caher Castle, Co. Tipperary. Despite its formidable appearance, the island fortress commanding the Suir and the town bridge was vulnerable to artillery attack and the garrison quickly surrendered to Cromwell in February 1650. The present castle owes much to nineteenth-century restoration work.

Bottom: Dunbrody Abbey, Co. Wexford. Abbey and garrison were quickly overwhelmed by Parliamentary troops in October 1649 as part of the operation to isolate Wexford. The large, rather plain cruciform church is roofless but otherwise almost complete; the cloistral ranges to the left have not survived so well.

cere negotiations. The Parliamentarian army had been greatly reduced by sickness and by the need to garrison towns and castles captured earlier in the campaign, and Cromwell felt that he could not storm the strongly defended town. Instead he settled down for a formal siege and sent out units to take the surrounding villages and strongholds. The Royalist garrison was well supplied and by the beginning of December it was clear that the siege would have to be maintained for several weeks. The onset of bad weather brought renewed sickness in the Parliamentary army – around this time Cromwell wrote that he had 'not above 3,000 healthful Foot in the field' – and Cromwell abandoned the operation and marched away on 2 December. Amongst those who had perished of disease before Waterford was Major Oliver Cromwell, son of Sir Philip Cromwell, and thus a first

cousin of the Parliamentary leader. The town eventually fell to Henry Ireton in August 1650 following a second siege.

Unlike many Irish towns, Waterford retains most of its medieval defences. Much of the town wall survives, complete with interval and angle towers; there are well preserved sections around St Patrick's churchyard and Patrick Street, by Bachelor's Walk and Newgate Street and along the north side of Castle Street. At the north-east corner of the old town, by the junction of The Parade and Adelphie Terrace, stands Reginald's Tower, a massive twelfth-century cylindrical tower, restored in the nineteenth century and now a museum. 'Cromwell's Rock', high ground overlooking the town, is traditionally the site of the Parliamentary HQ during the unsuccessful siege of 1649.

COUNTY WEXFORD

Ballyhack (271111) A medieval tower-house at Ballyhack guarded the ferry across Waterford harbour. It was held by Irish Royalists in 1649 but the garrison was bombarded into submission by Cromwell's troops in November in preparation for the unsuccessful attempt on Waterford itself. The castle was badly damaged and is today very ruinous.

Dunbrody Abbey (271115) In mid-October 1649 a detachment from the Parliamentary army was sent to Dunbrody to expel the small Royalist force which had garrisoned the medieval Cistercian abbey. The Irish Royalists fell back at the approach of Cromwell's troops and Dunbrody was taken unopposed. The abbey is now a picturesque ruin, the roofless but otherwise complete church surrounded by the more fragmentary ruins of the cloisteral buildings. Dunbrody Abbey is open to the public.

Duncannon (272108) A sixteenth-century fort, the latest in a succession of strongholds to stand on the rocky promontory west of the town, was held by Ormonde's Royalists in 1648–49. In mid-October 1649, immediately after the fall of Wexford, Ireton was sent with 2,000 men to reduce the outpost. The garrison, however, held out, even when Cromwell and reinforcements from New Ross arrived on 27 October. A week later the disease-ridden Parliamentarians abandoned the operation; Ireton and his men

marched away on 5 November though Cromwell, ill with malaria and dysentry, had probably returned to New Ross some days before. The fort was eventually taken by Ireton in the latter half of 1650, long after the departure of Cromwell and the main Parliamentary army. The Elizabethan stronghold has been repeatedly remodelled and the present building on the site is largely nineteenth-century.

Enniscorthy (297139) An important market town at the head of the navigable reaches of the Slaney, Enniscorthy grew up around the thirteenth-century castle which commanded the tideway. After a stormy medieval history, the fortress was repaired and largely rebuilt by Sir Henry Wallop in the late sixteenth century. It was garrisoned for the King during the 1640s but surrendered without resistance to Cromwell on 30 September 1649. The Parliamentary army probably spent the night quartered in and around the castle and left a small garrison here under Capt. Todd. The fortress was retaken by local Irish at the end of the year and the garrison massacred. Derelict by the nineteenth century, Enniscorthy Castle has since been restored and is now in good order. The original plan – that of a rectangular keep with large corner towers – has been retained and much of the medieval and early modern masonry survives. The castle now houses a small museum.

Ferns (301149)   Now a small, quiet town, Ferns was once an important political and religious centre, the capital of the Kingdom of Leinster. In the north-west corner of the town stand the remains of a quadrangular Norman Irish castle, built in the thirteenth century on the site of an earlier royal fortress. Partly demolished in 1641, it was held by a small Irish force in 1649 but was promptly surrendered on 29 September as Cromwell and the main Parliamentary army marched through. Three of the four angle towers remain, including the south-east tower, which contains one of the finest surviving medieval chapels in Ireland.

New Ross (272127)   The medieval port, defended by a circuit of thirteenth-century walls, was garrisoned in 1649 by Sir Lucas Taaffe and 2,500 Irish Royalists. Cromwell arrived before New Ross on 17 October and immediately summoned Taaffe to surrender. Negotiations were stepped up on the following day when Parliamentary cannon began to pound the walls, opening a breach near Bewley or Three Bullet Gate, and the town surrendered on terms on the 19th. Cromwell remained here during the latter half of October and returned after a trip to Duncannon in early November suffering from malaria and dysentery. According to tradition, he lodged at Francis Dormer's house in the main street; the building has long since disappeared. Most of the town's defences have also been demolished and today only odd fragments of the medieval walls remain.

Tintern Abbey (279110)   The Cistercian abbey was founded in the thirteenth century by William the Marshall as a daughter house of its namesake in South Wales. Most of the monastic buildings were demolished soon after the Dis-solution but parts of the abbey church – the west end of the nave, the crossing tower and the presbytery – were preserved and converted into a Tudor mansion, also known as Tintern Abbey. The house was held by Irish Royalists in 1649 but surrendered without serious resistance at the approach of Parliamentary troops in October. Remodelled in the eighteenth century, the house survives in good order.

Wexford (304121)   The county town at the mouth of the Slaney had served throughout the 1640s as a base for regular Irish Royalist forces and for pro-Royalist pirates, and its capture became Cromwell's first major objective in the south. He arrived before the walled town on 1 October 1649 with 9–10,000 men and established a base on a rocky outcrop south of the town still known as 'Cromwell's Fort'. Rosslare fort at the mouth of the harbour had been evacuated at the approach of the Parliamentary army and Deane's fleet was able to enter the bay unopposed and give Cromwell naval support throughout the operation. Governor Sinnot spun out negotiations for over a week until Cromwell lost his patience and ordered his guns to open up on Wexford Castle on 11 October. The garrison within the castle promptly surrendered and Cromwell's men swept into the panic-stricken town. The soldiers and civilians put up some resistance, particularly around the barricaded market place, now the Bull Ring, but the Parliamentarians carried all before them and took a fearful revenge. The bloodletting of Drogheda was repeated and up to 2,000 soldiers and civilians perished during and after the fall of Wexford.

Cromwell stayed in Wexford on 11–15 October; according to tradition, he lodged at Kenny's Hall, a castellated house in Main Street.

COUNTY WICKLOW

Arklow (324173)   Arklow Castle was besieged by the main Parliamentary army as they marched through on 27 September 1649 and was surrendered on the following day soon after Cromwell had rejoined his troops here. The ruins of the small medieval fortress survive on the outskirts of the town.

A CROMWELL ITINERARY

1599–1616	Huntingdon, Cambs.
Apr 1616–1617	Sidney Sussex College, Cambridge, Cambs.
1617–1618	Lincoln's Inn, London?
1618–1631	Huntingdon, Cambs.
(22 Aug 1620	St Giles, Cripplegate, London.
1628–1629	London.
Nov–Dec 1630	London.)
1631–1636	St Ives, Cambs.
1636–1640	Ely, Cambs.
Jan–Mar 1640	Cambridge and Ely, Cambs.
Apr–May 1640	London.
May–Oct 1640	Ely, Cambs.
Nov 1640– Aug 1642	London (active in parliament for most of the time, but probably returned to Ely occasionally, including the parliamentary recess of Sept–Oct 1641).
10–c.26 Aug 1642	Cambridge, Cambs.
29 Aug 1642	Huntingdon, Cambs.
6 Sept 1642	London.
mid Sept–early Nov 1642	probably marching with main Parliamentary army under Essex:
10–19 Sept	Northampton, Northants. Coventry, West Midlands. Warwick, Warks.
24 Sept–19 Oct	Worcester, Hereford and Worcs.
20 Oct	Stratford-upon-Avon, Warks.
22 Oct	Kineton, Warks.
23 Oct	Edgehill, Warks.
24 Oct	Warwick, Warks.
2 Nov	Northampton, Northants. Dunstable, Beds.
5 Nov	St Albans, Herts.
8 Nov	London.
Nov–Dec 1642	no record of work in parliament – probably at Ely, Cambs.

1643

6 Jan	London.
14 Jan	St Albans, Herts.
26 Jan–11 Mar	Cambridge, Cambs.
12–13 Mar	Norwich, Norfolk.
14–16 Mar	Lowestoft, Suffolk; lodged at Somerleyton Hall, Suffolk.
17–19 Mar	Norwich, Norfolk.
20–21 Mar	King's Lynn, Norfolk.
22 Mar	Thetford, Norfolk.
23 Mar–c.7 Apr	Cambridge, Cambs.
c.7–c.20 Apr	Huntingdon, Cambs.
22 Apr	Peterborough, Cambs.
25–28 Apr	before and in Crowland, Lincs.
28 Apr–c.8 May	Peterborough, Cambs.
(early May	visited Ramsey, Cambs.)
9 May	Sleaford, Lincs.
11–12 May	Grantham, Lincs.
13 May	marches towards Newark; fight at Belton; night at Syston Park, Lincs.
mid May–early Jun	Nottingham, Notts.

4 Jun	Bottesford, Leics.
c.8 Jun	Boston, Lincs.
10 Jun	Donington, Lincs.
11–12 Jun	around Newark, Notts.
3–16 Jul	around Nottingham, Notts.
17 Jul	Stony Stratford, Bucks.
19 Jul	Burghley House, Cambs.
26 Jul	Grantham, Lincs.
27 Jul	North Scarle, Lincs.
28 Jul	Gainsborough, Lincs.
29 Jul	Lincoln, Lincs.
30 Jul	Stamford, Lincs.
31 Jul–3 Aug	Huntingdon, Cambs.
4 Aug	Cambridge, Cambs.
6 Aug	Huntingdon, Cambs.
7 Aug	Stamford, Lincs.
8 Aug	Peterborough, Cambs.
28–29 Aug	Cambridge, Cambs.
early Sept	before King's Lynn, Norfolk?
4 Sept	Ely, Cambs.
5–c.11 Sept	Boston, Lincs.
22–23 Sept	Kingston upon Hull, Humberside.
26–28 Sept	Boston, Lincs.
2 Oct	King's Lynn, Norfolk.
3 Oct	Ely, Cambs.; Boston, Lincs.
4–6 Oct	Boston, Lincs.
8 Oct	Louth, Lincs.
10 Oct	East Kirkby, Lincs.
11 Oct	Winceby and Horncastle, Lincs.
late Oct	around Cambridge, Cambs.
2 Nov	around Newark, Notts.
early Dec	around Sleaford, Lincs.
12–31 Dec	Ely, Cambs.

1644

1–13 Jan	Ely, Cambs.
16 Jan	Cambridge, Cambs.
18 Jan–mid Feb	London.
early Mar	approaches Oxford, Oxon.
3 Mar	Padbury, Bucks.
4 Mar	Hillesden House, Bucks.
5–7 Mar	Padbury, Bucks.
8–10 Mar	Cambridge, Cambs.
25 Mar	Huntingdon, Cambs.
late Mar	Northampton, Northants.
11 Apr	Cambridge, Cambs.
late Apr	around Belvoir, Leics.
6 May	around Lincoln, Lincs.
	before York, North Yorks.
2 Jul	Marston Moor, North Yorks.
c.3–c.6 Jul	active in North Yorks – before Knaresborough Castle?
	Tickhill Castle, South Yorks.
c.25 Jul–5 Aug	Doncaster, South Yorks.
6 Aug–2 Sept	Lincoln, Lincs.
3–5 Sept	Sleaford, Lincs.
6 Sept	Peterborough, Cambs.
7 Sept	Huntingdon, Cambs.

11–16 Sept	London.
17 Sept	leaves London for Banbury, Oxon.
26 Sept–4 Oct	Banbury, Oxon.
5 Oct	towards Reading, Berks.
6 Oct	returns to Banbury, Oxon.
8 Oct	Syresham, Northants.
9 Oct	Sulgrave, Northants.
14 Oct	Reading, Berks.
17 Oct	Basing, Hants.
21–27 Oct	in and around Newbury, Berks.
28 Oct	Blewbury, Oxon.
29 Oct	Newbury, Berks.
1 Nov	Compton, Berks.
2 Nov	Blewbury, Oxon.
3 Nov	Harwell, Oxon.
5 Nov	Chilton Plain, Oxon.
6 Nov	Compton Downs, Berks.
8 Nov	around Newbury, Berks.
10 Nov	Shaw, Berks.
15 Nov	Newbury, Berks.
17 Nov	Reading, Berks.
23 Nov–31 Dec	London.

1645

Jan–Feb	London.
5 Mar	marches west.
9 Mar	Andover, Hants.
10 Mar	Amesbury, Wilts.
11 Mar	Laverton, Somerset.
13 Mar	Cerne Abbas, Dorset.
	Ringwood, Hants.
26 Mar	towards Bridport, Dorset
29 Mar	Ringwood, Hants.
31 Mar	Sturminster Newton, Dorset.
6 Apr	north towards Bristol, Avon, but returns to Shaftesbury, Dorset.
9 Apr	Salisbury, Wilts.
10 Apr	Wilton, Wilts.
17 Apr	marches east towards London.
20 Apr	Windsor, Berks.
21 Apr	Caversham and Reading, Berks.
23 Apr	Watlington, Wheatley and Islip, Oxon.
24 Apr	Islip and Bletchingdon House, Oxon.
25–26 Apr	Bletchingdon House, Oxon.
	Middleton Stoney, Oxon.
27 Apr	Bampton, Oxon.
28 Apr	Bampton and Faringdon, Oxon.
29–30 Apr	before Faringdon, Oxon.
2 May	Newbury, Berks; before Faringdon, Oxon.
3 May	Blewbury and Abingdon, Oxon.
4–5 May	Abingdon, Oxon.
6 May	Dorchester, Oxon.
7 May	Newbridge, Oxon.
8 May	around Burford, Oxon.
9 May	Hinton Waldrist, Oxon.
10–11 May	Woodstock, Oxon.
13 May	marches towards Warwickshire, but ordered back to Oxfordshire.
22 May	Marston, Oxon.
23–25 May	Wytham, Oxon.
29 May	Aylesbury, Bucks.
31 May	Cambridge, Cambs.
4 Jun	Huntingdon, Cambs.
5–10 Jun	around Cambridge and Huntingdon, Cambs.
11 Jun	Bedford, Beds.
13 Jun	Kislingbury and Guilsborough, Northants.
14 Jun	Naseby, Northants.; towards Leicester, Leics.; Market Harborough, Leics.
16 Jun	Great Glen, Leics.

18–20 Jun	Leicester, Leics.
23 Jun	Warwick, Warks.
24 Jun	Stratford upon Avon, Warks.
26 Jun	Lechlade, Gloucs.
	Highworth, Wilts.
	Wanborough, Wilts.
29 Jun	Marlborough, Wilts.
	Salisbury, Wilts.
	Blandford, Dorset.
3–4 Jul	Dorchester, Dorset.
5–7 Jul	Crewkerne, Somerset.
10 Jul	Long Sutton and Langport, Somerset.
11 Jul	Woolavington, Knowle and Knowle Hill, Somerset.
12–23 Jul	before Bridgwater, Somerset; base at Chedzoy, Somerset.
24 Jul	Martock, Somerset.
2 Aug	before Sherborne Castle, Dorset.
4 Aug	Hambledon Hill and Shroton, Dorset.
5–17 Aug	before Sherborne Castle, Dorset.
18 Aug	Castle Cary, Somerset.
	Shepton Mallet, Somerset.
	Chew, Avon.
21 Aug	Keynsham, Avon.
22 Aug–10 Sept	before Bristol, Avon; base at Stapleton, Avon.
11–14 Sept	Bristol, Avon.
15 Sept	towards Devizes, Wilts.
20 Sept	before Devizes, Wilts.
21–22 Sept	in Devizes, Wilts.
28 Sept–6 Oct	Winchester, Hants.
7 Oct	towards Basing, Hants.
9–14 Oct	before Basing House, Hants.
15 Oct	marches west.
16 Oct	Wallop, Hants.
17 Oct	Salisbury, Wilts.
	Longford House, Wilts.
21 Oct	Blandford, Dorset.
22 Oct	Cerne Abbas, Dorset.
23 Oct	Chard, Somerset.
24 Oct	Crediton, Devon.
late Oct–31 Dec	with Fairfax and main army in quarters around Exeter, with bases at Crediton, Tiverton, Ottery St Mary, Topsham and elsewhere in Devon.

1646

8 Jan	Crediton, Devon.
9 Jan	Bovey Tracey, Devon.
24 Jan	Totnes, Devon.
25 Jan–9 Feb	before Exeter, Devon.
10–13 Feb	Crediton, Devon.
14 Feb	Chulmleigh, Devon.
16–22 Feb	Torrington, Devon.
23 Feb	Holsworthy, Devon.
25–26 Feb	Launceston, Cornwall.
27 Feb	west through Cornwall.
1 Mar	St Tudy, Cornwall.
2 Mar	Wadebridge and Bodmin, Cornwall.
3–6 Mar	Bodmin, Cornwall.
10–20 Mar	Truro and Tresillian, Cornwall.
21 Mar	Bodmin, Cornwall.
25 Mar	Plymouth, Devon.
27 Mar	Tavistock and Okehampton, Devon.
29 Mar	Crediton, Devon.
31 Mar–9 Apr	before Exeter, Devon.
10 Apr	in Exeter, Devon.
22 Apr	London.
May–Jun	in Oxon for siege of Oxford.
Jul–Dec	London.

1647

Jan–Apr	London.
(20 Mar	Bury St Edmunds, Suffolk?)
2–20 May	Saffron Walden, Essex.
21 May–3 Jun	London.
4 Jun	Ware, Herts.; Kentford Heath, Suffolk.
5 Jun	Newmarket and Kentford, Suffolk.
6–9 Jun	Cambridge, Cambs.
(7 Jun	Childerley, Cambs.)
10–24 Jun	Royston and St Albans, Herts.
25–26 Jun	Berkhamsted, Herts.
27 Jun–2 Jul	Uxbridge, Greater London.
4–c.18 Jul	Caversham and Reading, Berks.
19 Jul–early Aug	with army at Bedford, Beds; Colnbrook, Bucks; Hounslow Heath, London.
Aug	London, with visits to army HQ at Putney and King at Hampton Court.
early Sept	Isle of Wight?
14 Sept–13 Nov	London, at Westminster and army HQ at Putney.
14 Nov	Hertford, Herts.
15 Nov	Corkbush Field, Herts.
19 Nov–31 Dec	London, at Westminster; and army HQ at Windsor, Berks.

1648

Jan–Mar	London and Windsor, Berks.
27 Mar	Farnham, Surrey.
1 Apr–3 May	London and Windsor, Berks.
8 May	Gloucester, Gloucs.
10 May	Monmouth, Gwent.
11–14 May	Chepstow, Gwent.
15–16 May	Cardiff, South Glam.
19 May	Swansea, West Glam.
24 May–10 Jul	before Pembroke, Dyfed.
11–14 Jul	in Pembroke, Dyfed.
24 Jul	Gloucester, Gloucs.
26–30 Jul	Warwick, Warks.
1 Aug	Leicester, Leics.
3 Aug	Nottingham, Notts.
6 Aug	Mansfield, Notts.
8 Aug	Rotherham, South Yorks.
9 Aug	Doncaster, South Yorks.
10 Aug	Pontefract and Leeds, West Yorks.
11 Aug	Wetherby, West Yorks.
13 Aug	Otley, West Yorks.
14 Aug	Skipton, North Yorks.
15 Aug	Gisburn, Lancs.
16 Aug	Clitheroe, Hodder Bridge and Stonyhurst, Lancs.
17 Aug	Longridge and Preston, Lancs.
18 Aug	marching south from Preston, Lancs.
19 Aug	Winwick and Warrington, Cheshire.
20–22 Aug	Warrington, Cheshire.
23 Aug	Wigan, Greater Manchester.
27–28 Aug	Skipton, North Yorks.
1 Sept	Knaresborough, North Yorks.
	Boroughbridge, North Yorks.
	Northallerton, North Yorks.
	Darlington, Durham.
7–8 Sept	Durham, Durham.
9–10 Sept	Newcastle upon Tyne, Tyne & Wear.
11 Sept	Morpeth, Northumberland.
12–15 Sept	Alnwick, Northumberland.
16–18 Sept	Cheswick, Northumberland.
19–21 Sept	Norham, Northumberland.
22–29 Sept	Mordington, Borders.
30 Sept–2 Oct	Berwick upon Tweed, Northumberland.
4–7 Oct	Edinburgh, Lothian.

8–9 Oct	Dalhousie, Lothian.
14 Oct	Carlisle, Cumbria.
17–19 Oct	Newcastle upon Tyne, Tyne & Wear.
20–24 Oct	Durham, Durham.
25 Oct	Barnard Castle, Durham.
28 Oct	Boroughbridge, North Yorks.
2 Nov	Byram House, North Yorks.
6–29 Nov	Knottingley and before Pontefract Castle, West Yorks.
6–31 Dec	London and Windsor, Berks.

1649

Jan–Apr	London.
30 Apr–1 May	Hursley, Hants.
2–10 May	London.
11 May	Alton, Hants.
12 May	Andover, Hants.
13 May	Theale, Berks.
14–16 May	Burford, Oxon.
17–c.20 May	Oxford, Oxon.
25 May–9 Jul	London.
10 Jul	Brentford, Greater London; Windsor, Berks.
11 Jul	Reading, Berks.
12 Jul	Marlborough, Wilts.
14–c.23 Jul	Bristol, Avon.
28 Jul	Tenby, Dyfed.
30 Jul	Swansea, West Glam.
2 Aug	Tenby, Dyfed.
4–13 Aug	Milford Haven, Dyfed.
15–31 Aug	Dublin, Co Dublin.
1 Sept	Ballygath, Co Meath.
2–10 Sept	before Drogheda, Co Louth.
11–12 Sept	in Drogheda, Co Louth.
16–27 Sept	Dublin, Co Dublin.
28 Sept	Arklow, Co Wicklow.
29 Sept	Ferns, Co Wexford; towards Enniscorthy, Co Wexford.
30 Sept	Enniscorthy, Co Wexford.
2–10 Oct	before Wexford, Co Wexford.
11–15 Oct	in Wexford, Co Wexford.
17–18 Oct	before New Ross, Co Wexford.
19–26 Oct	in New Ross, Co Wexford.
27 Oct–5 Nov	before Duncannon, Co Wexford.
6–23 Nov	New Ross, Co Wexford.
24 Nov–1 Dec	before Waterford, Co Waterford.
2–3 Dec	Kilmacthomas, Co Waterford.
4–c.6 Dec	Dungarvan, Co Waterford.
c.7–16 Dec	Youghal, Co Cork.
17–31 Dec	Cork, Co Cork.

1650

early Jan	based at Cork, but also visits garrisons in area: Kinsale, Bandon, Dunmanway and Skibbereen, Co Cork.
mid–28 Jan	Youghal, Co Cork.
29 Jan	Mallow, Co Cork.
	Kilbeheny Castle, Co Limerick.
2 Feb	Rehill Castle, Co Tipperary.
3 Feb	Fethard, Co Tipperary.
	Cashel, Co Tipperary.
	before Kilkenny, Co Kilkenny.
	Callan, Co Kilkenny.
9–10 Feb	Fethard, Co Tipperary.
15–17 Feb	Cashel, Co Tipperary.
24 Feb	Caher, Co Tipperary.
27 Feb	Kiltinan, Co Tipperary.
5 Mar	Cashel, Co Tipperary.

16 Mar	before Grenan Castle, Co Kilkenny.
17 Mar	Thomastown, Co Kilkenny.
18 Mar	Knocktopher, Co Kilkenny.
19 Mar	before Gowran Castle, Co Kilkenny.
20 Mar	in Gowran, Co Kilkenny.
22–26 Mar	before Kilkenny, Co Kilkenny.
27–28 Mar	in Kilkenny, Co Kilkenny.
1–13 Apr	Carrick, Co Tipperary.
23–26 Apr	Fethard, Co Tipperary.
27 Apr–17 May	before Clonmel, Co Tipperary.
18 May	in Clonmel, Co Tipperary.
26 May	sails from Youghal, Co Cork.
c.28 May	lands Bristol, Avon.
31 May	Windsor, Berks.
1 Jun	Hounslow Heath and Hyde Park, London.
2–27 Jun	London.
28 Jun	Ware, Herts.
29 Jun	Cambridge, Cambs.
	Northampton, Northants.
	Leicester, Leics.
	York, North Yorks.
	Durham, Durham.
10–15 Jul	Newcastle upon Tyne, Tyne and Wear.
16 Jul	Morpeth, Northumberland.
17 Jul	Alnwick, Northumberland.
18 Jul	around Rock, Northumberland.
19 Jul	Chillingham Castle, Northumberland.
20 Jul	around Haggerston, Northumberland.
21 Jul	around Berwick upon Tweed, Northumberland.
22–24 Jul	Mordington House, Borders.
25 Jul	Cockburnspath, Borders; Dunglass, Lothian.
26 Jul	Dunbar, Lothian.
27 Jul	Haddington, Lothian.
28 Jul	Musselburgh, Lothian.
29 Jul	Restalrig and St Leonard's Hill, Lothian.
30 Jul–5 Aug	Musselburgh, Lothian.
6–10 Aug	Dunbar, Lothian.
11–12 Aug	Musselburgh, Lothian.
13 Aug	Braid Hill, Lothian.
15–17 Aug	Musselburgh, Lothian.
18–25 Aug	Braid Hill, Lothian.
26–27 Aug	around Gogar, Lothian.
28 Aug	Blackford Hill, Lothian.
29–30 Aug	Musselburgh, Lothian.
31 Aug	Haddington, Lothian.
1–5 Sept	Dunbar, Lothian.
7–13 Sept	Edinburgh, Lothian.
14 Sept	Niddry Castle and Leith, Lothian.
15 Sept	Linlithgow, Lothian.
16 Sept	Falkirk, Central.
17 Sept	St Ninians, Central.
18 Sept	before Stirling, Central.
19 Sept	Linlithgow, Lothian.
20 Sept	Dundas Castle and Linlithgow, Lothian.
21 Sept–8 Oct	Edinburgh, Lothian.
9 Oct	Linlithgow, Lothian.
10 Oct	Kilsyth, Strathclyde.
11–13 Oct	Glasgow, Strathclyde.
14 Oct	Muir Head, Strathclyde.
15 Oct	Livingstone, Lothian.
16 Oct–26 Nov	Edinburgh, Lothian.
27 Nov	Livingstone, Lothian.
28 Nov	Blackburn, Lothian; Kirk of Shotts and before Hamilton, Strathclyde.
29 Nov	marches east.
30 Nov–31 Dec	Edinburgh, Lothian.

1651

Jan–3 Feb	Edinburgh, Lothian.

4 Feb	Leith, Lothian.
5 Feb	Falkirk, Central.
6 Feb	Kilsyth, Strathclyde.
7 Feb	Linlithgow, Lothian.
8 Feb–16 Apr	Edinburgh, Lothian.
17 Apr	Musselburgh and Livingstone, Lothian.
18 Apr	Edinburgh, Lothian.
19 Apr	Hamilton, Strathclyde.
20–29 Apr	Glasgow, Strathclyde.
30 Apr	Carnwath, Strathclyde.
2 May–late Jun	Edinburgh, Lothian.
30 Jun	Newbridge, Lothian.
1 Jul	Linlithgow, Lothian.
2 Jul	Falkirk and Larbert, Central
3–4 Jul	Linlithgow, Lothian.
5 Jul	Shotts, Strathclyde.
6–11 Jul	Glasgow, Strathclyde.
12 Jul	Monckland, Strathclyde.
14 Jul	Larbert, Central; Linlithgow, Lothian.
15 Jul	Callendar House, Central.
17 Jul	Torwood, Central.
20 Jul	Bannockburn, Central.
21–23 Jul	Linlithgow, Lothian.
24 Jul	Dundas Castle, Lothian.
26–28 Jul	Leith, Lothian.
29 Jul	Burntisland, Fife.
30 Jul	Fordell Castle, Fife.
31 Jul	around Loch Leven, Tayside.
1 Aug	before Perth, Tayside.
2 Aug	in Perth, Tayside.
4–5 Aug	Leith, Lothian.
8 Aug	around Kelso, Borders.
9 Aug	Eglingham Hall, Northumberland.
10 Aug	Whalton, Northumberland.
12 Aug	Newburn and Stella House, Tyne and Wear.
14 Aug	around Newcastle upon Tyne, Tyne and Wear.
15 Aug	Brancepeth, Durham.
16 Aug	Catterick Bridge, North Yorks.
17 Aug	Ripon, North Yorks.
19 Aug	Ferrybridge, West Yorks.
21 Aug	Doncaster, South Yorks.
22 Aug	Rufford Abbey, Notts.
23 Aug	Lutterworth, Leics.
24 Aug	Warwick, Warks.
26 Aug	Stratford upon Avon, Warks.
27 Aug	Evesham, Hereford & Worcs.
28 Aug	Moor, Hereford & Worcs.
29 Aug	Upton and White Ladies Aston, Hereford and Worcs.
30 Aug–2 Sept	Spetchley, Hereford and Worcs.
3–4 Sept	around and in Worcester, Hereford and Worcs.
5–7 Sept	Evesham, Hereford and Worcs.
8 Sept	Chipping Norton, Oxon.
9 Sept	Aylesbury, Bucks.
11 Sept	Uxbridge, Greater London.
12 Sept	London.

Thereafter, Cromwell very rarely left the confines of Greater London. In May 1652 he paid two brief visits to Kent – on 22nd he was in Dover and on 25th he travelled to Rochester – but there is little evidence that he ever returned to his old haunts in Cambridgeshire or visited the properties he had acquired in Essex, Buckinghamshire and elsewhere after 1651. Instead the last seven years of his life were spent around Whitehall, Westminster and (from 1654) Hampton Court, with frequent visits to the City, to Woolwich for the launching of new ships, and probably to Wimbledon to see Lambert. The itinerant soldier had become the settled, London-based politician.

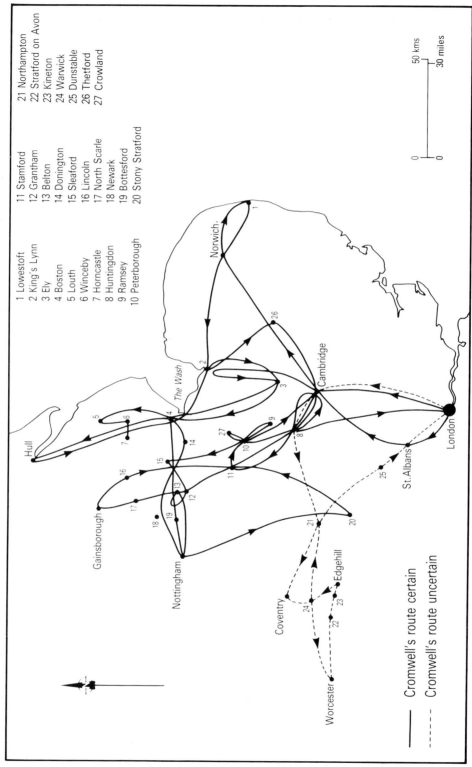

The first stage of the war: from London, January 1642, to Winceby, October 1643

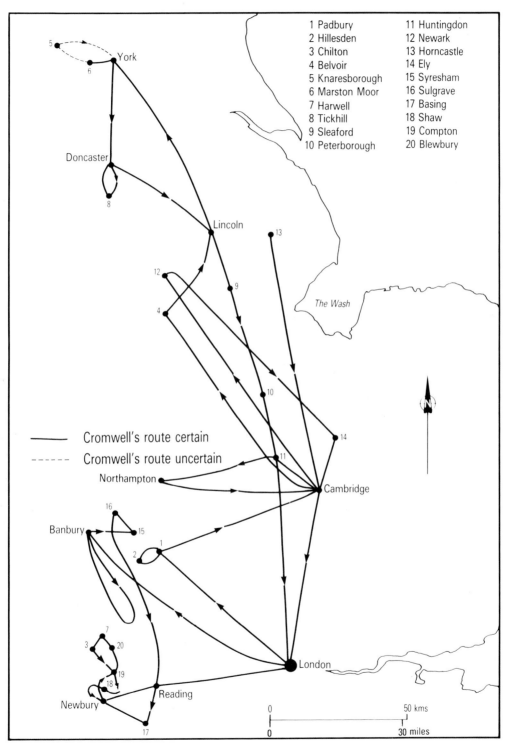

1 Padbury
2 Hillesden
3 Chilton
4 Belvoir
5 Knaresborough
6 Marston Moor
7 Harwell
8 Tickhill
9 Sleaford
10 Peterborough
11 Huntingdon
12 Newark
13 Horncastle
14 Ely
15 Syresham
16 Sulgrave
17 Basing
18 Shaw
19 Compton
20 Blewbury

York
Doncaster
Lincoln
The Wash
Northampton
Cambridge
Banbury
Reading
Newbury
London

Cromwell's route certain
Cromwell's route uncertain

0   50 kms
0   30 miles

Manchester's second-in-command: from Horncastle, October 1643, to London, December 1644

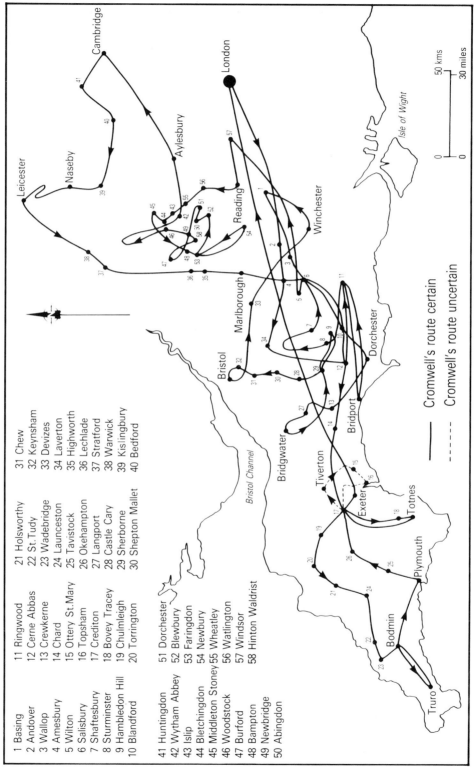

1 Basing	21 Holsworthy	31 Chew
2 Andover	22 St.Tudy	32 Keynsham
3 Wallop	23 Wadebridge	33 Devizes
4 Amesbury	24 Launceston	34 Laverton
5 Wilton	25 Tavistock	35 Highworth
6 Salisbury	26 Okehampton	36 Lechlade
7 Shaftesbury	27 Langport	37 Stratford
8 Sturminster	28 Castle Cary	38 Warwick
9 Hambledon Hill	29 Sherborne	39 Kislingbury
10 Blandford	30 Shepton Mallet	40 Bedford

41 Huntingdon	51 Dorchester
42 Wytham Abbey	52 Blewbury
43 Islip	53 Faringdon
44 Bletchingdon	54 Newbury
45 Middleton Stoney	55 Wheatley
46 Woodstock	56 Watlington
47 Burford	57 Windsor
48 Bampton	58 Hinton Waldrist
49 Newbridge	
50 Abingdon	

—— Cromwell's route certain

------ Cromwell's route uncertain

The last year of the war: on campaign in Oxfordshire and the South West, January 1645 to April 1646

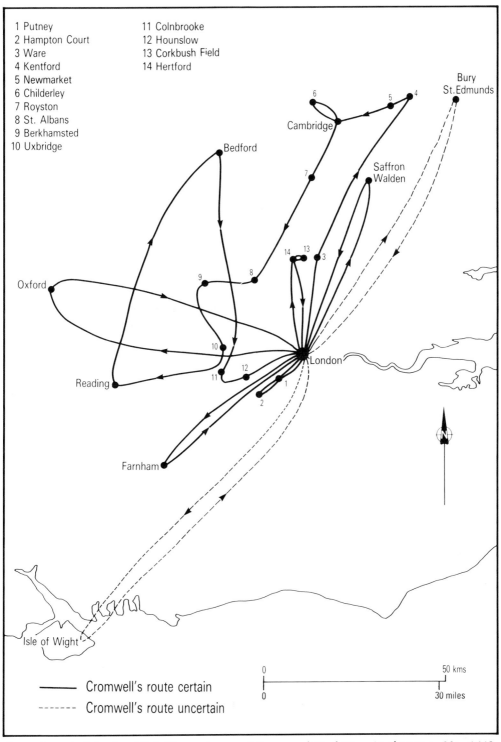

1 Putney
2 Hampton Court
3 Ware
4 Kentford
5 Newmarket
6 Childerley
7 Royston
8 St. Albans
9 Berkhamsted
10 Uxbridge

11 Colnbrooke
12 Hounslow
13 Corkbush Field
14 Hertford

Bury St.Edmunds

Cambridge

Saffron Walden

Bedford

Oxford

London

Reading

Farnham

Isle of Wight

N

0   50 kms
0   30 miles

—— Cromwell's route certain
- - - Cromwell's route uncertain

From the end of the first Civil War to the eve of the second Civil War, April 1646 to May 1648

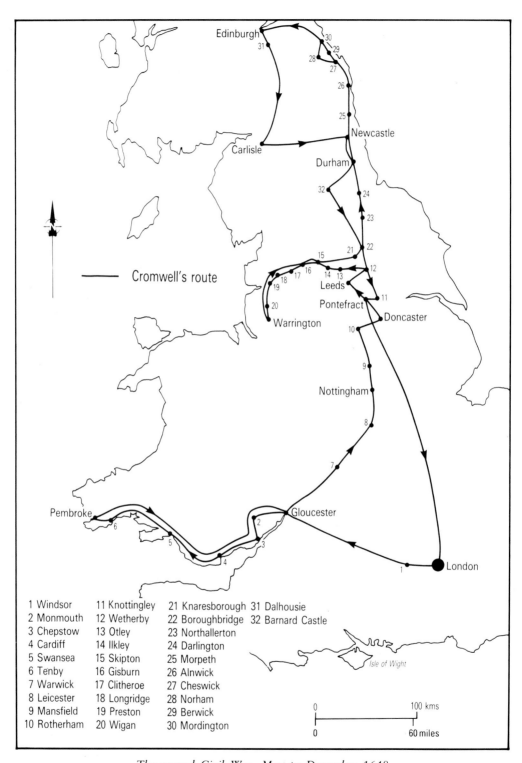

Edinburgh

31

30
29
28
27
26
25

Carlisle

Newcastle

Durham

32   24
           23
        22
    21 12
15 14 13
16
17 18   Leeds
19
20   11
Warrington   Pontefract

10   Doncaster

9

Nottingham

8

7

Pembroke
6

5
4

2   Gloucester
3

1   London

Cromwell's route

1 Windsor	11 Knottingley	21 Knaresborough	31 Dalhousie
2 Monmouth	12 Wetherby	22 Boroughbridge	32 Barnard Castle
3 Chepstow	13 Otley	23 Northallerton	
4 Cardiff	14 Ilkley	24 Darlington	
5 Swansea	15 Skipton	25 Morpeth	
6 Tenby	16 Gisburn	26 Alnwick	
7 Warwick	17 Clitheroe	27 Cheswick	
8 Leicester	18 Longridge	28 Norham	
9 Mansfield	19 Preston	29 Berwick	
10 Rotherham	20 Wigan	30 Mordington	

Isle of Wight

0   100 kms

0   60 miles

The second Civil War, May to December 1648

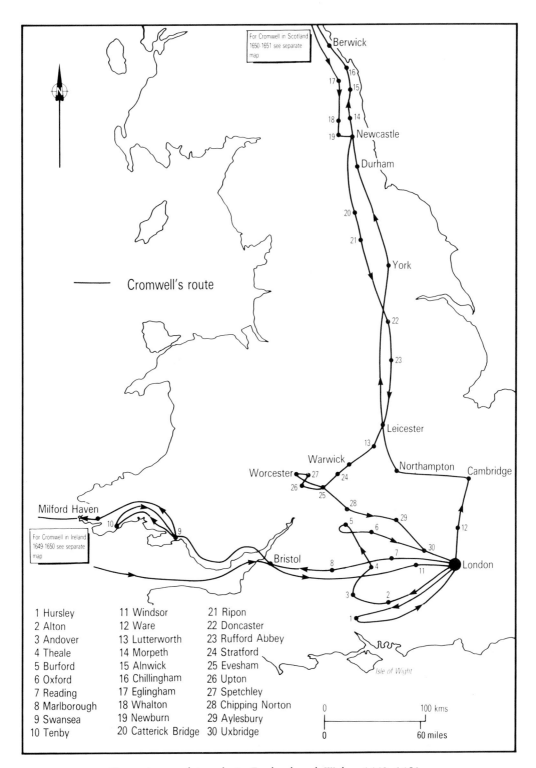

Berwick

16
17   15
18   14
19   Newcastle
       Durham

20
21
         York
22
23

       Leicester
13
Warwick   Northampton   Cambridge
Worcester   27
26   24
     25   28   29   12
                              30
         5   6
Milford Haven   7   London
10   4
     9   11
              Bristol   8
                    3   2
                                1

—— Cromwell's route

1 Hursley	11 Windsor	21 Ripon
2 Alton	12 Ware	22 Doncaster
3 Andover	13 Lutterworth	23 Rufford Abbey
4 Theale	14 Morpeth	24 Stratford
5 Burford	15 Alnwick	25 Evesham
6 Oxford	16 Chillingham	26 Upton
7 Reading	17 Eglingham	27 Spetchley
8 Marlborough	18 Whalton	28 Chipping Norton
9 Swansea	19 Newburn	29 Aylesbury
10 Tenby	20 Catterick Bridge	30 Uxbridge

Isle of Wight

0   100 kms
0   60 miles

Campaigns and travels in England and Wales, 1649–1651

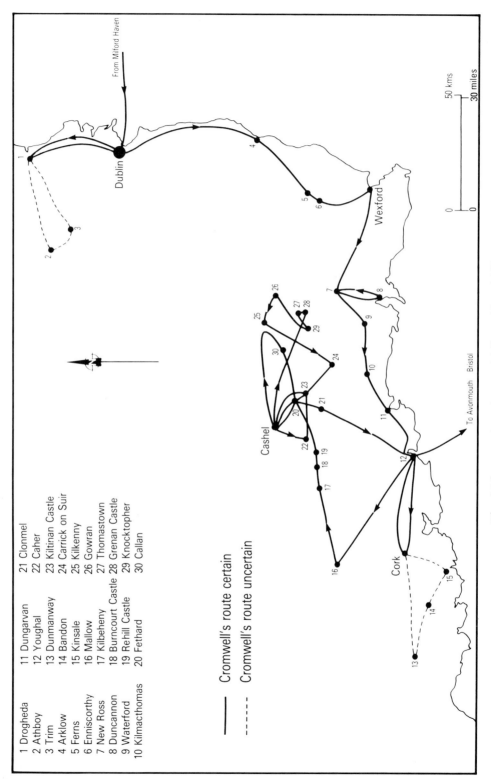

1 Drogheda
2 Athboy
3 Trim
4 Arklow
5 Ferns
6 Enniscorthy
7 New Ross
8 Duncannon
9 Waterford
10 Kilmacthomas
11 Dungarvan
12 Youghal
13 Dunmanway
14 Bandon
15 Kinsale
16 Mallow
17 Kilbeheny
18 Burncourt Castle
19 Rehill Castle
20 Fethard
21 Clonmel
22 Caher
23 Kiltinan Castle
24 Carrick on Suir
25 Kilkenny
26 Gowran
27 Thomastown
28 Grenan Castle
29 Knocktopher
30 Callan

—————— Cromwell's route certain
- - - - - Cromwell's route uncertain

From Milford Haven

Dublin

Wexford

Cashel

Cork

To Avonmouth Bristol

50 kms
30 miles

The Irish campaign, August 1649 to May 1650

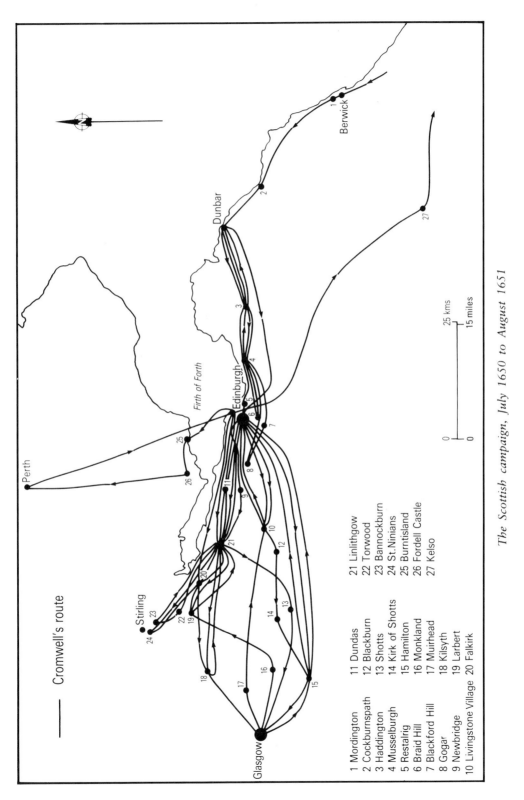

Cromwell's route

1 Mordington	11 Dundas	21 Linlithgow
2 Cockburnspath	12 Blackburn	22 Torwood
3 Haddington	13 Shotts	23 Bannockburn
4 Musselburgh	14 Kirk of Shotts	24 St.Ninians
5 Restalrig	15 Hamilton	25 Burntisland
6 Braid Hill	16 Monkland	26 Fordell Castle
7 Blackford Hill	17 Muirhead	27 Kelso
8 Gogar	18 Kilsyth	
9 Newbridge	19 Larbert	
10 Livingstone Village	20 Falkirk	

The Scottish campaign, July 1650 to August 1651

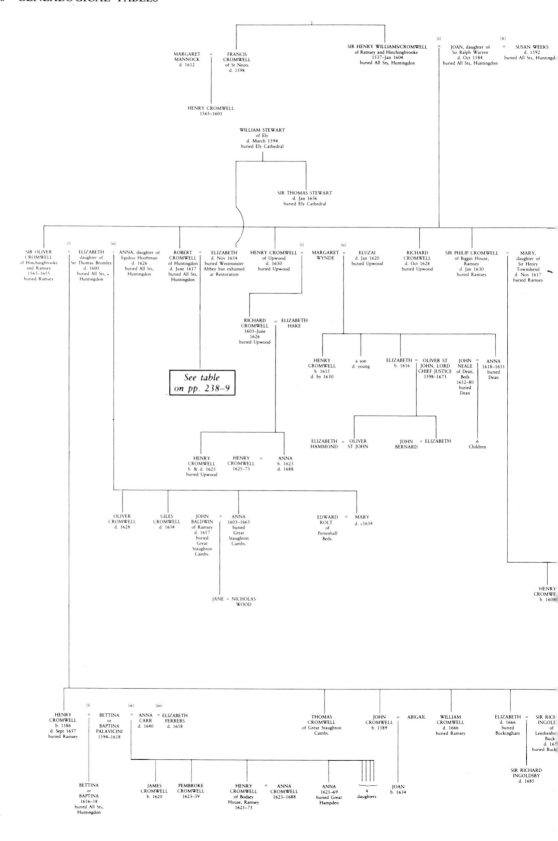

See table
on pp. 238–9

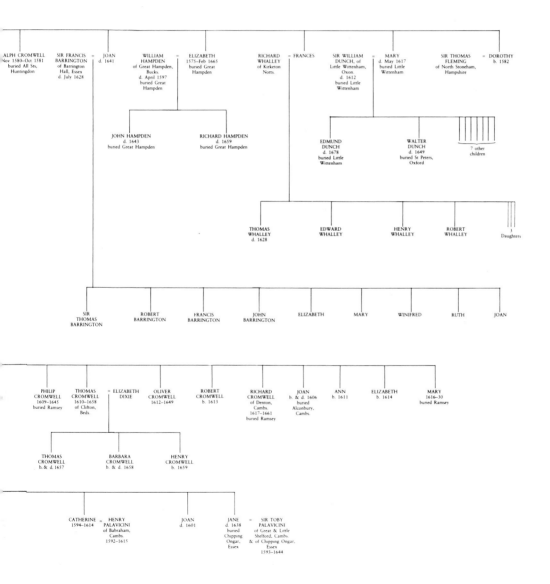

RALPH CROMWELL
Nov 1580–Oct 1581
buried All Sts,
Huntingdon

SIR FRANCIS
BARRINGTON
of Barrington
Hall, Essex
d. July 1628
= JOAN
d. 1641

WILLIAM
HAMPDEN
of Great Hampden,
Bucks.
d. April 1597
buried Great
Hampden
= ELIZABETH
1575–Feb 1665
buried Great
Hampden

RICHARD
WHALLEY
of Kirketon
Notts.
= FRANCES

SIR WILLIAM
DUNCH, of
Little Wittenham,
Oxon.
d. 1612
buried Little
Wittenham
= MARY
d. May 1617
buried Little
Wittenham

SIR THOMAS
FLEMING
of North Stoneham,
Hampshire
= DOROTHY
b. 1582

JOHN HAMPDEN
d. 1643
buried Great Hampden

RICHARD HAMPDEN
d. 1659
buried Great Hampden

EDMUND
DUNCH
d. 1678
buried Little
Wittenham

WALTER
DUNCH
d. 1649
buried St Peters,
Oxford

7 other
children

THOMAS
WHALLEY
d. 1628

EDWARD
WHALLEY

HENRY
WHALLEY

ROBERT
WHALLEY

3
Daughters

SIR
THOMAS
BARRINGTON

ROBERT
BARRINGTON

FRANCIS
BARRINGTON

JOHN
BARRINGTON

ELIZABETH

MARY

WINIFRED

RUTH

JOAN

PHILIP
CROMWELL
1609–1645
buried Ramsey

THOMAS
CROMWELL
1610–1658
of Clifton,
Beds.
= ELIZABETH
DIXIE

OLIVER
CROMWELL
1612–1649

ROBERT
CROMWELL
b. 1613

RICHARD
CROMWELL
of Denton,
Cambs.
1617–1661
buried Ramsey

JOAN
b. & d. 1606
buried
Alconbury,
Cambs.

ANN
b. 1611

ELIZABETH
b. 1614

MARY
1616–30
buried Ramsey

THOMAS
CROMWELL
b. & d. 1657

BARBARA
CROMWELL
b. & d. 1658

HENRY
CROMWELL
b. 1659

CATHERINE
1594–1614
= HENRY
PALAVICINI
of Babraham,
Cambs.
1592–1615

JOAN
d. 1601

JANE
d. 1638
buried
Chipping
Ongar,
Essex
= SIR TOBY
PALAVICINI
of Great & Little
Shelford, Cambs.
& of Chipping Ongar,
Essex
1593–1644

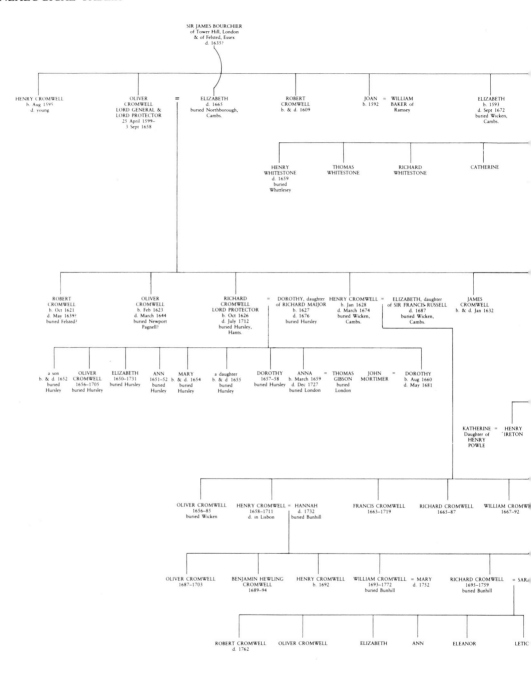

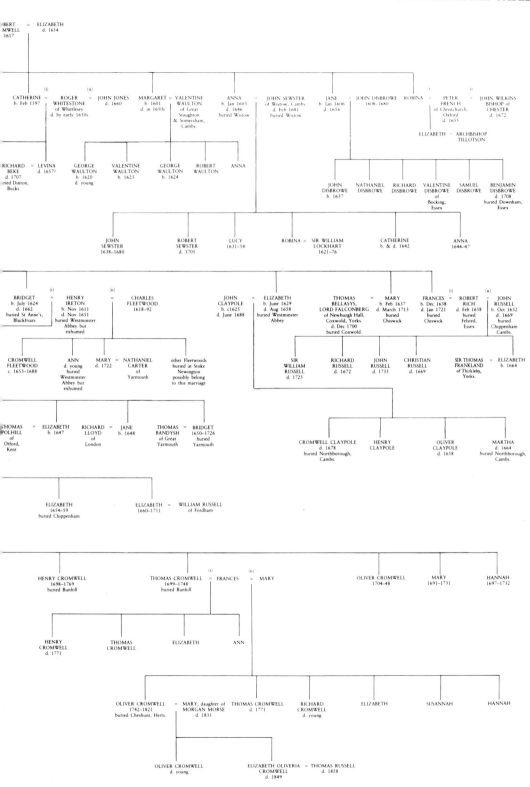

ROBERT CROMWELL 1617? = ELIZABETH d. 1654

(i) CATHERINE b. Feb 1597 = ROGER WHITESTONE of Whittlesey d. by early 1650s | (ii) JOHN JONES d. 1660 | MARGARET b. 1601 d. in 1650s = VALENTINE WAULTON of Great Staughton & Somersham, Cambs. | ANNA b. Jan 1603 d. 1646 buried Wistow = JOHN SEWSTER of Wistow, Cambs. d. Feb 1681 buried Wistow | JANE b. Jan 1606 d. 1656 = JOHN DISBROWE 1608-1680 | ROBINA = PETER FRENCH of Christchurch, Oxford d. 1655 | JOHN WILKINS BISHOP of CHESTER d. 1672

ELIZABETH = ARCHBISHOP TILLOTSON

RICHARD BEKE d. 1707 buried Dinton, Bucks = LEVINA d. 1657? | GEORGE WAULTON b. 1620 d. young | VALENTINE WAULTON b. 1623 | GEORGE WAULTON b. 1624 | ROBERT WAULTON | ANNA

JOHN DISBROWE b. 1637 | NATHANIEL DISBROWE | RICHARD DISBROWE | VALENTINE DISBROWE of Bocking, Essex | SAMUEL DISBROWE | BENJAMIN DISBROWE d. 1708 buried Downham, Essex

JOHN SEWSTER 1638-1680 | ROBERT SEWSTER d. 1705 | LUCY 1631-54 | ROBINA = SIR WILLIAM LOCKHART 1621-76 | CATHERINE b. & d. 1642 | ANNA 1644-47

BRIDGET b. July 1624 d. 1662 buried St Anne's, Blackfriars = (i) HENRY IRETON b. Nov 1611 d. Nov 1651 buried Westminster Abbey but exhumed (ii) = CHARLES FLEETWOOD 1618-92 | JOHN CLAYPOLE b. c1625 d. June 1688 buried Westminster Abbey = ELIZABETH b. June 1629 d. Aug 1658 buried Westminster Abbey | THOMAS BELLASYS, LORD FALCONBERG of Newburgh Hall, Coxwold, Yorks. d. Dec 1700 buried Coxwold = MARY b. Feb 1637 d. March 1713 buried Chiswick | FRANCES b. Dec 1638 d. Jan 1721 buried Chiswick = (i) ROBERT RICH d. Feb 1658 buried Felsted, Essex (ii) = JOHN RUSSELL d. 1669 buried Chippenham Cambs.

CROMWELL FLEETWOOD c. 1653-1688 | ANN d. young buried Westminster Abbey but exhumed | MARY d. 1722 = NATHANIEL CARTER of Yarmouth | other Fleetwoods buried at Stoke Newington possibly belong to this marriage

SIR WILLIAM RUSSELL d. 1725 | RICHARD RUSSELL d. 1672 | JOHN RUSSELL d. 1735 | CHRISTIAN RUSSELL d. 1669 | SIR THOMAS FRANKLAND of Thirkleby, Yorks. = ELIZABETH b. 1664

THOMAS POLHILL of Otford, Kent = ELIZABETH b. 1647 | RICHARD LLOYD of London = JANE b. 1648 | THOMAS BANDYSH of Great Yarmouth = BRIDGET 1650-1726 buried Yarmouth

CROMWELL CLAYPOLE d. 1678 buried Northborough, Cambs. | HENRY CLAYPOLE | OLIVER CLAYPOLE d. 1658 | MARTHA d. 1664 buried Northborough, Cambs.

ELIZABETH 1654-59 buried Chippenham | ELIZABETH 1660-1711 = WILLIAM RUSSELL of Fordham

HENRY CROMWELL 1698-1769 buried Bunhill | THOMAS CROMWELL 1699-1748 buried Bunhill = (i) FRANCES (ii) = MARY | OLIVER CROMWELL 1704-48 | MARY 1691-1731 | HANNAH 1697-1732

HENRY CROMWELL d. 1771 | THOMAS CROMWELL | ELIZABETH | ANN

OLIVER CROMWELL 1742-1821 buried Cheshunt, Herts. = MARY, daughter of MORGAN MORSE d. 1831 | THOMAS CROMWELL d. 1771 | RICHARD CROMWELL d. young | ELIZABETH | SUSANNAH | HANNAH

OLIVER CROMWELL d. young | ELIZABETH OLIVERIA CROMWELL d. 1849 = THOMAS RUSSELL d. 1858

SELECT INDEX OF NAMES

This index of names covers substantial or important personal entries only; passing references to military career, participation in battles and sieges, etc. are not listed.

Assheton, Sir Ralph 72
Axtell, Daniel 68, 69, 86

Baldwin, John 16
Barrington, Sir Francis 54
Baynes, Adam 110
Beke, Richard 10–11
Beaumont, Adam 168
Bellasys, Thomas, Lord Falconberg 62, 120, 123
Bennet, Robert 30
Birch, John 74–5
Blake, Robert 61–2, 68, 69, 92, 145
Bourchier, Elizabeth 12, 18, 54
Bourchier, Sir James 54
Boyle, Roger, Lord Broghill, 1st Earl of Orrery 214
Bradshaw, John 66, 68, 69, 72–3
Brereton, Sir William 61
Broughton, Andrew 94

Chute, Chaloner 78
Claypole, Cromwell 19
Claypole, John 14–16, 18, 62
Claypole, Martha 19
Cooper, Anthony Ashley, 1st Earl of Shaftesbury 49
Cooper, Samuel 64, 68
Cromwell, Anne or Anna (b1623) 20
Cromwell, Anne or Anna (d1646) 22
Cromwell, Anne or Anna (d1651) 5
Cromwell, Anne or Anna (d1663) 16
Cromwell, Anne or Anna (d1669) 11
Cromwell, Anne or Anna (d1727) 67
Cromwell, Bridget (d1662) 64, 127, 137
Cromwell, Catherine (b1597) 20, 191
Cromwell, Dorothy (b1582) 77
Cromwell, Elizabeth (d1654), mother of the Lord Protector *see* Stewart
Cromwell, Elizabeth (d1665), wife of the Lord Protector *see* Bourchier
Cromwell, Elizabeth (d1658) 16, 18, 62, 68, 69
Cromwell, Elizabeth (d1659) 14
Cromwell, Elizabeth (d1665) 10–11, 66
Cromwell, Elizabeth (d1666) 8, 11
Cromwell, Elizabeth (d1672) 22
Cromwell, Frances (d1721) 14, 16, 54, 61
Cromwell, Sir Henry (d1604) 16, 18, 19
Cromwell, Henry (d1630) 20
Cromwell, Henry (d1673) 19
Cromwell, Henry (d1674) 14, 22, 216
Cromwell, Henry (d1692) 22
Cromwell, Henry (d1769) 65
Cromwell, James (d1632) 16
Cromwell, Jane (d1637/8) 53
Cromwell, Jane (dc1655–6) 14, 68, 69
Cromwell, Joan (d1606) 13
Cromwell, Joan (d1641) 54
Cromwell, Margaret (d1655–6?) 20

Cromwell, Mary (d1617) 137
Cromwell, Mary (dc1634) 5
Cromwell, Mary (d1713) 14, 61–2, 65, 66, 123
Cromwell, Sir Oliver (d1655) 13, 19, 22
Cromwell, Oliver (d1649) 223
CROMWELL, OLIVER, LORD PROTECTOR passim, but see particularly 'Cambridgeshire' (pp 13–22) and 'Greater London' (pp 61–70)
Cromwell, Oliver (d1685) 22
Cromwell, Oliver (d1821) 86, 88
Cromwell, Sir Philip (d1630) 13, 19
Cromwell, Ralph (d1581) 18
Cromwell, Richard (d1626) 20
Cromwell, Richard (d1628) 20
Cromwell, Richard (d1712) 67, 76, 86
Cromwell, Richard (d1759) 65
Cromwell, Robert (d1617) 16, 18
Cromwell, Robert (d1639) 54
Cromwell, Robina (fl1640) 68
Cromwell, Thomas (d1658) 5
Cromwell, Thomas (d1748) 65
Cromwell, William (d1772) 65

Deane, Richard 68, 69
Devereux, Robert, 3rd Earl of Essex 62, 66, 68, 69
Disbrowe, John 14
Disbrowe, Samuel 14
Downing, Sir George 65
Dunch, Sir William 137

Elsyng, Henry 68

Fairfax, Ferdinando, 2nd Lord Fairfax 118
Fairfax, Sir Thomas, 3rd Lord Fairfax 62, 66, 67, 68, 118, 120, 123, 126
Fettiplace, Col. 139
Fiennes, Nathaniel 88, 134
Fleetwood, Charles 64, 65, 216
Fleetwood, George 10
Fleming, Sir Thomas 77
French, Elizabeth 68

Gell, Sir John 36–39
Gibson, Thomas 67
Glanville, Sir John 170
Goodwin, Thomas 65
Grey, Henry, 1st Earl of Stamford 102

Hampden family 10–11, 66
Hampden, John 8–12, 136, 139
Harrington, James 44, 68
Harrington, Sir James, MP 62
Hesilrige, Sir Arthur 50, 103
Holles, Denzil, Lord Holles 46–48
Hotham, Sir John snr & jnr 90
Hungerford, Sir Edward 146

Hutchinson, John 103, 130

Ingoldsby, Richard jnr 11, 110
Ingoldsby, Richard snr 8, 11
Ireton, Bridget 110
Ireton, Henry 62, 66, 67, 68, 69, 127, 137, 162, 216
Ireton, John 62, 127

Jones, John 191
Jones, Michael 214
Jones, Philip 193–4

Lambert, John 22, 44, 62, 65, 67, 110, 118, 120
Lawrence, Henry 20, 88
Lenthall, William 134, 137
Lilburne, John 22
Lilburne, Robert 44, 126
Lisle, John 76
Ludlow, Edmund 172

Maijor, Dorothy 76, 156
Maijor, Richard 76, 156
Marten, Henry 137, 186
Marvell, Andrew 67, 90, 123
Masham, Sir William 54
Massey, Sir Edward 56
Mayne, Simon 10
Middleton, Sir Thomas 176
Milton, John 6, 10, 60, 66, 67, 68, 137
Monck, George, 1st Duke of Albemarle 13, 42, 67, 68, 69
Montagu, Edward, 2nd Earl of Manchester 18
Montagu, Edward, 1st Earl of Sandwich 18, 69
Morley, Herbert 52
Mytton, Sir Thomas 144

Neale, John 5
Norton, Richard 77, 78

Okey, John 4–5, 68
Onslow, Sir Richard 156
Owen, John 65

Packe, Sir Christopher 102, 103
Palavicini, Sir Toby 53
Penn, Sir William 2–4, 62
Pennington, Sir Isaac 10
Peter or Peters, Hugh 13
Pickering, Sir Gilbert 114

Popham, Alexander & Edward 170, 172
Pride, Thomas 156–7
Purefoy family 158
Pye, Sir Robert 82
Pym, John 66, 68, 69, 146

Rich, Robert, 2nd Earl of Warwick 54, 66
Rich, Robert 54, 66
Rolt or Rolte, Edward 5
Rous, Francis 6, 61
Rushworth, John 67
Russell, Elizabeth 14, 22
Russell, John 14
Russell, Sir William 14

St John, Oliver 19
Scott, Thomas 8
Sewster, John 22
Sheffield, Edmund, 2nd Earl of Mulgrave 122
Sidney, Philip, Lord Lisle, 3rd Earl of Leicester 94
Skinner, Augustine 94
Skippon, Philip 61, 65
Stewart, Elizabeth 14, 20, 68, 69
Stewart, Sir Thomas 14, 20
Strickland, Walter 89, 90
Strickland, Sir William 89
Strode, William 68, 69
Sydenham, William 49–50

Thurloe, John 22, 53, 62, 67, 89, 137
Tillotson, John 68
Tomlinson, Matthew 94

Vane, Sir Henry jnr 52, 95, 104
Vane, Sir Henry snr 52

Waller, Sir William 2
Waulton, Valentine 20
Whalley, Edmund 132
Whitelock, Bulstrode 137
Whitestone, Henry 20
Whitestone, Levina 10–11
Whitestone, Roger 20
Widdrington, Sir Thomas 67
Wildman, John 139
Wilkins, John 68
Wolseley, Sir Charles 152
Worsley, Charles 69

PICTURE CREDITS

The publishers wish to acknowledge the following for their help in supplying black and white illustrative material and for giving their permission to reproduce it. Pictures are identified by page number and position (left to right, top to bottom).

Astley Hall/Chorley Photographic Society 96b;
Bord Fáilte 215b, 221a b & c;
The British Tourist Authority 3b, 9a, 17a, 25b, 31a, 37b, 43a, 75b, 93b, 105a, 112b & c, 165a, 171a & b, 177, 199b;
The Duke of Buccleuch and Queensberry ii;
John Clifford 101a;
Peter Clifford 57a, 96a, 181a;
Trewin Copplestone iii, 21c & d, 63a b & c, 71b, 87b, 119b & d, 125c, 131a, 151c, 215a c & d;
Alan Foulds 81a b & c, 187b;
Peter Gaunt 3a, 17b & c, 31b & c, 43b, 75a & c, 93c, 135a & b, 147a, 159a, 181b, 187a;
Gloucester City Museum 57c;

D.B. Good 15a b & c, 21b, 51b, 71a & c, 105b, 112a, 119c, 121a b & c, 125a, 151a, 207a;
The Guernsey Press Company Limited 25a;
Humphrey Household 9b & c, 21a, 37a, 47a & b, 105c, 117a & b, 125b, 129a, 131b, 135c, 143a b & c, 147b & c, 151b, 159b, 181c, 185a & b, 190b, 197, 199a, 203, 211;
A.F. Kersting 57b, 101b;
The Manx Museum 93a;
Crown copyright, National Monuments Record 129b;
Fred Spencer 119a;
Derek G. Widdicombe 51a, 161a & b, 165b, 190a, 207b & c.